The Civilization Trap:
Fading Into Sentient Senescence

by:

John C. Cornuelle

 Bluebell
Press

Table of Contents

Cover photo by author

Preface

Audience perspective. Never was this intended to be an arcane academic work. Some footnotes are provided, but every fact and calculation is not footnoted and justified; that would make this even more unpleasantly unreadable (and much longer). In manufacturing, there is an old bipolar attitude termed "inspect to accept/inspect to reject". What it means is that you can always, when inspecting parts or assemblies, find a cause or reason to reject the item if you do not want to accept it. Maybe you want to send the supplier a message (you are upset with him), or you have too many parts already and don't need these, or because the part inspector is having some contest-of-wills with the manufacturing manager and is going to show him he is not one with whom to trifle, or for some similar reason. So it will be with this book – factual support and footnotes notwithstanding, if your mind is already made up, if you believe otherwise, if you are simply human, you may just dismiss what you read here out-of-hand.

Approach. Fortunately for the non-fastidious author, this book did not require the adept assembly and subsequent orchestration of carefully-extracted, out-of-context quotes, partial truths, and urban legends to ex post facto justify some pre-established conclusion. The author instead was able to simply point to behaviors on the part of man so common and so obvious that everyone will recognize them in someone they know, if not themselves. If some of the categorizations here of man's nature sound original, it is only that their ubiquitously-boring ordinariness has caused them to appear non-apparent. The facts, behaviors, and processes presented here are observationally-obvious, scientifically-based, generally-accepted, and non-controversial, unless you are a person who lives in a belief-based world, which means you are prominently featured in this book. As this book covers 60,000 years of man's history, a period for 95% of which man's focus was on coping, struggling, and surviving, the concept of "permanence" was nowhere in his consciousness. Hence no history of these times was produced to fall back on, and so conjecture is a necessary part of this book. The conclusions contained in here must by their nature also be conjecture, since running coercive experiments on people, and especially planets, is not only frowned upon but budgetarily infeasible. But the conjectures are limited to the most plausible, reasonable, Occam's Razor explanations, not LGM (Little Green Men), and other such extravagant leaps. Yet, when confronted with the book's premise, that man has major issues when attempting to competently engage the modern world, a world re-made by man, and although agreeing with all the book's content, the reader may just say - "Well, I just don't believe in/agree with that," helping prove the thesis precisely.

Writing lean. References to individuals, events, scientific facts, established concepts, and physical laws are often made assuming that either the reader is already familiar with these items, or he will jump on his handy digital device and shortly make himself a nano-expert. Forcing the reader to struggle through that extra material in this book would be an excessive demand.

Words 2.0. In spite of what his grandmother sternly instructed, the author has utilized a few words that are not dictionary-legal, as there did not seem to be any appropriate alternative. If you stumble on such a word, and find yourself offended near-fatally, the author provides his sincere apologies. The astute reader will also notice that the author moves between addressing him as either "the reader" or "you", whichever seems more appropriate in the specific context, trashing another inviolable rule of authoring.

Sexing. Convention-wise, in almost all cases the author has defaulted to the generic "he" and "his". If it works better for your reading comprehension and enjoyment, please substitute "she" and "her" respectively, or whichever other individual or group sex that you prefer.

Numerology. All numbers cited in this work are point estimates – single values. Normally the author only thinks in terms of ranges – few numbers, especially historical values for things for which there are no accurate records or data, are meaningfully displayed with a single value. But almost no one thinks this way, and most people, if presented with a range, will ask: "Well, which is it, the bigger number or the smaller number?" So the author concedes defeat and goes with point estimates. But if you find this offensive, every number in here if it is an estimate can be converted to a range plus and minus 30% around the stated point estimate. So, for example, this book will often use the value of 60,000 years for how long modern man has been on the Earth. Plus and minus 30% means it could be 42,000 years or 78,000 years. No one knows when the first modern human appeared in effectively meaningful quantities – whether there were 30 or 2,000 or 12,000 humans 42,000 years ago really doesn't make all that much difference. It will not change the conclusion or the argument or the logic in which the number is immersed – none depend on the precise accuracy of the number.

Chronology. On the topic of the age of modern man, you will see 200,000 years ago often used as the time that the first person appeared. Subsequently some small number of individuals struggled for survival, undergoing a major threat 30,000 years later when the numbers dropped back to the point that we are all descended from a single, common mother from that date. In this book, 60,000 years is used for the time that a homogenous modern man has effectively been engaging his environment. It seems imprudent and unwise to count the experiences of man before this time, when man's numbers were so very small, and it is not clear if the version of man on the Earth 170,000 years ago was sufficiently-identical to the 60,000-year-old version. But if you would prefer to use 170,000 or 200,000 years for the effective experiential age of modern man, feel free to do so - it just makes the argument stronger.

Invisible hand. Somehow we ended up where we were 60,000 years ago, where we were a million years ago, and where we were 500 million years ago. Man, plant, and animal life behaves as it does; the world works as it does. To simplify the causative factors for all of this in as few words as possible, it is all assigned to Mother Nature. Wherever an explanation needs to be cited, Mother Nature is invoked. If you prefer a different agent – God, aliens from the planet Zargon, another set of deities, anthropic-principled universe, luck/good fortune – feel free to substitute as you see fit.

Originality. If the ideas cited in this book are not obviously in the common marketplace, or the source is noted, then the author developed them on his own. He is solely responsible for their reasonableness or lack thereof. The author made no effort to determine the originality of the ideas in this book. If a similar idea appears somewhere else, a most likely situation, it can simply be attributed to the inevitability of much common ground in a discussion of human nature. However, there was no intellectual theft involved in any portion of this work.

Frame of reference. The author was born and raised in the U.S. As a consequence, he is most familiar with U.S. societal-centric examples, and so these illustrate most of the characteristics of human nature in this book. Using third-hand representations, except in the cases where the historical record is clearly understood, seemed sub-ideal. But as the "no fault" paragraph emphasizes, this does not imply or hint that only U.S. society possesses these characteristics or such vivid examples.

Simplifying complexity. This book attempts to make simple something that superficially and at the margins can appear quite complex. As a result it falls right smack into the middle of the "all generalizations are false" swamp. Each such generalized statement in this book is certainly precisely wrong if nit-picked appropriately. But each is approximately right and for certain not misleading, and should be approached that way. Many statements are phrased "man is ..." - that does not mean that each and every member of mankind is, nor only men and not women, nor vice versa, nor only you, nor not you. It means that the vast majority of mankind, taken in the aggregate over the last 60,000 years unless stated otherwise, is... . Most likely you as an individual will not match up against all of the human nature characteristics listed here; some will be more dominant; others more quiescent. Your friends, neighbors, and relatives will match up similarly but with differences. For some people a few of the factors described here will not apply at all. For others they will have some fundamental characteristics not even mentioned here. This book is not intended to cover Michelangelo's, Michael Jordan's, Mozart's, Maxwell's, Mandela's, Moses', Mailer's, Mother Teresa's, Boudicca's, Bonaparte's, and Byron's. These people are just off-the-chart. Some people will have little sign of these characteristics in most areas only to have them show most prominently in surprising places ("I don't believe in ...", heard from scientists, is the most common example). But for most people, for every under-compensation here there is an offsetting over-compensation there. Overall these differences tend to wash away. So as you read along and find yourself saying wait, I am not like this – not to worry, someone else more than makes up for you. Few people will be right-down-the-middle average. And you may be in that relatively small group to which none of this, or only a tiny aspect of this, applies.

The oxymoronic challenge of an over-distilled encapsulation running to 350 pages. 60,000 years of man's experience on the Earth, 100 million years for everyone else, neuro-anatomy and molecular biology, brain functioning, epigenetics, psychology, along with lots of juicy examples - all had to be rammed, crammed, and jammed into this little book. If this works poorly for some readers, the author now provides his apologies. Lacking the laconicism of Hemingway, the author has over-simplified some technical aspects and deselected many details (no textbook psychology for example) in an attempt to manage the page count (and boredom index).

No excuses. This book is about the facets of human nature that make man; i.e. it is about nature, not nurture – these features are "built-into" man. But the fact that man has skills and tools and capabilities is unrelated to how and when he elects to use those tools. He can help himself and his family to

6

thrive, or destroy them, his neighbors, and neighborhood. It is his choice; his innate skills will work for either course of action. So stating that man has a certain nature does not in any way absolve man from responsibility and accountability for what he does. The author does not waste the reader's time throughout this book continually rehashing this message. Every time a feature of human nature is described there is no caution attached that reminds the reader that possession of this feature is no excuse for "bad" behavior on the part of any individual.

Blame-free, judgment-free, no-fault. Imagine picking up a high-quality book of the most stunning landscape photographs and trying to describe them to someone blind from birth. Or describe Handel's Messiah or Tchaikovsky's Piano Concerto Number 1 to someone deaf from birth. You can describe everything as extensively as you can but never capture the impact and beauty and feeling that these convey. It is no one's fault – the individual that is blind or deaf is unable to perceive things the same way you can. This book outlines the key features of human nature, most of which involve cognitive short-cuts and emotionally-driven, rather than logically-driven, thinking. An example is cognitive dissonance – people holding feelings that are positive about something cannot at the same time accept and maintain perceived negative or critical information about that subject, and vice-versa. In order not to have this book sound too theoretical and academic, it is filled with real examples from everyday life, examples that show how many groups of people think about certain subjects. But a reader that sees themselves described will, based on their human nature, respond to this description not in a logical, scientific way. They will instead utilize these mental short-cuts coupled with emotions and react by dismissing the statement as being untrue. Other readers may fault the group being described as being mentally defective, or obviously total idiots. In other words, it is difficult to explain man's own nature to man because his own nature has to interpret what is said to him. Many readers may feel that the author is "picking on", or has an "axe to grind", or has a "hidden agenda", every time they see an example of human thinking dissected that happens to be one that they "believe in" or "like" or "strongly support". But human nature ensures that just describing these cases will be perceived as "criticism". The author tried to select the most vivid examples of how human nature drives human thinking. There is nothing to criticize or judge – man is simply what he is. No fault or blame is being hinted at, implied, suggested, or to be read between the lines. But no matter how explicitly this is stated, similar to the example of explaining the symphonic work to someone deaf, simply to characterize will be taken by many as an effort to criticize. Infiltrating man's indefatigable nature may prove difficult if not impossible.

What is not here – this book is not about what drives and motivates man, nor how deeply or strongly he is driven, although the nature of how he thinks will sometimes affect his motivations. It is not about man's instincts, although it is about human nature and man clearly uses his nature in a instinctive fashion. And the book does not cover the nature of human consciousness, normal or aberrant. This is not to pretend that man's drives, when they align with his basic nature, do not compound and amplify both his drives and his basic nature. But because there is no interference between drives and instincts and consciousness and the aspects of human nature discussed here, to keep this book manageable in length and scope and complexity, only how human nature affects the way man thinks is covered here.

Rest of the blame starts here. While the author's wife and children assisted with both advice and editing, the remaining typos in the book are lovingly provided entirely by the author - no one else bears responsibility. The author intended to write a serious book about a progress-arresting issue for man, but in an attempt to make it somewhat readable, in some few cases tried to exercise his very wry sense of humor. So if you can't determine why you are offended, it may be the author trying to be humorous.

Short cuts – this book centers on techniques that are part of human nature that in effect operate as short-cuts, enabling man to decide and act more efficiently, rapidly, and effectively than his rational brain would normal allow. In this spirit, here are some short-cuts for a few of the chapters in this book:

Chapter 6 – The Irrational Man. Most of this book concerns not the logical, rational, problem-solving faculties that man has but those based on instinct and drive which man himself senses as emotion. To provide a causal and not just conjectural background, this chapter summarizes how man's brain is designed. The emotional processing capabilities in man's brain are not only intimately integrated into his rational side, but outnumber the centers dedicated to logical thought. If you do not feel you have the time; or you do not have any interest in reading about somatosensory areas in the prefrontal cortex; or about the causes for variations in sociopathic/psychopathic behavior then you can pass on this. Or if you feel you do not need to know the causal basis for emotions in the brain before you read about how they work; or you are the kind of person who is not going to change your mind no matter what you read – then you can skip this chapter and go to Chapter 7.

Chapter 13 – Alexander the Greatest. Alexander is used as a fundamental paradigm and baseline for several concepts in this book. If you are willing to accept that he was the most driven human of all time, and the greatest human of all time, "greatest" defined in the haziest way you desire, you can skip this chapter. Alexander also set the high water mark for the new paradigm for man – the man who spends all his energy going after his fellow man instead of enriching himself at the expense of Mother Nature - if you concur, then you can skip this chapter.

Chapter 18 – Mother Nature's Keeping Track. Consisting of two major sections: the first discusses Mother Nature keeping track during your individual lifetime, by making inheritable changes in your genome that is covered by new branch of science called epigenetics, which not too many people are familiar with. The second reviews Mother Nature keeping track from lifetime to lifetime through one's descendants, which everyone is pretty familiar with. Both processes are documenting man's interaction with this new world he has created, in ways that may not be so obvious at first glance. The epigenetics section, since the basis for the conclusions must be fact-based, necessarily involves some biochemistry – processes like methylation and promoters. If you begin reading this and it proves too dreary, what with too many concurrent distractions, or you don't feel you need all the supporting explanation, or don't have the time, then you can just read the summary at the beginning of the section.

Chapter 20 – Other Perspective's on Man's Run. Spengler and Toynbee are two other historians who presented theories about societies rising and then crashing, primarily because history repeats itself. This book also speaks about threats to man's success, but not because of cyclic reasons but because of specific aspects of human nature built into man. Summaries and a evaluation of these two author's work are included for the sake of completeness. If you cannot be bothered with any of this, then you can skip this chapter.

Introduction

The mammoths stood silently grazing, as they always did. It was a typical day 12,000 years ago. Suddenly one mammoth was violently slammed by two lion-like predators in a timed attack, both locking onto its trunk with their jaws, claws, and forearms. Much larger and stronger than lions, this was no desperation attack by small, starving carnivores. The mammoth instinctively reacted to this massive weight and compromise of its ability to breathe by lowering its front legs, dropping its right shoulder, and beginning a whipping motion with its head to throw off the lions. But as its head was just beginning to move, two more lions hit its trunk, and the whipping degraded into a slow drag. A fifth lion coming straight in leaped over its sisters (or maybe a brother or two) and locked itself in just below the forehead of the mammoth, its powerful forearms raking both sides of its head, blinding it instantly. Another bit down on the very end of the trunk, so that both breathing through its trunk and any head movement were just about impossible. A seventh lion now approached and bit down directly on its mouth, almost completely blocking its ability to breathe. Another two lions began tearing at its throat. In three minutes it was over.

By restricting their attack to its trunk and head, the cats avoided being struck by the feet of the mammoth, a solid blow from which would prove fatal, not directly but indirectly, since an injury would prevent competent hunting. And through the weight, strength, and timing of a large group, they effectively immobilized the head of the mammoth before it could utilize its tusks to spear its opponents, as well as keeping them inside the range of the tusks even if the mammoth were somehow able to attempt a thrusting movement. Four lions attacking an African elephant, by comparison, would not result in success.

For several million years the sabre-tooth cat was the dominant land predator. Weighing as much or more than a large tiger but living and hunting together in groups, as wolves do, enabled it to successfully hunt the largest plant-eating animals, and always without any threats to itself.

Yet in another 2,000 years the sabre-tooths were all gone. Done in by man, who possibly never struck at one with the intention of doing it harm. Man out-hunted the cats for the large animals that the sabre-tooths required to make their hunting equation work. That equation puts effort, calories expended, elapsed time, risk of injury, and chance of success against the amount of food gained per hunter per successful kill. Against large, relatively slow animals like mammoths, sloths, and camels the equation was favorable to the sabre-tooths. But when man hunted and ate all these animals to extinction, he could readily switch to deer, rabbit, fruit, fish, and the like. But the equation for the lions changed by about a factor of twenty – suddenly they were chasing smaller, faster prey that took more energy to catch, had a lower chance of success, had a greater chance of injury while chasing them, and would payoff with one-tenth or fewer calories per lion when caught than before.

If the sabre-tooth cats could have suddenly morphed into solitary hunters like tigers, could they have survived? Who knows; but they were not able to do this, and they did not survive; not one. They went from master of the planet to oblivion. They in effect obsoleted themselves because their skills, perfectly matched for one kind of world, became not just useless but an unsurvivable handicap when the world changed. Certainly, it was not their "fault" that the world became different; but Mother Nature is a no-fault eliminator. If your skills are mismatched, you vanish.

In the case of <u>The Decline and Fall of the Roman Empire</u> Edward Gibbon started with an overwhelming advantage As they say in science and in inventing in general, knowing that it can be done is half (or you pick the percentage) the battle. In Gibbon's case, everyone knew the Roman empire had fallen; he provided the reasons, though some (like Christianity) are still inflammatory enough even today to get the book put on the burn list of belief-driven people, who are featured here a little further on. This book is conceptually more challenging – caught in the midst of the brouhaha, it is not so obvious for us to recognize that man is most likely flaming, fading, failing, and falling. And not because he has some fundamental weakness, or has done anything wrong, or has changed in some ominous way. Man is quagmired because his nature is unchanged. Most of us are well-acquainted with at least some of the reasons for this. It is just that they don't seem like causes, and toward what conclusion, until they get the limelight treatment.

By way of introduction there are two thoughts that best set the context for this book. The first is: "Seek ye then to destroy he who is invincible? Make yourself a student of his strength – for in that greatness will you also find his weakness." (Anon.) Any organism, including man, whose dominance depends on a strength or set of strengths, has simultaneously made that strength a vulnerability, simply by its wholesale reliance on this strength(s). Poisonous snakes are absolutely invulnerable to all threats, except they are near helpless against those who have become resistant to their poison. The AIDS virus actually uses man's immune system, one of his most powerful weapons, as its entry point, since the virus is covered with proteins (gp120) that magically bind to specific receptors on one type of immune system cell (CD4+ T cells). History is replete with individual examples of this, whether one starts with Goliath, or Samson, or Achilles, Socrates, Alexander the Great,

Joan of Arc, Napoleon, Mozart, Nikola Tesla, Hitler, Rommel, or Lyndon Johnson. These people were too good at what they did, because they depended exclusively on their collection of ultra-deep skills. They could not change or adjust or be flexible if the need arose, and this innate rigidity based on their strength brought their eventual fall from "power".

Man is possessed of such strengths that they enabled him to conquer and subdue the world, something no other inhabitant has been able to match. From a beginning with a handful of individuals, man now fills the Earth with seven billion of his own, and much of the world is now literally man's creation with Mother Nature only providing vestigial decorations. Man lives, works, eats, and is cared for, protected, and entertained in structures, with machines, and under the rule of systems that could just as well be on another planet as exist on Earth. Mother Nature is a footnote for many, amounting to no more than an inconvenience or a fashion guide from time to time.

The strengths that enabled man to subdue the world are not disconnected tools that he picks up out of some magical basket – they are his fundamental nature. For 60,000 years man has demonstrated that he possesses a set of skills deeper and stronger than any other plant or animal on the planet. But now man has the same skills, but faces a world that he has thoroughly re-made, a world bearing no resemblance to the one that his skills were designed for. Protecting his family against all manner of savage threats, securing reliable supplies of food and water, surviving disease and drought, flood and famine, building shelter against wind, storm, and his fellow man – all this and more he was prepared to do. Making hand tools, then small levered tools, then manually-powered machines, animal-powered machines, metal and pottery-firing furnaces, then wind and water-powered machines, then finally fuel-powered machines – no problem for man. But today's problems are complex, fuzzy, diffuse, international, interconnected. Some, like global climate change, may have latencies and feedback cycles that play out over more than one lifetime. They are full of tradeoffs and may have unfavorable side effects. Nothing is simple or easy or clear or amenable to quick, forceful action. But man is near-perfectly designed for the ability to quickly size up a situation, to problem-solve with the facts he faces, and take rapid, forceful action. So man's innate strengths have enabled him to fashion a world in which his strengths are obsolete; he has produced a mismatch where his powerful talons claw haplessly for traction against his flawless glossy new world.

The second thought comes from the ancient Greek philosophers who had as much insight as anyone since:

"Know thyself" or "the unexamined life is not worth living"

These are credited to Thales of Miletus and Socrates and need scant re-interpretation here. Literature on this subject fills the self-help sections in all bookstores. Issues of values, attitudes, beliefs, morals, ethics, right or wrong, nature or nurture, spirit or spiritless, good or evil - all fall under this simple subject. Little of this will be covered in this book - countless other authors have already. But something does remain untouched, unheralded. Not *what* man thinks about, not what man "is", but rather *how* he thinks about it. Not what he feels or sees or hears, but how he comes to feel and see and hear. The way man thinks cannot be separated from what he thinks; in fact, what he thinks is often determined by the thinking process itself. The part of "know thyself" that is under-explored is the "how" of the cognitive processes in man. These processes are built-in (hard-wired), and as such are a part of man's nature. They are behind man's accomplishments and excellence.

Man is the result of millions of years of evolution, displacing and replacing previous versions of himself that were not as successful, efficient, and/or effective. The current version of man has been around for roughly 60,000 years (the exact time is unimportant; see Preface). For all that time man has successfully met the challenges of securing food and shelter against lions, tigers, bears, wild frontiers, uncontrollable and unpredictable Mother Nature, flood and drought, pest and plague, and most sadly, other marauding humans.

Suddenly, starting about half a century ago, everything changed. All the frontiers disappeared. Mother Nature was not only predictable but warnings of serious events were often feasible. Contrasted with earlier times, medical science has remedied many previously fatal diseases and conditions, at least in industrialized societies. Farming, either of crops or animals, has transformed from everyone's occupation to a minor activity. The average man during the last 60,000 years may have lived with a group of 200 people and travelled no more than 100 miles from his birthplace during his lifetime. He never saw a piece of machinery more complex than a lever, and never read a written word. Today, it is almost impossible to find anyone that meets these criteria unless you travel to the most primitive areas of the most underdeveloped countries of the world, and even there they may have cell phones, modern clothes, mass-produced goods, and some benefit of modern medicine and technology, like clean water, even if only indirectly.

Man has his carefully-crafted storehouse of tools, fine-tuned over the millennia, but all of them are for square-hole problems, and it is now a round-hole world. The best spear, knife, bow and arrow, and plow are not much help in dealing with the barrage of electronic information, climate change, complex international economic inter-dependencies, and focussed misinformation. What makes man distinctive is how he thinks, and the purpose of this book is to show that these thinking skills, designed for a world that is now only history, have now become a hindrance instead of a help. As these thinking handicaps begin to globally interfere with man's ability to successfully deal with social, economic, moral, and physical problems, then they begin to place limits on man's future.

This has already occurred.

The challenge is to overcome, somehow, the restrictions imposed by using our own perceptual and cognitive skills to evaluate how these skills work. Since our capabilities are limited, they will by their nature impact our view of ourselves, possibly compromising that perspective. It is a little like trying to understand why a camera takes out-of-focus pictures through photographs taken of the camera by the camera. Since the photos are out-of-focus, it is hard to determine what is wrong. Like it or not, we can only peer through our crystal, enclouded and dusky, to see what is inside.

If your initial reaction to the title and/or book concept is that the book and/or author are incompetent and/or clueless, then this book may be written both for you and about you. This reaction is probably binary and judgmental and tinged with cognitive dissonance and maybe even a belief-based view of the world, characteristics of human thinking key to supporting the premise of this book. If your reaction instead is one of no reaction, you probably already know most of this anyway, and can read the book quickly to see how many key points you are already familiar with, or were overlooked, or could have been better characterized.

The title of this book could well have been <u>Mismatch: The Civilization Trap</u>, but there all already too many books in existence with mismatch in the title. Sentient Senescence is intended to signify the effects of this mismatch, the trap that not necessarily man but any sentient race constructs for themselves by way of their advanced civilization. This mismatch between the skills that enable any sentient race to conquer their world and remake it, versus the skills that are needed to excel in this completely non-natural world of sentient-being-engineered systems, organizations, and environments, stultifies the progress of the race, stymies its ability to thrive, and results in the equivalence of senescence in an individual.

Chapter 1
Coincidence of Causes

The loss of life when the liner <u>Titanic</u> sank in 1912, over 1,500 people, was due to many factors. There was not sufficient lifeboat capacity because it was based on a legal but inappropriate algorithm. About 450 spaces in the lifeboats were left unfilled due to sloppy loading practices on the part of the ship's company. The captain decided to steam at full speed at night in iceberg conditions where the standard practice at the time was to stop and wait for daylight. There were no binoculars available for the watch – they had been locked up due to concerns about theft at their last port stops. There was no moonlight on the night of the sinking, and there was no wind, so the white water splashing from wave action at the base of the iceberg, which normally gives away its position, was absent. Immediately following the collision no attempt was made to steam at full speed in reverse toward the ship lights in the distance – most likely the <u>Californian</u> – this may have both slowed the water intake rate and gained the needed attention from this ship. The watertight doors into the engine room were never cracked open, which would have allowed the large pumps located there to go to work and would have extended the float time for the ship.

Had just any one of these factors not been present, most likely the <u>Titanic</u> either would have never sunk or would not have sunk with the loss of life that occurred. It took the simultaneous presence of all these factors for this catastrophe to take place.

Pilots on commercial airplanes make mistakes all the time, just because they are human, and because familiarity breeds contempt. Flying is incredibly routine and computer-controlled for the most part, and it is easy to lose what is called situational awareness – always knowing the plane's speed, altitude, and condition of all of its flight systems – or to skip a step or steps on a checklist or procedure and leave the airplane systems unprepared for a critical flight phase like landing, an inherently risky flight condition since the plane is flying so slow and low. Pilots can come in too fast (hot), land too far down the runway (past the threshold), or choose a runway with a tailwind (should have a headwind). They can forget to arm the spoilers (little flaps above the wing surfaces that destroy the lift and let the weight of the plane drop on the wheels so the brakes can work) or fail to pull the throttles all the way back to idle so the spoilers fail to deploy. They can engage the thrust reversers late, come on the brakes late or not hard enough, or ignore the fact that they are landing on a runway that may be wet, have standing water, and may be ungrooved (grooved runways provide better traction). With 30,000 commercial flight landings in the U.S. every day, pilots in roughly 1,000 of them will make one or more of the above errors while landing. However, you almost never hear of a plane running off the end of a runway in the U.S. – why? Because even if the pilots make all of these mistakes at the same time, if they land on a dry, long runway, which is typical, they will have sufficient distance in front of the plane to enable them to safely stop anyway, so that few except they, the tower, and some astute passengers will notice. But given a wet runway, they will come close to the end of the runway. And on a short, standing-water runway and everything worst-case, they will be off the runway, into grass or an engineered overrun area if lucky; over ditches and embankments and freeways if unlucky; and off a cliff if really unlucky. Those you hear about.

Catastrophic disasters seldom occur, yet things constantly go wrong. A genius it does not take to realize that the reason for this is that it takes many things to simultaneously fail to create a catastrophe. Since the odds of this are very low, catastrophes are thankfully rare.

This book describes seven key attributes possessed by man that, along with other talents like being able to think logically, abstractly, and solve problems, have enabled him, starting from a literal handful of specimens 60,000 years ago, to conquer and remake the world as he desired. Had a few of these skills not been present, man may have amounted to only a wisp of a presence. Struggling to be noticed over everything else that Mother Nature had to offer, he would have been no more impressive than say Neanderthal or Heidelberg man. But with this package of skills, man has been impressively successful.

But like the <u>Titanic</u> steaming at full-speed on a clear, windless day, what appears to be a dream voyage can become a nightmare if day suddenly becomes night. In man's case day became night not when darkness fell, but when man's victory over the natural world was complete. Seven billion people filling the world; buildings and houses everywhere; water, food, and sanitation for most everyone. Medicine, science, and technology conquering most every old problem. Weather becoming not preventable but predictable. And the threats from lions, tigers, and bears have all but vanished. Man's skills are designed for the world that he first entered, not the world that he has remade. Brave this new world is not – it is one of complex global problems, inter-relationships between countries and economies, the need to digest vast amounts of incomplete and often misleading information. And nothing during the last 60,000 years has prepared man to deal effectively collectively with this world. Everything was just right for man for the first 50,000 plus years; now, everything is perfectly out of alignment. Man's skill set is designed for the old world, for daylight, but in today's world, it is like night. And it is not just two or three key traits that have become unhelpful, but seven, so that like the rare airplane crash, everything has gone wrong simultaneously. It were as if the <u>Titanic</u> were sailing full-speed into the densest imaginable field of icebergs, each one representing a complex problem that man's nature was not designed to solve.

It is this multiplicity of causes coupled with the radical change in the type of challenges faced by man that results in this perfect storm. Had significantly fewer than seven of these fundamental factors been working against him, or if he had not changed the world over so dramatically, it might be only small craft warnings and thunderstorms. But instead the modern world is in effect presenting Category 5 hurricanes and F-5 tornadoes for man all prepared in his overshoes and umbrella, as he finds himself possessing anachronistic tools for an alien job.

Chapter 2
An Absence of Morality

The first extensive, acknowledged, and written set of laws is credited to the Code of Ur-Nammu, around 4,000 years ago, followed by Hammurabi's about 300 years later. It took another 300 years for the Egyptians to codify the 42 Negative Confessions, describing the proper ethical and moral behavior for a person with respect to his fellow citizens and himself, which did not have the sanction of the state behind them but the psychological pressure of eternal heaven versus much much worse. Then it took another almost 1,000 years for Solon to produce his law code.

Modern man has been around for approximately 60,000 years, so for 93% of that time, there was as far as we know no documented set of laws or rules for people living as a civilized group. Undoubtedly, as seen in primitive tribes, there had been informal codes of behaviors enforced by group elders that long pre-dated these formal expressions, but we need some place to draw a line in the dust.

For most of the 60,000 years that man has been on the Earth, Mother Nature's rules of the road were pretty clear. Looking at the world around him, if man back then had had the luxury of contemplation, he would have quickly noticed that Mother Nature's first Rule was the Living-Demands-Eating-Living-Things Rule: everything lives by eating something that is already alive. Every day he could see hawks, eagles, foxes, wolves, bears, crocodiles, snakes, antelopes, deer – no one was eating sand, pebbles, and dirt to stay alive. (The subtlety of nitrogen fixation and photosynthesis was probably below man's radar in the conditions of 60,000 years ago.) If it could fight back or run, you had to catch it or kill it first. If it just sat there, like an apple or berry, you only had to grab it. But all life seemed to be there so it could be eaten by someone else. In other words, Mother Nature's lesson to man was that life was a means to an end – the end being the survival of the eater. Man was designed by Mother Nature for this world, but man was not an observer. If you were not fast and careful or lucky, you would be eaten. But even if you escaped fangs and claws, you could freeze, starve, dehydrate, drown, fall, get injured, get sick, get lost, or die in childbirth. When the first few humans were scattered around the world, it was all they could do to survive. Man would take anything from Mother Nature that he could to assist himself or his family in his efforts to be present on the morrow. The concept of ethics, or morality, was an idea that would would not get much traction with man during this time. Mother Nature was only respecting one set of behaviors, or ethics if you wanted to use that term – if you did not look after yourself, you were nourishment for something else. Killing was not just sanctioned by Mother Nature – it was mandatory and obligatory. You had to eat to live, and you had to kill to eat. So did every other animal around you.

Early on, someone went to get the family dinner he had just brought down, by a spear or trap or rocks, and was confronted by someone who had just enlisted in the world's oldest profession, crime, based on man's inherent addiction to short-cuts. Or a family member ran to a father telling him that some stranger had just taken all the food that the women had been foraging for that morning. There was no shorter-cut to food 60,000 years ago but to pretend that someone else's success was yours. There would have been an escalating dispute, and if the hunter/father could not convince the intruder to catch/pick his own meal, then he would have to resort to violence, and if it were sufficient, the intruder would end up lifeless. But with the alternative - starvation for his family, and Mother Nature showing killing to be as right as rain - how big a leap was this? It was nothing. Most likely regret that the intruder chose to impose himself and force a confrontation, but as to whether it was proper to look out for his family – not remotely questionable. Similar situations would play out over the years – sometimes the criminal would take the initiative and resort to violence first. Other times he would be caught in the act or post facto and be dispatched with or without some rudimentary attempt at due process. For sure man did realize that he appeared to be different from all other animals, and that he should not be hunting himself for dinner (although obviously this did infrequently occur). But this perception and any resulting discipline and control was self-acquired and self-imposed – it was not in any way a reflection of an example displayed and exhibited and encouraged by Mother Nature.

At some point in time, maybe within the last 10,000 years, the numbers of man grew to the point that small villages would have appeared. As a result, there would be permanent contact between family groups of people instead of intermittent or haphazard contact. Man had already learned the benefits of division of labor – Thog was too heavy and slow to be much of a hunter, but he was a whiz at making super-sharp edged arrowheads, spear points, knives, and hand axes. So Rog would use his flint points for hunting and in return give Thog a share of what he brought down. Now it might be tempting, and easier, to steal Thog's fine flint points instead of trading for them. But everyone who attempted this found that Thog would either steal something of yours back, or move away, or put one of his fine arrows between your ribs when your weren't looking. So man realized that he could not treat his own kind like he could all the other animals that he normally preyed on. He could not follow the example set by Mother Nature, but had instead to invent an entirely different paradigm, which for simplicity's sake was the Golden Rule: "Do unto Thog how you would have him do unto Rog." Or you could call it the Rights Rule: "Rog's rights stop where Thog's rights begin." This was in effect practical ethics – if you treated Rog unfairly, you would pay for it, so there was a negative sanction against counter-societal or "unethical" behavior. As village civil structures became formalized, a village chieftain, strongman, clan leader, or the equivalent would have absorbed the administration and enforcement of their version of the Golden Rule - if you want to live in the village, you have to play by the village's, or the chieftain's, rules. Violate the rules, and you end up in the bog, leather laces tightly around your neck, or if the chieftain feels beneficent, simply exiled.

Said another way, in the kingdom of Mother Nature, the only accepted currency is killing, and whoever can kill the best survives. Man, of all those in her kingdom, has a clear monopoly on this currency – a killer of most superb excellence.

But in the "kingdom" of man, killing, unless excused or justified, is an abhorrence. Like not drinking or using chewing tobacco in church, this is a man-imposed rule, a cultural norm, a self-restraint that runs counter to everything that Mother Nature expects and demands. Man has to train himself to be Dr. Jekyll (Mr. Nice) among his own, and Mr. Hyde (the Monster) everywhere else. At least Jekyll had the benefit of his special concocted potion when he wanted to deconstruct into Hyde. It is the first, and grandest, nature versus nurture test, and the results are beyond obvious.

In another 4,000 years, some of these scattered little villages would become towns. This accumulation of people meant that a larger portion of mankind would now be having sufficient contact with other men in addition to Mother Nature that the need for some formalized consistency in the rules and codes to govern business and personal disputes and conflicts and bad behavior would have become universally obvious. Through trial and error each village would have developed their own rules, passed on from key individual to key individual based on some established tradition. But as people moved from town to town to trade and relocate, rules for acceptable behavior and punishment would vary, causing confusion and complaints of unfairness. For example, someone might commit a crime in one place and then return to his home area with a much more lax set of rules. These differences would be rationalized and consolidated to various degrees over time, eventually culminating with Ur-Nammu's Code, the beginning (as far as we can tell) of formalized, documented, regime-backed laws and punishments.

While there seems to be a biological basis for man's concern for and protection of his own family group (provided by the hormone oxytocin that is produced by the hypothalamus in the brain), its effect appears to become less strong as you move away from the family group to unrelated parties in the same clan and then drop away for perfect strangers. So man has developed a system of penalties administered by the group to prevent man-on-man destructive behavior from taking place, behaviors that would be perfectly acceptable if they were targeted against Mother Nature.

The bases for these "right" behaviors over time are now called ethics and morality. Some of them are codified and supported by law, some by religion, some by cultural norms, and some by personal values that are passed on generation to generation. But they are all in place to do one simple thing – to make sure that man does not treat his fellow man the same way that for nearly 60,000 years he was forced to treat Mother Nature in order to survive.

Now some readers at this point may be unable to suppress their apoplectic allergy to this – it has to be wrong – if man is designed by Mother Nature to kill, everyone would be killing all the time. Well, as they say, if you have such a reaction, you need to get out more. The first point is that simply possessing a capability has nothing to do with the frequency with which it is utilized. Some male lions may only rarely kill – when they take over a pride and eliminate all the cubs of the previous incumbent to remove his genes and to reignite the fertility of the female lions. The second is that Mother Nature's first rule in the Animal Kingdom is Avoid Injury, and any sprinting, attacking, or attempted killing involves the risk of injury. So animals are extremely parsimonious in utilizing their hunting skills. This is why you see prey and predator harmoniously coexisting on the Serengeti. And why the recommended defense for an attack by a lion or bear is to look large and noisy – in other words, potentially too dangerous a prey to risk attacking. The third point is that man's closest genetic relative, the chimpanzee, is also the animal that exhibits the most brutal savagery against his own kind (aside from man).

You can earnestly believe that man has some genetic restriction against killing (like bonobos, who appear to never kill), or hope that he does, or feel he must, but there is absolutely no evidence for this. And as there is abundant factual evidence to the contrary, the author is forced to go with what Mother Nature has provided and demonstrated, and not with what he might want to be true, or might prefer. Or what the reader might be happier to hear.

Chapter 9 mentions that over the past 80 years, the culmination of man's success on the Earth, he has killed about 100 million of his own fellow men, all civilians, some during wars but most for other reasons. The message is that man still readily retains his ability to treat his fellow man the way he was accustomed to treat Mother Nature for the past 60,000 years, in spite of whatever legal, moral, ethical, and other prohibitions and restrictions he may retain and/or produce to the contrary.

This book is about seven attributes of human nature that enabled man to conquer the world. And now that this newly-conquered world is so very different from the one that man struggled against for nearly all his time on Earth, he finds that these seven skills are now a handicap instead of a help. In certain circumstances, ethics and morality could be argued to assist in mollifying the effects on one of these seven aspects of human nature. But so could many other factors. Humans and how they think and act are extraordinarily complex. But just discussing complexity does not add value. Only in parsing out the fundamental characteristics behind why man acts the way he does brings insight. Ethics and morality, beyond the family group, are not "fundamental" human nature characteristics, in the sense and context of the attributes discussed here, and so they are not being included in this book. It is not that they do not exist, or are not important, or do not have value – absence of evidence is not evidence of absence. It is just that ethics and morality are not germane to what is being discussed here, and there is not the time, space, or readers' patience to include them.

So if you are reading some later chapter and find a behavior that you feel is immoral, or unprincipled, or unethical, and are dismayed or unsettled that the author has not made some comment or judgment to that effect; all such commentary has been intentionally excluded - house rules.

Chapter 3
Man is ...

"I decline to accept the end of man. It is easy enough to say that man is immortal simply because he will endure; that when the last dingdong of doom has clanged and faded from the last worthless rock hanging tideless in the last red and dying evening, that even then there will still be one more sound: that of his puny inexhaustible voice, still talking. I refuse to accept this. I believe that man will not merely endure; he will prevail. He is immortal, not because he alone among creatures has an inexhaustible voice, but because he has a soul, a spirit capable of compassion and sacrifice and endurance. The poet's, the writer's, duty is to write about these things. It is his privilege to help man endure by lifting his heart, by reminding him of the courage and honor and hope and pride and compassion and pity and sacrifice which have been the glory of his past. The poet's voice need not merely be the record of man, it can be one of the props, the pillars to help him endure and prevail."[1]

This is an excerpt from William Faulkner's Nobel Prize Acceptance speech. As a piece of brief oratory, it ranks with the best in the world. The theme is on constant display in his novels, indicating that it was not a concoction for Oslo. Based on his nature - his hope and pride and compassion and sacrifice - man will prevail until the end of time.

Here is a sampling of what other authors, most poets, say about man's nature. Much of this everyone's English teacher at some point made them read – this will save the reader the time of going back and looking it all up again.

Exuberant also were Shakespeare's praises. From <u>Hamlet</u>:
"What a piece of work is a man! How noble in reason! How infinite in faculties! In form and moving, how express and admirable! In action, how like an angel! In apprehension, how like a god! The beauty of the world! The paragon of animals!"

---

1   "William Faulkner - Banquet Speech". Nobelprize.org. 17 Mar 2011
    http://nobelprize.org/nobel_prizes/literature/laureates/1949/faulkner-speech.html

Sophocles notes: "Wonders are many, yet of all things is Man
        the most wonderful."

Even Sandburg is surprisingly optimistic:
        "The people will live on....
        Man will yet win."

The Bible is pretty clear: "And God said, Let us make man in
        our image, after our likeness." (The emphasis it
        should be noted is on appearance, not on what is
        inside.)

But there is another position, heavily represented. The Bible
        also says "Man that is born of woman is of few days,
        and full of trouble. He commeth forth like a flower,
        and is cut down; he fleeth also as a shadow, and
        continueth not."

Homer noted "Of all creatures that breathe and move on earth,
        none is more to be pitied than a man."

Shakespeare balanced what he said earlier with:
        "Life's but a walking shadow, a poor player
        that struts and frets his hour upon the stage
        and then is heard no more: it is a tale
        told by an idiot, full of sound and fury,
        signifying nothing."

From Swinburne: "In his heart is a blind desire
        In his eyes foreknowledge of death;
        He weaves, and is clothed with derision;
        Sows, and he shall not reap;
        His life is a watch or a vision
        Between a sleep and a sleep."

And Drummond: "This life, which seems so fair,
        Is like a bubble blown up in the air ...
        For even when most admired, it in a thought,
        As swelled from nothing, doth dissolve in nought."

From King: "Like to the falling of a star,
              Or as the flights of eagles are,
              Or like the fresh spring's gaudy hue,
              Or silver drops of morning dew,
              Or like a wind that chafes the flood,
              Or bubbles which on water stood:
              Even such is man, whose borrowed light
              Is straight called in, and paid to night.
              The wind blows out, the bubble dies;
              The spring entombed in autumn lies;
              The dew dries up, the star is shot;
              The flight is past - and man forgot."

From the Chinese proverb: "Man's life is like
              a candle in the wind,
              or like the frost
              upon the tiles."

And Arnold: "For the world, which seems
              To lie before us like a land of dreams,
              So various, so beautiful, so new,
              Hath really neither joy, nor love, nor light,
              Nor certitude, nor peace, nor help for pain;
              And we are here as on a darkling plain
              Swept with confused alarms of struggle and flight,
              Where ignorant armies clash by night."

So which is it, as someone said - are we to be optimistic, hoping this to be the best of all possible worlds, or pessimistic, fearing that it is fleetingly so? Is there an answer as to what man is and has/will/can become?

Not to throw too much brutal reality on the poets, but the answer of course is all of the above. Man can be simultaneously both full of promise and full of demise. But the first evidence of man's nature shows up in man's writings about himself – they all, without exception, reflect one extreme or the other. Man is great or garbage, a demi-god or dust. You never see some complex, hybridized, Janused, chameleon picture of man reflected in poetry – just pure, mono-thematic clarity. Chapters 7 and 8 will discuss why man's nature prevents him from embracing duality (or worse) and accepting only simple singularity – it's one or the other, but it cannot be both. But we will get to this in a moment.

There are answers to the poets' ponderings, they surround us, we live them day to day, but they are seldom singled out, and never assembled in one place for our review. Some of the reason for this is the old saying, familiarity breeds contempt, as we pay no attention to that in which we are immersed. Some may be what Gibran notes: "The obvious is that which is never seen until someone expresses it simply." But another fundamental factor was introduced by Sir Isaac Newton: "I do not know what I appear to the world, but to myself I seem to have been only a boy playing on the sea-shore, and diverting myself in now and then finding a smoother pebble or a prettier shell than ordinary, whilst the great ocean of truth lay undiscovered before me." Today, the beach is swept and piled with shells and pebbles of all varieties and attractions, bordered by many seas, and the seas by continents, and the continents by planets, and planets by galaxies. Finding the right places to start, and staying with it before being distracted by something else, is today's great challenge. Ironically, in Newton's day, in consideration of the tools and data available at his time, he had not near the problem of either distraction or the size of the ocean that we face today.

There are countless works - poetry, essay, philosophy, fiction - about what man is, both individually and collectively. Close by stand the issues of the meaning of life, and the "right" way for man to act and behave. Since man acts through conscious thought and subconscious impulse or both, how he thinks, the mechanisms by which he digests and uses incoming information and stored memories, are of great importance.

Why? Poetic license allows the poets to freely have their say above. But these are all speculative conclusions – artfully assembled, brilliantly sung to be sure – but you must take the poet on faith unless you understand how man actually thinks and behaves. Otherwise it is a "black box" appraisal – sort of a variation on a Turing Test for a species. Knowing precisely how man ticks allows you to tell if there is more than gears and silicon in the box.

In comparison to what man is and what he should be, there is much less written on how he thinks. Many, many tests have been performed on people that measure how people react to different stimuli, test protocols, and situations. But these do not so much tell you how man thinks as *what* happens when he thinks. In addition, the distillation tends to be missing. You can find books containing a summary of literally hundreds of different test results, but you are not left with a short list of say five key techniques that represent how man thinks that you can then utilize to predict what the average man will do in any future situation. Biological/neurological studies exist, but they are like a study of the kitchen of a great restaurant. The spoons and pans and ovens and counters and food storage are all described and cataloged, but this sheds no light on how a memorable dish is prepared to look and taste the way it does.

Yet even if this "how" is explained, something is still missing. A restaurant which opens when everyone is asleep, or serves breakfast when everyone is expecting dinner, will not be a success. It has to seamlessly mesh its internal machinery for preparing food with the accommodation of its patrons - opening at the right time, providing a pleasant environment, and ensuring that the right meal is served on time at the right temperature.

And so it is with the thinking process of man. It only has relevance when played against the particular time of man, the challenges and obstacles and goals that face him at that juncture. Many things do not change, but many do, and as the environment surrounding man changes, his ability to deal with it will also change.

Once the thinking process of man is integrated into man's environment, and evaluated from the dawn of man out into the future, a distinct message becomes apparent. And the message is troublesome and disconcerting. Based on what man is (how he thinks), effectively dealing with his environment is becoming more and more difficult. (Environment here is not trees and plants, it is meant to be everything that surrounds a specific individual, including other individuals.)

Where does all of this lead? Is the outcome as inevitable as it appears? Attractively-simple answers are just not going to cut it.

Man is a certainly great, possibly noble, and very much alive experiment in which everyone participates. But the outcome is driven by what man is, by his nature, and not what he believes or wishes or hopes or longs to be.

Senescence

Who was the most talented, brilliantly-skilled-in-multiple-areas human of all time? Without wasting a lot of space defining talented, most people would say Leonardo da Vinci. Some might say Newton, or Alexander the Great, or Jesus (religion is cheating here), or Ramses II. How about the greatest leader? – that would capture Alexander for sure. How about the smartest person ever? Some might go with da Vinci or Newton again, others might say Einstein, some might go with Tesla, or reach back to Aristotle. Let's try the greatest musical composer ever. A matter of taste for sure, but Beethoven normally comes out on top, with Mozart, Bach, Tchaikovsky, and another dozen or so in pursuit. How about the greatest painter of all time? Even more personal for sure, but let's stay away from what you would like hanging in your living room or what you would trade your children for. Michelangelo often comes out on top here, as do Raphael, Rembrandt, several of the Impressionists, Picasso, da Vinci, and maybe Caravaggio. How about the greatest sculptor? Well, Michelangelo generally wins this easily, with Praxiteles, Bernini, and even Rodin getting some votes. How about the best mathematician ever? Well, you get one repeat and some new ones – Newton, Fermat, Leibniz, Gauss, Hilbert, and another ten or so in close competition. How about the most beautiful building ever? Most people would take the Parthenon in Greece, although it has been badly damaged from warfare. Fans of history might also select Queen Hatshepsut's Funerary Temple, although it again is in poor shape, and others might select other palaces and temples which have entirely vanished – the Hanging Gardens of Babylon, Darius' Palace that Alexander torched in a move he immediately regretted, the Temple of Olympian Zeus, the Temple of Capitoline Jupiter, the great pyramid of Khufu/Cheops, the Taj Mahal, the Hagia Sophia, the Hermitage, and a few others. How about the greatest writer of all time? Shakespeare often ends up on top of such lists, but others might put Dickens, Tolstoy, Dostoyevsky, Hemingway, Faulkner, Melville, or Chaucer there instead. For the best poet ever, it is a real free for all, since poetry is probably more a matter of taste than art, including people that think all poetry is trash, and there is no distinct consensus number one. But those on this list would be Shakespeare (sonnets), Wordsworth, Tennyson, Byron, Dickinson, Keats, Frost, Homer, and obviously others. How about the best violins and cellos ever made? Well, now here for once is a category where there is no contest. 300 years ago, Stradivarius made an instrument at the rate of one every two weeks for years. These have never been equaled, nor for that matter understood, surprising considering the technology available today and the lack of technology in Stradivarius' hands. How about the best swords or knives ever? Well, most people will give the nod to Damascus steel, so sharp and so strong that it provided an unwelcome surprise to the visiting Crusaders in the 13th century, cutting right through their steel armor like it was tin. But the katana, the sword carried by the Samurai, had steel that comes in a good second. While the recipe for the Damascus steel is long lost, katana steel is still made today with the same conserved formula and techniques.

So what is the message here? All these responses have something in common. And no, its is not that they are all talented. It is that they are all long departed. Most have been gone for hundreds of years; some for thousands. The great pyramid of Khufu has been around for 4,500 years, not only one of the most remarkable buildings in the world but one of the oldest.

But this is not the half of it. A few hundred years ago the population of the world was not even one billion. Now it is seven billion. So somehow all the best people in all these categories emerged from a relatively small sample of mankind, way before we had any of the accumulated knowledge and experience that all of man benefits from today. It is almost that quality is inversely proportional to quantity – now that there are seven billion of us, talent appears to be thinned out; veneered over us in such a way that it does not have an opportunity to pool to any significant depth.

Is this just a coincidence? With most humans on the Earth being alive today, you would think that at least some of the "best" would show up. A few of the names do come close – Hemingway and Picasso are semi-recent. But too many names and buildings are hundreds of years old. Not even one name alive today? Something is amiss.

Now the statisticians will say that the total number of people who have ever been born is much larger than the seven billion alive today, so it is no surprise that the best of everything lies in the past. To buy that argument, you have to accept that someone born 1,000 years ago, or 10,000 years ago, has just as fair a chance of excellence as you today. That person was trying not to get smallpox, TB, pneumonia, or any other systemic infection, trying not to starve to death, trying not to be killed by some marauding band or army, could count on not being able to read or write, and was lucky if they made their 30th birthday (and that was if they made their first birthday). If you think about it for a moment, it is not a fair fight.

So it looks like Mother Nature could be sending us a message – she is done with us. The best has went and gone. A landscape of drooping senescence. It is a pretty stunning and unmistakable pattern.

A Word from Mother Nature

Homo sapiens sapiens (us) evolved roughly 200,000 years ago. This book is using 60,000 years ago as a figure for the effective date for modern humans in quantity on the planet, but technically and genetically we go back much further. Neanderthals also evolved in about the same time frame, but disappeared about 30,000 years ago, so they overlapped for on the order of 200,000 years. Denisovans, a relative of both man and Neanderthals, and who also disappeared about 30,000 years ago, may have only lasted 50,000 or so years. Homo rhodesiensis (an ancestor of modern man) lasted about 200,000 years. Homo heidelbergensis (an ancestor of modern man and Neanderthals) appeared to last about 250,000 years. Homo antecessor (possibly an ancestor of homo heidelbergensis) seems to have lasted about 400,000 years. Homo sapiens idaltu (an ancestor of modern man) appeared to last about 200,000 years, although this data is very speculative. Homo floresiensis appeared to last approximately 100,000 years, and may have been around until as recently as between 12,000 to 400 years ago.

So while there is no hard or fast rule, recent species of man, now that he has become sophisticated, seem to only last about 200,000 years (older, less-sophisticated versions lasted over one million years). And, surprise, surprise, what do you know, man has been around for just exactly Mother Nature's magic interval. So maybe we are not just on a senescence run, but an obsolescence fall, and Mother Nature is fiddling with the curtain and the next act.

Is there proof of this? You can't prove anything. All you have are the facts. All the greatest accomplishments of humans appear to have been in the past. 200,000 years have passed and that is about how long a particular species of man gets on the Earth. Some poets affirm this, that we are but dust. Now our brand of humans may in fact last much longer than 200,000 years. You can make a careful evaluation of the evidence and make a determination that this may apply and you should be cautious, or that there is no possible way this can be germane. Or you can simply choose to not believe this – a whole chapter in this book is devoted to belief-driven cognition – people who interpret the world through pre-held beliefs (such as: the world is flat, the Earth is the center of the solar system, evolution is pretend, the state of man is fine and only getting better). But Mother Nature has a tidy way of dealing with those who do not heed her messages, and man has even given them a name – fossils.

Dèjá Encore

Along the coast of southwest Italy, with a view of the setting sun across the Tyrrhenian Sea, are some lovely homes, available to any families with upper-middle class incomes. Some of these that the author remembers most fondly have a separate marble and mosaic pavilion along the shore used for seaside dining. Of course, people will complain about everything – here is how one critic complains about the bathrooms for example: "... and the tiny little bath ... situated in an ill-lit corner... Who is there who could bear to have a bath in such surroundings nowadays? We think ourselves poorly off, living like paupers, if the walls are not ablaze with large and costly circular mirrors, if our Alexandrian marbles are not decorated with panels of Numidian marble, if the whole of their surface has not been given a decorative overlay of elaborate patterns having all the variety of fresco murals, unless the ceiling cannot be seen for glass, unless the (hot tubs) into which we lower our bodies with all the strength drained out of them ... are edged with Thasian marble (which was once the rarest of sights ...), unless the water pours from silver taps. And so far we have only been talking about the ordinary fellow's plumbing. What about the bath(rooms) of certain former (workers)? Look at their array of statues, their assemblies of columns that do not support a thing but are put up purely for ornament, just for the sake of spending money.... We have actually come to such a pitch of choosiness that we object to walking on anything other than precious stones.... Nowadays 'moth-hole' is the way some people speak of a bathroom unless it has been designed to catch the sun through enormous windows all day long, unless a person can acquire a tan at the same time as he is having a bath, unless he has views from the bath over countryside and sea."[2]

This same critic has more to say about some of the more upper-end residences: "Is it not living unnaturally to hanker after roses during the winter, and to force lilies in mid-winter by taking the requisite steps to change their environment and keeping up the temperature with hot water heating? Is it not living unnaturally to plant orchards on the top of towers, or have a forest of trees waving in the wind on the roofs and ridges of one's mansions, their roots springing at a height at which it would have been presumptuous for their crests to reach? Is it not living unnaturally to sink the foundations of hot tubs in the sea and consider that one is not swimming in a refined fashion unless one's heated waters are exposed to the waves and storms?"[3]

You can probably tell from the language that this complaint is not about today's homes – this criticism is about the values and priorities of Roman society 2,000 years ago. Herculaneum, a non-distinguished middle-class town, had the luck (for us, not for them) of being hit with mud and not ash, so it was preserved and not crushed by Vesuvius, and you can see how these people lived for yourself. The author can't speak for other readers, but his bathroom does not actually have any marble, murals, silver, or windows larger than a couple of phone books. Now the author has heard that some people now, who have money to burn and have to be able to leave at a moment's notice, like some doctors, have installed heated driveways to melt snow and ice. But the author is a little shaky on people installing hot water underground to make roses and lilies bloom out of season, or installing hot water swimming pools open to the ocean. The author has also seen some condo buildings with some small gardens and a tree or two on the roof, but for people in individual mansions to have orchards and forests of trees on their roofs – that seems a little unusual nowadays also.

The point here is that 2,000 years ago, these average Roman citizens did not have any electrical or electronic devices, fancy automobiles, synthetic materials, antibiotics, or exotic vodkas. But they lived in houses much fancier and more sophisticated, if you subtract out electronics, than a comparable citizen lives in today. If you were very rich, or super-rich, there is no modern parallel. Have we made progress over the past 2,000 years? In some areas, clearly, but in others, we have probably moved backwards, maybe the inevitable result of having seven billion of us now. The Romans probably thought they were pretty cool, and they definitely were in many areas, and they lasted almost 1,000 years before they disappeared. So if you are reading this and feeling really comfortable in your society that has lasted a few hundred years, beware the Ozymandias effect.

---

2   Letters from a Stoic, Seneca, Penguin Books, 1969, pp. 145-146
3   Ibid., p. 222-223

Chapter 4
Mismatch

Man does not have any weaknesses. Man has come to dominate his planet and all other species on it in a relative short span of years. With all the technical prowess that man has been able to demonstrate, he still cannot even begin to comprehend the precise biological mechanisms behind his own competence.

This book is not an attempt to pretend to find vulnerabilities in man and exploit them. Man has nothing but strengths that even the world's best scientists have been unable to explain. Look at it from the perspective of everyone else in the animal kingdom: "What is it with this species man? No claws, no horns, no fangs, no hooves, not even any fur. Pound for pound we are stronger by about a factor of ten. We can jump higher, swim faster, out-run, out-fly, and out-climb man. But in a simple endurance race, he can run any of us down, run us into the ground. And everything about him is a trick. He chases us into traps, off cliffs, into box canyons, shoots us with pieces of tree and rock, catches us with hooks and nets, and always something we don't expect. Even though we are more capable than man by almost every measure, he always finds a way to avoid our strength and conquer us."

Man's powers developed over time to cope with the challenges that he was faced with. This book is not targeted at man's physical innovations – walking upright, fine motor skills in the hand, ability to hunt any animal to exhaustion, and the ability to talk are some key examples. But the mental developments that left all other species in the dust were equally profound – the ability to construct abstract concepts; to apply extended, logical thought, both deductive and inductive; to think in verbal (language-based) terms; to speak and write in the most complex fashions imaginable in many different languages; and to have a store of memories of events, feelings, colors, tastes, and smells with an almost limitless depth of details covering a span of seventy years or more. (Man has other talents, like the ability to paint, sculpt, write, and play music, but they do not seem to enhance man's ability to compete with his environment.)

Homo erectus was the closest direct ancestor of modern man, and through one or more of modern man's capabilities that they did not possess, homo erectus disappeared from the planet maybe 70,000 years ago. Neanderthal man, another direct or indirect descendant of homo erectus, lasted longer, until as recently as 30,000 years ago, but they too were finally completely displaced by modern man, even though physically their brain was about the same size as ours. Some think it was the ability to speak, some think it was the ability to think abstractly, but there was some critical trait or traits that brought about the complete demise of this race. Now, there are still many other species of apes around, many endangered, so it is rather stunning to think that this race of man was entirely eliminated just because of some missing man-like traits, considering all of the apes are obviously missing even more of them. Some anthropologists feel a more sinister explanation is the answer – a systematic elimination of the not-quite-perfectly-human race by our ancestors – the first genocide. But the most plausible, Occam's Razor explanation is found in Chapter 10.

But no other species or physical barrier or natural threat has been able to daunt man's supremacy. Even the most terrible disasters that nature could throw at man – famine, floods, earthquakes, disease, hurricanes, tornadoes, volcanoes – have just slowed things down a bit. Considering all other species can only come into balance with nature, it is pretty impressive.

Imagine a master carpenter with a truck full of tools if you are suddenly stuck in the wilderness. No problem, he can build you a shelter no matter how severe the weather. Or you happen to be sitting in a major hospital and you suddenly don't feel so hot – most likely you will be able to get your medical problems dealt with.

But if you ask the carpenter to help you with your medical problem, or the radiologist to help you build a weather-proof shelter, you are probably going to be out of luck. Not for their lack of skill, but it's the wrong skill for the the wrong problem.

And so we get to the concept behind this book. It is not about a lack of skills or competencies in man. Instead, it is about a mismatch of skills, about the wrong skills at the wrong time, about having an excess of round-peg skills but square-hole problems.

Man spent 60,000 years coping with a world that went through two enormous climate changes – into and then out of a massive ice age that put most of the Northern Hemisphere under a mile or more of ice. He then had to chase a dwindling food supply around the world for close to 30,000 years until it basically ran out. Faced with this new challenge, he had to invent agriculture, irrigation, and farming. This led to inventing cities and civilization. Civilization meant warfare, and so pressure-edged flint blades established over a period of more than 100,000 years had to be replaced with the invention and mastery of copper and then bronze and then finally iron weapon technology. But climate change had to be dealt with again, as the Fertile Crescent in Mesopotamia, and what is now Egypt, Iraq, and parts of Iran went from gardens to deserts. And again, when the sun seemed to go out during the Little Ice Age, when for 350 or so years every river and lake in Europe froze over during most winters, incidentally helping to ruin Napoleon's run into Russia. And now in the 21th century, the opposite challenge, warming, is here to stay.

Old growth forests in Europe and England were basically eliminated as the need for strong timbers for ship-building over-took the world's supply, leaving only second growth wood suitable solely for structures and firewood.

With ships man spread all over the rest of the world, exploring and settling until there was nothing left. Ships made of wood powered by sails that today would barely qualify as a small fishing boat would spend months crossing oceans in search of often the unknown, braving weather that at the time was a completely unmanageable factor. Hurricanes in the Atlantic, typhoons in the Pacific, cyclones in between – all these were routine challenges for these explorers and settlers-to-be. Many ships were lost, many died, disappeared, never heard from again.

Lacking water, men built wagons and used oxen to drag them across land not only inhospitable but but often impossibly steep and dry. Women and children often would walk. When the wagons or oxen gave out, everyone would walk. If they managed to find enough brackish water, they still had to find enough game until they could clear land and farm. If the weather turned against them, drought or excessive cold, they would all starve.

Not until around 1865 and Joseph Lister and Louis Pasteur did anyone figure out on a widespread basis that germs caused infection and disease (Jenner's smallpox vaccine was conceptually just a variation of the technique of variolation that had been around for hundreds of years, and while much more safe and effective was not a breakthrough in understanding). For the preceding 60,000 or so years, modern man had to deal with things like the black death (Bubonic plague), which killed about one-third of everyone in Europe in the Middle Ages, amounting to maybe 100 million people. Just smallpox and tuberculosis between them would take almost 1% of the population a year. Toss in pneumonia, strep, gangrene, leprosy, cancer, heart attacks, and childbirth, and most people seldom made it past thirty years old. And if you were unlucky enough to live in the tropics, the parasites and diseases were too long to list, resulting in blindness and incapacitation as often as death.

Of course, people still had to dodge lions, tigers, and bears, alongside wolves, snakes, floods, droughts, trails, cliffs, fording rivers, and every other imaginable hazard in a world lacking any kind of local improvements.

But roughly by 1900, all the world had been explored; as had all the world that people had a strong interest in settling in. Oh, people were still burning down tropical forests so they could farm for a year or two and then repeat the process, but that was just more of the same. The challenges morphed from lions, tigers, bears, rivers, and mountains to problems with neighbors, crime, economics, and government.

By 1950 medical science has had antibiotics and for the most part had indeed become a science. The last World War had passed. Cities that had once been wood and brick and then proudly stone were now concrete and steel. The Minoan invention of covered sewers was pretty much ubiquitous. Powered machinery performed most tasks that man or farm animal would previously have had to execute. Electrical power provided light, heat, and communication replacing darkness, firewood, and silence for most of the world. Transportation, for thousands of years the most expensive choice an individual could make, became routinely affordable for everyone. Food was not a chase but a trip to the market; housing not a hovel but a rental agreement. Large families, necessary for so long due to infant mortality and the need for extra hands on the family farm, became an expensive handicap. Clean water, a miracle a few hundred years ago, was now taken for granted by most everyone.

The challenges of today, many people would report, are job security, income level, retirement security, value of their house if they own one, quality of the education system, health insurance (in the U.S.), the level of crime, and if their children are going to end up in overall better shape than their parents. Beyond this you will find concerns on clothes, shoes, cell phones, cars, girls, boys, music, portable music players, movies, celebrities, sports, food, and social web sites. If you are from an Asian country, a quality education is going to be near the top of the list. In Western Europe, time off and quality of life are equally important.

Switching places with someone from 25,000 years ago, or 20,000 years ago, or 12,000 years ago, or 8,000 years ago, or 6,000 years ago, or 4,000 years ago, or 2,000 years ago, or 1,000 years ago, most people from today would last a few days best case. The person from that time period would do a little better in today's environment, it's just that they would be spending their time in jail or a hospital. But all the skills possessed by both would be totally irrelevant in their "new" world – other than finding a true alien, the differences could not be more exquisite. Even a switch from 500 years ago would not work, nor would one from 200 years ago. It is only when you get within 100 years of today that you can make a passing argument that the average person might survive such a switch.

What's the point? 100 years is just a few tenths of a percent of the span of modern man. All of modern man's experience, and his genetic predecessors' experience, going back millions of years, has been targeted, developed, tuned, and polished to attack and subdue an environment that no longer exists. The environment that exists today - one entirely of man's own making - one of seven billion people, global impacts from man's actions, where it is difficult for the actions of one person to not affect his neighbors, one of massive metropolises, intensive unstopping electronic information, people moving effortlessly over significant distances on a daily basis, where the daily struggles for food, shelter, and self-preservation that were the totality of life for every person for tens of thousands of years are today, for billions of people, as antiquated as basket-weaving, making fire, or curing hides.

Well, so what, you may say, man is if nothing remarkably adaptable, so he will simply adjust to these changes.

And cope man did. Dependent on the Nile flooding, the Egyptians built complex irrigation facilities over 4,000 years ago. Restricted to just one river, the people of Sri Lanka built a series of the largest brick structures in the world along with complementary irrigation channels and gates, watering over 100 square kilometers of agricultural land around 2,500 years ago. A little later the Romans built an even more extensive water supply system over thousands of lineal miles. 4,500 years ago the Egyptians somehow built a stone wonder of the world just to mimic the rays of the sun in the sky. The Chinese built all-told about 30,000 lineal miles of fortified stone walls in Northern China to protect themselves against invaders, including in that the 3,500 or so miles attributed to the Great Wall of China. Adjusting man did well, and thrived as the world changed and the threats presented by the world did as well.

But the world today is irreversibly and qualitatively different from anytime since its origin, and the tools that served man so well in the past will feel clumsy, dull, and counter-productive today. Give man a new frontier – an untouched land to settle, a life-and-death battle to wage – and he is unstoppable. But where it is a contest of the loudest, or most colorful, or most captivating opinion on social, political, or economic issues, no longer do these historically-demonstrated skills add value. Man's fight or flight instincts enable him to instantly assess and then escape from a potentially dangerous situation, but what happens when he has to use these to screen 15 second sound-bites of often intentionally-misleadingly-packaged misinformation, purposefully targeted to take advantage of these very instincts? Journalism as a profession used to dominate the sources of news, regardless of the media type, as late as 40 years ago. But the consensus today is that all such media is now part of the entertainment business, having made the decision that a media company with professional journalism as its number one goal/objective is not financially viable. Heavily-researched factual stories are out; headlines on celebrities and opinion pieces are in. It is back to the yellow journalism standards of a little over a century ago for about the same reasons. Only by intensive digging can the average person come up with an objective, complete picture of any complex problem. Few today have the time, motivation, or mettle to do so. Or how do man's rapid decision-making and problem-solving skills, allowing him to sift through irrelevancies to figure out how to build a better arrow, spear, knife, wall, roof, pot, shoe, shirt, plow, or kiln help him with problems only established through years of work by teams of experts, based on technology, science, and data that the average man has no knowledge of, contact with, interest in, aptitude for, or tangible personal evidence of – problems like global climate change; ground water depletion; air, water, and ground pollution; and economics on a (inter)national scale?

People often used the metaphor "a perfect storm" to describe a worst-case scenario where chance/fate/Mother Nature/luck seemingly let everything go wrong at the same time, creating a one-time catastrophic event. Welcome to today. Man has spent 60,000 years developing characteristics, encapsulated in his human nature, that can deal with any problem except those created by the world of today, a world that has not existed for 4.5 billion years. A stranger in a strange land, Richard Heinlein would call him. But this is not just a runaway Murphy's Law scenario. This convocation was orderly, predictable, and inevitable – once conquered, subdued, pacified, homogenized, and suburbanized, all of the threats and challenges possessed by Mother Nature effectively disappeared for most of the seven billion people on the planet.

This book is about why man has reached a critical point – and it is not that man has changed. The world, ironically through man's own success, now presents a set of challenges unlike any of those that man was designed or has experienced over the previous 60,000 years. Why man is now so jeopardized is because his skills are for the most part not just obsolete but a mismatch, a handicap, a negative, a limitation. What used to be a strength as recently as a century ago is now collectively a weakness for man. That is what this book is about.

Now Mother Nature has a way of dealing with these kinds of challenges, fans of paleontology will claim. No matter how severe the shock, life bounces back, aggressively and powerfully. Well, yes, but sometimes 90% of the life forms that are alive at one moment are gone the next. So man might drizzle down to a footnote and the meerkats will take over. There is no guarantee for a particular species, especially when they have the wrong tools for the job. As Gary Larson has the professorial dinosaur saying to his fellow dinosaurs: "The picture's pretty bleak, gentlemen... The world's climates are changing, the mammals are taking over, and we all have a brain about the size of a walnut."

Chapter 5
Man's Limiting Characteristics

There are seven principal characteristics of human thinking that fundamentally impact man's ability to interact with his environment: Taken together, (and toss in some additional flavoring), and we call the result "human nature". As powerful forces go, this one is a planet re-maker.

Some of you may remember the movie <u>The Crying Game</u> from 1992, most likely for the androgynous acting of Jaye Davidson. But some may also remember the movie for the amusingly confused state in which it left everyone about Aesop's Fables, for the movie has reference to a fable on human nature that was neither Aesop's nor anyone else's, although many will swear that it was.

A scorpion asks a frog to ferry him across a stream, goes the modern fable. But surely you will sting me and I will drown, says the frog. How silly, replies the scorpion, for then you and I would both drown, and it would be the end of me. So on climbs the scorpion and the frog begins to swim across the water. Midway across the stream, the scorpion stings the frog, and as the paralysis slowly creeps over him and he sinks into the water, the frog bitterly cries out to the scorpion, asking him why, as they are now both going to drown. "It's my nature" are the last words of the scorpion.

So it is with human nature – if it can be changed, it is not part of human nature. Human nature is inviolatedly imprinted; it is incorrigibly inked into the deepest fundamentals of what makes man man. The fable illustrates that human nature allows itself to be happily self destructive; reason and logic don't get in the building. Here are seven characteristics that both define human nature and limit man.

The Irrational Man

That man is capable of rational thought, logic, conceptualization, and the like is completely obvious unless you are a philosopher. But those abilities do not mean that man's thinking is exclusively rational, or always rational. In fact, countless recent physiological studies using brain imaging techniques, usually either fMRI (Functional Magnetic Resonance Imaging) or PET (Positron Emission Tomography), have shown that many areas of the brain are involved with conscious (and unconscious) thought, and emotional areas are always active along with what would be termed the exclusively "rational" areas like the cerebrum. In other words, the brain is designed to remember, present, recall, gate, color, twist, interpret, adjust, emphasize, and spin thinking, memory, and recall with emotional content. It is not designed to "think rationally" without emotional input.

For those who who are skeptical of generalizing from such studies, nature unfortunately (for them) provides us with a control group that convincingly makes the case. There are small groups of people who clearly, demonstrably, and in some cases with terrible consequences do not add emotional content to their thinking. At one extreme are the Aspie's, those with Asperger's Syndrome, a subset of Autism Spectrum Disorders, or ASD, who cannot perceive, relate to, or feel emotional context in others nor in themselves. At the other are most sociopaths and psychopaths. In order to "appear" normal and get along with the rest of society, these people must learn to mimic the emotional, non-rational content that is entirely automatic in the rest of us. Some sociopaths/psychopaths can excel at this mimicry, often with disastrous societal consequences. Aspie's struggle to maintain even a minimally-acceptable functional performance.

Sadly, there are rare individuals with more drastic damage, where the centers in the prefrontal cortex that link emotion into the thinking and decision areas of the brain are damaged or missing. These people are perfectly capable of thinking through any scenario as would any normal person, but they are incapable of acting or making a real decision. They can tell you what *should* be the decision, but they cannot implement what they know to be the right thing. Or they will debate endlessly about whether it is better to go to the store on Wednesday or Thursday. Without the linkages to the emotional side of the brain, the rational side has no motive power to take the action that it can imagine or deduce.

Of the following seven human nature traits, five are firmly based on emotion, one is strongly impacted by it (self-first orientation); and one is based on the physical limitations of the human brain. None are intellectual or rational traits.

Short-Cut Thinking

Man is a short-cut machine. We use a variety of cognitive short-cuts to speed up our thinking and decision-making processes. We are driven to seek closure, an answer, an explanation, even if it means filling in the blanks where information is simply missing. We almost automatically sort the world into what is most important and then everything else. There is an innate tendency to look for the best, the most popular, the number one, the winner. To help speed up this short-cutting process, we save and recall most information judgmentally. We preferred it or we did not, we enjoyed it or we did not, we agreed with it or we did not, we like it or we dislike it. In addition to this judgmental tagging, we generally use a thinking and remembering short-cut with only two possible opposing choices to remember. This can be called bipolar thinking. Judgmental tagging is almost always bipolar, but so is most everything else - right or wrong, attractive or unattractive, fits well or fits poorly, too much or too little, rich or poor, conservative or liberal.

Because both judgmental tagging and bipolar thinking reflect your personal outlook, they may be (and generally are) different from person to person. This often leads to sharp, emotional, and logically-lean differences of opinion - since each side has fallen automatically and unconsciously into one of two emotional opposing views.

Man's preoccupation with modern electronic technology is but a reflection of his own nature's proclivity toward short-cuts of any kind. With a smart phone or video game or web-enabled computer you can jump anywhere, communicate with anyone, see and experience anything, read and play anything, and become anything, without so much as moving, and at the speed of light, and with accompanying sound that makes the experience forcefully compelling.

Cognitive Dissonance

"The test of a first rate intelligence is the ability to hold two opposed ideas in the mind at the same time, and still retain the ability to function. One should, for example, be able to see that things are hopeless and yet be determined to make them otherwise." This quote is from the writer F. Scott Fitzgerald. By Fitzgerald's standards, few of us can genuinely pass this test. Being "genuine" forces one to keep both poles of the two opposing beliefs simultaneously intact, and not to pull back/soften/ameliorate on the one by addressing the other. So in Fitzgerald's own example, almost all people, once they make the determination to take actions to remedy the "hopeless" situation, will automatically feel that things are less than hopeless.

The term for the characteristic in human nature that automatically re-adjusts some aspect of your belief structure as soon as an opposing fact/belief arrives on the scene is cognitive dissonance. Like it sounds, when a dissonance appears on the scene, the human mind automatically re-normalizes the conflict, leaving only the primary belief in place. If this happens to you, you don't have to do anything overtly to have these conflicts rectified. Do you intensely dislike a particular TV show, TV characters, breakfast cereals, fast food restaurants, and the like? Just raise a couple of children, have them go wild for these exact same things, and after a while you will notice that they are not nearly as bad as you once thought they were. Do you dislike a particular type of software, cell phone, or computer? Just have your company standardize on and mandate the use of it, and it will appear to be much more tolerable. Everyone probably remembers Aesop's use of this trait in his fable of the fox and the grapes, where the fox, denied access to a bunch of grapes that are so high they are beyond his reach, frustratedly walks away with the new determination that they were most likely sour and inedible anyway. The thought of a delicious meal being denied him because he was unable to leap sufficiently high was too much dissonance to take – he was starving due to his own lack of strength and/or willpower. This was unacceptable, and had to be resolved by making the grapes in effect vanish. Better that than yummy grapes and an incompetent fox – Aesop knew he would seldom bump into someone who would make that selection. But whatever the choice, it is one or the other, and not both – Aesop and Fitzgerald (and a landfill of psychologists) are pointing out that almost no one is walking away thinking I'm perfect, the grapes are perfect, and I'm still starving.

Belief-Driven Cognition

Belief-driven motivation in man is a great strength. What we call "hope" is the most powerful result, carrying man through situations where rationality alone would most likely call for surrender. This developed most likely as a way to compete on at least an even footing with other species who, without the ability to think, would never think of surrendering.

Being driven by belief means a motivation that has no factual or rational basis. In the absence of facts or reasons, belief is entirely appropriate. Faced with a drought, or famine, or absence of game, or a plague, or a town or city attacked by marauding bandits, or caught in a storm on a sailing ship – hope that somehow they would survive the calamity would provide the motivation to keep people going instead of capitulating.

But being driven by belief when the world is filled with facts reverses the situation. What was a strength in the absence of facts now becomes a handicap in the presence of them. If a person comes to a belief, and then accepts only the facts that appear to support their belief, rejecting those that appear in conflict with them, then they have belief-driven (or belief-gated if you prefer) cognition. If a person comes to a belief, and then rejects basically all facts since most seem to conflict with their beliefs, then they have belief-driven cognition.

Belief-driven cognition means that cognition, or thinking, is first screened by the person's beliefs before anything is interpreted, decided, or remembered. The simplistic model is that people react "rationally" to everything – in fact, the opposite is true, and only the most innocuous items involve a non-belief driven reaction. Utilizing belief-driven cognition is how many think, and people who depend on it – politicians, lawyers, advertisers, governments, demagogues, religious zealots, cult leaders, conspiracy theorists, and many people who earn a living in the radio, TV, and cable program business – are fully aware of its effectivity and power, and utilize it competently.

Hard-Wired Capabilities

Because of man's impressive powers of learning and adaptation, he can and does thrive in the shadow of massive change. This capability falters when it runs up against a limit that is physically built-in or hard-wired into man. An example would be reading speed. Mother Nature provided man with the gift of language, a tool he wielded masterfully to cooperate with his fellow man and subdue Mother Nature herself, exploding from a few thousand 60,000 years ago to a population of seven billion today. But along with this magical skill came a caveat, a limit, that 60,000 years ago was not even a whisper on the wind - whether there are ten books to read or ten million, man's reading speed is relatively constant. As the number of critical things to read has expanded, man has reacted not by reading more, but by explosively expanding his mechanically-assisted indexing and recall systems, by specializing in more and more narrow fields, and by getting by with more condensed summaries (like "sound bites"). A knowledge-retrieval system does not make you into a competent practitioner. It still takes the same amount of time to train a doctor, an auto or plane mechanic, or an electrical or software engineer. When changes in the world overwhelm a capability that is hard-wired in, man will struggle seeking work-arounds, but he cannot change what he is, and he remains overwhelmed.

Self-First Orientation

Everyone has some selfless and some selfish tendencies. From a global perspective, the important measure is the summed impact of all the significant activities that affect the world around a specific individual. The point here is not to become tangled in moral judgments, but to make a dispassionate assessment of the whether a person's activities sum up as a self-first or a selfless contribution. In many cases, this is not that difficult a call.

If something is obvious, it is probably that man is fundamentally self-first. Were he not, then he and his family would not last, eliminated sometime over the past 60,000 years, either by nature or another human. There is no safety net in nature. Some would even say the slope is greased. Any miscalculation - no water/bad water, no food/bad food, poisonous or dangerous animals, excessive heat or cold, falling or drowning - can result in destruction. Man must make sure that he has planned and prepared and acted in a fashion that will ensure his survival, and only after that will he have the time to concern himself with others and other things.

This does not at all imply that being self-first requires man to disadvantage nature or other humans as he looks out for himself. There are most often a lot of ways to obtain food without stealing it from your neighbor. How a given man elects to look out for himself is a function of that specific man and not man as a species. Self-first does not necessarily mean others-last. However, if a man is only focussed on himself, by definition he is not paying attention to anyone or anything else. That benign neglect will lead to whatever materializes, not necessarily bad, but not necessarily good.

By his very nature man is self-first. He can recognize this, he can attempt to and sometimes succeed in overcoming it, but the trait remains. Because it is so painless, automatic, and often appropriate to be selfish, the self-first side dominates in man. As man's numbers and power increase, so does the impact of this net selfishness, eventually resulting in significant social and environmental damage.

Ease of Adaptability

One of man's most impressive capabilities is his adaptability to a change in the environment around him, if it is perceived to be in his favor to so adapt. The good-natured adaptability of the English to the prolonged air bombardment at the beginning of World War II was a turning point in the conflict. In most cases, you can take a young man from the most agreeable of social circumstance, place him in the most terrible of combat conditions, and repatriate him a few years later with nothing but heroic behavior all the way around. In the face of the most severe natural disasters ever to have occurred - be it earthquake, flood, fire, famine, massive political or economic change, man recovers and thrives almost without a noticeable interruption.

In the cases where to adapt is not in man's best interest, resisting the temptation is at best difficult if not impossible for most people. Being an airline pilot has been described as years of intense boredom interrupted with seconds of sheer terror. For some pilots, the realization that the situation has moved from the ordinary to extraordinary arrives too late - they have adapted too well to the everyday routine. It is just about impossible for anyone to remain in a state of readiness for anything dramatically different from the environment they are normally surrounding by. Living in California and being constantly prepared for an earthquake that never comes is another example. Keeping both hands on the steering wheel in case a front tire ever blows is impossibly difficult for almost everyone. The everyday, no matter how bizarre to an outside observer, becomes the norm, and man will creatively, ferociously, and effectively adapt to it.

Chapter 6
The Irrational Man

The Biological Basis

It was an epiphanic moment. The leading edge of the tightly-bunched herd of wildebeests hesitated, mulling, turning, colliding with one another. More than a million were on their annual migration, leaving behind the dry summer Serengeti for the wetter, fertile feeding to the north-northwest, a trek near a thousand miles. But they had paused just short of this low shrub and grass-covered rocky outcrop, where hidden except for their heads were six lions of the dangerous kind, lionesses, disguised about as well as a harp on a harlot, staring intently at the endless wildebeest panorama.

After maybe a ten second delay, the herd began to move forward again, passing no more than thirty feet in front of the motionless lionesses in their outcrop. After another fifteen seconds the lionesses leapt into the herd.

Wildebeests don't "think" in the sense that man does. They do not make calculations, review alternatives, weigh the odds, and the like. Mother Nature has instead equipped them with something else equally effective, or you might say, more effective, to accomplish the same thing. The molecular biology of each wildebeest provides them with instincts and with pre-established neural pathways. They act like simple Boolean logic statements: if this, then that. If you run out of grass and water, walk north. If you see a lion, maintain a watchful safe distance and stay close together. The epiphany is what happens when both of these pathways light up simultaneously and both instincts are activated. Mother Nature long ago figured out a solution – if the herd does not migrate, wildebeests cease to exist; if the wildebeests ignore the lions, a few wildebeests will be lost. So migration trumps fear, and the herd moves forward.

No "thinking" is involved. Mother Nature instead uses pre-established pathways in wildebeests, and in all animals for that matter, to deal with situations like this and any other. The animal senses something, it sets off a pathway leading to an instinct, and the animal responds in milliseconds. No wasted time, no delay that might endanger the animal, no agonizing about what you know or don't know, no what if's, no regrets, just action and response. This set of instinctive reactions is Mother Nature's equivalency for the thinking capability that man has. And before you feel sorry for these poor animals, stuck with such a shoddy, half-baked set of mental processes, remember that when you see an animal like the crocodile today, you are looking at the same unchanged animal that was on the Earth before the dinosaurs were here. This is no jury-rigged system, this is pure perfection – this is exquisite excellence. If you want to ask for whom the bell is tolling, it is not for the crocodile.

There have been countless species (hundreds of millions) on this planet, culminating with man after a span of over two billion years. For all the others, Mother Nature elected to remain strictly in control, utilizing biochemistry, molecular biology, and instinct to keep her fingers deeply enmeshed in the behavior of, and fundamental nature of, each and every individual organism.

But man was uniquely provided with the ability to operate autonomously, to provide self-direction through his ability to logically and systematically think, utilize language, and problem-solve. Man himself, realizing these capabilities, from the very beginning began to assess himself, and realized that he alone of all other living organisms was a rational, sentient being. Consistent with his nature (which is the subject of this work), man tends to classify things in black or white fashion – one or the other – nothing gray or fuzzy. So man is always referred to as rational, as thinking, and contrasted against other animals which clearly cannot do what man can do.

But do you really think that Mother Nature, in her sixth or so experiment making a homo something (modern man), would just drop all of the techniques that had worked for her so well for the prior two billion years and several hundred million species? Would all that molecular biology, biochemistry, and instinctive control that Mother Nature had hard-wired into other species get shuttled off into the Recycle Bin?

There are some easy ways to see what man is really like. You can observe him in toto over the millennia. You can run tests on people, especially people who have certain areas of their brain damaged, to see what parts of the brain are involved in which activities. You can anatomically compare the brains of people with other animals to see how much of what Mother Nature put in is actually conserved.

If you purchase a computer today (a real computer and not a web-browsing device), you most likely will have a CPU chip with two or more cores (dual-core or quad-core), meaning that it has two or more processors that are calculating independently at the same time, speeding up those operations that are limited by the CPU (unfortunately, few for the average user). The advertising competition, sometimes with a financial payoff, that involves building the fastest computer in the world, takes this to an extreme, paralleling many identical simple computer chips in racks with software that splits the work up among all the processors. All the studies performed on the human brain show that, simplistically (?), it is an eight-core system. Portions of the right and left cerebral hemispheres along with the cerebellum control all movement including speech and are the first core. Other regions in the same hemispheres along with the critical areas of the ventromedial prefrontal cortices, the right somatosensory cortices, and the anterior cingulate cortex enable you to select what action or movement or decision you are going to take, and they represent the second core. If it is a physical action, it would then instruct the first core to move or speak. Personality resides in this core, and consciousness may reside here also, but if so it is highly dependent on the support and interaction with other cores in the system. To minimize the number of cores, we will toss factual, non-emotional memory storage into this core also.

Anything involving fears, phobias, or terror is part of the third core, the amygdala-mediated system, with the amygdala sitting deep down in the center of the brain. The fourth core is assigned to memories associated with any emotional feelings, whether from the amygdala-mediated system or others (to be mentioned next). These are called implicit or non-declarative memories to distinguish them from memories made of things, events, and people. People who have amnesia and cannot remember a bloody thing can still form emotional memories – there is this independent system operating. The fifth and sixth cores are the two parallel thalamus systems. The first feeds sensory inputs from the eyes, ears, and the like to the cerebrum, the part of the brain that turns them into sensations that we can comprehend. The second feeds the same data to the hypothalamus system that produces all the emotional content aside from fear in parallel with the "factual" comprehension of the same sensation in the cerebrum.

The seventh core is the hippocampal system. It provides the explicit memories surrounding emotional events in memory, meaning the circumstances, the context, what happened, and how you remember feeling, but, not the actual feelings themselves. The eighth core is the balance of the brain that runs the body on an autopilot basis as far as we are concerned – heart, lungs, digestion, immune system, and everything else – which is primarily located in the brain stem at the base of the brain with components like the midbrain, pons, and medulla.

Now the brain as you might guess is more complex that this simplistic characterization, for there are an abundance of nuanced interactions across areas not mentioned here. For example, a small part of the amygdala helps give weight to positive factors during the exact moment a decision is made and feed it back to the orbito-frontal cortex in the prefrontal area, even though the amygdala's main function is best-known for dealing with fear stimuli. But if these other linkages all get listed we end up with a brain textbook, even more bored ex-readers, and no real improvement in the eight-core model above, so we will stick with it. But if you are craving for more, it is out there.

If you are physically doing something, and that activity engages any emotional reaction at all – even boredom – or concurrently you are listening to music you enjoy, or thinking about something else you would rather be doing, or something you previously did that you preferred to this, then all eight of these cores, these processors, are working simultaneously in parallel, just like these fancy supercomputers you hear about.

There is a high degree of interconnection between the emotional systems in the brain and the decision-making and sensory systems in the brain. The sole purpose of those three specific areas, like the ventromedial prefrontal cortices called out in the second cerebral core that makes decisions, is to obtain emotional input to decide how best to take the next physical or logical step. That emotional input can be as basic as what you prefer, what your friend or spouse expects to hear or see, what your boss wants to hear or see, what your work group wants to hear or see, what the waiter or clerk expects to hear, or what perfect strangers around you expect to see or hear. Or it can be what you work on next in your job, whether you say you agree or disagree if someone asks you a question, what you put in your cart at the grocery store, whether you buy a new car or a new house. People who through injury or cancer surgery have these areas or the areas feeding them damaged are incapable of either doing anything at all, or doing anything appropriate or doing it reliably or correctly.

If you think of something that happened to you that resulted in an emotional feeling, then the seventh core, the hippocampal system, is activated to bring up the context for the emotional events. The fourth core is activated which brings up the emotional memories themselves; they will both feed into the second core, which is where you are thinking and making decisions. If fear or phobias were involved, the third core, the amygdala system may be reactivated. If the emotion is strong enough, the fourth core tells the pituitary gland to release a cascade of hormones that includes adrenaline. This creates systemic body effects that the fifth and sixth cores, the dual thalamus systems, pick up and feed back to the first core, telling you that you feel agitated, afraid, sad, or whatever. Even if no hormones are released, if you react physically to your memory in any way – smiling, making a sad face – your body also reads this and feeds it back to you as input. It doesn't miss a thing. If it is not a memory, but is happening in real time, the same process occurs, it's just that the stimulus comes directly in from the fifth core, the input sensory system.

If you ignore the eighth core, which few of us have intellectual control or contact with, the first and fifth cores are not directly involved with emotion, and the other five cores are, so 70% of the brain on a subsystem basis is providing emotional capabilities. And if you sever the connection of the action and decision part of the brain with the emotional part, which can be seen if either specific areas in the frontal areas of the cerebrum or key emotional areas like the amygdala, thalamus, or hypothalamus are damaged, people become effectively incompetent. So the human brain, both anatomically and from a performance perspective, places a high value on emotional content.

If you pick up a book on brain function sometime, you will not find the authors talking about the brain in terms of a multi-core processor, since those authors have goals different from those here. But they all make the point that man's thinking is basically emotionally-based.

So let's get back to the point at hand. Mother Nature produces this exquisite creature, the crocodile, so perfected that it has remained basically unchanged since the dinosaurs were just developing more than one hundred million years ago. Crocodiles don't think – they are all drive and instinct, they do what is in their genes, generation after generation, millennium after millennium. We ask the question again – when designing man, is Mother Nature going to just toss out what has worked so well for so long in animals, or will she build on this base, adding new capabilities?

Obviously this is a rhetorical question, since you already know the answer. Without wasting time on an anatomy lesson, all of the brain structures in crocodiles are found in man. It is just that many, especially the cerebrums, are much larger and have new capabilities. All the emotional drives and instincts that represent all that an animal is are found in man, sharing the stage with thought, reasoning, and decision-making. But they are wholly-integrated, not dominant, not subordinated, just intimately incestuously inserted into every part of man's thinking and memory-making and recall.

Why? Not having a lot of direct access to Mother Nature's thinking, this must unfortunately be conjecture – but we can take a better shot at this than you might think. There were several attempts that we know of at modern man, none of which but us, Homo Sapiens Sapiens, was successful. It is possible (and probably highly likely) that there were many other attempts that went nowhere that we have no record of. This balance between thinking and automatic action based on instinct is not quite as simple as it may appear. Too much instinct and you just have a better chimpanzee; nice but it is not going to conquer the world. Too much rational-thinking emphasis and you have someone like these people with damaged prefrontal areas – unable to make effective decisions. They would be chewed up by the dangerous world in minutes. Getting the balance right was most likely very difficult, and took many false starts until the right formula was found.

Thinking, problem-solving, rational thought – these things all take time and require knowing things about the world around you. For man 60,000 years ago, most of the world and how it worked was either an unknown or misunderstood. So the advantages that this new set of capabilities brought had to be carefully tempered, limited, curtailed, managed, controlled, and restricted. On the other hand, instinct and basic drives work in total opposition to calculated thought – they represent an automatic stimulus/action mechanism – no intermediate step of judgment or evaluation.

One solution is to have instinct work for some behaviors; thinking for others. This would result in a kind of schizophrenic organism, and for obvious reasons was not selected for full implementation by Mother Nature. What Mother Nature did instead is use instinct, drives, and emotion as the compressed spring and/or dynamite that enabled man to act instead of continuing to think. And she used them to color, weigh, provide emphasis, tag, and stress observations and memories so they could be prioritized, ranked, assessed, and triaged effectively and efficiently, all in the spirit of quick decisions and action. So the weaknesses that thinking can bring are offset by drawing from the ancient pool of drives and instincts. Thus the potential whatlessness of sights, sounds, and memories are overcome by tagging all of them with feelings that are drawn from the same pool.

Put another way, instincts, emotions, and drives in effect act as a short-cut for the implicit delays associated with rational side of man. Depending on the situation, emotion can enable man to skip most all the thinking steps before he acts, or compress the process into a very brief engagement. It is person-specific – two different people may handle an identical situation in a radically-different manner. Some people are ready-aim-fire; some are ready-fire-aim. Some are driven and never stop; some seem to never get started. Some people seem dominated by their emotions, pushed and pulled as they hear from friends or as new events occur. Others seem coldy-focussed on a self-established purpose and are undisruptible.

The people who have damage to the critical areas in their prefrontal areas that break the links to the emotional areas which as a consequence prevent them from making any decisions are in every other measurable way, normal. They pass with flying colors every psychological test they can be given. When asked how they would act in a given situation, they choose all the right answers. The intellectual parts are all in place – what is missing is the oompf – there is no go, no action. They know which door to go through, but they cannot actually get up, go to the door, open it, and go through it. Now this is the extreme case, but it shows that without emotion, nothing happens. The rational side is fundamentally incompetent – wheels or gears without an engine; a boat without a sail; I/O (input/output capability) without a processor.

Individuals whose prefrontal centers that make the connections to the emotional areas are missing have been connected to a "lie detector". It measures their reactions to a series of photographs, a mix of mostly bland pictures of landscapes and cityscapes with every-so-often an alarming photo of a murder, horrific automobile accident, war crime, and the like. Compared to the average person, these people show absolutely no emotional reactions to the photos – the lie detector is flat-lined. Yet when interviewed afterward, they are fully aware of what they saw, know they represent unsettling images, and know they should react to them, but also know they do not react. So the cognition side is present and working, but the linkages to the emotional side are completely interrupted.

There is an even more serious reaction in people who have damage to an area called the anterior cingulate cortex. They become completely inanimate and unresponsive, although they are fully-conscious and technically fully-aware. Those who have been questioned about this, whose condition was temporary, described being in a trance-like state with absolutely no interest in any sensory observation or information presented to them. The world going by is like watching the most boring movie in the world over and over while on some powerful tranquilizer – you just see and hear and are not bothered in the slightest by anything, including your condition. Without the impetus, the power, the motive force that emotions bring through connections into this area of the cerebral cortex, the brain cannot do anything with the intellectual input it receives. In other words, it is another confirmation that the brain is designed on an integrated but dependent basis with the rational part of the mind providing all of the smarts, but the emotional side providing all the go.

When the term emotions is used here, it means connections to all of the parts of the brain, the cores, the processors that are dedicated to emotional reactions. Exactly what "emotion" you might feel, if any, is not the point. It is the connections to all these cores that is a prerequisite for acting like a normal human; break or disrupt them, and you become incompetent.

Now while complete damage to these areas is most illustrative of the behavior of the mechanism, partial damage is also well-documented. These people have feelings and emotions, but their management of them is not compatible with what is socially acceptable and constructively viable. They behave inappropriately and erratically, saying and doing things that others find totally offensive, and so they cannot hold a job or live with anyone except family. They are unable to make reasonable judgments or decisions that are in their best interests, nor can they make timely decisions. They will waver and consider and internally debate the smallest choice ad nauseum. Someone encountering them briefly, knowing little of their background, would simply write them off as being "crazy". Those afflicted with frontotemporal dementia, an Alzheimer's-like (but different) disease, will often have these symptoms.

Those individuals with Asperger's Syndrome and high-level autism have a much more narrow interruption of activity in the prefrontal area. They can make decisions and do not behave in an unacceptable or abnormal fashion. They can have normal emotions except for one area – they completely lack the capability to perceive, comprehend, demonstrate, respond to, and reciprocate any interpersonal social communication, whether it is toward a group of strangers, friends, family, or a significant other, although such a personal relationship tends to become almost an impossibility. Many of these people have written micro-autobiographies, and they all sound the same – they were a stranger in a strange land. They have absolutely no idea what others are doing, or why they are doing it. They do not understand any of the nuances of everyday communication that everyone else takes for granted – humor, sarcasm, exaggeration, figurative versus literal, figures of speech, or slang. They have no interpersonal feelings toward others. Observers will describe these people as "loners" - they are always by themselves, simply because they are clueless as to why others behave and speak the way they do. Most of them end up coping by building notebooks filled with "if, then" instructions to themselves. If someone says this, you should say or do this in response. These notebooks can be 50 or more pages long On all their lists, at the top, is never try to tell a joke. They are incapable of discriminating between what is humorous, what is the appropriate context for humor, and the difference between humor and offense.

What is the point of all this detail on the human brain and brain dysfunction? The first message is that the successful functioning of humans depends on Mother Nature's decision to completely integrate her ancient toolkit of instinct and drives into man's new capability of thinking and problem-solving. All of man's thinking processes are infiltrated with emotion, Mother Nature's nuanced representation of instinct and drives. Take away emotion, which happens when the specific areas in the prefrontal areas in the cerebrum that make the integrated connections are damaged, and man is either no longer man or completely incompetent. He is not just "unemotional".

The second point is that the reason man becomes incompetent when emotion is removed is not that he is "unemotional" - it is that he becomes enervated, unable to make a decision, unable to take an action. The connections to the emotional processors of his brain provide the motive force, the energy, the push, the avalanche of momentum that gets man off his agony of indecision and forces him to commit. In the context of this book, in effect, it is a short-cut to action – depending on the circumstances and the person, the action can come instantly or with some latency. It can cease after a half-hearted effort or it can be ceaseless, unstoppable, unbeatable. People with a "short-fuse" can react with what to others seems an imperceptible stimulus. Mystics in a cave or the equivalent may have given grave consideration for years and then made one, substantive, life-altering decision.

The third point is that the smallest damage to these brain areas can cause effects that while allowing a person to remain physically and orally "active", handicaps them with social and interpersonal difficulties that can range from troublesome to challenging to debilitating. It is almost "better", or "easier", to have a stroke or equivalent damage to other areas of your cerebrum that you use to think or move with. Often with physical therapy you can train your brain to find alternate pathways to regain some or most the facilities lost in the stroke. But lose any of these emotional connections, and no repair or recovery is possible. Emulation can be attempted, as the Asperger's individuals do, but that is qualitatively different from re-establishing what is not there.

Consequences

Every second, for everything you think and do, you are fully wired into all of the emotional and instinctual parts of your brain. Whether you think you can "feel" what it is telling you is probably a waste of time – you do not have a way to see how you would "feel" if these cores were somehow to be removed. This is the most important take-away from the previous discussion.

You are working or talking to someone and a deafening explosion slams into you – your natural tendency is to duck, freeze, and try to figure out if you should run, and if so, where. The same thing happens if you hear gunshots or someone yells "fire". You are busy and you feel something crawling on the back of your neck, or on your leg, or the back of your hand – before you can think your reaction is to shake it off or brush it off. You are walking down a path and some small animal shoots under your descending foot – so fast you cannot in that instant tell if it is a snake or a ground squirrel or a small bird. You leap backward or over that area on the ground without thinking. All these actions are automatic – they are instinctive. In these cases the senses feed cores five and six, the thalamus systems, which then ignite the amygdala system, core three, which lets you know, though core two, but at the same time makes you move, by exercising your muscles using core one. Because fear is involved, the amygdala gets to participate, and so it takes over and gets you to physically take action without waiting for your cognition to get on board. It also wakes up your endocrine system, pumping in adrenaline and other neurotransmitters, so you feel fear, agitation, and are physically ready to run or fight. If something like this has previously happened – you have already been stung by a spider, or almost stepped on a snake before, your emotional memories in cores four and seven will be activated also, and this will reinforce the intensity of your reactions to these stimuli.

Mother Nature gave emotion/instinct the right of first action in these and similar cases because fundamental safety is at stake. 60,000 years ago, you can probably surmise, the ones who were thinking instead of running would all end up getting eaten, so either Mother Nature finally got it right or we were left with a self-correcting gene pool.

But while the initial reaction is reflex and instinct, Mother Nature quickly returns control of an energized, adrenalized human to its rational, thinking owner, although depending on the situation, some may stay fully emotional and panic. But as anyone in this situation can testify, it becomes difficult to think in a calm, cool, logical manner in a stressful situation. Mother Nature, through the demand for action coming from the emotional side, is constantly calling for an early termination of the thinking process. Making good judgments in such situations is difficult. It is said by professionals that you can never predict in advance who will act calmly and rationally in an emergency, and who will succumb to panic.

If we switch to a situation that one clear step short of an emergency – a serious situation, meaning the ramifications involve you or your partner's career, or your child's education or health, or a major financial decision or risk, or a medical treatment choice, the exact same brain systems are invoked. It is just that the sense of panic and fear and agitation may be missing or only indirectly apparent – you may get a headache or an upset stomach or lose your appetite or overeat or some other (for you) atypical behavior. But just because you do not feel panicked, these systems have not disconnected. They are all still there, running normally, feeding your rational side emotional inputs to help it make quick decisions using the information and the memory of past events that are most important to you.

Then if we move to the most mundane of activities – what you order for lunch, whether to exercise or not, what comment you make back to some co-worker who makes some less-than-complimentary comment about you or your work in a meeting or in front of another co-worker – the same systems are still running, always full-on. If you are tired, "off your game", having a bad-hair day, or you are sick, your rational side may not be as carefully screening what is going on. Your emotional processors, which do not by the way fall asleep or get tired, may decide to skip exercising since it's a big hassle, decide to have a tuna melt instead of a salad for lunch, and make some snarky comment back to your co-worker that the next day you will regret.

Everyone is not a cookie-cutter copy of everyone else. There are maybe 200 quadrillion synapses, meaning junctions of two or more nerves, which is what creates memories and stored patterns like instincts, in the brain. With just 20 odd thousand genes, it is impossible for the genes to come close to controlling what a brain ends up looking like. "All" the genes can do is specify the process for how the nerves cells grow, and the relative sizes of each part of the brain, and their location, and what connects to what where with what kind of intensity. After that, the neurons just grow, using chemical gradients as a guide just like a plant grows toward the sun, and the white matter, the connections between the neurons, fills in underneath. This is why no two people are alike in personality, skills, or temperament. This is a grand oversimplification, since obviously some things are inherited to a degree. Professional athletes sometimes have children who are also professional athletes; professional musicians sometimes have children who are professional musicians.

But most all the variation that we observe from person to person, and that makes the world go 'round, what is it based on? It is what we like the most, who sounds the most appealing, who is the most likeable, who seems the most respectable, or acts the most statesmanlike, or makes us feel the best, or makes us feel the most patriotic. Or is the best example, or makes us laugh or cry the best, or makes the music that we most enjoy listening to or dancing to, or acts in the movies that we most like watching. Or lives the life that we would most like to live, or says the things that we wish we were smart enough to say, or writes the books or columns that we most enjoy reading, or who our children most enjoy watching or listening to. Or is the best-dressed, or lives a charmed life, or lives a disastrous life, or makes the most money for us, or whom we depend on for our livelihood. Or tastes the best, or smells the best, or looks the best. What do all these have in common? They all invoke the emotional side of the brain, not the rational side. All the decision-making that we do is precipitated by a push or kick from the emotional side.

Man is an irrational being. Not in the sense that he is necessarily illogical per se, but that he is per se emotional before he is rational. He can *be* rational; but he cannot *act* rational without invoking his emotional machinery that enables him to make a choice or a decision and move forward.

Now the cynics here will be saying now wait a minute, there are plenty of places where decisions are made purely objectively, just using facts and science, with no emotions or subjectivity visible. Possibly. But many of these examples, if rigorously investigated, will be found to have had their initial settings made through emotionally-driven reasons, so that while the subsequent decision-making may appear "objective", the overall result is biased to accomplish a subjective, emotionally-motivated set of goals. Or the criteria, even if initially set up objectively, are re-interpreted on a subjective basis by each user. This is why we end up with women with different pay for the same work than men; or fire departments with high black memberships always have only white firefighters pass the test for lieutenant; or separate but "equal"; or performance reviews in business where the people that the boss likes are always rated the highest and the ones that he does not are always ranked lower; or votes are carefully tabulated in districts that have been gerrymandered to always reelect the incumbent, and whose borders look like a steam-rollered cancerous tumor. Then there are the cases where you may have expected objectivity, but receive something a little different: history and science textbooks that are re-written for religious reasons; government scientific reports that are "adjusted" for political reasons; information from the government, paid for by taxpayers, that is edited and spun to accomplish political results for the party in power; and financial audits of public companies paid for by the companies themselves that surprisingly (?!) fail to detect major risk areas that later result in bankruptcy for the companies, causing drastic financial losses for other individuals, organizations, and governments.

It is difficult to find a non-subjective view of anything – written or oral, fiction or non-fiction. In just the selection of what material to include and exclude subjectivity haunts; in where the emphasis should rest or in any conclusions it has mastery. Only people and not Nature produce conclusions. Man is simply built with a structure that laces logic with emotion, inseparably. Resistance is futile; man must embrace himself.

Still unconvinced? How do you, or your friends, or society in general, feel about nuclear power, or nuclear radiation, or x-ray radiation of food? Chances are, unless you are an expert, in which case you are disqualified from consideration, you are somewhere between guarded and terrified, and your position has little to do with science, logic, reason, and calculated decision-making. Nope, people have responded so hysterically to the portrayal of deadly, insidious, mysterious nuclear radiation in movies and media that their emotions have been saturated and slammed to one extreme, and their rational skills may as well have been donated to the Smithsonian. Just an example or two – live within 50 miles of a nuclear plant, and your annual exposure to radiation increases slightly. But if you live within 50 miles of a coal plant, your radiation exposure goes up three times faster – there is more radiation from coal than nuclear. You get as much radiation in an hour flying in a commercial airliner as you would get living next to a nuclear power plant for 50 years. And you get 80% more radiation living in Denver than San Francisco (one year in Denver is 9,000 years next to a nuclear power plant) – but you don't find "Danger – Radiation" signs all over Denver. Logically and scientifically coal kills more people every month than nuclear radiation ever has since the beginning of time, including WWII atomic weapons, but as they say, where emotion is king 'tis folly to be wise.

People think rationally, but they *move* on emotion; they think logically, but they are *driven* by emotion; they problem-solve systematically but they most often *decide* based on emotion. The logical part of man is the passive, intransitive side; the action part is the emotional side. This is man's nature – he cannot help himself. Just a mention that radiation has been detected near you, even if it is at a level that is say one-millionth the natural background rate you receive automatically, and the average person will go into a near panic. They may even worry about it all during their next airplane flight, accumulating hundreds of times more radiation that they would ever receive from any radiation incident. Logic and reason just cannot buy a ticket to this game.

Even in the Three Mile Island nuclear disaster, there was no citizen exposure. In the Fukushima disaster in Japan, the citizens of town of Iitate had to evacuate due to the radiation levels, which were approximately equal to one month of normal radiation exposure at sea level per day at Iitate. So say you ignored the authorities for whatever reason and stayed behind for four extra days, or sneaked back for two hours a day for a month or so, and received four extra months of radiation. That is the same as living in Denver for just one year instead of at sea level. Is this a "problem" - well, yes, to the same degree that living in Denver is a "problem". Even the Chernobyl exposures, created by a government that had a wanton and barbarically-dismissive attitude toward its citizens, utilizing and then uncontrollably-experimenting with a carbon-moderated reactor without a containment vessel, and then not even notifying them of the disaster nor evacuating them after the fact, were equivalent to about 12 years of living in Denver.

A second important conclusion that comes from all of the tests and studies of man's brain and how it works are the implications of variety. Asperger's and autism are generally noticeable. These individuals are classed as having a medical disorder, since there are enough people with similar symptoms. But what about people with short tempers, or who are indecisive? Short-tempers are tolerated if the person is "successful" or "famous"; indecision is most often not. What about those who are single-mindedly focussed on something, to the exclusion of all else? If it is about making money, many people think it is great. If it is about writing music, or painting, it's fine if they are successful, but they are wasting their time and have their priorities all messed up if they are not. And what if their focus is on washing their hands? Well, then they are obsessive/compulsive, a disorder right out of the DSM-IV (Diagnostic and Statistical Manual version 4, the "bible" for psychiatrists), and they are "nuts". What if they are shy and introverted, or extroverted and very social? These are just normal person-to-person variations. What about if the extroverted person is a master at being charming and social, and sweeps people off their feet? He dazzles people with stories of who he knows and what he has done, wears expensive clothes, drives expensive cars or is transported in jets and limousines. Oh, did we mention, he has a special investment fund only open to privileged, by-his-permission-only investors? He could be what he hints at, or he could be what everyone knows as a sociopath or psychopath – someone that appears exceptionally charming (although it is all an act), who lies pathologically, who believes that he himself is a minor god, who is manipulative and cunning, has no feelings of remorse or regret for any damage he may be doing, acts impulsively and irresponsibly, and has to live on the edge, driven to take advantage of others wherever possible. He is not the least dismayed, distracted, or slowed by negative, poor, or disastrous results, or even by punishment. These people have only the "now" emotional connections in their brain – they always and forever simply live literally in the moment, because all the memory, history, judgment, and planning emotional connections in their brain are missing. So while they always sound convincing, and they actually sincerely mean what they say in the moment, it has absolutely no connection with the actual reality of what this person has previously said and done. That momentary "commitment" has absolutely no value a moment later. But since, for them, no "faking" is involved, they are often absolutely, and unquestionably, convincing. Even psychiatrists who know their history, have their file open in front of them, cannot resist their siren-song of remorse and repentance.

And if this sociopathic/psychopathic-like individual does not possess all these characteristics, he may possess only half, or one-quarter of them, or just two. Maybe he is not selling investment products but used cars, or weight-loss pills, or something at a street fair or too-good-to-be-true web site. Maybe he is selling some kind of charity, and wants your money that will only go to cover his "expenses". Or he is selling some kind of religion, and needs your money to cover his "expenses", since if he is seen living rich it is just a sign that God is showering His blessings on him. Or he is selling gold coins with outrageous markups so most likely you will lose money on your purchase, no matter what happens to the price of gold. Seem familiar? You may run into one of them at work, or at some social event, every day or once a week. What's "normal"? There ain't no such thing. We are all just one of an endless parade of variations. Only if a cluster of us has our behaviors become so extreme, and so anti-self or anti-social, does medical science tag us with a syndrome or a disease or condition.

You may be inclined to pass this off as only applying to criminals and social deviates – Ponzi's and Madoff's and the like. But the second President Roosevelt, FDR, was a master of several of these skills, coldly and some have said ruthlessly using people to accomplish his goals, without emotion, love, caring, or concern ever in evidence, except in his well-compartmentalized world where maybe only Sara, Daisy, and Lucy were able to develop a relationship that had some genuine emotional content, and even there it has to be emphasized only maybe. And he demonstrated the typical pattern - as a small boy intentionally setting a trap for his nanny that tripped her and sent her falling down a flight of stairs - his goal to eliminate her as a competitive threat to his intense drive and need to dominate and control all those around him. Luxuriating in his own excellence, excessively overconfident, when he was good, he was very, very good. But when he misread people whom Roosevelt thought he could manipulate and control, like Stalin, the results were disastrous (FDR's goal was to win WWII; Stalin's goal was to dominate the post-war world. FDR missed Stalin's goal until he became somewhat uneasy just before his death – he desperately wanted Stalin's help to defeat Japan. Estimates at the time were that it could take up to two million American lives and until 1947 [this was of course pre-atomic bomb]). As Roosevelt seriously degraded in March of 1945, unable to make decisions so the government had to "run itself", Roosevelt's nature persevered until the very end. Never involving, informing, or updating Truman and others on the critical strategic issues facing the U.S. - like Stalin greedily eating Eastern Europe almost without opposition - Eisenhower ended up in effect fighting the wrong war, a military war instead of the geo-political war that Stalin was waging.

The individual described in the previous paragraph, the one who is charming, manipulative, without conscience, and dangerous to all is what used to be called a sociopath or a psychopath, depending, and 1% of us are them. The DSM-IV now calls it Antisocial Personality Disorder (they have dropped the sociopathic/psychopathic terminology in typical psychiatrist twisted wisdom), but their description is fairly skimpy, not useful in predicting behavior, and for the author, inadequate. The master of this is Dr. Robert Hare's Psychopathy Checklist - Revised (PCL-R), that has twenty characteristics elaborated. He has developed a similar one for children, since you are born with these "features" of your emotional side in full prominence. Hare gives the example of a five-year-old girl whose mother comes across her flushing her new kitten down the toilet. When the mother cries out "Why?" in shock, the daughter calmly responds that she was bored and hence done playing with the kitten. Asked later by her father about the incident, the child denies that it ever took place. But she is a relative angel compared to six year old Tess, who asked if she was collecting knives from the kitchen, said "Yes, big, sharp ones." As to her intentions: "Kill Mommy and Benjamin (her younger brother)." Asked about her interest in small animals, she said she liked to "Stick 'em with pins, a lot, (to) kill 'em."[4]

What happens when one of these two young girls, or some variation on their theme, grows up? She may get prompted to have a baby, and then enjoy the child for a year or two until she becomes bored – the newness has worn off, it is a lot of responsibility, she wants to be single again and free to do what she wants. She will look for some way to "avoid" the burdens of parenthood, and she might feel pressure to do it quickly before the child begins to observe keenly and speak competently, reporting her irresponsible parental behavior to others. If the child is lucky, this might involve leaving the child with a grandparent or father. If the child is unlucky, it may end up deceased. And in a subsequent trial, the jury is totally confused – the mother

---

4 <u>Without Conscience</u>, Robert Hare, The Guilford Press, New York, 1993, p.171

was reported to be so happy with the child – how could she have caused its intentional death? For a sociopath/psychopath, living always and only in the moment, this is utterly natural and effortless – like the frames of a movie film spinning swiftly by, once they are on the take-up reel, those scenes and thoughts and emotions are dark, lifeless, and gone.

If the child has a milder collection of sociopathic traits, and uncritically-observant parents and friends (normal), they may pass invisibly through society until they participate in some major event – say she spends a riotous night consuming chemicals and liquids with her latest boyfriend, arrives back at her own apartment the next day with the front door wide open, blood on the floor and their roommate's door locked and unresponsive - and she would have no reaction, which would be typical – no concern for others. When someone later finally kicks in the door and she finds her roommate ferociously slaughtered, her reaction would not be to join a vigil of distraught friends a few hours later, but to shop for adults-only underwear with her boyfriend, speculating on its usefulness. Her statements to police might say that maybe she was there, maybe she wasn't; maybe she saw her boss at her part-time job kill her roommate, or maybe not. She may not firmly recall anything that happened in the 18 hours that preceded finding her roommate dead. Living only for her own pleasure in the "now", where there is no difference between the "truth" and a nicely-fabricated story - an uncareful sociopath is a mess. So the police would have to decide if they have a psychopathic killer on their hands, or just a regular, run-of-the-mill, sociopath.

Fortunately for society, most sociopaths/psychopaths, since they just live in the moment, are poor planners, and often get themselves into irrecoverable problems. If they cannot talk their way out of them, which they are superbly adept at, they will be trapped, tried, and imprisoned. Unfortunately for society, judges and juries in almost all cases have not a clue that when facing a sociopath/psychopath as a defendant, they are really participating in a science fiction movie, with a defendant who is human by all appearances on the outside but is in effect an alien on the inside – no recognizable human emotions or behavior patterns. In The Mask of Sanity by Hervey Cleckley are a large number of case studies of sociopaths – amazing reading for a non-psychiatrist.

Similar to those with Autism Spectrum Disorders, or Asperger's, or selective prefrontal lobe damage, only a few of the emotional connections in the brain are undisrupted in sociopaths and psychopaths. They do not feel any emotions other than disdain toward others, and for themselves are generally only motivated by self-gratification, fulfilled almost always by an activity that feeds and reinforces their already abundant ego and self-importance at the expense of others. If society is lucky, this is restricted to writing bad checks, being a con artist, stealing, faking romantic interest in women to relieve them of their money, or getting drunk which makes them feel more invulnerable and all-powerful. If unlucky, society finds a serial killer or worse on the loose. Neither able to read emotions in others nor feel emotions themselves, they must learn to "fake" all social interactions. Those who study hard at this, and are good learners, can become excessively charming, and hence psychopathic. Others just learn enough to get by, and will be perceived as still rough around the edges and socially "off". But someone may not be technically "sociopathic" (it requires you to have a certain number of the specified traits) but still have some sociopathic traits – no feelings of remorse about hurting others; excessively self-focussed; pre-occupation with today with no concern about what happens tomorrow; excessively charming; does not learn from failure. And these are variations on just one of hundreds of formal named conditions noted in the DSM. The fact that the DSM or someone else does have a name for a group of personality traits does not mean it does not exist, rather there is just too much complexity and clutter to name every variation of every condition. Just like variations in physical capabilities, mathematical capabilities, reading, art, science, music, and everything else, the emotional side of man has variation upon variation, all easily recognized, seen by everyone every day, just not given fancy names and numeric scores that people proudly put on their wall or in their scholastic record.

Alexander the Great, Chapter 13, had all kinds of talents, among them being driven, maybe driven more than anyone else has ever been. To claim his brain was "normal" or "average" would be inappropriate. Edmund Hillary, along with Tenzing Norgay, was the first to climb Mt. Everest in 1953. The difficulty of this endeavor, with the equipment of that time, and lack of any precedent or knowledge of what challenges they had to face on the mountain and at that altitude, is almost unimaginable. If you read his account of this expedition, you would think he was collecting wildflowers in the foothills somewhere. Hillary had been a beekeeper in New Zealand before climbing, not exactly the background that one might expect would be the most optimal preparation. Hillary, who actually did refer to himself as "average", was average only in comparison to Alexander. If you read the descriptions of what Audie Murphy or Daniel Inouye did to earn Medals of Honor in World War II, while they may have just seemed like average Americans at the start of the war, there was nothing remotely average in how they behaved. Take Mozart, Van Gogh, and Poe. All driven artists, all enormously talented. (Mozart luckily found a sponsor while Van Gogh and Poe did not; both died basically miserably and penniless while Mozart was given time to produce more work before he self-destructed.) But the same emotional energy that drove their artistry also drove the balance of their personality, causing enormous social and personal problems for all three, living erratic, disruptive, abbreviated lives. Look around the world today (many people are not real fans of history) – make a list of everyone that you are aware of who is really wealthy (billions) and is not aggressively still pursuing acquiring more, working as hard as they possibly can. Any names on your list? Even at the age of 65, or 70, or 75, or 80, or 85, or older they do not stop until they die. Why? One explanation is that they all are in some special secret contest only open to billionaires, seeing who can be the first one to spirit away their wealth to the next world, to take it with them. The other is that the same emotional structuring in their brains that has resulted in the ceaseless push for money and power has nothing to do with age – it is immutably innate in their brain biology. This loaded spring that drives these people is never going to diminish; they can only redirect it, and few seem to so choose. There is intrinsic, as-yet biologically-unmeasurable variation from person to person that most likely accounts for much of these behavioral differences that are observed, at least those that cannot readily be attributed to differences in upbringing, education, and opportunity.

We are not just different for arbitrary, random reasons. All it takes is a tiny tweak of these prefrontal areas from person to person, and who knows what the consequences could be. The focus on people tends to always center on intelligence and IQ, but most of the cores, the independent processor systems in the brain, are based on emotion, not intelligence. Obviously the different manifestations of intelligence are important, but Mother Nature elected to hinge the ability of man to act entirely on the emotional side of the brain. Failing to give this contribution its due, simply because it is currently impossible to adequately measure, is maybe consistent with human nature but not acceptable.

The theme of this book is that there are seven facets of basic human nature that have allowed man to conquer the world in which he found himself, and now that he is immersed in his remade world, they have become a limitation. Of these seven critical attributes, five of them are based on the emotional side of man and one is impacted by it (self-first orientation). A book's worth of information on how man's brain works was crammed, jammed, and rammed into this chapter as a preface and prologue for the following discussion on the five emotion-based traits that are now affecting man's ability to cope with the modern world.

Chapter 7
Short-Cut Thinking

Man- The Decision Machine

Recently an extraordinarily expensive, custom-made, fabulously fast computer was able to defeat the best chess player in the world. (A computer named Watson also plays Jeopardy, but it can't "think" – it's just a big on-line reference book.) Is this computer smart? It can evaluate 200 million potential moves per second, or 36 billion in the three minutes it has before it has to make a move. It is said that a human player can evaluate maybe three moves per second, so the computer has a 70 million to one advantage in speed. But with that speed advantage, it can just barely win. All the previous computer versions lost to a human player. But this computer cannot do anything that a one-year old baby or puppy can easily do. It cannot plug itself in; it does not even "know" that it has won. Computers don't think, they just do things, fast. They don't get bored; they are consistent; they don't make "mistakes". But they cannot come to a decision, make a choice, or express a preference. Only living things can do that. The most unsophisticated of life forms can make decisions and survive in their day to day living, something even the most powerful of computers cannot do.

People, as well as most animals, are decision machines. With very little information and only an instant of time, people can make effective decisions. This capability has enabled man to thrive and excel. The computer that defeated man in chess was incapable of making a "decision". It could evaluate move after move, score each one, and then present the one with the highest score at the end of its time period. But if you changed anything - started another game, changed the kinds of chessmen or their individual moves, the human could respond instantly. For the computer, hordes of programmers and months of time would be required before it could function again. The computer is not deciding, it is just doing things fast.

This point is of great significance. Man is capable because of his decision capabilities, not his mental power. Every day is a weave of decisions - most made with no time or data. Is it safe, will it work, can I do it, what's next, am I lost, did I remember - such is the foundation of human civilization. Consistently making the wrong decision, or unable to make a decision, would have resulted in a world without a significant presence of man.

In baseball or tennis, the ball is often coming at the other player at 100 miles per hour, which is around 150 feet per second. This player has to determine where the ball is going to be in a fraction of a second later, move his body into position, and then make proper contact with the ball so it goes in the direction he intends. This happens successfully most of the time. Players cannot explain how they do this, for it occurs so quickly that they have no time for calculated thought. They just "react" and it works. The same thing can be observed in American football, where adjustments for wind, weather, the opposing players, the relative height of the two players, and the quarterback's own passing situation (relative grip on the football, throwing position, arm strength) have all to be made in a fraction of a second. Slow-motion video of the pass receiver often shows the ball landing right in the receiver's outstretched hands, even though he is running at full-speed and the quarterback had to throw the ball before the receiver made his last change of direction and the ball has flown 40 yards through the air. A similar thing can be observed in basketball, where the complex relative motion between the player, who may be running at near full-speed and then turning or spinning, and the rim of the basket, must be accounted for at the instant the player releases the ball, so that it can drop through a small hoop fifteen or twenty feet away. If you had to replace a football quarterback or basketball player by a computer-controlled machine, it is hard to estimate what the development cost and time would be, or if it would even be feasible at all. (The author does not think it could be accomplished with today's technology at any cost.)

Most large ships in the American Navy are protected from close-in attack by a system referred to as CIWS (Sea-Whizz) or Phalanx. This system is a radar-controlled gun that shoots 75 rounds per second. The radar tracks the target and determines where to aim to hit it (since it may be moving extremely fast), and then measures how far it misses the target. It makes the appropriate adjustment and then fires again, in effect "walking" the rounds from the gun onto the target. For even a target only half a mile away going Mach 2, the gun gets maybe four attempts before it is too late. Rounds from the CIWS are really moving also – 3,600 feet per second, which is over Mach 3. The reason it fires 75 rounds per second is the obvious one – things are happening rapidly at these speeds (closing speeds of a mile a second in the example above). Granted the targets are moving fast, but this gun has a big computer that moves a lot faster than the target. In the sports examples noted above, man gets only one chance to hit the target with the ball or the ball with his racket or bat, and often less time than Phalanx gets, and yet he often succeeds.

The mental shortcuts that man is able to make are spectacular and basically unbelievable. We accept them because we see them every day - but this does not make them any less amazing. Man has an under-recognized and powerful ability to make accurate, complex calculations in a way he cannot describe, since they happen so quickly that there is little conscious methodology involved. As the contrast with the computer examples indicate, this process is completely unrelated to what a computer would do. It is a brilliant short-cut mechanism built in to man that he can readily use but never comprehend.

Animals appear not to be conscious. Animals do no hesitate. They do not sit and calculate. If threatened, they either run or attack. If they need something, they go off and seek it. All without any apparent deliberation, since no deliberation is possible. Most animals appear well-suited to their environments - thriving unchanged over tens of millions of years of time. Crocodiles, sharks, insects, and dinosaurs are examples (dinosaurs lasted over 100 million years – the asteroid took them out, not some internal weakness). Their ability to react quickly and appropriately, along with their offensive and defensive skills, is the basis for the endurance of their species.

Much of this also applies to man. Intensive thought, analysis, and deliberation generally are the most useful when applied against fundamental, long-term situations. Man has been able to insulate himself more and more from the day-to-day, season-to-season variations of nature and society through deep thinking and study. Improvements in shelter, clothing, agriculture, health, and technology are examples. However, the dangers and risks of minute-to-minute living can only be survived by rapid and effective actions and reactions, and not deliberation. "He who hesitates is lost" is the key. A poor choice of what to eat, when and where to go out alone at night, or just driving, walking, hiking, or swimming can injure and kill without warning. Seldom is the luxury of extended thought available or possible in most dangerous situations. Deliberate thinking will tend to put you in harm's way - in the wrong place at the wrong time. However, it is most likely the momentary decision of starting out instead of waiting, leaving instead of staying, that actually results in your injury or death.

While man is equipped for deliberation, he is designed for action. The wide range of complex brain activity observed for the simplest of tasks is not remembering or thinking. It is attempting to come to a conclusive end or decision as quickly as possible. In most critical situations, man does not have time for his serial left brain to methodically evaluate all the potential risks and issues and factors. Instead, he can count on his right brain to perform an indefinable, integrative, non-verbal appraisal and provide him with an immediate decision as to what to do.

This decision-making process is no random choice process. People who earn a living coaching people who take tests advise them to always go with their initial guess or hunch if they are unsure. In fact, they are encouraged not to over-analyze problems - they will probably lower their score. This instant-answer gift in man is eerily accurate and unaccountably dependable.

Can someone ignore this capability and go against its prompting? Can you replace it with only an explicit analytical (left-brain) approach? Can you self-disturb (drugs, medication, alcohol, sleeplessness) or let others disturb (other-directed) its functioning? Can we be born or raised with an inadequate capability? Yes. But for most people this skill is obvious and effective.

There are some people whose decision processes stand near the one extreme. Their process is so enhanced and dominant that the analytical approach is most often set aside or only used half-heartedly. These people are called intuitive. Everyone know someone like this. They cannot explain how they do it. It takes no time. They are not always right, especially when the situation approaches a purely-logical set of conditions (like a high school math problem). But their capability is more than admirable for someone mired in the sequential, logical approach.

At or beyond the extreme are those called "idiot savants". These people cannot function independently, in most cases cannot communicate, and absolutely are unable to explain what they do. Without practice, training, or time, they can instantly calculate impossibly-long math problems, play music, sketch, and perform unmatchable memory and mental calculation feats. These people have lost control over their brain to this powerful process. In a specific area they have gained what we would call genius capability; but at a terrible price - their inability to control or moderate the process. But it is an insight, a hint, at the enormous power of this non-verbal, primarily right-brain capability that we all have to widely-varying degrees.

Partially in this camp are many artists. In almost all cases their capabilities are intuitive, un-thought, non-analytical. Poetry, words, or music just appear in their minds and are put on paper; painting or sculpture comes from their hands without planning or thought. But many appear to pay a price - this same strength that brings talent also penetrates and influences the conduct of their daily lives. When it brings artistic creativity it is a blessing; when it brings anarchy, self-destructive behavior, weak self-control, and emotional instability it is often the premature end of the artist. Uncontrollable feelings applied to a canvas may result in a work of art; applied to one's daily life may result in drug/alcohol dependence and broken personal relationships. The masterpieces of music and art in the world's museums are a testament to the power of this capability - as are the tortured and shortened lives of many artists.

Examples of man's short-cut thinking skills surround us on a daily basis. Everyone is both a user as well as an observer, although lacking an identified name these skills seldom come up in most discussions. "Conspiracy theories" are an excellent example. The attractiveness of conspiracy theories is that they offer a conceptually simple explanation for a complex or even unknown situation. Deaths of famous people or transportation disasters are excellent candidates for such theories, since often critical information is simply unavailable, the situations are complex, and the event was notorious enough to attract their attention. Offering a conspiracy theory accounts for the missing information by implying that it was all carefully worked out by the conspirators. UFO's/alien abductions are perfectly explained by this. But such theories are not figments of modern life. Religious groups have been historically blamed for many events, and such concerns arose as recently as the 1960 presidential election in the United States. Since the beginning of human history and before, explanations for natural events, which unfortunately for them was most everything, was attributed to gods of every sort, sometimes with capricious natures. Only the advent of monotheistic religions brought an end to this. Conspiracy theories are a direct reflection of man's need for a simple, unequivocal short-cut explanation for events that otherwise appear slightly unbelievable, vague, puzzling, uncertain, inexplicable. Unbelievable because man's nature is looking for an instant, categorical cause for the event. And if the facts, or in most cases the absence of key facts, excessively delays this, then man's nature forces him to create an explanation to fill the intellectual vacuum.

This drive in man for a non-inconclusive picture of an event should not be underestimated. Ask yourself or anyone you know how well you would enjoy a book or movie if the last ten pages or minutes were removed. Most likely, almost no one would read or see the work. Or instead, take a hundred pages or a half-hour out of the body of the book/movie - you would have a conclusion but it would not necessarily make sense, depending on what was omitted. The same drive for conclusivity applies to everyday events, especially those deemed significant.

This innate human demand for an "answer" is not limited to "conspiracies". Forty-five hundred years later, there is no consensus on how the great pyramids in Egypt were constructed, or their significance if any beyond that of the rays of the sun in the sky. Lacking a miracle find, it is most likely we will never find out. As a result, people have put forward detailed arguments including the involvement of supernatural forces and aliens. And new theories arise from time, showing just how much of a logical vacuum there is to fill. The deaths of a substantial number of well-known historical figures with political or military positions are always being questioned as to whether they died a natural death or were poisoned by someone or some group. Egyptian pharaohs, Alexander the Great, Roman Emperors, Napoleon, and Marilyn Monroe are at the top of this list. In some cases, the explanation is that the person in question did not die at that time, but went off to some other little-recorded set of activities. This includes figures in the Bible up through Elvis. With the advent of DNA testing, there has been discussion and some occurrences of exhuming people to check the validity of some of these theories.

There is the old cliche that truth is stranger than fiction. If stranger, and without all the answers, people will not buy it, and will look elsewhere. There is still controversy over how the Lusitania sunk as quickly as she did after being torpedoed close to shore off the English coast, and why the battleship Maine came to explode in Havana. The Titanic sinking still raises questions over how the lifeboat count was determined, how many ice messages the captain saw, how hard they tried to fill the early lifeboats, and how the third class passengers were treated. Many people remain unconvinced that President Kennedy was assassinated by Lee Harvey Oswald acting alone, and maybe the same percentage are convinced that the U.S. government has a systematic, decades-old procedure to hide visits and crashes by aliens in spacecraft. And there are those that attribute historical financial problems, political events, and even wars to a conspiracy of certain ethnic/racial groups.

The reason that quick, short-cut explanations are so attractive is not that everyone is an idiot. It is man's drive for a rapid answer combined with the problem that the truth is often very problematical; complex; complicated. In John 18:37 Jesus speaks to Pilate: "To this end was I born, and for this cause came I into the world, that I should bear witness unto the truth... Pilate saith unto him, What is the truth? And when he had said this, he went out again ..." The Bible records no answer, but it records the question. In a way, Jesus is saying that the truth cannot be simplified to a few-word response. But a few-word response is what man is craving; is dying for.

The NTSB in the United States will spend whatever it takes to identify the cause of a plane crash that results in a significant loss of life. So will NASA for a major manned spacecraft failure. Sometimes the identification of the fundamental cause, ascribed to an insignificant event years earlier, like Apollo 13, is so ingenuously done that you can only marvel at the result. Sometimes, like TWA Flight 800, every cause save one can be excluded, but the suspected reason that is left can still not be proved. The lesson is that even years and tens of millions of dollars cannot guarantee that the cause of a disaster can be absolutely proved. Since few groups in the world can support years and millions of dollars, proof, or the truth, can often be infeasible. So jumping to a conclusion, blaming a conspiracy or some other vague causal agent, is just filling an empty space that may not be filled to anyone's satisfaction any other way.

There is an old saying that for every complex problem there exists a simple, but wrong, explanation. Simple, neat, tight and quick - this is the way we like our world. Many of us know people that are lucky (or unlucky) enough to live in such a world - everything in its place, and a place for everything. If something does not quite fit in its little compartment, then the offending pieces are brushed off and left behind: politicians are corrupt, a Ford is the only car to own, Democrats are spendthrifts, (another race) is lazy, the private sector always solves problems better than the government can.

Bipolar Thinking and Judgmental Tagging

Make a mental list of the first twenty decisions that come to mind that you have made, maybe recent, maybe really significant. It could be the last place you went out to dinner, or piece of clothing you purchased, or where you live. Summarize the decision to yourself - you are happy with what you bought or unhappy, you liked the restaurant or food or you did not, you got in the right line or the wrong line at the store. Most likely, your recollections of these decisions are in the form of:

> It was good or bad
> It was right or wrong
> It worked out or it did not
> You liked it or you did not
> Your were happy or unhappy with it
> You agreed or disagreed
> You would support it or you would not
> You would do it again or not

If the decision was trivial enough, or has little personal impact on you – like how many ice cubes you put in your water glass, how you chose to perform a simple task at work, or the exact chair you occupied in the conference room - then you will not have much of a reaction or recollection or colored memory.

There are two fundamental characteristics about most any decision important enough for you to remember. You remember it as one of two opposites, and the opposites are judgmental in nature. By judgmental is meant that you have measured and scored its value to you. This is not something that can be measured with a piece of equipment or a photograph. It is emotional, integrated, and holistic; it puts a meaning or significance on the event that was not part of the event itself. Remembering only "whats" about the event is not judgmental; remembering how you felt about it is. For significant decisions and events, the "how you felt" part is always stored along with the other details. As the event ages, the "how you felt" part may be the dominant thing that is retained.

The two opposites, one of which is selected to represent how you feel about the decision, are usually simple, obvious, common contrasts - good/bad, right/wrong, happy/sad, exciting/boring, new/old, in/out, conservative/liberal. With only two extremes or outcomes to select from, this kind of thinking is bipolar. Having two opposite representations of things tends to be the rule, rather than the exception. There are male/female, plants/animals, land/sea, flat/hilly, above ground/below ground, hot/cold, wet/dry, still/windy, cloudy/clear, sweet/sour, salty/bland, light/dark, tall/short, heavy/light, empty/full, noisy/quiet, hunter/prey, plaintiff/defendant, House/Senate, Republicans/Democrats, rich/poor, labor/management, us/them, heaven/hell, night/day, hungry/full, tight/loose, love/hate, rough/smooth, busy/idle, introvert/extrovert, tense/relaxed, weak/strong, fat/thin, wild/tame, cheap/expensive, city/country, yes/no.

A full list would be very long. In fact, the whole universe is in a sense itself bipolar - it can be split into two groups of things: those that are bipolar, and those that are infinite in variety. For the average person, contact with the infinite class of objects is primarily restricted to the senses - colors, sounds, etc.

Of course, this is an exaggeration. Most things in the world are not necessarily bipolar; instead it is our perception of these things that is bipolar. But this overly-simple classification does work. With nothing but bipolar words you can readily communicate with someone else on anything that concerns itself with day to day existence. Most of the world's activity is tolerant and receptive to bipolar descriptions. If it were wide of the mark, it would not be in such overwhelmingly-common use. Its ubiquitous nature comes from its dramatic effectiveness as both a thinking and communication short-cut.

Nature itself is often bipolar. There are only two electrical charges, positive and negative, and two magnetic poles, north and south. In particle physics, there is matter and anti-matter, up and down spin, leptons and bosons, and other abstract concepts. There are two sexes, two sets of chromosomes, two lungs, two kidneys, two eyes, two ears, two arms, two legs, and two brain hemispheres. There are two nucleotide chains that contain genetic information, RNA and DNA, and DNA itself is itself double-stranded. All proteins and sugars used by living organisms are right or left-handed – life on Earth can only utilize left-handed proteins and right-handed sugars.

It is not just our descriptions of the world that are bipolar. Man's view of himself and the world are deeply colored bipolar. Try to name a game or competition that does not have a winner and then everyone else (losers). There are hundreds of card games, games with tokens or pieces like chess or go, sports contests of every variety, beauty, talent, and humor contests, even pet and car competitions. All have only one winner. And many people have even observed how unfair this is - for small children who do not really need a lesson in winning and losing, for teams that have both played extremely well so that neither deserves to be a loser, for skaters or gymnasts who consistently make a jump or move only to miss it in competition. Man cannot invent and sustain a contest without a winner, a clear measure of this facet of his nature. In the few cases without a clear winner, for example in college football in the United States, in years where there is no clear consensus on the number one team there is a outburst of complaints about and requests for a playoff game to clearly determine the one team that is number one.

From another perspective, bipolar thinking is a rejection of the vagueness and uncertainty of multiple or missing explanations for things that man perceives in the world. Bipolarity forces a choice, like some test methodologies, of one or the other. This brings an answer or conclusion rapidly, without any gray complexity or open issues.

Sometimes bipolar concepts are referred to as duality, sometimes as dialectics. Janus was the two-faced Greek god - happy on one side, sad on the other. Dr. Jekyll and Mr. Hyde in the Stevenson story refer to the two contrasting sides of human nature. The "good cop/bad cop" duality is a cliche in books and movies, and maybe in real life. St. Augustine talked of the City of God versus the City of Man. The medical term for people that have manic-depression is a bipolar disorder. Heraclitus theorized that harmony resulted from a blend of two opposites. Aristotle in his Ethics discusses the concept of the golden mean, a middle ground between two extremes. These would be stingy and profligate, starvation and gluttony, cowardice and recklessness. Either extreme is perceived to be a vice by Aristotle; a blend in the middle is the proper behavior. Even the Koran in the Al-Furqan notes "True servants of the Merciful are those ...who are neither extravagant or niggardly, but keep the golden mean...." Hegel and other philosophers stress the idea of opposition or dialectics - that every idea begets its opposite, and that through the resulting conflict a composite idea results. It is also referred to as thesis, antithesis, synthesis. Marx extended the idea into political economics with well-known results.

Bipolar thinking and judgmental tagging are the two dominant characteristics of human decision-making. Try to imagine someone without these characteristics, attempting to work through their day. Without bipolar thinking and words, describing something for someone else would take forever. You would have to very carefully choose words that conveyed the intended meaning. This is not as easy as it sounds - many bipolar words are only used to make an impression, and do not literally have much meaning. What is a "light" lunch, a "good" book, a "shy" look, a "bad" feeling, the "high" road, a "poor" attitude? Their meaning is derived from being "not" their opposite. Someone conservative is not liberal, someone poor is not rich, someone drunk is not sober, someone Type A is not Type B, someone young is not old. These terms are not meant to be precise. This communication is effective because its meaning is so quickly grasped. Most of the time, the precise nature of the thing described is not required to talk about it. Calling someone who just bumped their head tall, or someone with a cane old, is sufficient to convey what is intended. If you were forced to use non-bipolar terms in a conversation, it would take so long to make a point that the listener would lose interest. Trying to explain a "light" lunch in terms of your basal metabolism, body weight and type, other caloric intake, general activity level, and caloric assumptions based on assumed serving sizes and caloric content is unnecessary overkill. The same problems would arise if describing someone drunk, or conservative, or Type A. Someone who does not communicate using bipolar terms would not be able to come to the point, would take forever to describe something, and would nit-pick everything that you said and how you choose to say it.

People who hold strong opinions with no facts to support them are called idealists, zealots, lunatics. But people who cannot maintain an opinion or feeling or passion or preference are almost not there - "the lights are on but no one is home". Without the anchor of judgmental tagging, people appear gray, conviction-less, morally-bankrupt, spiritually-ephemeral.

Consequence

Every so often the Gallup organization polls Americans with the question "Who do you regard as the greatest U.S. president?" In 1956, the responses in order were: Franklin Roosevelt (FDR), Lincoln, Washington, and Eisenhower, who was president at the time of the poll. In 2011 the responses by Democrats in order were: Clinton, Kennedy, Obama, FDR, and Lincoln. For Republicans, the responses in order were: Reagan, Washington, Lincoln, Kennedy, and George W. Bush. Unfortunately, Gallup was not doing his survey in 1922, but if he had been, it probably would have looked like this: Teddy Roosevelt, Lincoln, Washington, Harding, Grant. Harding of course was the president in 1922, and history would regard him as one of the worst ever.

Translating the results, what this means is that while as students most Americans were taught American history, they retained precious little, and when asked this question, immediately commingle who they like, or have a favorable impression of, or have a distinct recollection of, with those whom they actually have some dim performance memory of. In 1956, Washington and Lincoln were on Mt. Rushmore, FDR just got them through the Depression and WWII, and Eisenhower was their current president, so he was the best anyone could come up with for fourth place. Plus, Ike was likeable – he helped win WWII as the Supreme Allied Commander, and did not say or do anything as president to make anyone angry or upset. His style was easygoing, friendly, and down-to-earth. In 2011, the Democrats are picking Clinton because he is so likeable, and Kennedy because he was so tragically lost. Then Obama because they like him, but also because he is now their president. FDR is the most famous Democratic president that they can think of so he goes next, and then finally they get to Lincoln. The father of our country, Washington, is being chiseled off Mt. Rushmore as this is being written. For the Republicans, it is Reagan as number one, because everybody loves Ronald Reagan; no matter how many bad things happened during his watch, he always had a positive, America-is-the-greatest attitude. Washington and Lincoln were next, so the Republicans for some reason allow their history lessons to intrude here much sooner than the Democrats do. But then the somewhat shocking choice of Kennedy before George Bush, Kennedy for the Democratic reason and Bush because he was likeable and was the last Republican president they can remember, like Eisenhower.

What this signifies is that people answer performance questions with whom they like, or can fondly recall, or recall at all. It is a popularity contest, not a thoughtful evaluation of strengths and weaknesses, a consideration of the president and the times and events he had to contend with. When asked a question that requires thinking, man's short-cut processes take over instead and he responds with a judgmental response. It is his nature – he cannot help himself.

The comedy/pseudo-reality TV show <u>American Idol</u> has a nominal objective of selecting the "best" young singer, established through the voting of a TV audience biased to the very young side by the predominance of text message voting. The total number of votes ranges from 30 to 50 million per episode, so a fair number of people are involved, although multiple votes are accepted. Almost without exception, the singer with the most singing talent never garners the most votes and wins the competition; in fact, winning is sort of a "kiss of death" from a career perspective with a few exceptions. Setting aside for the moment that it is the entertainment business and the goal is to make money for the show, and not really to choose the best singer, the real reason that the "best" singer does not win is actually captured in the name of the show - "idol". Fatefully, or ironically, the wizards who chose the name of the show subconsciously anticipated that viewers would not choose the best singer, otherwise the title would have been "singer" rather than "idol". By dissecting the comments from those that vote, the voting is clearly not based on musical talent but on likability – who the viewer would like to have sitting next to them on the couch for an hour; who they would like to introduce to their friends as their new boyfriend (boys tend to win). Viewers are so dominated by their bipolar and judgmental natures that they cannot even evaluate something as simple as musical talent, even when it is placed directly in front of them in a plain apple and apple comparison. For this reason, the winner of the competition is often a singer from whom no one would ever really want to purchase music (and does not), but they are certainly friendly, cute, polite, humble, and likable.

Many bipolar descriptors are also judgmental, especially the ones used most frequently - good/bad, right/wrong, excellent/poor, positive/negative. The more judgmental words that are used in a comment, the faster the point is made. With the information overload clearly evident and getting more severe, there is a clear incentive and a clear movement to use more and more words that are judgmental and bipolar. This emphasis has been so intense that there is now a backlash against words that are perceived to be judgmental - that of "political correctness". If a word or phrase contains judgmental content that a group feels is pejorative, then there may be a formal emphasis to eliminate the words from use in the offensive context. Substitute words or phrases need to be found and used.

Because most languages have only a very few words to convey a certain meaning, and inventing new words in a language is not easy to accomplish, the politically-correct words are often awkward and strained compared to the incorrect version. An example would be "fireperson", along with most any racial, ethnic, or male/female terminology. Political-correctness is the best example of words being considered exclusively for their judgmental content, ignoring completely their actual meaning or informational content. Those offended by perceived political incorrectness will not even get to the stage of considering the point that was being made - they are so completely put off by the emotional content of the words. That this sensitivity has become so pronounced is an indication of the depth of judgmental thinking and content in the language of common daily usage.

Some issues are so polarized and emotional that they are excellent representations of this characteristic in man. The Pro-Life/Pro-Choice movements, the gun control pro and con groups, religion in the schools groups, and the restriction of material deemed "obscene" groups are in this category. Almost by definition, there is no middle ground, only extremes, and every issue related to this is charged with emotion and an absence of genuine rational dialogue - "you are either for us or you are against us." Note that these behaviors represent the basic nature of man, and the issue of who or what is "right" or "wrong" does not have to be considered.

To be clear, judgmental tagging, like other aspects of basic human nature discussed in the subsequent chapters, is a beneficial feature, not a defect, in man. Someone without judgmental tagging is unable to communicate with his fellow man in today's world, using today's languages. Individuals with Asperger's Syndrome do in fact take words literally, with no connotation, and they have an almost impossible time surviving socially without constructing for themselves a guidebook that explains what "regular" people mean when they use words in certain ways. To say someone is "hot", or something is "cool", totally confuses them. But the words do not have to be slang – how about calling someone a liberal, or a socialist, or a murderer, or an enemy sympathizer, because you disagree with their politics? These words are not used for their literal content. There are a huge number of pejorative words that apply to race, ethnic origin, and sexual orientation. Ideas, events, actions or comments by public officials will be routinely referred to as "bizarre", "insane", "unusual", "ridiculous", "stupid", "dumb", "idiotic", or "moronic" and the like by individuals and journalists, all of which are utilized for their judgmental content. If every time someone had to make a point, they were not allowed to use a judgmentally-tagged word but to instead convey it with an objective analysis or descriptive paragraph full of neutral words, the world would collapse until someone independently invented judgmental words. Someone asks you – what did you think of the President's/Senator's/Governor's speech? - under only special circumstances do they expect a ten minute analysis of its strong and weak points. Nor do they expect you to say it was short or long – one-word descriptors without judgment. No, they want you to say it was wimpy, or whatless, or pablum, or a reiteration of his campaign platform, or politics-as-usual, or a sell-out to the special interests, or a shameless attempt to hide behind patriotism. Your listeners want it short, distilled, and colored with some kind of emotion or judgment to show how you felt about it. If not, it most likely would not be brought up at all – like religion or politics in a general work situation.

Readers who are skeptical of this need to keep careful track of their casual conversations and see if they can avoid all words with non-neutral connotations and with any emotional content. You can, but you will lose your listener. You can have one or the other, but not both.

Now, having said that, there are those who only speak/write with words that have the highest incendiary content all the time. To some degree, this is the exception proving the rule, although it is far from an exception today. In an interconnected world of sound-bites and video-clips and twittered-bits, it is not the well-turned phrase that makes the grade but the hell-tuned rage.

Backwardation of Biography (and more)

Biographic descriptions of famous individuals from the historical literature shows how bipolar thinking has actually degraded the quality of our characterizations over time. (Backwardation refers to futures prices; so here we are applying it to the standards of good biography.)

The earliest biographers seemed to take a special effort to record all aspects of an individual's personality and behaviors – both strengths and weaknesses, positive benefits and negative outcomes. This often if not always provided a complex and non-simplistic view, something that was not easily subject to sound-bites and simple generalizations. Today, in a world that wants everything distilled down to 10 second parcelettes, polarity is the tool of choice to do the distillation, and most everything and everyone can only have one or two key simplistic attributes. And they better be self-consistent. Meaning, you can be sweet and cute, or mean and nasty, or big and brutish, or cerebral and pensive, but you can't be sweet and mean, or cute and cerebral. No one today has time for this complexity – bipolar thinking has come to the rescue and enabled rapid uni-dimensional characterizations of everything for easy, quick tagging and memorization without any thought required.

Here are a few representative examples from 2,000 year ago:

"Syria was governed by Licinius Mucianus.... Mucianus' character was a combination of self-indulgence and energy, courtesy and arrogance, good and evil. A libertine in idle moments, he yet showed remarkable qualities once he had set his hand to a thing. To the world his activities might seem laudable; but there were ugly rumours about his private life. Yet by a supple gift for intrigue he exercised great influence on his subordinates, associates and colleagues, and found it more congenial to make an emperor than be one."[5]

"Such was the fate of Servius Galba (Roman emperor).... His own personality was something of a compromise; he had good qualities and in equal measure bad. Having won a reputation, he neither despised nor exploited it.... A tolerant attitude toward courtiers and officials attracted no censure when they happened to be honest; but his lack of perception if they were not was quite inexcusable. However, distinguished birth and alarms of the time disguised his lack of enterprise and caused it to be described as wisdom.... Indeed, so long as he was a subject, he seemed too great a man to be one, and by common consent possessed the makings of a ruler – had he never ruled."[6]

"As for Titus Vinius, during a lifetime lasting forty-seven years he played many parts, both good and evil. His first tour of military service won him notoriety. The wife of his commanding officer Calvinius Sabinus had an unfortunate passion for inspecting the campsite.... She had the shamelessness to commit adultery, in the headquarters building of all places. The man involved was proved to be Titus Vinius. So he was put under close arrest by Gaius Caesar (Emperor Caligula), but when times changed soon afterwards, he was given his freedom, rising smoothly in the public service as praetor

---

5   The Histories, Tacitus, Penguin Books, 1993, p. 21
6   Ibid., p. 46

(government official) and then as a legionary commander who proved his worth. His reputation was later sullied by a scandal unworthy of a gentleman. He was alleged to have stolen a gold cup at a banquet given by (Emperor) Claudius…. Still, he proved a strict and honest proconsul of Narbonese Gaul, and after that his friendship with (Emperor for a few months) Galba carried him irresistibly into the abyss. Unscrupulous, cunning and quick-witted, when and as he made up his mind he could be either vicious or hard-working, with equal effectiveness."[7]

"So (Emperor) Tiberius died, in his seventy-eighth year…. His character … had its different stages. While he was a private citizen or holding commands under Augustus, his life was blameless; and so was his reputation. While Germanicus and Drusus [his children, the former adopted, at least one (Drusus) murdered] still lived, he concealed his real self, cunningly affecting virtuous qualities. However, until his mother died there was good in Tiberius as well as evil. Again, as long as he favored (or feared) Sejanus (a vicious murdering Machiavellian), the cruelty of Tiberius was detested, but his perversions unrevealed. Then fear vanished, and with it shame. Thereafter he expressed only his own personality - by unrestrained crime and infamy."[8]

Here is a another glowing description of a Roman emperor: "(His) accession seemed to the Roman people – one might say, to the whole world - like a dream come true… most provincials and soldiers, many of whom had known him as a child, and the entire population of Rome as well, show(ed) extravagant joy that he was now Emperor…. An equally popular step was the recall of all exiles, and dismissal of all criminal charges whatsoever that had been pending since earlier times…. (He) drove from the city the perverts known as *spintriae,* and could with difficulty be restrained from drowning the lot. He gave permission for the works of Labienus, Cordus, and Severus, which had been banned by order of the Senate, to be routed out and republished – stating it to be entirely in his interest that posterity should be in full possession of all historical facts; also, he revived Augustus' practice, discontinued by Tiberius, of publishing an Imperial budget; invested the magistrates with full authority, not requiring them to apply for his confirmation of sentences…. (His) creation of a fifth judicial division aided jurors to keep abreast of their work; his reviving of the electoral system was designed to restore popular control over the magistracy…. He twice presented every member of the commons with three gold pieces (maybe $600)."[9]

7   Ibid., p. 45
8   The Annals of Imperial Rome, Tacitus, Michael Grant, Trans., Barnes and Noble Books, 1993, pp. 226-227
9   The Twelve Caesars, Suetonius, Robert Graves, Trans., Penguin Books, 2003, pp. 156-158

This guy sounds pretty good, and certainly an improvement over Tiberius, although it was said that Augustus selected Tiberius because he was the worst of all possible candidates available to succeed him, chosen to make Augustus to look so much better in comparison.

But this emperor is the same one who, during lunch and dinner, had people slowly tortured and killed in front of him while he ate. He insisted that his soldiers kill everyone he selected for death, and there were many, as slowly as possible so that it was as painful as possible. He regularly reminded his closest friends, officials, and even those he loved that with just one word he would have their heads struck off. Anything he saw or heard would cause him to react explosively and destructively. If he saw someone with beautiful hair, he would have them scalped. If they looked fit and strong, he would have them tossed into the Colosseum to fight gladiators. His arbitrary viciousness, depravity, and bloodthirstiness were unmatched – but he lasted almost four years before he was stabbed to death. The Roman people knew him as Gaius Caesar, but we refer to him by his nickname, Caligula.

So even a consensus-catastrophe like Caligula receives a "fair and balanced" treatment in the hands of historians 2,000 years ago, certainly the dawn of biography and history as a profession. Two emperors later we would have Nero, who while not as bad as Caligula had extravagant waste and ego as his greatest assets. He also received the same biographical treatment as Caligula by Suetonius – listing all of his strengths and accomplishments alongside his disastrous behaviors. So now, in the present day, building on the example and leadership of these early biographers, after the opportunity for two millennia of improvements and enhancements, you would expect that we would have the science of balanced biography, or for all history and analysis for that matter, refined to the point of exquisite excellence.

But rather than the dramatic leap forward that one would anticipate, collectively we seem to have moved backward. Today, it is extremely difficult to find a summary of a person (or political or religious belief or economic system) free of bipolar or judgmental taint. The evenhandedness that Tacitus and Suetonius gave to their subjects is a rare find nowadays. Other chapters in this book discuss the examples of Presidents Kennedy and Reagan, capitalism, and various aspects of Christianity, so we will pick a few other examples. President Lyndon Johnson is generally characterized only as a terrible President. He was in office by assassination, with a background of all the wrong skills. Adept at compromise and negotiation as the Majority Leader of the Senate, he was incapable of the leadership needed as the Chief Executive of the nation. He adopted the alternate-reality techniques normally used by celebrities of refusing to speak to anyone bearing unfavorable news, in this case not about themselves like a celebrity but about how the war in Vietnam was going. This fostered the fabrication of favorable reports of progress in the war and so prolonged a hopeless engagement. His woefully-low favorable rating prevented him from running for a second term. But President Johnson also pushed through a legislative agenda that included Medicare, Medicaid, Food Stamps (making pilot programs permanent), the Job Corps, the Public Broadcasting Act (basis for NPR and PBS), the National Endowment for the Arts, various Federal funding programs for education, and most importantly, the Civil Rights Act of 1964 and the Voting Rights Act of 1965, giving true equal rights to blacks for the first time in 400 years, an amazing step for a many-generation Southerner. So was Johnson a great President or a disastrous one? He was both at the same time, a mental-meltdown characterization that ancient historians were willing to engage but that no one today will touch.

How about President Nixon? He had to resign from office over the coverup of illegal acts following the break-in by Republican operatives to the Democratic offices at the Watergate building. He selected Spiro Agnew, the only Vice-President forced to leave office because of criminal charges (bribery). He selected John Mitchell, the only Attorney General ever to be found guilty of criminal charges (conspiracy, perjury, obstruction of justice) and end up in prison. He nominated G. Harrold Carswell for the Supreme Court, maybe the most amazing nomination of its kind; and he was the only President to dress the White House staff in uniforms reminiscent of a cheap Hollywood dictator movie (but for only one day). Most everyone you would ask would rate Nixon as a disastrous President. Yet he was the one who extracted the U.S. from the war in Vietnam; who was the first to initiate diplomatic relations with the "inscrutably-evil red China"; was the initiator of detente with the Soviet Union that produced the first SALT treaty, the ABM treaty, and the outlawing of biological weapons (BWC). He was responsible for Title IX (Patsy Mink Act), the Clean Air Act, and the EPA; and he was the President under whom for the first time public schools in the South became desegregated to a substantive degree. So, like Johnson, Nixon was both quite excellent and terribly bad, and concurrently. It is not one or the other, it's both, as utterly fingernails-on-a-chalkboard unbearably unacceptable as that may sound.

Saddam Hussein and Osama Bin Laden, for many Westerners, are the epitome of evil, killing thousands of civilians for their own self-centered agendas. Yet if you drop back a decade or so before they earned their current reputation, they were both the dearest of allies of the United States, the former waging war against Iran, the latter against the Soviet Union in Afghanistan. So they have to be looked on as friend and foe, not just the single flavor.

But this movement toward the polarized classification of people and events is not restricted to modern times. Just look at Richard I of England, often referred to as Richard the Lion-Hearted. This is the wonderful king whose return Robin Hood is always credited to be faithfully holding out for, fighting off all manner of evils in the process. Hogwash. This guy may have been lion-hearted, but he disliked the English climate, only spending time there when recalled by his father; was French-speaking and loving, dwelling in Aquitane, his mother's portion of his father's kingdom; spent all his time and energy conspiring first with Louis VII and then his son Philip Augustus to raise armies to overthrow his father, Henry II, and take over his empire. Each time Henry defeated him, he would grovel, beg forgiveness, and promise never to repeat his bad behavior, and Henry would forgive him without sanction. When Henry II died due indirectly to Richard's actions, Richard sacked England for all the money he could obtain, went on a crusade, ended up captured by the Holy Roman Emperor, and had to pillage England again to pay off the ransom demanded, a sum equivalent to several year's worth of the royal income. England was a ruin at the end of Richard's reign compared to the way his father had left it.

Animals tend to have homogenous, pure natures. You raise a dog or a horse a certain way and they will conserve those behaviors, and assuming you prefer them that way, you are happy with them, it's "good dog", and "nice horse". But if they get a new owner, or a visitor with different expectations, the same behaviors might suddenly occasion a negative reaction. The dog or horse is not to blame, although they always are – man is always right even when he is not. But man is not the same. He is fluently schizoid by design. He can effortlessly compartmentalize his behavior – play with his children sweetly all afternoon and then poison them that night, like Joseph Goebbels. He does not have one nature – he has many natures. Now he may have a distinctive personality type – aggressive, passive, loving, cool – but everything else is a grab-bag of youthful errors, just plain mistakes, miscalculations, desperation, over-exuberance, intoxication, opportunities taken, over-reaching, influence of others, rush to judgment, blood thicker than water, decisions made out of love, or hate, or jealousy, or rage; selfishness, miserliness, or altruism; a lust for fame, for popularity, for power; for political advantage, for geo-political advantage, because the ends justify the means; coveting that which someone else has, greed, security, or fear. People take actions all their lives for these and many other reasons, and the consequences of these actions accumulate for 50 or more years. Maybe during your life, or maybe 10 years after you die, someone makes some assessment and determines that you were OK, or good, or bad, or useless, or whatever. A more useless endeavor, simplifying a complex life into one simplistic word or phrase or label, cannot be imagined, save in man's world of bipolar thinking and judgmental tagging, demanding short-cut summaries. Man's nature insists that for most everything a giant ledger must be assembled, on one side the "good", on the other the "bad", determined subjectively by historians and pundits and commentators, and then a hellacious subtraction exercise must take place so that we are left with only a single net resultant outcome – overall "good" or overall "bad".

Now, to be sure, there are scholarly works that do not sound like this, that attempt to portray a balanced view of individuals and historical events. But it is swimming uphill – if you query the typical citizen, or litmus test the average characterization that floats around in the daily press, electronic, aural, or print, this balanced portrayal is never recalled – it is always the polarized, single-concept, one-color paintbrush version.

There is not sufficient time to walk through example after example – hopefully this is self-evident. Hitler was responsible for the deaths of 20 million or more people, but he may have been one of the most skilled interpersonal communicators/manipulators, both one-on-one and with massive crowds, in history. His propaganda minister, Joseph Goebbels, a major assist to Hitler in creating the mindset necessary to make the killing machine most effective, invented propaganda techniques so cunningly effective they have been used by every government, company, and politician since, be they tyrant or freely elected, Democrat or Republican. Winston Churchill, while given credit for his oratory and leadership during the Second World War, was responsible for the Gallipoli campaign in WWI, a poorly-thought-out invasion of Turkey that cost the British over 200,000 casualties. He also fought the Second World War with the goal of restoring to Britain all of the colonies that it had prior to the conflict, and was deeply disappointed but powerless to protest when Roosevelt refused to support his anachronistic demands. Napoleon, hailed generally for his control-freak remodeling of France and Paris specifically, without whom we would not have the preservation of ancient Egyptian artifacts, including the Rosetta stone, nor the Napoleonic Code, but also without whom we would not have wasted the lives of a million French soldiers invading Russia, and who knows how many other lives, both French and others, in his attempts to conquer the rest of Europe, which hardly needed conquering.

Consequence - The Mono-Polarity of Celebrities

Historical figures make for better examples since not only is all the data in, but they tend to have a higher recognition factor. But celebrities, taken as a class, also support this point. Many celebrities who produce assessable work - musicians and actors for example – have a favorable or strongly favorable impression in the eyes of those who like/enjoy their work. So, the first thing these celebrities do is use this favorable view to both plaster over bad behavior on their part – driving under the influence, unfaithful to their spouses, public displays of destructive or negative behavior, private abuse of their staff, waiters, hotel staff, small business people, contractors, anyone they come into contact with. Because human nature means you can only hold one view of these people, the favorable view "excuses" all the bad behavior. The celebrity's agents and other third parties may then decide to start selling merchandise – "me too" over-priced blandness that if sold stand-alone by Walmart or Sears or JC Penney would hardly move, yet by simply branding the product with the celebrity's name, even though the celebrity most likely never saw the product before it was ready for sale, it will sell fine to the those followers of the celebrity. Celebrities that have not been in a movie for 30 years hawk financial products like no-questions-asked life insurance, unsecured loans, and reverse mortgages, all of which require a sophisticated knowledge of the terms and conditions since the financial costs and restrictions are quite high, but the companies involved are calculating that the "good" impression the celebrity has will obviate any questions a customer might generate. But then reporters begin to ask these celebrities about their thoughts and opinions on current events, on politics. Now many of these people did not get to college, and if they did, were certainly not interested in learning, and once they left school, for certain do not spend any time on staying informed. Sure they have opinions, and have the right to opinions, but so does every one of the other seven billion people on the planet. Yet their favorable label as a celebrity provides sticking power for their opinion, regardless of the degree of insubstantiality that lies behind it. People pay attention; they are widely quoted; some run for political office; some even get elected; few amount to much. In a non-bipolar/judgmentally-tagged world, celebrity fame would be just one compartmentalized facet of a person's attributes. Whether anyone would buy their credit cards, perfume, handbags, or opinions would be an independent calculation.

In subsequent chapters, other features of man's nature are described that sometime overwhelm even these black/white oversimplifications of bipolar thinking and judgmental tagging. But here are two characteristic examples that could just as well appear later on. President Clinton served two terms that, without getting into any details or taking sides, would be considered "typical" as presidents go. No major wars, no major national financial calamities. Clinton's main skill was his communication capability, especially one-on-one, but also as a public speaker. Well into his last term he let his personal life intrude into his Presidential, and had a sexual relationship with a young intern in the Oval Office at the White House, which utilized White House security staff and regular staff to both facilitate and cover-up, and to compromise the integrity of the intern system. He was impeached for this, and in a bipolar/judgmental world, "Monica" is the characterization the average American would assign to his presidency. Once the impeachment proceedings were over, Clinton, who only too well knows that that man thinks in this bipolar way, spent the balance of his presidency furiously trying to reach a Palestinian statehood agreement with Israel, calculating that it would result in a Nobel Peace Prize for him. People, who he knew would remember his presidency for one thing, would replace "Monica" with "Nobel Prize", and he could rest easy. But the Middle East negotiations were not successful, and then Clinton was unable to deny his nature as a politician at the end of his term, providing pardons to those to whom he owed political favors and were undeserving of pardons on any other basis, further besmirching his already smirched reputation. Since leaving office, Clinton has embarked on efforts to re-win the Nobel Prize, raising money from all kinds of interesting sources, showing up in places and areas of need on his jet, making appearances in front of the cameras, not letting heart surgery slow him down. Critics (of the above) characterization will say that Clinton really "cares" about what he is now doing. This may well be true, but is not germane; the goal is to win a Nobel, the means is to run around and to do charitable work. The only way to win the Nobel is to do an exceptionally good job on the charitable side, and the only way to do that is to be motivated and to "care" about it. A cynic here will say – well, what's the problem – Clinton's finally trying to do good things - what's there to complain about? The precise response is: Mother Teresa was trying only to do good things, and ended up with a Nobel Prize. Clinton is trying to win a Nobel Prize, and is choosing to do things that will make him look deserving of it. It is not clear the two individuals, starting with two completely different goals, end up in the same place. The author is not trying to, and does not have the capability of, judging, but is only pointing out that one cannot assume that acting in a certain way necessarily mandates motives, competency, or sincerity.

Sarah Palin was Governor of Alaska, the easiest state to govern since it obtains all its revenues from petroleum royalties and the Permanent Fund, when she resigned in the middle of her term. While she had some legal difficulties they appeared to fall far short of impeachable offenses. For a politician this is extremely rare behavior, since "quitting" is the concept from which most want to keep a vast distance. Why would Palin do this? Two of her explanations at the time were "I love Alaskans too much to put them through a lame duck session," and "that huge waste that we have seen with the countless, countless hours that state staff is spending on these frivolous ethics violations." Others have speculated that she left for financial reasons (she had a rich book deal but the Alaska attorney general had said she could not do a book tour as governor), and for celebrity/fame reasons, based on her exposure to the national scene as the Vice-Presidential nominee for John McCain. But let's try another perspective. Like Clinton, Palin does well with teleprompter speeches to large groups, and with the assistance of speechwriters during the Presidential campaign found that she garnered solid support and resonance with a certain segment of the political spectrum.

But when you are Governor, you have to make decisions every day – you are Chief Executive of the state. Some people will find fault with every decision, regardless. You can declare it American Flag Day, or Grandmother's Day, and someone will grouse that it is a waste of money. With every decision some number of people are upset, you have to make twenty decisions a day; pretty soon your approval rating is 35%.

But if you stop being Governor, and just become a "talking head", a commentator, then now all you have to do is criticize the others who are making decisions every day, who do have real jobs. You simply wait until they do something, or don't do something, that you can say something critical about that your base of supporters will really love, and then sing out. Or take some other philosophical position that could never become real legislation but makes for a great sound-bite. If you have the luxury of a group of supporters, it is a magical position.

Palin knows people think in a bipolar/judgmental manner. As Governor, the negatives were only going to accumulate, as they already had. She had seen when campaigning as Vice-President, with no "baggage" in terms of a previous track-record of actions, the freedom that talk alone, without having to make decisions, brought. For the subgroup of the population that she was targeting, she was only getting positive responses. So she realized that if she remained in a "decision-free/talk-only" mode, she could count on just accumulating favorable reactions (from those she was targeting). Human nature, where people were going to react in a simple like/dislike, for her/against her manner, would work strongly to her advantage.

So Palin quit the Governorship, which would normally appear to be political suicide, and went with human nature, an advantage that is undeniable and unstoppable. As measured by her ratings among her supporters, she appears to have solidly accomplished exactly what she had intended. In Palin's own words, "I know when it's time to pass the ball for victory" (using a basketball analogy).

Now there are many other commentators who also talk instead of act, relying on its inherent safety. But no one aside from Palin has voluntarily quit an elected office, which is why she makes for such a crisp example.

In a non-bipolar, non-judgmental world, such things as these Clinton and Palin activities, or celebrities hawking debit cards, would not occur. People, ideas, events, and institutions would not be assessed simplistically but complexly, multidimensionally. One could not flip their image from bad to good by selling Girl Scout cookies for two years in front of the local church, or deciding to talk instead of do, or expecting that their favorable aura would spill over to some otherwise unsavory financial product. But human nature puts us in another world, one that requires that every politician giving a speech must have five American flags in the background, who has unpopular American presidents choosing to speak at U.S. Armed Forces bases. It is a world that has people intent on taking away someone else's rights always talking about how much they love the U.S. Constitution, and people who want to stamp out someone else's religious rights always waving the Bible, bearer of the of the long-forgotten words of Jesus: "Blessed are they which are persecuted for righteousness' sake" (Christians feel they only apply if Christians are being persecuted). Like Motherhood and apple pie, these things for most people draw positive reactions, and those speaking want to associate themselves with that reaction, even though their message may be far afield, if not in direct contradiction. In these examples the speakers are looking for people to make a judgmentally-favorable bipolar choice about them, and immerse themselves in or hold up a symbol that will hopefully garner that response regardless of what they say.

Individual word use is just a microcosm of this same effect, except that there is no independent symbol or image – the word itself has to convey the "logical" content (if significant) as well as the judgmental content. You can say something is boorish, crass, or indecent, or inappropriate, or in poor taste, or a poor choice, or I-wouldn't-have-done-that, and all of these words/phrases have some judgmental or emotional content in addition to the word/phrase itself. It is the nature of the beast, man in this case – Mother Nature has given us the power of a color or flavor that rides along with most every word conveying other meanings that it might take a much longer explanation to otherwise convey. By your choice of say "crass" versus "I-wouldn't-have-done-that", you are specifying a particular flavor or color in that emotional dimension that serves as a communication short-cut. Replacing these words with "garbage", "trash", or "crap" moves the coloring even further afield, and of course you can go as far as you wish with words with even more dramatic emotional content if you wish. Going the other direction, finding words with no emotional content, is extremely difficult. The reader should give it a try if they think this is a trivial exercise.

Consequence – Education

In April of 2011 The Wall Street Journal had an article[10] which some readers may have seen on the state of education in India, a BRIC (Brazil, Russia, India, China) country, and important because it contains one-sixth of the population of the world. Indian companies cannot, using the millions of

---

10 "India Graduates Millions, But Too Few Are Fit to Hire", The Wall Street Journal,
   April 5, 2011

recent graduates from Indian universities, find acceptable candidates to meet the qualifications for thousands of entry-level jobs that require basic reading, typing, speaking, and comprehension skills. Slightly over half of fifth graders can read at a second-grade level, so the problem begins early. India's global businesses like information technology find that only 25% of the graduates from India's technical universities are employable. Some companies report that only three percent of their applicants can meet their minimum standards. At the university level, there is a tacit understanding that the professors do not expect much from the students, and the students should not expect much from the professors. Classes can be skipped with little consequence; a few days of studying at the end of the semester are sufficient to pass the final exam. And if not, if you write your cell phone number on the exam paper, the test grader will call you, and for a fee of about 10,000 rupees ($225) he will give you a passing grade.

Now part of this is certainly due to India's deep and systemic commitment to bureaucracy (the License Raj, in spite of attempts to remove some aspects of it), along with cricket the major vestigial remnants of its British occupation. Everything in India requires one to navigate many-layered roadblocks of rules, procedures, and red tape, most often accompanied by an exchange of cash if progress is expected. And a portion will be due to the problems that any organization develops which has functional instead of performance goals, where its members begin to select sub-optimal personal goals that replace the original goals of the organization, personal goals like less work, more money, job security, and more power, But aside from the anti-Darwinian impact (more on this in Chapter 18) of students failing to meet either the requirements of the educational system or the businesses that depend on the educational institutions, softening the standards of the academic institutions, having teachers back off their responsibilities, allowing classes to be skipped without academic consequence, enabling a few days of studying to equate to the learning needed for the full semester of a class, or allowing the payment of a fee to achieve a passing grade – these are all short-cuts. Like cheating on any school test or assignment, which are all short-cuts, the cheater is the one who ultimately loses, since by not learning what they should have been learning their future competency is impaired and diminished. But the temptation to cheat, to utilize the drive to seek and take short-cuts that is built into man's nature, has in this case for India become a national catastrophe.

Consequences – Health

If you are "average" or "typical", especially if you have children, you have personally experienced this. You notice that drinks with food coloring make your children go absolutely hyper, or certain foods cause you health problems, or taking vitamins or supplements seems to improve some health challenges. Certain over-the-counter medicines appear to work much better than others, or only work at dosages different from the recommended amounts. Some prescription medicines do not help you at all, or bring on near-catastrophic side-effects, unmentioned by your doctor. If the doctor directed you to take the item in question you may get a polite hearing, but for everything else you will be told that your observation is total nonsense, that there is no scientific evidence to back up any of this, that it is all in your head (the placebo effect). But you stay with what works in spite of what the physician says, slightly frustrated and disappointed but unable to quarrel with success.

One problem of course is that doctors are not scientists - they practice medicine – and doctoring and science tend to be unrelated disciplines. But the other complexity is that through genetic differences (kitchen ingredients), through gene expression (recipes, chefs, and cooking), and epigenetics (gene expression changes passed on to your children), we are all quite different from one another. Molecular biologists exploiting PCR (polymerase chain reaction to explore genetic differences) know this, but this complexity is just too great for your family physician. But it is not fair to blame the family doctor - the technology to establish these differences across individuals is prohibitively expensive at this time. Only a few major diseases/syndromes attributed to single genetic change have been identified - a few dozen to date.

A single drug or vitamin test on a large group of people to see if something is effective or not will often show it is not a factor. Even though 1%, or 2%, or 5% of people may benefit, or be favorably impacted, by something, since everyone else is not, or some may even have an unfavorable reaction, the study overall shows a negative result.

In a world that did not look at everyone as identical, that appreciated the painful and distressing complexity that almost everything – allergies, vitamins, supplements, diet - are affecting the population at somewhere between the 1% and 20% level, problems that people are now forced to self-treat would have the support of the medical profession and research community.

Man - the Short-Cut Master

The ubiquitous nature of wireless-capable devices, their readily portable size in many cases, serves them well as a mechanism to enable man to instantly connect himself to whatever he wants whenever he wants effortlessly. Even in countries with no infrastructure – no roads, electricity, water, sewage, or visible effective government, cell phones are available and work. But fundamentally, the attractiveness of all these devices is that they represent the fastest way to accomplish that which an individual prefers to do on the spur of the moment, moment to moment, often with no pre-planning or preparation.

Some people think man is just preoccupied with technology, but this cannot account for the countless high technology devices that the market has rejected because the complexity/difficulty of use versus benefit ratio was too unfavorable. Some people think that man is just lazy. While someone texting on their smartphone unendingly, or enthralled in a video game on their phone/computer every spare moment may not get enough physical exercise, they may well be "lazy", if by that is meant in poor physical condition, because they are addicted to what their technology delivers. But they are not first "lazy" and then pick up a piece of electronic technology out of boredom. Someone truly lazy will pick a fully-passive activity, like watching television, and not playing a game or working a smartphone that takes continuous attention and effort – the machine must be fed.

While the competition in technology always demands more performance and more features for something close to the same price, the consumer does not want to put up with more of a hassle to obtain those features and performance. A classic example is in personal computers, where people are willing to pay well over twice as much for the same raw performance from a manufacturer whose computers are recognized as being easier to use. Their market share is relatively small, but it shows the immense utility people place on ease of use. Ease of use is just another way of measuring how good a short-cut the particular technology is. When the iPad was first released, a purchaser was quoted as saying "It's the elegance, the simplicity, and the way you interact with it is beautiful. This will kill the laptop." When you get through all the hype and fluff, what Apple has figured out is how to be the market leader on short-cut technology, even if performance disappears in the process. People will gladly trade away performance, and pay a lot of money, to obtain a short-cut, perceived as ease-of-use. The iPod Nano, in its sixth generation, has been reduced in size two-dimensionally to not much larger than the screen size, which is now a multi-touch color screen, so you can whiz around using your fingers instead of the five previous versions with a rotating click wheel. With the appearance of an even faster, more sophisticatedly-sexy short-cut, it is the must-have portable music device. That is, unless you choose to actually *use* the touch-screen to select the music you want to hear next on the Nano – then you get about 45 minutes of playing time out of it (author data). Apple is betting, and seemingly winning, that customers will buy on short-cut appeal even if that means a massive degradation in performance.

If you go to a supermarket today, the smallest portion of the store is dedicated to foods that have not been pre-processed in some way. Tapes, whether 8-track or cassette or VHS, were doomed the second that laser-encoded discs came out. Even setting the performance advantages aside, why would you want to spend time rewinding a tape if you did not have to? Until digital cameras became available, Polaroid film sold well – extremely expensive lousy small photographs – but, you had them in two minutes, a short-cut that many would accept all the other technical limitations and cost to obtain. Some people claimed you were buying convenience with Polaroid – but it was completely inconvenient – you had to do sticky wet chemistry on the film yourself. It was the short-cut people were buying. Many fabrics now are permanent-press/no-iron. Cordless tools are everywhere, but expensive. Wireless navigation devices for automobiles, so much easier to use than maps, are common. You could buy a car full of maps for the cost of one. You could not populate a modern building today if it had only stairwells and not elevators. Microwave ovens are now used more than conventional ovens because of their speed, a better match for the almost-ready-to-eat food now widely available. You can buy a moderately-priced do-everything coffee machine for home use, but most people would rather stop at a popular coffee store and pay twenty times as much for apparently the perceived convenience of not having to do it themselves, although the actual time saving is probably negative.

While the argument will be made that these examples just reflect people's careful consideration of the value of their time, if you look carefully, there are enough exceptions to indicate that it is the addiction and fascination with the idea of a short-cut that man is attracted to, and not the cold-blooded calculation of a short-cut.

Been to a parking lot lately? People will drive around in their cars for many minutes, or double-park along a traffic lane, waiting for a parking space to open up right near the door of the store they want to visit. They could have parked at an open spot, walked in, and have completed half their shopping in the time many of them waste doing this. But they are irresistibly drawn by the opportunity of a parking space right in front – it would be like winning the lottery. Availing themselves of a possible short-cut is worth waiting forever for. The same people, or their soul-mates, will queue up at elevators to go up or down just one floor. If they were really only interested in saving time they would be on the stairs. Fast-food restaurants often have drive-up windows – you never have to leave your car to order or get your food. Cars will line up eight or ten deep and wait for for one-at-a-time service. If you parked and took the ten second walk inside, there are maybe one or two people in line with two or more order-takers. But people will wait forever for the perception of the "convenience" of the drive-in window, the short-cut of not having to open your car door and stand-up, even though it actually takes much longer. Now if you have three children in the car under 18 months old, or someone in a wheelchair, it might be easier to stay in your car, but that is not the explanation for this, nor for the parking space preoccupation. Now some would say that the three previous classes of people are not seeking short-cuts, but are just "lazy". Well, lazy is first of all a pejorative word, but it is describing in a non-complimentary fashion the intense desire to avoid work or the expenditure of energy. An effective way to do this is to look hard for short-cuts, regardless of the consequence or logic thereof. "Lazy" is an observation about the result; but seeking short-cuts for many people is the facet of human nature that enables them to end up in the condition that we term laziness.

People will wait in line for days before the "special" sales the day after Thanksgiving, in order to save what?, maybe $50 or $100 best-case on that equivalent product, valuing their own time at say $1 an hour, and missing Thanksgiving with their family. Or getting a great price on a large TV whose quality is so bad you would never want to buy it under any normal circumstance. (The data actually demonstrates that the best prices show up the week following Thanksgiving, and that on-line comparison shopping can match or beat almost any in-store price.) Ignoring the data, the attraction is in effect getting a better deal than anyone else, a short-cut to savings that the rest of the world cannot obtain. That it costs you overall more than it is worth is never calculated. The purchased coffee versus make-it-yourself example was already given – it is the perception of a short-cut that the customer is buying, not any real time or money savings. He walks in, does nothing, and gets a fancy concoction in a big cup a few minutes later – magically! Doing it at home – where's the magic in that? People will take the family out for pizza, or hamburgers, or whatever other fast food, because it is perceived to be quick and easy, a short-cut. Or they will buy TV dinners or equivalent pre-processed meals at the grocery store and warm them up. But if you want to get as easy as possible, toss a bunch of fresh ingredients in a big crock pot and let it cook all day. Unless you have a family of eight, it will make more than one meal, it will taste a whole lot better than what you can get anywhere else, it will impress the living bejesus out of your family, it will be a lot more nutritious for them, and, taken over the number of days it lasts, it will take less time than putting everyone in the car and running off to a restaurant. But no one does that – it is perceived as "more work" - the short-cut of "fast-food" is always taken, even if it actually takes a lot more time.

Man is short-cut addicted. Show him one and he is on it, whether it actually saves him any real time or not. Many young people now spend their whole lives keying into and listening to a digital world, and the attraction is that it is such a short-cut compared to any other way of doing the same thing. Of course, they have lost all track of time and invest much more time than they ever would have had the short-cut not been available in the first place. They do not use the short-cut to save time, which is what would happen if they were simply interested in saving time; rather they are drawn hypnotically to the short-cut itself, which in this case is the digital technology. Since the short-cut is there, always, it has to be used. It is too much of an attraction to be ignored. Only 15% of American mothers breast-feed their babies for the first six months, even though it is highly recommended by physicians for the short-term and long-term benefits for the child. Formula in a bottle is too irresistible an alternative.

One can see the biological evidence that Mother Nature has hard-wired cognitive short-cuts into man in the form of pattern recognition. Whether a concept, a behavior pattern, or a level of expectation, only a brief exposure will often result in an almost complete understanding of what is happening and an identification who is involved. People can be exposed to only a few notes from a song and and recognize it. A still photo from many movies is often sufficient to enable it to be named. People can guess the artist, or class of artist, or general time period from a view of a single painting or sculpture. Shown only a few ingredients, most people who cook can recognize what the recipe is for. Exposure to a few lines from a poet or writer who is well-known is often sufficient to recognize the author. Still photos of ordinary people in ordinary situations will almost always be properly identified as to their activity - driving, cooking, sports, music, tinker, tailor, soldier, sailor, doctor, lawyer, Indian chief. Where the observer has not seen the exact painting, or read the exact words, or recalls the musical phrase, they can be identified only because they are part of a pattern previously learned. Few people will confuse Faulkner and Hemingway, Joyce and Shakespeare, Whitman and Cummings, or Tennyson and Dickinson due to the distinctive nature of their style, and not because they remember or recall a specific sentence or line. It is the pattern that is recognized, like the pattern of the pace or intensity of the sound or music in a movie predicts what is about to happen. Many people can guess what is going to happen next in a movie or book, or how they will end, not because they are clairvoyant, but because the pattern that is being developed appears to move in a predictable way. Even intentional non-predictability is predictable, like the most unlikely person being the one who committed the offense. People can readily (and sometimes aggravatingly) fill in the next word for someone when they pause in speaking, and husbands and wives are really good at it.

Pattern-recognition is a powerful shortcut - it enables understanding with almost no investment in time or effort. A few brief slices of a science-fiction movie shown to an aficionado would allow them to guess reasonably accurately what was happening. Showing the same movie over and over to someone in 1850 would never communicate anything except utter confusion - none of the material would present a recognizable pattern. It is the pattern recognition that applies the cognition, the understanding. Without the pattern recognition, all you have is memorization, like someone memorizing a song in a foreign language. With cognitive short-cuts operating so effectively on image and sound memories, it should not be surprising that Mother Nature utilizes short-cuts in verbal thinking as well.

But this feature does not always work to man's advantage. As reported in The New York Times, in the first 250 wrongful convictions overturned through the use of DNA evidence, in other words, overturned after the trial was concluded and the individual was serving their sentence, it was found that in 190 of the cases, the convictions had been based on eyewitness testimony. And these eyewitnesses, in their own words, had "positively", "conclusively", and "without any possibility of error or doubt", identified the wrongfully-convicted individual as the perpetrator of the crime. This means that man's short-cut talents also apply when he is making a memory of a new face during a stressful and possibly brief time. The mind fills in whatever information was missing or misperceived, but the witness nevertheless leaves supremely confident in his fabricated memory.

For the most convincing evidence of the durability and invincibility of man's drive for short-cuts, you can look at any period, any society, any group, at any time. Even today, there are nations where more of the economic output is based on this particular short-cut than any other activity. And this is in spite of man's best attempts to discourage, quash, and obliterate this short-cut by penalizing its use, by putting harsh sanctions on anyone having been found to have utilized it, by making participants outcasts and pariahs. Prostitution is often given the honor of the world's oldest profession, but that title was assigned by humorists and not historians. Prostitution is ironically one type of transactional short-cut (both for the client and the provider), but there is an even older short-cut that predates it, that has been an evil tied to mankind from the time there were at least two men, and that is crime. The first events in the Christian Bible center on crime. Crime is simply taking a short-cut to obtain some tangible good not by hunting for or mining for or building it or making it, but by simply taking it without permission from your neighbor who has already done that hard work himself. Speculation has gone on forever about whether man is inherently evil because he engages in criminal activities. While some criminals are psychopathic monsters or drug-driven pseudo-sociopathic robots, most crime is man just caving in to his drive for short-cuts. His nature is to be drawn to any short-cut; he cannot help himself. But social convention tells man that while he can use any short-cut he can find against nature and objects without owners, he shall not use them to take possession of something owned by another man. But for some people, this facet of human nature, this drive to utilize short-cuts, just cannot be constrained by social and civil rules. They cannot help themselves and take what is not theirs.

Social networking sites realize the same thing that Apple has, that man is driven to seek short-cuts. People will be drawn to them, even becoming in effect hypnotized or addicted if the short-cut experience is expansive enough. So the movement by these companies, whether hardware or software, is to expand their offerings, their capabilities and features, so the client/user/customer hopefully never leaves, never stops using their device, site, or game. These sites and devices offer utility to be sure, but that is not the attraction, the drive. Utility does not get people to stand in line and pay lots of money, or to carry on near-hysterically about the wonderfulness of a particular technology as if it were the prettiest sunset over the loveliest atoll. Utility by itself is boring; efficiency taken alone is uninteresting. For every product or website or game that is wildly popular you can find competitors that do the same thing. But no matter how powerful the alternative is, if it is perceived to be less of a short-cut, its attractiveness will fall off exponentially. Just an extra step or two and its potential as a competitor vanishes. You can do the same thing with a photo on most phones or cameras as you can on an iPhone except instead of quickly swiping a finger or two you have to push a button or turn a wheel. How much extra effort is that? Well, it is just enough to make people want to acquire an iPhone instead of an alternative device. Analysts credit the man-machine interface that Apple uses for being "cool" and "elegant" and "intuitive", but all these are just reactions to the attractiveness of the short-cuts that it presents. If you were to take the same interface and just modify it oh-so-mildly so it was slower to use than comparable devices, it would lose most all its panache. If you had to swipe at a photo five different ways to zoom it, the iPhone would have ended up in a Lisa-like landfill. The iTunes store sells close to 90% of the digital music on the web even though it prices its music higher than all other music sources, and for many years, the songs were digitally programmed to only work on Apple products, like buying socks from Macy's that would only fit if you wore Macy's shoes. Why? Because it so convenient, so easy to use. The iTunes software also runs all of Apple's digital music players, and the music is instantly available to purchase, integrate into the buyer's music library, and load onto their music player. You can do the same thing with the competition, it is just not quite as easy. That missing short-cut is all the difference between a 10% market share and a 90% market share. People are addicted to the temptation of a short-cut, even if the alternative is only ever-so-slightly less of a short-cut and less costly.

How did this fascination with short-cuts become part of man's fundamental nature? For 60,000 years man has continuously found ways to do and make things better. He is an improvement machine, and many of those improvements were gained by finding short-cuts. He would study the existing activity or item and figure out how he could do it faster by skipping a step, by doing more than one at once, by making it sharper, or stronger, or more durable, or smoother, or using a tool, or a better tool. For most of this time, people were not living in cities of one million people. They were in extended family or maybe three family groups of ten or twenty people. Those who could innovate the most rapidly and creatively, who could find the most short-cuts, thrived. Others not so capable would be struggling to survive, and would have a difficult time being represented in succeeding generations. 30,000 years ago most likely there were less than 100,000 humans spread out across the entire world. That is about 200 square miles of livable land (grassland and cultivatable land) per person. If people were in 20 to 40 person groups, that would be 2,000 to 4,000 square miles per group. (Fewer than 20 would have made division of labor and backup in case an adult was unexpectedly lost more challenging. More than 40 would make securing enough game on a daily basis too demanding, and differences of opinion about what the group should do would begin to tear it into factions.) Bumping into someone else was possible, but not likely unless you intentionally sought contact – for trading or worse. Unless you really wanted to be in a larger group, and they wanted you, you were on your own. Your group had to perform well to survive. In some cases techniques may have been traded between groups, but it is also possible that products were traded and the technologies that produced those products were kept a group secret, proprietary information that enabled a group to sustain a competitive advantage over their neighbors.

You make the best-edged flint knives and hand-axes in your group and trade them to others for food and skins. You keep the best ones for yourself, and notice that the ones that last the longest have cutting edges consisting of the most small chips, meaning you make them using a small tool and tap gently. You tap more and more softly – eventually you find that if you just press hard you can chip the flint – you don't need to pound at all. It's faster, easier, you don't have to throw as many away, and the overall performance is better. Your group is barefoot and you bump into some group who is wearing animal hides on their feet. Incredible. This will vastly speed up your ability to move around after game, berries, and water, so you figure out a way to make them yourself. You are fishing and you see your daughter trying to catch fish in the shallows using a basket. You realize if you make a really large open basket so the water goes through it but not the fish this just might work. Later you improve on it by using twisted fibers instead of the reeds that you used in the basket-based net. This net fishing is so much faster than using a hook. You are making shell necklaces and made a little bone drill that operates using a small bow with a twisted fiber cord that spins the bone drill back and forth. You happen to notice that the small wooden cap that secures the other end of the drill gets smoking hot, and you wonder if it could get so hot you could start a fire. You find that it can and suddenly you have a brand new quick fool-proof way to create a fire, an absolutely critical skill. You have caught a huge number of fish, but they are going to spoil unless you can somehow preserve them. You know that dry things seem to last longer than wet things, so you hang some filets high over the fire and leave them there. Others you pack in salt that you made by evaporating sea water in shallow pools since you know salt seems to pull the water out of everything wet. Both work to some degree but you keep working on both techniques until you can save most all the fish you catch during the summer. Now you don't have to go out hunting during severe winter weather.

Cooking is a big hassle – someone has to continually tend to it or it will burn. Even so, some is always over-cooked, some under-cooked, and it is often tough and hard to eat. You sometimes chop it into uniformly-sized pieces so they all cook evenly, but that is even more time-consuming. You notice that the rocks always stay hot for a long time after the fire burns down, so you try wrapping the meat in wet grasses and reeds to protect it, and then cover it with hot rocks and pile some of the coals on top. That doesn't work too well – the grass dries out – so you try putting the meat in a shallow trough with a few inches of water to keep the grass wet. The meat under the water is cooked OK but the top is not, so you figure all of it has to be in the water. So you hollow out a log that will completely cover the meat when it is filled with water. This works great – the meat is cooked uniformly and it is tender and easy to eat. But after a few uses the outside of the wooden trough begins to char through from the heat of the fire. So you try it without the coals, just using the hot rocks, and eventually realize that you only need to drop the rocks in the water – the ones outside the trough don't help. Adding a simple open basket over the meat greatly speeds up replacing rocks when it takes more than one set to fully cook the food. Then you start putting vegetables in with the meat, and now it all comes out tender and delicious and everyone is able to eat most anything. It takes hardly any effort, anyone can be trained to add a hot rock every 15 minutes or so to the water, you can do other things while it is cooking, and you don't have to worry about it being burned or half-raw or too tough or too hard to eat. While other groups are not doing as well, yours is healthy and well-fed.

You move heavy loads with your sledge and your inventory of a dozen and a half carefully selected round, straight, similarly-sized, light logs. It works pretty well except it is slow – after the sledge rolls over one set of logs you have to drag the previous set in front of the sledge again by grabbing and pulling on the twisted fiber cords you have attached to each one by having cut a circumferential groove around the outside near one end of each log. You made a toy version for your son and permanently attached two small logs to the bottom by using the same cord in the same groove, but cut into both ends of each log. It works fine with a light load but if another kid jumps aboard it freezes up and will only go downhill. You can put leftover animal fat on the log rollers to make them roll easier, but it wears off after a few minutes. You have to keep the rollers tied to the toy sledge, but you also have to find a way to keep the grease from rubbing off. So you figure if you put the grease just into the groove where the cord is, and put a spacer in there so that is the only place that the sledge rubs on the log rollers, the grease won't wear off as fast since it is not in contact with the ground. That actually works, so you deepen the groove, and shape the spacer to keep the log rollers from moving forward or backward. That works so well that you modify your own sledge so your rollers are permanently attached, using just two rollers like the toy for your son. That works but your sledge keeps bottoming on the uneven ground, so you add a third roller in the center. Now you need to grease it each time you use it, you have to keep your loads lighter because it does not roll as well, and you still have to be more careful about bottoming, but overall it must be more than ten times as fast, since you don't have to constantly stop to move the rollers. Now that you have the time, you decide to fix the bottoming problem by putting on much thicker log rollers, since you will only need two. You put on just the front one and find that it is a real hassle to fight the much bigger and heavier log roller over rocks – it's much harder than with the small roller log. You had already cut two deep grooves in it to hold it against the sledge, so you figure you will just cut some more grooves in it to make it lighter. You start cutting the first one and it dawns on you – why are you being so careful? Nothing has to fit in this groove. So you decide to make two giant grooves, leaving about eight inches of original log in the center. You build a fire about the length of the groove you want, put the log in for twenty minutes, pull it out and cut the burned part off with your flint axe, and put the log back in, turning it to get a different side each time. While you are cutting the front roller you have the back roller in the fire. While you are doing this your wife asks you what you are doing. "If you want the roller small in the middle and big on the outside, why don't you just stick a piece of the big log on the end of the little log?" she asks. You explain why you can't do that; you know what you are doing. When you finish and attach the two large roller logs with the big grooves cut into them to your sledge, you are amazed. Being lighter and being higher, while better, is not what is astounding. What completely surprises you is that the big grooves in the large rollers, instead of rolling up against rocks and uneven ground, now just roll right over them since there is clearance between the ground and the roller. So now if you steer your sledge carefully so the larger rocks go between where the rollers touch the ground, the effort is much, much less. After a time, you wonder if you really need the full-width of the roller in the center, and so you chip one away as an experiment. It works fine so you chip away the other one. Now you are amazed again to realize that this large roller looks a lot like your wife's ridiculous suggestion. So when you have time you cut a piece of large round roller log about ten inches wide, pile hot coals in the center, cut out the burned area, and repeat the process until it makes a hole all the way through. By cleaning out the hole and reducing the diameter of one of your old thin roller logs you get it to fit snugly on. You wrap strips of wet hides on the outside of the roller log and let them dry to keep it in place. One seems a little loose when you are done so you wrap some cord tightly around the roller also. Now this works even better. You don't have to stop, you don't get stuck hardly ever on obstacles, and even your son can take turns with his friend towing each other around on his toy. Every once in a while one of your large roller log pieces at the end of the small rollers splits, and you have to put on a new one, but you learn which wood makes for the most durable large roller. Also with time you notice that some of the large roller pieces end up being loose and turning on the small rollers as the sledge moves, but rather than a problem this actually seems to make the sledge easier to pull. You notice that when the large rollers move, it is easier to change the direction of the sledge, since one roller can turn while the other one can stay motionless, so eventually you allow all the large rollers to move and grease the small rollers so they easily can. Eventually to eliminate the problem of the rollers breaking someone makes one out of solid wood pieces pegged together with the grain oriented so they won't split. At some point someone calls it "the wheel".

Now whether this was really one single person in one place, or 20 different people in 20 places, or five generations each improving on the previous generations' work, or all kinds of idea cross-fertilization mixing across wide areas – does not really matter. One way or another this process, or one very close to this, took place. Documentation for most of the last 60,000 years entailed explaining it and showing it to your son and maybe your brother; writing it down would have been a total waste of time.

Whether cooking or wheeling, man was driven by trying to save time, to find a short-cut for what he was up against. Most everything man has accomplished is due to this – small incremental but continuous changes that led to time savings upon time savings, short-cut on top of short-cut, advantage upon advantage, until the advanced technology and civilization of today appears. Breakthroughs and brilliant innovation were also present, but much more common was Edison's 99% perspiration.

Chapter 8
Cognitive Dissonance

An Example

Most people have heard of <u>American Idol</u>, or its equivalent in Great Britain. With the format of a live talent show dedicated to young singers, one contestant is eliminated every week by a vote of the TV audience until the last contestant is declared the "Idol". As an instant injection into a professional musical career, fame, fortune, success, maybe adulation – it is just what the doctor ordered for man whose nature is addicted to short-cuts, as featured in the previous chapter.

The first few shows of the season are allocated to those who meet and exceed, or miss terribly, the minimum criteria during the preliminary tryouts held in major cities across the U.S.

Potential contestants fall into three groups – those that have talent to varying degrees, those that have no talent but want to be on TV for their 10 seconds of national fame, and those that have the same singing talent as the average German Shepherd but absolutely believe they sound better than an Elvis/Sinatra/Mathis hybrid. When this third category of contestant is told by the panel of music professionals that they should stop singing, should not ever think about singing again, cannot carry a tune, and have no musical talent, they almost always react by getting angry, swearing at the judges, and telling the TV camera that the judges obviously cannot recognize real talent when they see it and are utter idiots.

Firmly carrying a belief in your mind, for example that you are a superb singer, and then receiving feedback from music professionals to the contrary, results in a conceptual clash of ideas that human nature demands be reconciled to a clash-less condition. You can either believe you sing well, or badly, but not both simultaneously. In the <u>Idol</u> case, most of those in the third category opt to resolve this clash by tossing out the opinion of the judges – leaving them again with the untarnished belief that they sing wondrously.

Now if you are in the first group of singers – you have talent but maybe it is not quite exceptional enough to make the cut, or you were too nervous during the tryout, or the judges feel you were not quite ready, or you sound too much like you are trying to imitate some established singer – you can retain the idea that you are a capable singer; it is just that you were not able to make the Idol cut this time. Maybe next year (many in fact do). No clash – and no subconscious overpowering urge to fire the judges, and get angry, or to refuse to accept the judges' constructive criticism about their singing.

The singers in the third group who cannot sing, but nevertheless hold boldly and passionately to their belief that they can, are often said to be living in a state of denial. The trait in human nature that supports their residency in this state is called cognitive dissonance, the mental process that gives strongly-held beliefs immunity against rebuttal, refuting, conflicts, inconsistencies, and opposing experience and views. Cognitive dissonance demands that most people only hold one pure view of anything in their mind at any time – so if they know they are a great singer, any information or experience that is in conflict with that is rejected and dismissed.

Recently there was a terrible tragedy in New York – after a disagreement with her boyfriend, a young mother intentionally drove her car into a river along with her four children, after first coolly telling them that she planned for them all to die together. The oldest child escaped through a window and was able to report what happened – otherwise they may have never been located, since there had apparently not been any warning signs. As expected, there was a huge amount of media coverage – and a relative told a reporter "She was a *good* mother." Well, of all the characterizations possible, this was one that, no matter how you squint or twist, was clearly not applicable. The relative was simply reflecting cognitive dissonance – what she had experienced with this mother over the years could not be cognitively rationalized against this reported heinous, monstrous behavior, so she went with the mother she had lived with, not the one in the media. Someone might say she was just trying to bolster and burnish the mother's reputation – but this was just a relative, not a PR professional, and salvaging her reputation is going to take a lot more than a comment like that – more likely a truckload of psychiatrists proving beyond a doubt that she was somehow excused by way of diminished capacity, drug use, abuse, Twinkies, evil spirits, and the like.

Mississippi recently concluded a most successful experiment involving convicted murderers and the governor of the state. Prisoners with good behavior could serve their time working in the governor's mansion, in personal daily contact with the governor. Now one can hardly imagine a better incentivized situation – if your behavior is exemplary, you are not in a Mississippi prison but the governor's mansion, a place few wealthy, law-abiding Mississippi citizens ever get to see the inside of. And if the positive inducement is not sufficient, if you do anything even remotely threatening there are probably fifty state policemen ready to put so many bullets into you that your weight would double. Following the conclusion of this experiment, the governor, by all reports a firm law-and-order supporter, announced that he was giving a full pardon to the convicted murderers that had worked with him in the governor's mansion. Cognitive dissonance irresistibly overwhelmed all sense of logic, perspective, and reasoning in the governor – the murders, trials, and convictions – all these were bypassed; short-circuited. He formed his opinion of the convicts based on that most artificial of environments inside the governor's mansion: The-Truman-Show-like, yes-sir-governor-sir one that intensely constrained and manipulated the behavior of the convicts, and one which bore absolutely no relation to the world that the convicts committed their murders in and would return to when pardoned. But to the governor, never seeing the convicts murder anyone, never seeing them act on their own in the real world, only seeing them fawning over him in the governor's mansion – to him, the convicts were little angels.

Should the citizens of Mississippi have been disappointed in the behavior of their governor? Absolutely. Should they have been surprised? No. This was human nature at its finest.

Psychology 1A – Welcome to Cognitive Dissonance

You don't get this in the first week in introductory psychology, but that is only because of the number of other concepts competing for attention. Cognitive dissonance - it's a little bit of a misnomer, but it was named by psychologists, so what can you expect? It really should be called Cognitive Assonance - the absence of dissonance. When people hold one belief, and they then have an experience that appears to demonstrate that that prior belief is wrong/incorrect, something has to give. Usually, it is the prior belief (unless you are one of the special contestants on Idol), simply because it is older and presumably less current, less fresh, and less defensible. Human nature does not allow for two conflicting opposing beliefs to be held simultaneously by almost all people. (If you are schizophrenic or have Asperger's, however, you probably do have the skills to do this.)

This belief/attitude adjustment is automatic – like breathing. In some cases, this process is straight-forward. You have a favorite restaurant that you really like. But suddenly the most recent meal you have there is not at all what you expected – the recipes seemed to be cheapened with no explanation; things did not taste as good; the experience was a disappointment. The next time someone asks you about this restaurant, your recommendation is going to be more conditional, milder, equivocal; and this revision will not take any effort on your part.

Cognitive Dissonance is an integral part of the marketing plan of all brand managers in Western countries. If by the use of a free sample, or a coupon, or a low sale price, they can get you to try their product, and your experience is positive; enjoyable; surprisingly good; then you are going to change your view of that product to a more positive attitude. You can't help yourself – the marketing guys/ladies, sitting in an office perhaps 7,000 miles away from you, are directly working on your mind. It is almost like action-at-a-distance, that crazy crap that physicists talk about.

Now if you think this is just more mumbo-jumbo psycho-babble nonsense, then you need to think for a moment as to why these people would be investing billions of dollars a year, every year, in these freebie/coupon and the like mechanisms. You could just dismissively declare that they are all idiots. But alas, before they parted with their billions, they hired some of the psychologists in the landfills and had them test out this concept. They took people off the street, tricked them (psychologists always mislead their subjects when they run tests so they won't have a clue what they are really being tested on), and then ran them through a set of procedures that would activate the cognitive dissonance process (if it in fact worked as advertised). They would test these people on their views (attitudes/beliefs) of various products, and would then have them verbally recite the equivalent of a positive testimonial about one product. In all cases a second survey would show a more favorable view of this product, just due to this clearly artificial testimonial. The activation of the cognitive dissonance mechanism was due simply to the fact the they, the individual, had taken this action on their own volition.

Now this is the mildest form of cognitive dissonance. If the subjects in the testing get paid to say or do something, or get to choose an object as a gift and then rate its value, or any similar permutation, the results are even stronger.

Note that while they do not make this distinction in the literature, there are two categories of Cognitive Dissonance, divided by how the new information is obtained by the individual. In all the cases described above, the individual actively participates in the development of this new information/opinion/belief by personally experiencing something. The second category is the indirect method, where there is no experiential effect, and the individual in question is just forming opinions due to reading or hearing or seeing something through some kind of media or an exchange with a friend or acquaintance. The reason for the second category for this type of Cognitive Dissonance process is that, in contrast to the hard and indisputable process of first-hand experience, the second-hand interpretation of someone else's experience is a soft process. As a consequence, it depends on the individualized credibility of your acquaintance and the credibility and effectiveness of the particular media and its content, something that cannot be assessed or generalized in any societal manner. While the first kind of Cognitive Dissonance is action-at-a-distance, meaning your belief structure gets automatically changed without your conscious intervention, the second kind of Cognitive Dissonance often results in the reverse result: the individual's original belief is conserved and the new input is dismissed.

Views that an individual holds about themselves and their beliefs and values are critically important to most people. Accepting positive, complimentary, or supportive new information is fine; but critical, negative, conflicting, or pejorative input is extraordinarily problematic. The Cognitive Dissonance model forces something to change if people suddenly find themselves possessing two conflicting beliefs. If the beliefs are about themselves, then this change process is aggravated and accelerated. But there is a crucial difference here - because the individual has not experienced this negative/conflicting information, and only received it, the rules allow them to hold on to their original belief and instead discard the new input as non-credible. Since they did not experience it first-hand, it is easy to create an explanation that rationalizes why what they heard or saw does not in their case apply to them, or does not matter, or can be ignored.

To keep it all straight, we will call Cognitive Dissonance that is experiential Active Cognitive Dissonance or ACD. If the individual instead just sees, observes, hears, notices, reads or otherwise indirectly obtains the conflicting information, then we will term it Passive Cognitive Dissonance or PCD. You are not going to find this distinction in the literature because the literature is generally interested in describing cognitive dissonance as a stand-alone phenomenon. The purpose of this book is to clarify how the way man thinks affects his ability to cope with the world, and cognitive dissonance directly interferes with the ability of man to understand the world around him and make informed decisions. Cognitive dissonance assists in holding tightly to beliefs, in spite of facts to the contrary, and beliefs formed with ACD are much more difficult to dislodge than those with PCD, so this distinction is critical.

Going back to the example at the start of the chapter - the mother who drove her children into a river – the relative that called her a "good mother" had undergone PCD, so she had not changed her attitude about the mother. However, if somehow through the use of exotic science-fiction technology this relative could have been inserted into the car while this event had unfolded, and watched the children drown in front of her, and was then whisked out again to safety, most likely she would not have made this same statement. That's because she would have undergone ACD by living through this awful experience, instead of just hearing about it second-hand after-the-fact.

As you will read in several places in this book, it is not intended as an academic work on history, psychology, or anything else. That would make it boringly unreadable. But the author does not want to make statements unsupported, so some of this explanation is obligatory. If the reader is already weary, just skip ahead a paragraph or two once in a while.

Every time a perception that is in conflict with their existing beliefs arrives in someone's consciousness, the test that must be made is whether the previously-acquired beliefs were ACD or PCD-produced, and if the incoming conflicting perception was picked up through ACD or PCD. If the existing belief was ACD and the new input is PCD nothing changes. If the old belief was PCD and the new information is ACD then the belief adjusts to the new view. If it is a tie, ACD on ACD or PCD on PCD, then it is a matter for the details – how much, how intense was the new input versus the accumulation of previous experience and exposure. The ACD/PCD distinction enables us to more clearly understand how man changes (or does not) his beliefs in response to information and experiences.

Origination

Why would Mother Nature add this feature to man's skill set? From today's perspective, it may seem perplexing, but from the vantage point of 60,000 years ago, the choice was obvious. Mother Nature had created every other animal that man would contact, whether they be food or foe, to operate on instinct – automatic, instant responses to anything that approached them. All the while man was utilizing the thinking, planning, considering, evaluating, and deliberating skills provided by Mother Nature, his animal co-occupiers of the world would be fighting or fleeing. Even some of Mother Nature's own hazards – floods, hurricanes, forest and plains fires – would be intolerant of delay. Others, like a drought or a lack of game, would penalize those who hesitated, uncertain if the drought or game scarcity were real or transient. So Mother Nature had to make sure she did not allow these new strengths to become weaknesses, and buttressed them with an action bias, an inherent tendency move forward instead of pondering and contemplating.

Let's step back say 50,000 years to attempt to obtain an appreciation for the environment our ancestors faced. A simple number exercise will help. If you assume that the average age of a generation is 22 years (few made it past 30 in these times), meaning that half the children will be born before the man and woman average 22 years old, and half born after the age of 22 (those born at the average age of 22 wash out), then if after one generation two people produce one extra person overall, in other words, three live to an average age of 22 years old, then the population growth rate would be 1.86% annually. Starting with say 250 humans 60,000 years ago, how long would it take to get to around two million people, which was the population ten or twelve thousand years ago, just before it began to grow quickly? Well, at that growth rate, just 500 years, not 50,000. Uh-oh, let's try one new person net for every two generations, which would be 44 years. This gets us to a couple million in one thousand years, still not even close. So let's go to one new person every ten generations – that means it takes 220 years for one new person to be added for every two. Even with that, the population would go from 250 to two and a half million in 5,000 years. We have to extend the time it takes to add one new person to a family of two to 100 generations – that is

2,200 years - before we get the population numbers to come out right.

A rocket scientist it does not take to figure out what this means. It means that Mother Nature's top priority was population control – by making sure that you either died in childbirth, or died as a baby, or died from childhood diseases. Or if you made it that far, you died from injuries, or infections from injuries, or adult diseases, or starvation, or predation from wild animals, or cold, or drought, or heat, or floods, or whatever else Mother Nature threw at these poor people. It had to be somewhere between hazardous and horrific. 100 generations to add one new member to a family of two does not literally mean that if you have say a family group of six people, three couples, that after 2,200 years they will find themselves at nine; no, it means that many of these groups will at some point during that 2,200 year period vanish without a trace, or that maybe one or two survivors may be lucky enough to join up with another group. With the odds of survival so low, everyone is not going to make it.

Lacking of course any written records for most of man's history, these gross statistics have to suffice. The first time we get any individual data is 3,500 years ago in Egypt – Queen Ahmose-Nefertari had nine children, five of whom never made it out of childhood, and that was with the best food and care that came with being the children of the Pharaoh. Her oldest, Amenhotep I, made it maybe to 30. A few hundred years later Ramesses II, regarded as the greatest pharaoh of all, went through 13 sons with who knows how many wives before one, Merenptah, lived long enough to survive him.

With survival so questionable, a singular focus on preservation of oneself and one's family was paramount. Clarity in goals and action was a necessity. The causes of disease, infection, fertility, and health were a total mystery. Weather, the seasons, and the availability of game and fruits and vegetables were only slightly less murky. Without any writing, every skill and warning and successful bit of advice had to be passed from father and mother to son and daughter, and if they were missing, it had to come from an older brother and sister, or uncle or aunt, or maybe a cousin. If it did not come, you did not make it. Whether it was about avoiding threats like snakes or wolves at night, or how to remain safe while moving around during the day, or how and when and where to hunt what, and where and when to find what, these lessons literally meant life and death. No nuances, no mixed messages, no speculation; just black and white brutal clarity. Cognitive dissonance, as well as the other aspects of human nature described in these other chapters, enabled man to survive in this environment. They were all cognitive short-cuts – all Alexander-the-Great-Gordian-Knot solutions to the potential problems that man's thinking machine presented. Whenever someone might start thinking along the lines of "Well, I learned this at my father's side, but maybe it's not like this all the time after all ...." and the possibility that the gray fuzzy area of complexity would drape itself over the landscape, bipolar thinking and judgmental tagging already discussed in the previous chapter, cognitive dissonance, and other traits yet to be mentioned would come to man's assistance, rescuing those who could be salvaged from this mental mire.

Cognitive dissonance is a short-cut that attempts to restrict the acceptance of information in conflict with the pre-established beliefs or views in your mind. It is a short-cut in the sense that it "cuts out" or "short-circuits" the rational, logical, thinking part of man which, on paper anyway, is supposed to review incoming data objectively and accept or reject it on that basis. All these people had for over 50,000 years was the knowledge their parents could pass on to them, often by either living it or showing them how, before they died. Were they careless with it, the statistics say they had no chance of making it. Cognitive dissonance was Mother Nature's way of, as the economists put it, of making the barriers to entry high for conflicting information, information that could threaten their existence. You can overwhelm cognitive dissonance certainly, but the default setting is that possession counts for 99% of everything – whatever beliefs man has pre-installed take precedence over those requesting acceptance.

Whether they were written 2,500 or 3,500 years ago, the books of Deuteronomy and Leviticus in the Bible are some of the oldest specific, documented evidence of how man thought prior to the modern day. Entirely prohibited are rabbit, goat, lamb, pig, bison, venison, antelope, and catfish, eel, shark, abalone, shrimp, lobster, clams, scallops, and oysters. In a world without cognitive dissonance, and in a hungry world, you might expect instructions more along the lines of: only eat shellfish in certain months, or make sure the meat is well-cooked, or eaten the same day it is cooked, or similar types of conditionally-restrictive provisions. Instead, the list simply specifies total prohibitions, indicating that the conceptual complexity of a foods that you can eat at some times but not others, or if prepared in certain ways but not others, was still too challenging for these times, only yesterday on the scale of 60,000 years. These lists also prohibit foods by what appear to be classes or general classifications, which is a clear sign of a desire to avoid cognitive dissonance Allowing some foods within a class of foods but not others, like shellfish, might lead to cognitive dissonance (how come it is OK to eat all these shellfish but avoid these others sitting right alongside?), so it was avoided, even though there might have been a sound foundation for this (red tide hazard for shellfish that filter for their dinner).

Implications

Going back to where we were before we diverted off to explain the derivation of cognitive dissonance, the fundamental key distinction being made about the importance of cognitive dissonance today is that what people are, how they view themselves, is based on their accumulated experience of living, experiencing, working, playing, struggling, yearning, failing, succeeding. It is all, in the previous context, earned experientially. So to have any chance of modifying this requires additional experience, in other words, it requires Active Cognitive Dissonance, or ACD. In another vernacular, you have to fight fire with fire. If just exposed to PCD, chances are the person will not change their beliefs or attitudes. So if a person passes a billboard or a subway sign telling them they might be fat and should lose weight and get more exercise, it is not going to have any impact. Or if they meet someone in a bar who tells them they should dump their Chevy truck and get a Toyota, they probably won't be rushing out to do it. Now everyone already knows this is the case; this is just common sense you are all thinking, but this is the psychology model behind your common sense.

Going back to the brand manager people, when they get you to try a free sample or use a coupon they are purposefully engaging ACD. They know that it works much more effectively than media ads that, regardless of their cuteness, are all PCD. Anyone else selling something that gives you a free trial period or the equivalent first is also engaging ACD. Companies advertise constantly, but the dirty little secret is that while some people may remember the ad, few remember the product, and no one changes their attitudes or beliefs, simply because PCD is all that is in play.

While psychologists will use different terminology for each different nuance of PCD, the underlying mechanism is the same. An anorexic looks in the mirror but sees only the invented image in their mind – the mirror image is not experienced, it is only visualized, so in a PCD process, the original belief, which is that the individual is fat, remains, unaltered. Conversely, someone who wears the same clothes that they did twenty years ago but has gained 70 pounds since then sees only the person of twenty years ago when they put on those same clothes. Others of course see a fashion debacle. Destructive habits, like overeating, excessive alcohol or drug consumption/dependence, smoking, lack of exercise, obsessive fascination with games or hobbies, and similar time and behavior traps are examples that most everyone has either first or second hand experience with. If people join a group so that their value as perceived by society now rises and falls with the value of this group, then the PCD process will apply to any criticism or negative facts about the group or the people who run it. Is the preacher collecting money on cable TV a not-so-nice person that maybe should not be getting these funds? Forget trying to sell that to someone who believes in him, even if you have facts from an investigative journalism report. Are reports suddenly out about your priest molesting children two decades ago? You are going to have a terrible time with parishioners who have so fondly liked him for those twenty years. How about a mother whose child is arrested for murdering three people in cold blood, with witnesses and surveillance camera footage. Oh no, no way, says the mother, no way could my son have possibly done this. All the facts in the world will not get through the PCD screen.

Yes, it can be more complicated. Teenagers, due to hormonal and cultural factors, are very "other-directed", to use the David Riesman term. If a sub-group of classmates appear to, or intentionally, say critical or pejorative things about a teenager's physical appearance, dress, behavior, choice of friends, race, religion, or other choices, the teenager feels that he/she is bathing in this "criticism", takes it to heart, and will re-adjust his/her view of themselves. Fat, loser, pariah, dork, whatever – what for an adult might be a PCD event for a teenager is an ACD experience. And some grown-ups are equally fiercely "other-directed", for obvious reasons that do not need to be elaborated. And as de Tocqueville pointed out in <u>Democracy</u>, even some elements of American society can themselves be very inner-directed-intolerant, so that those who fail to heel to the societal norms are ostracized.

But let's look at classic PCD: "My country, right or wrong." It would be pretty hard to over-state the amount of damage caused by that particular aspect of PCD. There is not a country in the world that does not have a litany of wars and internal injustices on its conscience; but if you ask many of it citizens, its country is great, and these past ills are exaggerated, blown out of proportion, misunderstood, in some cases, they never happened. People (other than immigrants) grow up in their country, they live it, and so their feelings about it are all experiential, and almost always positive and favorable. And, since they personally identify themselves with their country, their feeling and beliefs about their country automatically transfer to themselves, just like they do for members of any group or organization. If their country is a problem, then they are the citizen of a problem country, and this plays poorly with most people, so most end up feeling that their country is great. Any information just heard to the contrary will not change their beliefs, since that process is PCD. A citizen generally has to live problems to become disillusioned with his country, an ACD experience. So if they are discriminated against or unfairly treated by their country, an experiential process, their attitudes will change.

One of the crispest cases of PCD is the United States. Nominally a country with the free-est press, one would initially think that its citizens would have the most accurate appraisal of its history. Since the U.S. never had colonies, but in its own hemisphere and later on in the world had great power, in the slightly over two centuries of its existence the U.S. has either invaded or overthrown through violence more governments than any other country in the world (excluding world wars). Yet were you to ask the average citizen on a multiple guess test how the U.S. would rank (on invading and overthrowing), they would put the U.S. down as the least offensive. Even if presented with the track record, starting say with the U.S. making war on Mexico in order to get California, Texas, and New Mexico in the 1840's, making war on the Hawaiian monarchy to steal Hawaii in the 1880's and finally 1890's, making war on Spain to get Cuba in the 1890's and the Philippines in the 1900's, all the way through JFK approving the coup against the president of Vietnam Ngo Dinh Diem in 1963 (leading to the assassination of his brother and him), the support of anti-democratic forces in Nicaragua by the CIA in the 1980's, the invasion of Grenada in 1983, the invasion of Panama in 1989, and of course the invasion and occupation of Iraq in the first decade of 2000 – the average American is still going to tend to stay with the opinion and belief that their country is the greatest in the world.

It is not that this information is unavailable – it is taught in most standard history courses. Many citizens even lived through the most recent examples. Kennedy is on audio tape, memos, and documents, and Reagan testified about selling drugs and arms to Iran for illegal purposes. It is not that it is up for dispute. For most Americans, it is just blotted out; compartmentalized, like JFK's liaisons; shrugged off; discounted. It is the classic collision of PCD against beliefs that have to be ACD'd out. And it is the poster child for Fitzgerald – you can't believe that the U.S. is the greatest country in the world and at the same time believing that it is also the world's worst international citizen – minding everyone else's business through force of arms.

The U.S. was also one of the last modern nations to make slavery illegal. Germany, Russia, Poland, Azerbaijan, Belarus, Hungary, Latvia, Lithuania, Kyrgyzstan, and Estonia among others all gave women the right to vote before the U.S. did. Right now the average U.S. citizen needs to practice the following Cognitive Dissonance exercise, saying to themselves: "My country is the best, plus it sucks on imperialism, sucks on slavery, and sucks on suffrage." Doesn't quite work, does it? If you are from another country, like say Japan, just use the rape of Nanking. It's not hard to find similar examples.

What is the point of all this? It is not to criticize patriotism or your native country. The point of Cognitive Dissonance, whether PCD or ACD, is that it prevents conflicting information from being held in people's minds. Why is this a problem, you ask? Well, because compartments overflowing with conflicting information is another word for "welcome to the real world." The U.S. is what it is, warts and all. What Cognitive Dissonance means is that people cannot hold reality in their minds – their nature forbids it. In other words, human nature forces people to live in a permanent "state of denial". You might have thought that this was some kind of a joke, or something just reserved for idiots. Unfortunately no, it is welded into the brains of all normal humans. No matter how good you think you are, no matter how objective, no matter how rational, etc. ad nauseum, your nature is conspiring 24/7 with this ACD/PCD process to knock all the sharp corners off anything that conflicts with your core beliefs and attitudes. Unless of course you are that highly unusual and rare personality that meets Fitzgerald's criteria.

The classic example where PCD and ACD make the real world disappear is in American political election campaigns. Americans vote for national representatives every two years. Let's first outline how the evaluation process of a political candidate should work. We are using politics here as an example, but this could apply to any important decision that has to made by an individual that involves the interplay of complex factors and considerations.

Every candidate (or issue, or problem) will have a variety of positions on issues (sometimes multiple positions on the same issue); a track record of past performance both in and out of politics which will involve both favorable and unfavorable aspects, accomplishments and failures; and a set of qualifications that will be more complete in certain areas and incomplete in others. Each citizen would need to take all of this information on each candidate, match them up side by side, match them up against the job that the candidates are running for, the problems facing the district and the country, and make an estimate about which candidate would most likely meet the voter's prioritized goals. The voter will have to factor in their degree of credibility associated with each candidate, both on their proclaimed positions and the expectation that they will hold to what they promise once in office. Their final choice will be a trade-off – the voter will have areas of agreement and disagreement with each candidate's issues; they will be comfortable and uneasy with portions of each candidate's background, character, and credibility. There is nothing new or sophisticated about this – it is just Decision-Making 101.

Now let's move to a cognitive dissonance world.

Contrasted with other countries, the U.S. limits neither the time nor money spent on elections, with more than the GDP of Greenland and 40 other countries being invested by those who want to make sure that the spoils are split with their interests in the most-favored position. And the only reason that this is done is because Passive Cognitive Dissonance (PCD) works so well. Otherwise, election spending would probably drop by a factor of 50.

Political advisers know that if a voter supports a candidate for logical reasons – specific issues, a platform, prior experience – they can create PCD by inserting a conflicting idea into the voter's mind. Hence negative advertising. PCD demands that something has to give if the voter supports a candidate, but then has to absorb something that they are uncomfortable with and cannot support about that same candidate. The negative advertising is always targeted at an emotionally-held issue – patriotism, religion, financial security, fear, race – something that in the PCD competition in the voter's mind will ensure that it will dominate, and the previously-held view of the candidate will change to something negative. These political advisers know that if they can get a strong enough negative in there, PCD requires the voter to change their mind on the other candidate. Negative attacks are not just acts of desperation or dirty politics – they are an affirmation of the wondrously reliable magic of cognitive dissonance.

Now let's go at it from the other direction. Take a candidate with little going for them – no experience, no qualifications, many negatives in their background - except for sophisticated political advisers and barrels-full of money. The advisers will not even worry about building a platform with long, detailed statements about what the candidate's position is and what action they will take on a wide variety of issues. Instead, they will run surveys on the voters to find out what core values are most strongly held by those most likely to vote – the old standards are variations on religion, patriotism, national security, race, financial security – and then put together a simple set of "sound-bite" "one-liners" that the candidate can use in speeches, signage, and press interviews. These core-value one-liners will stick with a certain number of likely voters, creating a favorable impression. But in contrast to facts about various issues and information about the candidate that the voter has only an intellectual attachment to, these few, vague core-value issues are emotionally held. So when the campaigning starts, and the PCD process plays out in each voter's mind, the contest is between some dispassionately-held information versus some passionately-held beliefs. PCD allows for only one winner, and passion wins every time. The potentially more experienced and better qualified candidate has a logical advantage, but cannot overcome the PCD handicap.

Or, if it is feasible, the advisers might want to try to reach for a piece of Active Cognitive Dissonance (ACD). A raw candidate could run as the "anti-politician", pushing their complete lack of experience as a positive. The advertising emphasis to the voter would be that this candidate is "just like you". If this works, then voters see the candidate as an embodiment of their life experiences, goals, and desires. Since they want their beliefs and goals to be realized, they develop positive feelings/attitudes/beliefs about the candidate, who becomes in effect an avatar for themselves. Attack their candidate and it is similar to attacking the voter personally, which means that it is now a case of ACD instead of PCD. Since ACD requires the conflicting information to be strong enough to overcome beliefs and attitudes produced through life's experiences if it is to make an impact, it almost never succeeds. Thus by having voters identify with the candidate as one of their own, the ACD process is invoked and with it near immunity from negative advertising from the opponent. Polling will show what subgroups will respond strongly to this kind of identification process – in addition to being the anti-politician, race can work, or religion, or gender, or even sexual preference.

So what happens? Realizing their disadvantage, the experienced candidate also goes negative, trying to point out the flaws in the raw, moneyed candidate. But in the PCD battle, a strongly-held value like religion or patriotism is going to withstand a negative ad pointing out that this candidate has demonstrated, for example, zero credibility. If in addition the other candidate has adopted an ACD position - "I'm just like you" or the equivalent – it is really an uphill swim. The only winning strategy for the experienced candidate is to drop their focus on specific issues and experience and grab another fundamental emotional issue not taken by the raw candidate. So if religion is taken, then take patriotism. But by this point in the campaign it is usually too late for such a jarring change.

Now this is just an example of one specific case in one specific voting environment. Each political race has different contenders and factors that give one side or the other of the PCD equation more innate weight. With two equal candidates, both experienced or both inexperienced, the negatives may cancel and wash out, since each candidate is equally known or unknown. With a overall satisfied electorate, issues may dominate; with a dissatisfied electorate, negatives aimed at incumbents will be especially effective. And candidates always have the opportunity to commit self-induced political suicide due to gaffes and missteps.

Going back to try and find the basic point of this discussion, American citizens often think they are voting for the "best person", but the PCD process in fact forbids this. People with money know that it can buy shifts in attitudes and beliefs, which is why so much is spent during the election cycle in the U.S. By creating the appropriate advertising and messaging for a candidate, those with enough money to spend know they can almost guarantee an election win, especially when taken in the aggregate (for example all U.S. House of Representative races). The result is a skewed representation favoring the wealthiest at the expense of those who cannot afford to buy election attitudes. The reader can make a decision about the non-optimality of this, but it is probably not what those who founded the country had intended.

For Americans let's try another test case on basic PCD, a self-test. Most Americans laud either Presidents Kennedy or Reagan for a bunch of good things they are supposed to have done. Now in some cases, like giving Reagan credit for the breakup of the Soviet Union, things were just tossed in by supporters to burnish his reputation. (Talk to anyone actually from the Soviet Union and see how they react if you mention Reagan had something to do with its demise. Their response is: who is Reagan?) But let's for the moment assume they did all the wonderful things that you think they did. So then for Kennedy we need to add in the Bay of Pigs disaster, meaning he let these Cubans patriots die when the U.S. had promised to help them; the launch of the war in Vietnam; his incompetent PT boat boatmanship (while idling, sliced in half by a destroyer); the nepotistic appointment of his brother as Attorney General, who could only show a few years serving as an attorney to various Senate subcommittees as his entire legal background; the incredible treatment of his wife by his multitudinous liaisons; and the undisputed fact that everything famous he ever said, including his <u>Profiles in Courage</u> book, was "co-authored" (amusingly, the Kennedy's vast and vivacious legal resources require that we all use the euphemism "co-authored" instead of the more appropriate ghost-written - if I suggest the subject and you write it, then it is co-authored per this definition) by the very talented and more loyal Theodore Sorensen. For Reagan, we already mentioned the drugs and weapons for Iran, which may have eventually been used to kill Americans; the Savings and Loan debacle, where deregulation of this industry allowed them to run amok, wasting the savings of hard-working Americans to the tune of over $150 billion, and nobody went to jail; the overbuying of defense items, a gift to defense contractors, for items that nobody needed or wanted; the firing of all the air traffic controllers, permanently and dramatically reducing the safety of flying in the domestic United States, reflected in near misses, confusion, errors, and a contributing factor in crashes and deaths; the Strategic Defense Initiative, another gift of free money to defense contractors for the technological equivalent to fighting a guy with a gun by catching his bullets – even if it worked he could beat you by just firing more bullets; and the little imperialistic escapades mentioned previously.

So if Cognitive Dissonance does not work, you will be able to absorb this negative information about your favorite president, set it neatly alongside your opinion that he is a great or one of the greatest presidents, and everything is fine. If Cognitive Dissonance works, something has to give – you are going to toss out this information, or change your view of your president. Run the test and see how well Cognitive Dissonance works on you. If you are the average human being, you have tossed out all the information that does not fit your image of your favorite president (and, funny thing, if you did not like the other president, notice that you happily accepted all of his negatives).

Your reaction will probably be, wait, this is bull-crap, Cognitive Dissonance doesn't work me, I am totally in control of my mind and my beliefs. The reason I threw out all that information about my dear favorite president is because it is all wrong, or because it is all lies and slander, or because it was all justified, or because he did not know about it and had nothing to do with it and was not accountable, or because it did not matter in the grand scheme of things. Right, that is PCD in action. It works every time. People cannot hold conflicting ideas in their mind simultaneously, especially if they have any kind of emotional feelings about the ideas. As Arnold replies to his wife's questions as they stand together under terrorist gunpoint in <u>True Lies</u>, after she has just found out that he has been a spy during their entire marriage: "She: Have you ever killed anyone? He: Yeah, but they were all bad." That wraps up the potential ACD problem.

For the previous 60,000 years, ACD and PCD were one of the many short-cuts built into man to enable him to quickly dispatch the problems that faced him in the world. Other chapters in this book cover others. Once a person has their belief structure in place, human nature makes sure that it takes quite a shock to disturb or re-align it. The ACD process will generally toss out conflicting information that would otherwise muddle, confuse, and delay a person who might be tempted to start questioning whether they should be doing what they were doing, or had the correct priorities, every time such information showed up. Going with your pre-established beliefs and attitudes is fast, clean, and simple; setting up an evaluation process to factor in conflicting and contradictory information is slow, complex, and difficult.

In yesteryears, if you created a toxic waste dump next door you could eventually just move on and start over. There was plenty of room; it did not seem to matter. If you needed to cut down all the trees in the forest, there was always another forest. If your (water or oil) well ran dry, move on and dig a new one. If all the abalone or oysters seemed to disappear, move over to the next bed. If all the fish seemed to vanish, just sail on another half an hour. If the soil crapped out – not enough nutrients or too much salt due to your farming techniques - just move on a mile or two and start over. If you need more watts, just burn more coal. If you need more coal, just do more digging.

But today, the world is both full and limited. Whatever one person does affects all his neighbors and his descendants. Few things can be treated as simple, straight-forward, mono-dimensional yes/no choices. Now most problems are multi-dimensional, and deriving the proper valuation algorithm to appropriately factor in all germane considerations often seems as much art as science. How do you factor in the cost to tomorrow's generation of today's pollution? There is no *right* answer; just complexity, uncertainty, estimates, probabilities, guesses. Take coal. It is not clean. It pollutes when it is mined; it kills miners when it is mined; it kills miners later from black lung and from emphysema. It puts twice as much carbon dioxide into the air when it is burned as natural gas per unit of heat obtained; it puts out way more sulfate and nitrate pollution than any other energy source, producing acid rain that leaves forests and lakes dead; it leaves behind an accumulated waste product of fly ash that is a toxic waste dump. But coal is available and is not expensive. All these factors have to considered when coal is evaluated as an energy source, and not just the advertising from the coal companies that they sell "clean coal" (which of course they do not).

But take alternatives to fossil fuel, what proponents call renewable energy, like solar and wind. Supporters want to tag these with one simple color, green, and use ACD to blow off any negative issues, focussing instead on the negatives of fossil fuels. But it takes non-renewable resources to manufacture and install wind and solar installations, and they both are visual blights. Wind systems, those who once supported them now find, are also audible catastrophes as well as raptor disasters. Cost for both wind and solar shorn of their government subsidies are an issue, long-term reliability/maintainability are questions, their intermittent nature is inherent and unfixable, and the infrastructure to feed this power back into the grid is just not available. This does not mean you do not pursue renewable energy, it just means all the plusses and minuses of coal, oil, natural gas, nuclear fission, and renewable sources have to be considered together in making decisions about the future. You can't jump into renewables just because they are "green", using PCD to ignore all the other problems, any more than you can dismiss nuclear power because it is "dangerous", another ultra-simplistic belief that many people hold because they have used PCD to toss out all the other facts surrounding it.

The reason the reader always sees these issues reviewed in the media mono-dimensionally – they are renewable, infinite, free, safe, clean, etc. - is that the companies in these businesses and their advertising agencies know full-well that Cognitive Dissonance is alive and well and in full-force. They want to create and maintain that simple, favorable belief about their product – they do not want any negatives or complexity in play. And they make sure that the politicians who have some control over where funds are going know that jobs for their constituents and their political contributions depend on the politicians drinking and selling the same Kool-Aid. The media people themselves know that most readers do not want to read about the complexity of these issues because whatever they write will just be perceived as PCD flotsam against their readers' extant belief structure. Sure, every so often a writer will publish a well-researched story, and they will get credit for its quality and depth. But that is not what sells today.

In the U.S. the most vivid examples of PCD and ACD are seen in two societal issues – the two groups which are anti-abortion and anti-gun-restriction-laws. Both groups have a core of supporters who fervently believe in their respective positions. If information filters through the media, these groups are not concerned that it will, through the PCD process, change the beliefs or attitudes of their supporters. As has been outlined earlier, information alone is usually never strong enough to overcome the accumulated life experiences of individuals, especially for strongly-held issues.

However, both groups want to bring others around to their positions, others who may not feel as strongly, who may not start off initially with a belief structure that is necessary supportive of their position. These others, contrary to the core of dedicated believers, may be influenced by information – the PCD process. So both groups constantly put out streams of information that have as a goal utilizing the PCD process to change the beliefs of everyone else to match the beliefs of their respective groups. As an ancillary benefit, this information will reinforce the beliefs of their core membership, but that is not the prime intent.

But much more dangerous to the singular purity of their platform would be actions, not information, that are in conflict and/or inconsistent with their beliefs. So for example, say the anti-gun-restriction groups were to allow for some legal restrictions on firearms in some situations. On the one hand the group is absolutely against something; on the other hand it allows it – two positions in complete opposition. Facing this conflict, the membership would have to make an adjustment in their beliefs – and one outcome might be that a few/some/most restrictions are OK. Both groups (guns and abortions) have concluded that they cannot risk this, so they have decided that they will not allow any exception, no matter how logical or reasonable, to their core positions.

This "no exceptions" position, taken to ensure that ACD is never invoked, leads to these groups being forced to take positions that they themselves do not "truly" support – a classic dammed if you do/damned if you don't predicament in all senses of the phrase. But both groups must maintain pristine-pure positions, refusing to allow that any circumstance or condition would be a sufficient reason to put any limit on gun ownership or use or allow for an abortion. Such a concession would present a conflict to its membership and to potential supporters, and they know that cognitive dissonance requires that all such conflicts be avoided at any cost.

The anti-gun-restriction groups point at the 2nd Amendment to the U.S. Constitution as the basis for their group's position: "A well regulated Militia, being necessary to the security of a free State, the right of the people to keep and bear Arms, shall not be infringed." The context for this statement was the conclusion of a war for independence as a colony from Great Britain, where the colonies had only volunteer militias versus the standing armies of the British Empire, and this accounts for the first two phrases in the amendment. A flintlock pistol in 1780 had a useful range of maybe 15 yards, a very low velocity bullet, and a reload time of maybe 18 seconds if you were accomplished. The only meaningful firearm in 1780, whether for self-defense or hunting, was the long rifle, which had a useful range of about 100 yards. Captain Cook was killed in Hawaii in 1779 by the unharmed Hawaiian into whom he had just fired his pistol at point-blank range.

A little over two centuries later, the U.S. has a standing national army and local national guard, obviating the concept of a militia as an anachronism. A 9mm (.36 cal) handgun today is much smaller and lighter than a flintlock pistol, holds 17 rounds (or more with a high capacity magazine) that can be fired in a few seconds, and can kill at over 100 yards, so it has roughly the firepower of 200 to 500 people carrying 1780-vintage flintlock pistols. Those who wrote the Constitution had not imagined and could not imagine the conditions of today. It would be as if they had written traffic rules for horse and carriage traffic and we were trying to apply it to jet aircraft.

But if you read the most recent Supreme Court ruling on the 2nd Amendment, DC versus Heller in 2008, you can see a classic case of ACD. If you can find pure cognitive dissonance in an opinion of the Supreme Court of the U.S., its robustness is undeniable.

The intent of the majority opinion in Heller was to demonstrate that the intent of the 2nd Amendment language was to allow individuals unrestricted access to any handgun. The issue was restrictions put on handgun ownership by a locality. Handguns in crowded U.S. cities are often used by teenagers in gangs to either enforce gang territories, eliminate illegal drug competition, or as part of the gang initiation process, issues (cities, drugs, gangs, semi-automatic handguns) not present or contemplated in 1780.

Supreme Court opinions are generally authored by clerks under the guidance of a judge – Justice Scalia authored the majority opinion so he most likely gave guidance to the clerks as to what he wanted in the text. Over 60 pages are devoted to this, stepping carefully though every word and phrase of this brief amendment, analyzing its meaning and proper interpretation from a historical perspective. With only 27 words in the amendment itself, that is over two pages per word. Yet if you read this majority opinion over carefully, you will not find one phrase, statement, idea, comment, or question that addresses the difference between today and 1780 in weapon technology, standing armies, state militias, cities, gangs, drug sales, murders, and the like.

For the issue that weapons technology is completely different from what the writers of this amendment could have imagined, the majority opinion simply dismisses with one word: "frivolous". In other words, a refusal to engage the subject. On the issue of the militias today being obsolete, this is similarly dismissed by utilizing legal logic. The militia statement is in a prefatory phrase; prefatory phrases do not have to be interpreted as restrictive (they can just provide context); so this one is going to be taken as context and will be ignored. The opinion admits that militia members brought weapons from home to use as their "military weapons"; that today's handguns have no military applicability is unmentioned and unaddressed. The opinion refers to and agrees to the legal precedents that the weapons protected were those "in common use at the time", and that "dangerous and unusual" weapons are prohibited. But after declaring this, these points are just left dangling and unaddressed. The opinion admits that all military weapons are not suitable for home ownership, but without making any attempt to state or define the boundary. The opinion does say that the right to own guns is not unlimited, similar to the right of free speech, but does not discuss whether any of today's situations that did not exist in 1780 would invoke one of these limitations. The opinion quotes several other legal opinions that the right to bear arms was established so the people could develop a familiarity and skill with the firearms that they will need to use when they are called up to form a militia – but then makes no comment about the fact that today this concept is completely obsolete.

After systematically walking through all of the above differences between today and 1780, the majority opinion declares "But the fact that modern developments have limited the degree of fit between the prefatory clause and the protected right cannot change our interpretation of the right." No reasoning, no explanation, no justification, just another case of "that's my opinion and I'm sticking with it."

The other pattern that emerges is a careful selective picking and choosing of quotes and portions of quotes that support a particular argument without addressing the loose ends, conflicts, and consequential damage that these raise. For example "the Second Amendment confers an individual right to keep and bear arms (though only arms that 'have some reasonable relationship to the preservation or efficiency of a well regulated militia')". Revolvers and small caliber handguns (less than .36 caliber) have no equivalency or use for the military or police; their use is pretty-well accepted, yet this quote, used in support of the main argument, would make their use unacceptable. And another example: "The right of the whole people, old and young, men, women and boys, and not militia only, to keep and bear *arms* of every description, and not *such* merely as are used by the *militia,* shall not be *infringed,* curtailed, or broken in upon, in the smallest degree; and all this for the important end to be attained: the rearing up and qualifying a well-regulated militia, so vitally necessary to the security of a free State." The opinion utilized this quote from the Georgia Supreme Court in 1846 to emphasize that gun rights are to be absolutely unabridged. But in doing so it leaves unmentioned the qualifying phrase at the end of the quote - the whole reason for doing this is to be able to call up an effective militia that can preserve the security of a free State (no professional armies back then).

The opinion quotes drafts for the 2nd Amendment submitted to James

Madison; here is Virginia's, almost identical to New York's: "That the people have a right to keep and bear arms; that a well regulated Militia composed of the body of the people trained to arms is the proper, natural and safe defence of a free State. That standing armies are dangerous to liberty, and therefore ought to be avoided... That any person religiously scrupulous of bearing arms ought to be exempted, upon payment of an equivalent to employ another to bear arms in his stead." Both show that because of the anathema that a standing army represented, a militia had to be maintained, and that the right to bear arms was inextricably tied to this need to avoid an army and replace it with a militia. Yet in the opinion this hard linkage, quoted by the majority, is just left awkwardly begging for an answer – once the need for a militia is removed, the impact on the right to bear arms must be affected to some degree, but that impact is unaddressed.

What this means is that this opinion was written by individuals who were themselves acutely aware of the need for the content, all 60 plus pages, to meet the requirements of cognitive dissonance. Everything that these writers found was in support of the final conclusion without exception; anything in conflict was dismissed without any serious intellectual engagement. What emerged was 100% pure, cleansed of any possible conflicting ideas. This is what cognitive dissonance demands – no concurrent conflicts, only calming consensus. The differences between 1780 and today are so great in so many dimensions that some would have been expected to show up in this opinion, but its purity, almost at a Platonic level, confirm the almost magical efficacy of cognitive dissonance.

Another clear indication was the inability of the writer(s) of the majority argument to refrain from using adjectives and modifying phrases, many of which tend to be pejorative about the minority argument. Considering that the minority often quotes James Madison, who wrote most of the Constitution, as well as other legal opinions and scholars, just as the majority opinion does, characterizing the minority opinion through the use of words and phrases like "bizarre", "is unknown this side of the looking glass", "is dead wrong", "uses the same excuse", "there is nothing to this", "no support whatever", "it is dubious", "flatly misreads", and "wholly unsupported assertion" seems only intended to disparage and insult the minority opinion, rather than present measured logic. A typical sentence would start out like this: "Other than that erroneous point, JUSTICE STEVENS has brought forward absolutely no evidence ..." All of this would be a tactic consistent with someone who has a strong emotional allergy to the opposing opinion, and not someone who is simply collecting, presenting, and digesting legal precedents.

In a non-ACD world, assuming the same conclusion, all of the points mentioned above would have been satisfactorily addressed, even if that result would have been evidence contrary to the final opinion. A final tally would show so many points in support of the argument, so many in opposition, and then a final conclusion that would affirm both the positive and negative contributions. There still has to be an opinion in spite of a diversity of views and prior findings; but in a non-ACD world artificial purity is not demanded.

In the spirit of full-disclosure, attributing the depth of debate surrounding the 2nd Amendment in the U.S. Constitution to just one aspect of human nature, cognitive dissonance, is too simplistic; like the rarity of Titanics, the discourse on the 2nd Amendment is a simultaneous compounding of several fundamentals. The next chapter discusses Belief Driven Cognition. One problem with presenting this book that the author has not found a way around is that ideally the reader would be reading seven chapters simultaneously, since the contents of all interrelate, and many characteristics of man's thinking involve several of these factors at work at the same time. The Belief-Driven Cognition model would say that the writer(s) of this opinion first came to believe in no-gun-restriction-laws on a personal basis, and then wrote the majority opinion by pulling only the positions that supported their starting belief into the argument. The result would probably look much the same. While these two human nature characteristics are certainly complementary and consistent, it is the author's experience that people and groups utilizing cognitive dissonance end up with a more comprehensive and systematic sweep of all possible factors. Belief-Driven Cognition arguments generally tend to be more narrow, limited, less careful, less sharp; since individuals, being captured by their belief (blinded, some might say), see everything framing that belief, even connections and reasons that to others may make no sense or seem unrelated. ACD/PCD-aware individuals, on the other hand, are the opposite – they know that the argument must be robust and apparent-conflict-free. But, if you as a reader after getting through Chapter 9 are convinced that either or both of the previous examples represent Belief-Driven Cognition behavior rather than ACD/PCD then you should keep that conclusion.

But there are other belief-driven aspects. Almost all supporters of the 2nd Amendment believe that the less government the better, and that government is inherently, potentially, worst-case dangerous. A citizen needs some fail-safe personal way to ensure that they can stave off an intrusion by the government that they would perceive as so invasive as to be life-threatening or freedom-threatening or constitution-threatening. Possessing their own weapon is their personal fail-safe fall-back solution against the government, in some unanticipated way at some time in the future, crossing this invasive line. They believe that freedom and liberty are always at risk, and that not only does having a gun enable them to protect these rights, but that the very right to have a gun is a litmus test or bellwether or "canary in the coal mine" of all those rights. Any limit of any kind on firearms or ammunition kills a canary and sets off the belief alarms. This belief-based view demands that the 2nd Amendment be supported without condition or compromise, and cognitive dissonance assures that this support will in fact be so. Now note why this 2nd Amendment support is exclusively a belief-based view. The last time period in which personal firearms would have been a conceptual match for government firepower was in the 1880's – when reliable repeating rifles and revolvers were available but before the invention of modern military weaponry, armored vehicles, and unmanned vehicles. The only defensive weapon useful today against a modern army is other civilians (you hope the government will refrain from offensive weapon usage to prevent collateral civilian damage). The only effective offensive weapons useful today are large buried bombs that can overcome any armored vehicle, explosively-formed penetrators (EFP's) that are hard to buy retail, and cyber weapons, which are the most easy to deploy and the most devastating but are too nerdy to be attractive. But because the individual with his own firearm knows that he is in full control of its usage, he believes that it will protect him, and he will argue that it will, regardless of the facts. The efficacy of belief-based thinking is absolute.

Many of these same individuals who fervently believe in the 2nd Amendment also believe that carrying a firearm protects them against someone else with a firearm intending to do them harm. This is a belief-based view – so what happens if you test it with a little logic? American soldiers in combat are heavily armed, are protected with body armor, know they are in combat, and yet are frequently killed by friendly Iraqi and Afghan soldiers. How? Because of the element of surprise – they do not view these soldiers as the enemy. U.S. Presidents are extremely heavily guarded, but no one who wanted to shoot one has ever been stopped before or during the attempt. How can this happen? Because it happens too fast for anyone to react. About 60 law enforcement agents are killed and many more wounded by gunfire every year (it used to be twice as high before they began wearing body armor), yet they are always armed, and always well-trained and prepared for the potential of contact with an armed and dangerous individual. This is because the element of surprise always trumps preparation, armament, and body armor. In much of the West before there was a formal police system, people carried weapons for self-defense. And yet armed people were killed all the time. How was this possible? Because they were most all shot in the back. So here is the lesson. In the real world, not in the belief-based world, people who are going to kill other people walk up to them quietly, and then quickly pull out a gun and shoot. There is no time to do anything; most will not even see their attacker. In a belief-based world, 2nd Amendment believers believe that those who might attack them are going to first stop thirty feet away, take out their handgun, loudly announce their intention to commit murder, and then walk over to their intended victim. This will give the victim plenty of time to pay attention, stop what they are doing, turn around, drop what they are holding, unholster their firearm, chamber a round and shoot the murderer-to-be. Now it is possible that this might sometime happen, but it is more likely you will need your handgun for an attacking shark first. But no matter what the logic may be to the contrary, these people absolutely believe they are safer with a gun. You can hold it, you can feel it – it can obviously kill – you must be safer. Belief is all-powerful – it is not subject to logic or reason or argument or debate or discussion.

One other fundamental factor is at play here, and that is man's Self-First Orientation, covered in Chapter 11. All other things being equal, man's innate nature is to choose and protect himself and his family instead of the faceless, impersonal world around him. He has had to do this for 60,000 years and it has worked just fine. So in the back of these individuals' minds is this factor – if it comes down to deciding between what appears to be my family or the government, I am not going to hesitate for a second – I have already chosen.

The complex issues of today are the ones that have the most consequence for individuals and the planet itself. Economics – fiscal, monetary, and trade policies on a national, regional, and global scale – the deeply-complex trade-off of how spoils are split on an inter- and intra-national basis. Energy production, pricing, and pollution. Food versus forest. Who owns the water and who gets to waste it? At what cost medical care? What are the long-term implications of oligarchical wealth concentrations in many countries – Russia, Middle East, U.S., China? The needs of today versus the obligations toward tomorrow. How about trying to grapple with the ultra-complex uncertainties, long-term issues, and high-consequence outcomes of global climate change on an international basis?

The whitewashing nature of cognitive dissonance makes successfully engaging any of these a most treacherous uphill swim. All involve a tradeoff of issues - plusses and minuses that have to be simultaneously investigated, studied, evaluated, weighted, and equated. But for someone whose beliefs are already firmly implanted, and whose autopilot feature of cognitive dissonance is smoothly running in the background, most effortlessly dismissing and disposing of any non-conforming fact - rest easy, all is well.

Chapter 9
Belief-Driven Cognition

You Must Believe...

Some readers are unfortunately ancient enough to remember the old joke about the new prisoner who finds his new mates calling out numbers and then all laughing – they have been together so long all the jokes have been memorized and assigned identification numbers. That man is goal-oriented is so well-established and familiar to every reader that the author, like the prisoners, is not going to waste your time trying to establish the proposition. That to be successful you must believe that you will attain your goal; that the most successful athletes (or whatever other example you want to pick) are the most confident and most self-assured that they will attain their goal is universally accepted. Babe Ruth spent most nights drinking and smoking cigars, and a hard workout for him was staying up late playing cards. Yet we can be pretty sure that he did not stand in the batter's box saying to himself "Well, I'm tired and hung-over; hope I can see the damn ball." No, he was probably saying "Ohhh - fastballs. Peachy." Everyone has heard this from their favorite sports hero or sports psychologist (or self-help guru person) – you have to visualize yourself attaining the goal, you must believe that you will be successful. Yoda actually gets it succinctly right in the second <u>Star Wars</u> movie "No. Try not. Do... or do not. There is no try." If your goal is to try, that's what you'll get - effort. Your goal has to be success - results. Martial arts practitioners break boards, bricks, and concrete paving blocks by absolutely believing that they can put their hand, forearm, or foot through them, by visualizing the location in space where they want it to be after the object is broken and then snapping it there. If they only try, they may end up with a broken body part. The U.S. record for broken concrete blocks is 17 at one time with the forearm – you have to be pretty confident to be positive that you can accomplish that.

Being goal-oriented, being confident, being positive – it's all about attitude and belief. In more formalized settings, where lots of money is at stake, the word used is "commitment" - "believe" sounds a little too airy-fairy. It's not about facts and capabilities and tools and skills. You can have plenty of capabilities and unlimited potential but if you feel that the best you can do is try, someone else who is certain that they can succeed and win and conquer will be more successful than you most every time. Over man's time on the earth, the lions, tigers, bears, floods, droughts, and famine picked off those with less confidence and faith and belief in their ability to accomplish things.

Sure, luck is involved, and lots of skill and low confidence will sometimes win over no skill and lots of confidence. Absolute desperation and total terror take over in some circumstances, but almost always these involve escaping danger and not social advance or progress. But these things average out over thousands of years and millions of situations. "Hey, Thog, come with us, the game (water/fruit/sea-life) is drying up – we have to find something better," or "Thog, we're building a stockade to protect against the (bears/wolves/neighbors) and then we'll move inside it – do you want to be a part of it?", or "We're not going to eat all our wheat so we can plant some next year and have even more to eat – do you want to go in with us?", or "Thog, I've come up with a spear-thrower that I think will let us take down a mammoth – I'll show you how to make it if you help me in the hunt," or "Thog, I think we can trade our flint arrowheads for the bows and arrows made by Roth – they're the best I've ever seen? Will you help me make more?" If they were not the instigator, which would be those who were the most-goal-driven, then all the middle-of-the-pack Thogs had to make decisions like this over and over. Those who were sufficiently goal-oriented to realize that they had to act to feed or protect or save their family would wake up and go with the leaders. Those who were not goal-driven would be asleep at the wheel would stay behind, run out of food or water, get eaten or killed or otherwise fall by the wayside.

Being goal-oriented, being driven to succeed, is a subset of man's belief-driven nature. Belief in something, or accomplishing or attaining something, is what drives and motivates man. Problems require skills, and man possesses skills to solve problems, but problems per se do not motivate man. Man tells himself that for the sake of his survival, or his family's, or his community's, a goal has to be met, and he believes he can accomplish that goal, he commits himself to that accomplishment, and that requires certain problems to be solved, and then he goes about solving them. It does not happen in some other order, or without the motivation of the goal and the commitment to meeting it. The goal is the end; man's skills to solve problems are a means to the end.

Some animals use tools to solve problems – dolphins, chimpanzees, sea otters, crows, even some fish. But the key distinction between man and everyone else is that man believes he can accomplish his goal. Dolphins and chimps use tools because they have seen others do it and observe that it works. Belief is not involved. Man first believes it is possible, believes he can do it, and then he looks for a way to do it. Necessity is the mother of invention, but necessity is *not* the problem that you are faced with; necessity is the belief that you do not have to live with the problem as it is. Animals in principle have the capacity for much greater tool use, but they lack belief – they are unable to picture themselves in an improved state. It takes that vision to precipitate the search for tools, or other problem-solving activities, and this is the key man/animal dividing line. You can see the same thing in man if the situation is completely without possibility of improvement – you are caught in the open sea in your small sailing ship in 1300 AD and you are going to have to wait it out. Trying to put up sail or wishing you were 500 miles away are not alternatives. You arrive at the well but it is dry – the next one is another day's walk – you keep on walking. You just brought down dinner but ten really hungry wolves just showed up. You can stay and probably be dessert or pass on this one. In all three cases you basically keep on going because you do not believe that you can do anything to make things better. You have plenty of tools and skills, it is the belief machine that is doing the thinking for you.

Belief – It's Man's Nature

Modern man has been around in a major way for about – pick a number - 60,000 years. You can use a different number if you would prefer; it won't change the point of this argument. Let's try to imagine a representative day time-averaged over those 60,000 years. The man, most likely a father with one or two older male children along with another family or two, will be out hunting or fishing. The woman, a mother, will be out initially gathering some vegetables and/or fruit with the younger daughters, and then will be back preparing food for the next several meals. The oldest daughter will be baby-sitting. A grandmother or adult relative will be making/repairing clothes, tools, or hunting weapons. When the men are back with more food, most will help with its preparation. After meals, there will be discussion on the relative availability of food; whether the change in the weather seems temporary or more permanent; whether they need to move temporarily or permanently; whether the new group of people nearby pose a threat; whether the injury that one of them suffered a week ago is healing or not; whether the baby seems healthy or not.

After maybe 52,000 years of this, there would have been a slight change. The family would have been in or near a small town, making a living farming or in a trade. Or even possibly as a sailor. Moving would still be an issue, but it would now be based on better opportunities rather than a lack of game. And in another thousand years or so, another threat would arise – organized groups of men whose goal was to terrorize, pillage, and take from those who had more and could defend themselves less. Sometimes they were bandits; sometimes pirates; sometimes the government itself. It was a much more tangibly dangerous threat than a wild animal now and then, or a change in the weather, and one almost impossible to defend one's family against. People would band together; build fortified towns; accumulate food and water storage in case of attack; but they would always remain vulnerable; watchful; fearful.

To have any real change in this picture, you have to move within a few hundred years of the present day, and even then, only in the most advanced societies.

Certainly it was man's rational capabilities that allowed him to make steady incremental improvements in agriculture, transportation, housing, tool and weapon design and construction, metal and ceramic fabrication, food storage and preparation, and infrastructure (water, drainage, roads, and public structures). The accumulation of these small changes over tens of thousands of years are the basis for the modern technological societies of today. Yet skill in any of these areas is experience-based, and not a logic-driven process. The basis for learning how to do anything well after you are coached on how to do it the first time, or to teach yourself if you must, is a trial-and-error, skill-building process. Logic works the first time; after that, it is practice makes perfect.

But even the command of problem-solving skills and rational thought by man was not sufficient. While logic created improvements and punctuated innovation, it did not provide a drive, or a motivation, or a catalyst. Fear, or terror, or hunger, or cold, provided that incentive, and once incentivized, man would create a goal, then use his tools, among them problem-solving and reason, to attempt to better his situation through attainment of that goal. Man was not driven to create the bow, or metal tools, or ceramic pottery because his problem-solving side made him create these things. Instead he was driven by the need to survive, and to not starve to death, and to defend himself. Possession of skills per se is whatless without the drive to accomplish something stemming from the belief that you could improve your lot.

For almost all of this time, man has lived in an environment where the large systemic factors that he has depended on for life and survival and success have never been responsive to attack by his problem-solving skills. While he could always find a way to make an improved axe, knife, arrow, brick, wall, shoe, wheel, irrigation channel, or roof; short-term and long-term weather, natural disasters, health, and economics were not just confusing, but in many cases misunderstood, and defied both explanation and exploitation for the common good. Justifications for these phenomena often invoked deities, lacking no other logical explanation, or just plain incorrect causality, due to a dearth of adequate testing and experimentation.

Without the ability to apply logic, man had to apply his other great strength – that of belief. If he only had himself, then he had to believe in his ability to succeed, to find food and water, to clothe, shelter, and protect his family, and to accurately discriminate between friend and foe. Belief in himself is normally called self-confidence. If he was paired with a relative, or acquaintance, or small group, and he was not the "decider", he had to have faith in the group's or the group leader's decisions. That faith is another form of belief, commonly called trust. And for the outcomes that he could not control, he and his family would depend on their belief in a host of other invented concepts. Each time someone left to go hunting, or to search for food, or got sick, or went to sleep each night, or strangers appeared, there was always the unanswerable but life-and-death question of whether they would safely return or wake up the next day or survive. He believed that the this god or that would bring the rain, the Nile flood, the birth of new game animals in the spring, the wheat harvest, good hunting, protection from enemies, or whatever else was important. He would believe that the shaman or witch doctor or small magical figure, or maybe a combination of herbs, bark, leaves, and animal parts would bring health or fertility (and eventually found that a few of them would bring some help). He invented good luck charms and rituals and superstitions to give himself a tangible focus for his beliefs to help him cope with the random uncertainties of life, and everything that he could not understand nor control. People created and believed in fairies and good and bad spirits to explain the behavior of people that they could not rationally understand. Sailors invented and believed in sea monsters to explain the loss of ships that never came home. The Chinese invented Feng Shui over 5,000 years ago, believing that designing their dwellings in a certain manner would bring them good fortune, having no other way to influence the events of life. Fortune tellers of all kinds, using hands, cards, and stars, provided something to believe in for people where no other avenue could provide an answer. And for all of that time religion, tautologically, has been a matter of belief. So have most of the basic philosophical questions that religion often speaks to – what is man?, why is he here?, what should he be about?, and how should he go about it? Until the last few decades, much of what Mother Nature offers – hurricanes, typhoons, tornadoes, earthquakes, tidal waves, volcanoes, droughts, floods, and the weather in general – have been completely resistant to the application of science, and so any alternate approach from the Farmer's Almanac on one end to witch doctors on the other often seemed to suffice. (a footnote: Faith could be used interchangeably with belief if the religious connotation normally associated with faith is withheld. But because this connotation is ubiquitous and hard to shake, belief is the better word.)

Out of 60,000 years, even 1% is 600 years. One-tenth of that, .1% is 60 years, which would mean that for 99.9% of man's existence, weather has been a factor dealt with not by logic but by belief/prayer/hope (or just ignored, but if you are a farmer, you cannot ignore the weather). Medicine only began to leave a stage slightly north of the witch doctor level onto a slightly scientific basis maybe 150 years ago (so it spent 99.6% of the time in the witch doctor mode). While a small percentage of the world's population lives with some form of representative government and fundamentally non-corrupt public institutions, historically most of the world has always lived under unrepresentative, dictatorial if not totalitarian, governments whose goal has been to enrich and empower a very few and keep everyone else suppressed. Economics has been a disaster until as recently as about fifty years ago (99.9% of the time in the irrational mode). Even in farming, which benefitted from the plow and irrigation, agriculture spent 99.8% of the time without pesticides, and 99.9% of the time without sophisticated fertilizers and genetically-modified seed. Philosophy and religion of course remain in the belief mode.

So the use of problem-solving and logic are relegated to a relatively small part of man's universe. For most of man's time on the earth, and for all of the most consequential threats that he would face, logic would not help. Whether it was belief in himself; in family's personal gods; in his tribal gods; in his culture's or religion's gods; or belief in whatever other icon or magical figure struck his fancy; or in another person (group, political, or religious leader); it was belief that helped man get through life. Man is a belief-driven machine. He has many skills and tools: language, abstract thought, multi-step evaluation/planning, and logic among them, but belief is what drives, carries, and preserves him. His problem-solving skills were powerful, but it was his ability to believe that made him unstoppable and undefeatable.

At this point some readers may say, wait a minute, this is just self-confidence. True, but since we are searching for the basic components of human nature, confidence is a symptom, or an effect; belief is the cause, the reason. Confidence does not just appear – it derives from the belief that you will be able to better yourself, to improve your circumstances. Deprived of that belief in the possibility of improvement, confidence will not materialize. So belief is the egg and confidence the omelet, which is why belief, and not confidence, is the fundamental factor being featured here.

Belief-Driven Cognition – The Natural Progression

With belief such an ingrained and valuable part of man's skill-set, a trait without which he may not have been a success, meaning today instead of seven billion people there might still be only a few thousand of us, like the Neanderthals, it was entirely plausible that Mother Nature chose to borrow belief and use it as another cognitive short-cut. And it was more than easy.

In the previous chapter on cognitive dissonance it was outlined how, once a belief is established, it can only be dislodged by contrary information that is stronger than the experiences, whatever they were, that established them originally. But if the beliefs are based on non-facts anyway – myth, superstition, what his father or the village elders or the shaman told him –

then there is no competing experience that is going to supplant these original beliefs. If everything were based on facts, then logic would have a chance; but for most of the last 60,000 years, on most things facts and science were in very short supply. So belief became the placeholder for facts, filling in until there were some better explanation, which for man until maybe 60 years ago collectively never came. So people believed that the world was flat, that the brain was just used to cool the blood – for thousands of years they believed this without question in spite of the fact that a little thought experiment or real experimentation would readily make it not the most likely explanation.

Once belief settles in, if a lonely fact shows up, cognitive dissonance does its thing and the fact is dismissed, unless it has such a dramatic entrance that it can adjust or reverse the belief. So cognition, the process of thinking and perceiving the world, is driven or gated or pre-processed by the pre-established belief structure that each person carries. If it can pass the cognitive dissonance threshold then it will be incorporated; otherwise it is rejected or possibly parked for re-review at a later time. In a world with a dearth of facts, what else was Mother Nature supposed to do? For a monument to the singular effectiveness of belief-driven cognition, look only to this example: the Egyptian and Roman civilizations, for thousands of years and millions of people, depended every year on the flooding of the Nile, caused by snow melt in the mountains that fed the river. Yet in all this time, after periodic droughts during years of low flooding would kill many people, no one ever went up the Nile to try and figure out the real reason why it flooded. Not one person, not even the Romans. They stayed instead with their primitive beliefs.

Mother Nature has also provided belief-based thinking to man as a short-cut, one of many, that ensures that his strength, that of logical thinking and problem-solving, remains a strength and does not become a weakness. You have often heard the advice that in certain situations people should not "over-think" a problem – it can lead to "analysis paralysis" - where one's mental wheels are spinning uselessly without any traction while valuable time is lost, and the lack of any clear analytical result creates indecision and uncertainty. The lack of clarity leads to dismay, frustration, demoralization, discouragement, procrastination, and timorousness. Often there is either not enough hard information, or the information is conflicting or uncertain, or there is not enough time, to make a solid decision. So a man only depending on his logical, rational side in a life and death or equally serious situation, where facts are either absent or it's a flip-of-a-coin decision, may be at a serious or fatal disadvantage. So for example in the Thog scenarios a few paragraphs previously, you either believe in these propositions being made to Thog or not. There were not enough facts to make a decision, no matter how long Thog wanted to agonize over each scenario. Mother Nature's solution is belief (or trust if Thog is depending on his friends) – you simply believe in the idea being proposed and go with it. No quibbling about what you know or don't know – belief allows you to skip over all that and move on. It is tidy, neat, fast, automatic, and Thog ends up committed and positive, with a goal to attain. If man had to fall back on his rational side for every situation, he would be hung up every time a nebulous uncertain problem arose. His natural strength, his rational side, would become a weakness. Mother Nature found a way to side-step this, and that was to invoke belief wherever some uncertainty entered the picture. Logic is for those situations when man is buried in facts and information; belief is for all the other scenarios. Mother Nature made sure all the bases were covered, and she did good, and man proved to be a great success.

Now a cynic might jump in here and also object, claiming that since man never knows all the facts surrounding any decision he makes, some things are always taken on faith, so belief technically is involved in every decision. True, but that is not the point of all this. Belief-driven cognition requires that the framework for making decisions is built log by log, beam by beam, from beliefs and not facts. As facts stream by and rain down, they are always discarded, and never incorporated, unless they are pre-screened against the belief structure and deemed 100% compatible and supportive. On the other hand, if man's thinking is based on all available facts, constantly incorporating new information as it arrives, regardless of whether it will require a change in thinking or not, then even if belief is used to bridge some missing information, belief-driven cognition is not being invoked.

Consequences

As the modern aphorism goes "If you can fake sincerity, you've got it made." Sincerity is nothing more than credibility, believability. While the context of this originated with acting, it was the province of politicians, con men and women and others long before verisimilitude became a factor in acting. The largest Ponzi scheme on record, managed by Bernard Madoff, was entirely belief-based. Investors followed Groucho Marx's taunt to the letter - "Who are you going to believe – me or your lying eyes?" - and went for belief, ignoring the complete impossibility of Madoff's fund producing consistent returns even when the markets declined. Sure, investors were greedy, and did not want to miss out on a good thing, but it was not the numbers that were convincing, quite the opposite, it was wholly belief. And many of these people were not financially illiterate, nor inexperienced, nor uneducated, nor not bright. But Madoff is just the most savage and dramatic example. There are thousands like him every year, selling credibility, convincing people simply through their words, behavior, clothes, and cars that they are for real. If you read the statements of countless people who lost portions of their life savings to these charlatans, there is one theme that consistently appears - "we believed him", or "he seemed so sincere", or "we were convinced he was who he claimed to be." If you can fake sincerity, fake believability, you have a master key that unlocks all of man's defenses and provides direct access to his fundamental nature by way of belief-based cognition. Once hooked, your victim sees reality only after it is filtered and sieved by these beliefs, so potential warnings, danger signs, too-good-to-be-trues, explanations that do not check out are all rejected as debris, flotsam and jetsam, by the belief machinery that is in charge.

The implications of all this are profound. Man, as much as he would like to think so, is not automatically a rational, logical, systematic thinker as he moves through everyday life, event by event. After 60,000 years of success driven by his use of belief, it is utterly integrated into man's nature. It is not an afterthought, or a side exercise; rather, belief *is* man. Belief is automatically invoked at every occasion – man has to attempt to suppress it if he wants to disengage it, but possibly surprisingly that does not work well at all. He is rather a belief-driven thinker, with belief-driven cognition. His strength is belief – everything is screened first against his internal belief structures, and then passed to the rational side if it is safe and appropriate to do so. If the question is clearly of wholly rational content, like: which end of the sharp knife do I grab?, or should I look before I cross the street?, then the belief machinery does not get involved. But all you have to do is change things ever so slightly, pass a law saying that cars have to stop for pedestrians as soon as they enter a crosswalk, and pedestrians will not even look before they cross a street - they drop back to belief – they now "believe" that cars will stop for them, even if they abruptly step out in front of a moving car. And if the issue is what would be termed a "hot button" issue, or one involving "political correctness", or racial something, or homosomething, or heterosomething, or feminine something, or ethnic something, or religious something, political something, or liberty something, or another in an almost infinite list of similar items, then the subject matter is almost always handled by a person's internal belief machinery. Belief-driven cognition means that the way an individual perceives, interprets, remembers, and responds to something is driven wholly by their set of beliefs on this subject, and almost always not just the facts that were actually presented to the individual at the time.

The reason these subjects are termed "hot button" issues is simply because these preferentially engage the belief-driven cognition system instead of the logical, problem-solving side, and the Belief-Driven Cognition side is the one that has allowed man to move mountains, conquer empires, and is not to be denied. "Hot button" is an understatement. Nature designed this for its equivalent of total thermonuclear war. It is not supposed to be reasonable, balanced, objective, or unbiased. And you don't have to turn it on – it is always on. What you have to do is find a way to disengage it if you need to. Most people learn ways to do this for certain parts of their lives, but it requires conscious control and choice. If you choose to run on autopilot, you are running in Belief-Driven Cognition mode.

The reason for this is that people actually do not want to engage their rational side on these issues. They want to use their belief-based side. Using their rational side means they have to go through the laborious process of listening, considering, evaluating, studying, etc. - and they do not want to do this. They have made up their mind – they do not want to be confused with the facts. Belief allows this to happen effortlessly – skip over all the details and go with what you know to be right. Belief-based thinking is the short-cut provided by Mother Nature that is precisely what the doctor ordered.

The evidence for this is, as legal counsel would say, res ipsa loquitur (loosely translated, as obvious as Marilyn Monroe's lack of masculinity). "I don't believe in that" or "I believe that ...": how many times a day do each of us hear that from someone? And we don't hear it about cream cheese versus cottage cheese, we hear it about the most important issues for man, society, and the planet. "My party/candidate/issue/religion/country right or wrong" is a representative example. Once people buy into a particular party/candidate/issue/religion/country because it matches up with their personal belief structure, they generally will not change their level of support or their belief/opinion regardless of how much contradictory factual input they are presented with. With Belief-Driven Cognition, if the facts contradict the belief, it is the facts that are tossed. It is trivial to rationalize a good excuse – the facts must just be wrong; the person reporting them is either mistaken, biased, or a liar; there is a good explanation for this that we just haven't heard yet; this is part of a campaign by the enemies of my "whomever" to tear them down; this is part of a conspiracy of .....; and so on. Everyone has seen people who, in defending their beliefs, will not listen to anything, will not discuss anything, will not concede anything, and only protest and defend their beliefs harder. Any concession on anything, regardless of its factual underpinning, is a slippery slope in their view to an eventual abandonment of their belief. To give away anything is to show that their doctrinal fortress is built on sand and not stone, and so not a grain is to be forgone. People fruitlessly and frustratedly attempt to present rational arguments when debating issues with people who hold their positions for belief-driven reasons. But this is about as effective as explaining to a squirrel why they should leave the bird seed alone and instead eat the ten zillion acorns in the oak trees – neither is playing by, relating to, thinking, or even comprehending logic.

Pick an issue that is tied back to some fundamental belief, one that is looked upon by people as right or wrong, or one that they simply "believe in" or "firmly buy into", and everything that can be linked back to this in any way will then become affected by Belief-Driven Cognition. Does the person believe in small government? Then any expansion of government, no matter how severe a wrong that is being righted, will be fought vigorously. Does the person want low taxes? Then no matter how many tax decreases may have come in previous good times, or how dire and temporary the current financial situation may be, this person will never be convinced that a measure that may result in higher taxes is a good idea. Does the person believe that every word in the Bible is literally true? Then anyone who can say that a particular social phenomenon or issue, proposed law, or candidate for office contravenes anything in the Bible is automatically bad; out; unacceptable; regardless of how logical or reasonable it may be, and regardless of whether or not the Bible goes against even itself at times. Pro-gun rights? Then if anyone wants you to oppose something, they just need to say that it will impose on your gun rights. No details or logic need to be provided, nor would they even be read if they were. Fervently pro-life? Just point out that someone or something is not and you will oppose them, reasons not needed. Conspiracy theorist? Just cite a conspiracy to explain something and everyone will nod knowingly. Believe the media is all under the control of the liberal left? Just point this out any time you hear a negative story about your candidate to explain away any problems, regardless of their severity or the substance behind them. Believe that your political candidate is "different", and represents just your personal values – freedom, the American way, capitalism, low taxes, God, the American Flag, a strong America, America as the best country in the world, etc., etc., - because your candidate tells you so and that they are against all those other evil politicians who are socialists or worse; are for big, incompetent government; are for wasting your money; are for a weak America; etc., etc.? You are going to accept whatever your candidate says and not even listen to any facts that come out that might be show problems with your candidate, no matter how accurate and substantiated they may be.

You can tell that some individuals are aware of this because it is commonly used by people who need to depend on public opinion to keep their job and/or earning power – politicians, lawyers, advocates for individuals and groups, and business people. Whether on the offense or defense, when you watch these people you can see that they almost always dip into the Belief-Driven Cognition tank for sound bites. "Patriotism is the last refuge of a scoundrel" goes the old saying, but in modern America, as most would recognize, the version has been updated to read "Patriotism is the first refuge of a politician; rehab for everyone else."

And not to seem to be picking on politicians and the like, even those who are commonly recognized as the brightest among us are just as likely to be belief-driven. Einstein, if you recall his "God does not play dice" misquote, was speaking about quantum mechanics, which says that when you get to tiny little things, like say electrons, you have to talk about probabilities instead of certainties. You can specify exactly where a marble is inside a shoe box, but you can only specify the relative likelihood that an electron is in any particular part of the same shoebox. Einstein did not "believe" in quantum mechanics – he simply rejected it on philosophical grounds. Not based on math, or science, or having an alternate theory – he just did not "like" it. How could one of the most insightful and brilliant scientific minds of all time reject a scientific idea on the basis of belief? Ah, simple – because he was human. If you think this is unusual, it is only because you do not travel in scientific circles. Try reading the correspondence among scientists when new and moderately radical ideas or theories are proposed, ideas like string theory in particle physics, or someone saying a fossil bone means a new branch of early man, or plate tectonics which is why Africa fits into South America. While some will mull over the new ideas and review the strengths and weaknesses objectively, just as you would expect, others react like 3rd graders on too much sugar, raving about how insanely stupid and moronically foolish this theory is, that it has no merit at all, that only the theory they believe in has any value, etc., etc. When asked about these new theories that question an existing premise, quite often you will hear "I don't believe any of that" or the equivalent, dressed-up in fancier scientific language. Now scientists are supposed to "devil's advocate" new ideas to death, because this road-testing is the only way to assess the viability of these new theories. But there is a thick, dark line between harsh, brutal testing and wholesale condemnation and rejection. The former is good science; the latter is human nature.

Now there is an important distinction to be made between people who have beliefs, and are belief-driven. How to distinguish the two? The former does not screen facts, contrary beliefs, and other opinions through their belief structure prior to considering them, so they can often accept someone with a different belief or opinion without rancor or distress or any signs of irrationality or undue emotion. There will just be differences. Belief-driven people, on the contrary, will tend to always appear as if their beliefs have had to attack any non-conforming input, comparable to the way that the immune system responds to a foreign protein. Nothing seems to just "pass" quietly by. But the most telling discriminator is that people with beliefs will generally have an unconditional, homogenous view of that belief, which is usually a simple, fundamental concept, freedom of this or that for example. Belief-driven individuals, however, since they do not believe in the belief in its pure, philosophical form, but have simply incorporated it into their thinking as a tool, have a view of the belief that is conditional, selective, and restrictive. So for example, they may say they believe in freedom of speech, but this certain other group should be restricted because its views are too unorthodox. Or they believe in the Bill of Rights except for this group of people whom they don't like that should not have any rights. Or they believe in freedom of religion as long as their religion is given prominence at the expense of others. Or they believe in small government, except in these four specific cases where they want the government to proscribe these personal activities they don't like and prescribe these that they like and want everyone else to follow. Or they want to reduce government spending, except for any spending that happens in their own district or affects any local companies that have money and provide political donations. Now some will simplistically call these people hypocrites, and some that act like this are, but although a belief-driven individual will act as if he were a hypocrite, that is not a useful or causal description of what is actually occurring. These people, led by their belief-driven views, are almost always unaware that they appear to act in conflict with what they claim to support.

The most well-known and notorious example of a belief-driven individual in recent times is Adolf Hitler. This is somewhat unusual, since the only other co-temporal totalitarian dictator, Joseph Stalin, was probably his polar opposite – a pragmatic with a few sociopathic qualities. Stalin's top three goals were identical – self-survival. Hitler's top three were also the same – the creation of the thousand-year Reich, a belief-driven goal. Hitler ran his person life on a belief-driven basis – he was a hard-core vegan and a teetotaler. He did not believe he would live to see the full realization of his ideal Germany, and as a consequence was not distracted by accumulating wealth and material goods like many of his staff, making him even more focussed and dangerous. He believed in racial purity and systematically eliminated everyone who would compromise this – those who were mentally unwell or physically handicapped, those who were criminals, those who were homosexuals, those who were not hard-working (Gypsies for example), those with the wrong political beliefs (Socialists and Communists), and then eventually including the Jews. Although he was just a message-runner in WWI he believed from that experience that the only military strategy and tactic to be used at all times was to hold the ground you were on and fight to the last man. This unwavering belief cost the unnecessary loss of huge quantities of men and materiel and may well have resulted in a different war had it not been in place. He firmly believed and insisted that Germany needed technical superiority in weapons first followed by quantity, and this proved to be the case except for the Soviet T-34 tank (only because Hitler refused to listen to input from his tank experts). This openness to new weapons systems enabled Hitler to recognize the value of projecting force through high-speed self-contained armored groups (so-called blitzkreig), which he supported over the outspoken objections and resistance of the German High Command who felt it was not sufficiently traditional. Hitler believed, and wrote explicitly in his book <u>Mein Kampf</u>, that he only respected power, not weakness, which unfortunately Chamberlain and others did not have on their reading list. Unchallenged as he invaded country after country year after year, Hitler, the German High Command, and the German people were altogether shocked when the Allies declared war on them after the invasion of Poland in 1939. The High Command had been given 1945 as the date for war, when their technically-superior armaments would be available in sufficient quantities. Had power been used against Hitler earlier, he would have stopped. Hitler believed in the effectiveness of terror on civilian populations, taking a page from the father of "shock and awe" Vlad the Impaler. He supported the conventional bombing of Britain and then the development of the V1 and V2 terror weapons which hit both Britain and Belgium, most unfortunately teaching Britain to improve on the technique and use it against German cities. Hitler believed that the Soviet Union would fall following his invasion just as rapidly as Western Europe had, believing that the population hated communism as much as he did and would welcome the Germans as liberators, and ignored the fatal differences of dirt roads, long supply lines, and the advantages of Soviet men and materiel. He believed that the United States, distracted by a society based on chasing money and power, and divided by racism and excessive Jewish influence, would falter and not be a dangerous foe. Hitler absolutely believed he was infallible, because for many years he appeared to be so. Hitler invaded area after area prior to Poland without opposition as he predicted, reading the French and British politicians with flawless accuracy. Each time his generals had warned he would not succeed, and his insight and foresight slammed them collectively with shock and awe. This was reinforced by much of his staff, who had great weaknesses, by Hitler's ability to read and manipulate individuals, and by Hitler's photographic mind which could and did often embarrass the best presenters by quoting verbatim inconsistencies from their own testimonies months earlier. Hitler believed in the existence of fully-manned and outfitted regiments and divisions that were supposed to be staffed with men pulled from divisions that had been torn up on the Eastern Front, or back from medical leave, or drafted from some other targeted population group. The High Command knew these did not exist, but Hitler insisted that these be thrown into combat to stem the Soviet advance, and became hysterical when the results were invisible. Hitler believed that if Germany was not competent to win the war, then it and its people did not deserve to survive, putting many ground commanders toward the end of the war in the impossible position of disobeying an order from Hitler, which was instant dishonor and execution, or carrying out an order that would result in the deaths of their own people. Now Hitler did not get into and hold onto his position without other capabilities, but those are not germane here. What is important is that the individual responsible for the deaths of the third largest number of people in the history of the world was possibly one of the most belief-driven people that we know of.

Your reaction may be, hey, I know someone even worse than this. But everyone knows Hitler, and few know your acquaintance. This makes a far better public example.

Tragically, Hitler's success was made possible solely by belief-driven cognition on the part of politicians leading their clueless constituencies in Britain, the U.S., and France. From the 1920's through the mid-1930's, these three countries took the position that the only sure way to peace was through rigorous disarmament.[11] The logic of this belief-based position was unassailably sound – remove all weapons, and you remove all war. Britain was the most aggressive, the U.S. second, with France often passively cooperative, with an initial goal of matching the punitive targets set for Germany in the Treaty of Versailles and then going even lower. The Washington and two London Naval Conferences were utilized to work out the details. There was only one little tiny problem – the belief-driven people running things missed one nuance in their unassailable rule – they should have chosen instead: remove all weapons *from all countries* and you remove all war. But the beauty of belief-driven thinking is that facts and research are never required – you just hold onto your belief, knowing that you are safe in your rightness. And who did they forget about? Germany of course, who simply either blithely ignored the Versailles restrictions or, in the case of submarines, asked and incredibly received permission to match one for one Britain's submarine count. But – and here is the catch – Germany had to *promise* not to use them to attack other ships. Now for those of you sharing brain genes with those who were running Britain at that time, a submarine has only one use – an offensive weapon to sink other ships – and, oh, yes, it fills up holes in the ocean.

Ironically, or coincidentally, or providentially, the U.S. President FDR was also belief-driven: "To believe is to be *strong*. Doubt cramps energy. Belief is power. Only so far as a man believes strongly, mightily, can he act cheerfully, or do anything that is worth the doing."[12] This favorite quote of the Reverend Peabody, founder of the Groton School attended by Roosevelt, became one of FDR's favorites also. When Roosevelt spoke of America having nothing to fear but fear, and always acted positive and upbeat in public and private, it was based on his absolute acceptance of this belief. The nod to cognitive dissonance in the Peabody quote should not be overlooked: doubt - having reservations that your beliefs may be based on assumptions that might

---

11 Memoirs of the Second World War, Winston S. Churchill, Houghton Mifflin Company, Boston, 1987, pp. 37-38, pp. 42-43, p. 45, p. 57, pp. 69-70

12 Franklin and Winston, Jon Meacham, Random House, New York, 2003, p. 17

not all be soundly-based – this will create cognitive dissonance that will compromise the purity and intensity of your beliefs. So doubt, meaning obtaining facts, studying contrary points of view, evaluating weaknesses in your position, must be avoided.

But let's use a more current example, one that can be seen operating on a national scale. Most people in the U.S., and naturally almost everyone in Israel, believes that Israel is a good country, an ally of the U.S., and a bastion of democracy and freedom in an overall autocratic Mideast. Many Christians also believe that Jerusalem has special religious significance, and that Israel, by keeping Jerusalem non-Islamic, is preserving that significance. Jews, which are what the nation of Israel is all about, have been historically harshly discriminated against and deprived of their rights for around 3,000 years, more systematically and severely than any other cultural or religious group in the history of the world. The genocide against European Jews in World War II was physically and ethically devastating (although the treatment of early Jews by Jews recorded by Josephus, himself a Jew, was comparably terrible). While much of the non-Jewish population in and surrounding Israel is peaceful, two groups, one centered in Gaza and the other in Southern Lebanon, espouse violence against Israelis as a way to accomplish political and economic goals, among them a sovereign Palestinian state. They have bombed civilian targets and attacked, killed, and kidnapped soldiers. Israel declares these groups to be terrorists and aggressively and proactively fights against them. All of the above factors – the history of discrimination against the Jews and now Israel's current efforts to fight terrorism, reinforce a belief-based attitude that Israel is in the right. But if we jump back a little over 60 years, making sure that we do not forget the lessons of history, we find that the exact same situation was occurring. A group of people, looking for their right to have their own nation, was being oppressed by an occupying army, and had resorted to terrorism to force the granting of their independence. Except that things were reversed – the Jews were seeking nationhood, and were having their rights deprived, and were resorting to terrorism, in this case against the British. The circumstances were identical – the British clamped down on all the Jews due to the violent efforts of a few to pressure the British in order to grant them Jewish independence.

To deal with the two terrorist groups, Israel has harshly sanctioned the entire populations of both Gaza and Southern Lebanon, allowing basically unlimited collateral damage. In the name of internal security, land and property possessed by non-Israelis is regularly taken without due process or fair remuneration. Walls and security checkpoints with restricted entry are installed that deprive non-Israelis of their ability to earn a living. Individuals suspected of activities incompatible with the security interests of Israel are imprisoned with no access to a tractable legal system. The British sanctions had been much milder – jailing captured terrorists and depriving the population of their general civil rights. While the impact of the two violent groups targeting Israel today have been somewhat limited due to the effectiveness of the Israeli security and countermeasures, the Zionist terrorist groups were magnificently-effective, achieving their goal of independence for Israel. Zionist patriots actually invented and perfected modern terrorism in the 1940's, with their two main groups being the Irgun and the Lehi (which was sometimes referred to as the Stern Gang). The Lehi specialized in targeted assassination to create the maximum amount of terror. Ex-members of these groups have written books on their activities; Menachim Begin, the head of the Irgun, went on to become a Prime Minister, as did a member of Lehi (Shamir). British soldiers and a high U.N. official were targeted for kidnapping and execution; hotels and public areas were bombed.

But now that Israel finally has a nation to call its own, and rule it as it wishes, it is depriving the Palestinians with whom it shares the land of their civil and legal rights in precisely the same manner in which these rights were previously denied its Jewish ancestors, and in some cases, even themselves, by the British when the Jews were subject to British rule before 1948. So with this historic parallel in mind, and using just logic, you would think that first, the people in the U.S. would be looking askance at the hypocrisy of a country attacking both the identical methods and goals of people that it, Israel, used against the British, and defending the use of the same and much worse techniques than those that had been used against it by the British. And second, you would think that Israelis, seeing people in the identical plight that they were in just 60 years ago, and using Israeli tactics to try and improve their lot, and seeing Israel using even worse tactics than the British used against them to clamp down on all this; you would think that Israelis would be saying "Hey, wait a minute, we just walked that same mile in their shoes – we need to fix this situation." But, if viewed across the U.S. and Israel in general, this logical view does not prevail, and this is attributable to the belief-based view of Israel. The unconditional acceptance of this logical inconsistency can only occur where one's belief-driven cognition, which says that Israel is a great country and in the "right", enables you to toss out any conflicting information to the contrary (to be fair, judgmental tagging and bipolar thinking, covered in Chapter 7, and cognitive dissonance, discussed already in Chapter 8, all come into play to push people into having a one-sided emotional view).

Hence, if an Israeli civilian is killed by a non-Israeli it is termed terrorism and accepted as such by Israeli and U.S. populations; if non-Israelis, including innocent women and children, are killed by Israeli actions it is called self-defense and similarly accepted. No matter how many thousands of cases, no matter how extreme the circumstances; no matter what weaponry was utilized; no matter how young, unarmed, and defenseless the casualty - it was always reasonable force. Only in a belief-driven-cognitioned/cognitive-dissonanced environment can you find such a perfect score - not one single exception. The top priority for the Israeli "information" infrastructure is to ensure that Israeli actions always appear virginally-unblemished to the average U.S. citizen, so that there is no resistance to the funding of the state of Israel by U.S. politicians. This vast stream of funding, totalling to date $230 billion in 2010 dollars, is close to life and death for the state of Israel. If there were ever the perception that Israel had done something "bad", or "wrong", or "inappropriate", this funding might be jeopardized, so you will never hear less than perfection describing Israeli activities, at least in the U.S. See if you can recall the last time you saw the Academy Award/Emmy/Golden Globe winning movie <u>Exodus</u> starring Paul Newman broadcast anywhere. While it most favorably depicts the Jewish struggle to create their state, it was made in a polychrome era (see Chapter 21) and so (accurately) includes Jewish terrorism. 50 years later, that accuracy is today incompatible with the monochromed world that Israel and its supporters want portrayed, and so <u>Exodus</u> has been excised from public view.

The point is not whether or not you are allowed to have opinions about Israel and how it operates, and evaluations of the strengths and weaknesses of the behaviors of individual countries are not what this book is about. Israel may be "right" or "wrong" or some combination. The point is that the views of people are most often not based on facts, they are first filtered through their belief engine (and/or judgmental and bipolar tagging engines) which assigns polarized emotional values and filters out that which is incompatible with the belief-based world-view. The point is not that belief-based views are "wrong" - it is just that they are there, they are human nature, and reign supreme. If you know someone who is "pro" Israel, or if it reflects your own attitude, you will be able to personally validate the previous paragraph. It is rare to find someone whose views on Israel are not belief-based. Attitudes on Israel just make for a great example since the contrast between the facts, both historic and current, and opinions, stands out so starkly.

In the spirit of full disclosure, all of this cannot be ascribed to belief-based thinking. Cognitive dissonance, covered in Chapter 8, plays some role. The actions of Israel, for its citizens and supporters, must be all "good" and "justifiable", untarnished by the complexities and discomfort of any past behaviors identical to those that it today condemns. So this part of Israel's history, while just as much a fact as the Holocaust, is suppressed and unaddressed, ensuring that no cognitive dissonance is engendered.

A portion of those opposed to the possession of nuclear weapons also vividly demonstrate belief-driven cognition. Those who have a rational basis for their opposition, say one founded on the risk of an unstable, risk-oriented group or government obtaining such a weapon offsets the advantages that stable, risk-averse governments gain by possessing them, are excluded from this category. But those whose opposition is entirely belief-based, who believe that such weapons are simply morally wrong, or "evil", are unable to accept any use or possession as acceptable under any circumstance at any time, since that would blemish the conceptual purity that belief demands (and also invokes cognitive dissonance – you cannot be against it but also for it sometimes).

At the conclusion of World War II there were about 11 million German prisoners of war but only about 100,000 Japanese, and that was because the Japanese soldiers, and civilians as well, were told to fight to the death and not surrender (carrot: honor to die for the emperor; stick: Americans kill all prisoners anyway, which of course was false). Rough estimates at the time were that it would take another two million American military deaths to cause Japan to surrender without using atomic weapons, through an invasion and continued mass incendiary bombing of cities, along with ongoing efforts to intercept all supply ship traffic. Even if you most optimistically used the lowest number of combat deaths that the U.S. ever had during the invasion of a Japanese-held island, Guadalcanal, 3.5 deaths per square mile, and used it for an invasion of Japan, it would put U.S. deaths at half a million, obviously unrealistically-low, since Guadalcanal was not their homeland. Tinian, the next and still unrepresentative lowest fatality rate at 8 per square mile, would put the U.S. deaths at over one million. More typical was between 30 and 1,100 U.S. deaths per square mile. And of course those against the use of atomic weapons are not against the killing of military combatants, or even civilians for that matter, it is just the use of this specific weapon. The Japanese civilian and military death rate in Okinawa, probably more representative of the what the combat situation on the Japanese mainland would be since it was the closest large Japanese island near Japan proper, was 400 deaths per square mile, and there are 144,000 square miles in Japan (that comes out to 56 million). The reader can make their own estimates.

The firebombing of Tokyo on a single night produced more deaths and injuries than either atomic bomb, and the mass targeting of civilians was none too popular at the time. But the destruction of city after city by incendiary weapons, and proportionate deaths they produced, caused dismay at best among the people running the war in Japan, and rather than hastening the end of the war, brought about about the use of suicide tactics – kamikaze aircraft and instructions to civilians, especially women, to kill any invading U.S. military they came in contact with. The use of the two atomic bombs, on the other hand, produced shock, not because the casualties were any greater (they were not), but just because this weapon was so different and unbelievable. It was psychologically sufficient, where conventional casualties had not been (familiarity breeds contempt), to cause the government to agree to surrender. But if you hear this bit of history described by a belief-driven opponent of nuclear weapons, they must reinterpret history because they believe that such weapons are never justified. Belief-driven cognition always wins over fact-based logic. So these believers will give you some variation of the theme that if you had just kept up the conventional warfare, everything would have worked out fine. Kamikaze planes, kaiten torpedoes, disproportionately-terrible American casualties, fight to the death, no POW's, civilians becoming combatants and the wholesale slaughter this would have engendered – all this is discarded in a belief-based world. Once someone has established a belief-based frame of reference, almost nothing can penetrate, infiltrate, adjust, revise, or tamper with the belief.

In a rational, non-belief-based world, it would be simple – atomic weapons brought WWII to an end with the least casualties possible; and, if you so choose, that should have been the last use or possession of them. You can say the use of them to end a terrible war was the right decision; and you can say that the decision to have them go away thereafter is the right decision. But in a belief-driven world, people just cannot accept the belief that use of nuclear weapons is wrong, but at the same time allow their use as appropriate, just once. Belief-driven cognition, especially when coupled with bipolar thinking, generally means all or nothing, my way or the highway, for me or against me – a world of polarized extremes.

Another place to find exclusively belief-driven environments, and therefore individuals, is in cults and organizations that behave in a similar manner, but call themselves something else for obvious reasons. These groups force their members to behave exclusively within a rigid set of rules based on the beliefs of the leader(s) of the organization, who himself can set whatever rules he wants and does not have to follow any particular rules. Often these have a high pseudo-religious content as framed by the group leader, since the invocation of higher powers or deity brings more pseudo-authenticity to bear. The Peoples Temple Christian Church of Jim Jones was the most prominent recent catastrophically-disastrous example of a belief-based organization. The First Church of Christ, Scientist is a benign, non-coercive belief-based group with a central focus of spiritual healing, a belief-based activity, with on the order of 100,000 members. Somewhere between these two extremes most readers will have had either first or second hand experience with individuals whose lives are dominated by belief-based constraints, or, if you will, belief-based "features". Most unfortunately, the cult leaders of the coercive cults know well that they can only hold on to their membership through strict adherence to their belief-based rules, which ensure that logic, questioning, and debate are excluded and replaced by unquestioned allegiance. This results often in tragedy – members must be isolated from all non-member contact since that would dilute the cult message and encourage questioning, and members once in cannot be released since they might poison future potential members or bring the authorities in to investigate. People use the term "brain-washing" - but these groups simply use the belief-based faculties that are built into man as part of his basic nature. They may abusively feed an artificial belief structure to their members, but there is nothing unusual or unnatural about the cult process, which is why it works so well, much to the apparent surprise of some who fail to appreciate (or ironically not believe) that man is fundamentally belief-driven.

But there are much less dramatic examples that affect the average individual as they live their life each day. The concept of Prince Charming is found all through "happily ever after" stories and fables for children, made unforgettable by Disney having Snow White sing about him in the animated cartoon in 1937. Dorothy Parker wrote an equivalently-sophisticated poem for adults, portraying that for many women, the man they choose as a husband represents their moon and sun, their lord, their prince - the best of all possible men in all the world. Because they are positive they made the best choice, they know it to be so that their man is their prince, and they believe it also; the belief machinery is automatically invoked. So when Princess Di married her prince, she and the not quite one billion people who watched believed that this was a fairy tale come true. But later on in the marriage, when realities and problems and troubles arise, and the facts begin to indicate that a perfect prince the husband is not, belief is still in place, unimpeached, untarnished. Behaviors and actions are irrelevant – the woman is still going to see the lord, her prince. Cognitive dissonance, Chapter 8, certainly is a reinforcing element here, since if one's mind holds an image of a person as a flawless prince, it will not allow the simultaneous recognition of any negatives, weaknesses, or frailties. And believing that she originally made the best possible choice in selecting a mate, the woman cannot accept, with both belief and cognitive dissonance working together, that she in fact made a flawed choice. You may say – well, so what, where's the harm in such image fabrication? It's between two people in the privacy of a marriage. The danger comes when, in a relatively small but serious number of cases, the husband becomes violent or abusive toward or begins to take unreasonable advantage of, maybe through substance problems, not only the woman but children if they are present. The abuse will be tolerated, even when extreme, and relatives and public agencies often have extensive difficulties extracting women from these relationships. People on the outside wonder why this is so difficult, why some women seem "trapped" in abusive or negative relationships, and the responsibility lies with human nature, with belief-driven cognition, which is substituting a prince for the person that everyone else thinks is some kind of minor devil.

In the Princess Di case, of course, none of this occurred. When she soon observed that "there were three of us in this marriage, so it was a bit crowded," both the fairy tale and she dissolved, with the most terrible of results.

Now let's go back to the average person again, and some variation on, as they say on the comedy shows, "that's my story and I'm sticking with it." You try to discuss some factual issue and you are cut short with "Oh, I don't believe in that." Could be some aspect of religion, abortion, gun control, global climate change, taxes, deficit spending, irradiating food for e. coli, vitamins, fluoride, vaccinations, gay marriage, legalizing marijuana, politics, race, crime, or countless others. And in many cases you can also expect to receive the same emotional content as from someone who has strong pro-Israel beliefs, showing that the additional factors of judgmental tagging and cognitive dissonance are engaged as well. And what, says the skeptic, is the problem with this? Everyone is entitled to their opinions, and the world has done just fine so far in spite of this.

Has it? About nine hundred years ago, several powerful Western national leaders and the even more powerful Pope Innocent III got together and decided that the spreading threat coming from Islam from the south needed to be arrested and reversed. It would demand most all the money that their countries could collect, require them to assemble and arm a massive multi-nation army, march thousands of miles away to a land that neither they nor their ancestors had ever set foot in before, and attempt to take ownership of it, killing anyone who interfered with their endeavor. No negotiation, no due process, no rule of law – just raw force and, oh, one other thing, the utilization of belief-driven cognition – that religious beliefs justified killing and taking by force. This of course was the disaster known as the Crusades.

Now the skeptics again will say, no, these people were just fighting for what they believed in, for their religious beliefs. It is indeed important to make this distinction. When the Romans asked the early Christians to renounce their faith in exchange for their lives, the Christians did die for their religious beliefs. When people voluntarily agree to serve God by becoming nuns, priests, ministers, monks, and the like, and spend their life in constructive, self-less service, they are living for their religious beliefs. But when someone attacks a town 3,000 miles from his own country, a town whose people may have never before seen a Christian, breaches a gate and storms from house to house, slaughtering each and every unarmed man, woman, and child, they are not following their religious beliefs.

There are three basic ways to provide yourself with sufficient confidence that you can accomplish something. One is by experience – you can watch others do the same thing and predict that you will also be successful. Or you can calculate, model, measure, experiment, or otherwise do a scientific attack on the problem and determine that your approach will work. The third way - in the absence of either experience or an rational or logical basis – is that you can go on faith or belief. Belief fills in all the missing information and gives you the same equivalent level of certainty. Belief is like a granite foundation – it elevates your confidence in lieu of any other factual data. But belief is passive – it is just a support - it is a fill-in – it does not launch you or propel you. "I believe this will work," or "I believe we will find water," or "I believe she will live." It just provides you with an answer in the situation where no rational conclusion is available.

The soldiers that went off on the Crusades had strong religious beliefs, but those were not sufficient to catapult them anywhere. For the Crusades to happen, they had to be provided with a belief-based justification by those who organized the Crusades: a simplistic, Christianity-themed argument saying that God had demanded that they free the lands of Abraham and David and Solomon and Jesus from the evil infidel. The soldiers that went off to destroy and kill were butchering because they believed that God wanted them to so do, as they were instructed by both their secular and religious leaders. Those that sent these armies knew it was simply a power play, nations fighting other nations. But they could not convince their soldiers to march and fight thousands of miles from home with only that as a reason. These leaders needed to produce a motivation in their soldiers that would overwhelm all rational and logical objections. Why on Earth would these people want to go and fight someone thousands of miles from their lands who would never be a threat to them? Well, that would be a religion-based explanation. The soldiers all had a deep Christian faith, but that was not what drove them. Instead, it was the abuse of this faith by their leaders who concocted an argument that said that God demanded that those who had true faith would follow their direction and go off and attack these far-way towns and people with a different faith. Religious belief does not get you to go off and kill helpless, innocent children, quite the opposite. Only a belief-based argument, belief-driven cognition, which takes that faith as a motivator and ties it to some irrational but self-consistent set of actions will create the perfect storm where the ends justify the means, and will enable you to end up with a soldier with a cross on his chest, a sword in one hand and a dead child in the other.

Religion-based wars make for such picturesque examples since they are so conceptually oxymoronic – most religions have core values based on doing nothing but good to your fellow man. Since Martin Luther arrived Catholics and Protestants have been murdering each other justified by belief-driven arguments down through the present day, and Jews have had the benefit of persecution and worse for belief-driven reasons for several thousand years, and for their beliefs for even longer. The belief that the white race was inherently superior to all others led to a host of belief-driven cognitive problems of world-wide consequence lasting almost half a millennium. Colonies were set up in non-white countries with complete disregard to the impact on the indigenous populations; in some cases, the result was their virtual elimination. The civil and legal rights of these peoples, rights ironically critically important to the colonial masters, were ignored. Slavery of black people, who were deemed in effect sub-human, was rampant. Manifest Destiny was the term for the version of this belief utilized in the expansion of the United States, enabling it to do away with all Native American people as quickly as possible. Millions have been slaughtered, made homeless, treated abysmally, inhumanely, and all entirely because of the effectiveness of belief-driven cognition. Blaming the "bad" behaviors themselves, or some inherent "fault" or moral weakness in man, misses the point. It is not in man's nature to be "bad", or immoral – but it is in his nature to be belief-driven.

The last century saw tens of millions of people killed because of mild variations on one belief-based theme – that the ends justified the means. With that in place, any plan could be implemented, its depravity unbounded. More than six million Jews and many other ethnic and social groups were killed in Germany because their existence was incompatible with a belief in a homogenous, racially-pure Third Reich. Stalin's similar struggle for his classless society appears to have claimed about 20 million human lives through direct killing and indirect means (starvation, disease, cold). The Khmer Rouge slaughtered a little over a million in their quest for an unblemished society. Mao Zedong, in his remaking of China, currently gets credit for somewhere around 50 million deaths, including 30 million from starvation during the Great Leap Forward in the late 1950's. The Rwandan genocide of the lighter-skinned Tutsi's by Hutu's was an ethnic purge brought about by the belief that the Tutsi's were a lower class of people not worthy of any human rights or considerations. While the Empire of Japan did not initiate hostilities in World War II for belief-driven reasons, the unspeakable barbarity and depth of its killing of civilians and prisoners was based on a belief-driven cognitive view that was taught to all soldiers – that everyone was morally inferior to the Japanese soldier, and were therefore deserving of the worst possible treatment that could be imagined or contrived. The Japanese Army gets credit for the unnecessary and unimaginably brutal killing of about 11 million civilians during this war, contrasted with maybe half a million of their own, even if you include the atomic bombs and mass firebombings.

Now not all wars in the past century were based on a belief-driven set of logic. World War I was a classic war for power and territory. And as was mentioned above, the Asian portion of World War II was not initiated on a belief-driven basis, although almost all the casualties were attributable to belief-driven reasons. Similarly, many of the casualties on the Soviet-German front in that war can be assigned to belief-driven views by the respective political party structures of both countries. They took advantage during the invasion of each other's territory to purge it of citizens considered incompatible with the standards of its party, and to remedy the accumulated backlog of past perceived damages, sins, evils, illegal acts, and the like that had been committed against its own citizens. Between Russia and Poland, estimates of civilians who were killed by German actions are in the range of 20 million people, a number that dwarfs what was done to any other group. The Korean War was not a belief-driven war, but the U.S. war in Vietnam was entirely belief-driven.

Vietnam was perceived by the U.S. through the lens of the Domino Theory, a belief-based argument that said that communism was like a contagious disease that could be caught by nations physically adjacent to an existing communist country. At the first sign of an illness, medical attention was required; in this case, a half-million U.S. soldiers. Of course, the Domino Theory was purely belief-based, not logic or fact-based, and did not take into consideration the country by country specific differences and histories. In a world not dominated by people driven by belief-driven cognition, even if the Domino Theory were the default position lacking evidence to the contrary, each case would be looked at individually, and the facts for and against the Theory would be considered objectively. The people in a country like Vietnam, long dominated by colonial masters, would be resentful of yet another powerful country intervening in its government and internal affairs. They would not so much be drawn to communism for what it was but for what it was not – it was indigenous and not someone else taking charge of their government. It is like the draw of a labor union for workers long weary of feeling that they are helpless in their ability to influence the policies and practices of their management. The union might well have "feet of clay" and present many problems of its own, but at least it is their union, and the company management is clearly not theirs. China supported the North Vietnamese with arms and money in its fight against the U.S., but it was either lucky or wise to not send in Chinese troops to occupy Vietnamese territory. That most likely would have created the same negative reaction against foreign occupiers as the U.S. incited. So that war ended poorly for the U.S. and the South. And it produced that famous quote from Major Booris: "We had to destroy Ben Tre in order to save it," a tidy encapsulation of the ends-justifies-the-means cognitive approach.

The Soviet Union invaded Afghanistan for purely pragmatic reasons. But the U.S. decided to support the Afghan resistance fighters for belief-driven reasons: "the enemy of my enemy is my friend" – a non-logic, non-scientific, purely belief-based pseudo-heuristic aphorism without either sense or proof. So the U.S. fed the ISI, the Pakistani intelligence agency, arms and money for the mujahideen, the Islamic fundamentalist fighters, who eventually prevailed.

Then two decades later both the ISI and the mujahideen, rechristened as the Taliban and al Qaeda, caused all kinds of damage to the U.S., Europe, Africa, East Asia, and India. Again, one might argue that this U.S. policy was not belief-based but part of a carefully-calculated foreign policy strategy. But this could not have been true, since there was no follow-through plan on what to do with this religion-driven mujahideen/ISI machine once the Soviets left. Nor was there a plan on stabilizing Afghanistan once the Soviets left.

The war between Iran and Iraq was completely non-belief-driven. But the U.S. decided to again utilize the belief-driven rule of "the enemy of my enemy is my friend", and supplied Iraq with all manner of dual-use technology, conventional weapons, chemical and biological weapons technology, biological weapons themselves (anthrax), and intelligence on Iranian troop positions, although Saddam ended up using the poison gas on his own people as well as Iranians. This WMD support for Iraq would serve most conveniently for part of the public explanation for the U.S.'s belief-based invasion and occupation of Iraq a decade later, whose belief-based justification was only revealed several years later in interviews given by President Bush. His belief-based logic was that freedom and democracy were fundamental values that should not be denied the people of Iraq regardless of the cost or consequence. Of course, he was buttressed and reinforced by a cacophony of other belief-driven views by his administration that "evil" Iraq would fall like a house of cards, providing much to boast about – victory over one member of the "Axis of Evil" - views all held without benefit of vetted facts, investigation, or challenge. But like other-belief-based wars, that belief alone is never sufficient to garner support for the war, so other reasons have to be assembled. In this case, the overall theme was the war on terrorism, so it was thought it should be easy to tie the amount of weaponry that had historically passed from the U.S. to Iraq to a current terrorism threat. Since in the intelligence business, if you advertise what you want, you can get five guys willing to swear (for a price) that they saw Elvis having dinner with Marilyn Monroe and Adolf Hitler in downtown Baghdad with Saddam last week, this was readily accomplished. It's like the old lawyer joke – ask a lawyer what time it is and he responds "What time do you want it to be?" No inventing of information is required. You just have to not care too much about who you accept as intelligence sources, nor screen the information very carefully, which is what was done. A couple of decades ago someone in the U.S. reported that they had found a razor blade in a can of Coke. Then another report came in, and another. The total number of razor blades in cans ended up around 15, so you would think that this had to be a real problem. But after an investigation, it turned out that every single one of these reports was false – 15 separate, unconnected, individual fabricated reports. And there was no payoff involved here except some amount of fame or notoriety, or the opportunity to do some publicity damage. It represented a classic example of the difference between raw and thoroughly-verified intelligence information.

In this specific case, it was Rafid Ahmad Alwan, known by his German code name of "Curveball", who invented most all of the information about WMD in Iraq used by the U.S. to justify its intervention in order to obtain permanent asylum and/or residency, since he had embezzled money while in Iraq and was desperate to avoid going back. He had a degree in chemical engineering, although at the bottom of his class, and so had enough technical knowledge to fabricate superficially-plausible weaponry stories. Coming from an area renowned for producing the best rug salesmen in the world, Rafid produced stories which were simply unvetted, unvalidated, and unverified by a government which was not operating on a fact-based basis. It was a little like the government going into a holding tank in a jail full of drunks and saying: "Hey, have any of you guys had any solid contact with UFO's and extra-terrestrials? If so, we can not only permanently guarantee that you will never be arrested again, but will give you an unlimited line of credit at three locals bars. Oh, and by the way, we won't be doing any checking into what you will be telling us." And the beauty of both the WMD and UFO cases examples above, the government can "honestly" say – no information was faked to produce the final report – since the faking was all done by the source, not the government.

Rafid continues to live under police protection in Germany.

The U.S. invasion of Iraq was a classic example of the consequences of using belief-driven cognition as the basis for making decisions. Knowing that the decision to invade was being made on a non-factual basis, the intelligence information was screened on a belief-based basis – allowing sources supportive for the presence of WMD to be inadequately vetted and retained. Politically-inclined Iraqis who wanted U.S. support for their bid for power after the overthrow of Saddam concocted artificial stories about Iraq consistent with the U.S. belief-based view in order to curry favor. Iraqi's wanted the U.S. to occupy their country and would welcome them warmly. The belief-based view that Iraq wanted the U.S. to invade and occupy the country drove the absence of any plans by the Pentagon for control of civil order or military armaments post-invasion, and the absence of any occupation plan to operate the country effectively, restore its infrastructure, maintain a police force and local governments, maintain security, provide jobs, avoid sectarian violence, and deal with the intrinsic vacuum that the absence of a dictator in an innately tripartitely-schismed country.

A belief-based approach overlooked the credibility problems that the U.S. in general, and specifically Vice President Cheney, Paul Wolfowitz, and anyone connected with the first Gulf War had with the majority Shia population and Kurds that resided inside Iraq (not those few outside that the war planning was based on). President George H.W. Bush, speaking over the Voice of America radio system, had encouraged the Iraqi's to overthrow Saddam Hussein after the U.S. pushed Iraq out of Kuwait, but then Cheney as Defense Secretary did nothing when Saddam used helicopter gunships and ground troops to slaughter on the order of 10,000 Kurds and Shia and make refugees out of a million that had rebelled, creating enormous bitterness at what was felt was a double-cross by the U.S. The U.S. had almost no credibility as a consequence as an occupying power after the invasion. It was eerily-parallel to Stalin's treatment of the Warsaw uprising in August, 1944, encouraging the Poles to revolt against the Germans and then standing by while they were slaughtered. But Stalin was operating out of Chapter 1 of the Totalitarian Handbook - kill off all the patriots to make a subsequent communist state that much easier to install. Cheney's motives are as yet unannounced.

Operating on a belief-based basis resulted in the U.S. deciding that anyone associated with the old regime was automatically "bad", and by decree depriving them of their jobs and livelihoods and income – the military, police, government workers – basically anyone paid by the state. Desperate to support their families, many of these people would end up planting IED's, not for ideological reasons, but just for money for food. The basis for the selection of people sent to administer Iraq by the U.S. was not an intimate knowledge of Iraq, nor an intimate knowledge of their specialty, but rather absolute political loyalty to the Bush Administration and its belief-based policy. In other words, the sole criteria for the job was to pass a belief-based test. And strategically, probably the most telling sign that the invasion of Iraq was carried out on a belief-driven basis was the apparent absence of thought given to the gift it provided to the most dangerous country in the region – Iran. By removing Saddam and his completely secular Sunni Ba'ath party from control of Iraq, the U.S. in a few days did what Iran through a ten-year war had never been able to accomplish: the fundamentalist Shia powers in Iran now had a sympathetic Shia majority in Iraq to work with, something they may have never dreamed would have been possible. In a non-belief-based world, this outcome would have been avoided at most any cost.

As a result of so much of the thinking in Iraq being screened by belief-based cognition, it is logical that the results turned out as unfavorable as they did. Some people accuse the Bush Administration of changing its mind on the reasons for the Iraq invasion, but that is simply a commentary about the variety of public reasons provided by the government, not the President's private reasons of freedom and democracy for Iraq – these were never disclosed but also never wavered.

The U.S. invasion of Iraq and the German invasion of the Soviet Union had much in common – the belief-driven invasion justifications were identical.

Each invaded country would fall like a house of cards, limiting the duration to a month or two – the invaders being happily welcomed by the invaded populations. Intelligence information not in support of these premises was conveniently allowed to disappear. Working off the belief premises, neither country prepared for the conditions they would find – dust, mud, and cold (no winterized equipment or clothing) in the Soviet Union; chaos, sand, and resistance (inadequate armored vehicles and clothing) in Iraq. Both invading countries paid a catastrophic financial price for their decisions; limited in resources, fighting a full-out war on many fronts, Germany was unable to weather their belief-driven decision.

Assuming that the U.S. had suddenly found its Army in Iraq, but had been operating on a rational, logical, fact-based manner, civil order would have been preserved, preventing looting and the loss of so much electrical power among other things. Military armament bunkers would have been secured, preventing the wide dissemination of small arms, RPG's, and 155mm shells used in IED's. All the existing government institutions would have been maintained and left to a new Iraqi government to deal with; and security and jobs would have been the number one priority, as they would have been in any country at any time. Even if it had been the wrong invasion of the wrong country for the wrong reasons, there would have been minimal chaos and casualties if a non-belief-driven cognition basis had been utilized.

But it is not only nations who go to war for belief-driven, ends-justify-the means reasons. "Borrowing a page from U.S. foreign policy, I decided to send a message to a government that was becoming increasingly hostile, by bombing a government building and the government employees within that building who represent that government. Bombing the Murrah Federal Building was morally and strategically equivalent to the U.S. hitting a government building in Serbia, Iraq, or other nations.... Based on observations of the policies of my own government, I viewed this action as an acceptable option." This statement, part of a letter to Fox News by Timothy McVeigh, is not a reflection of someone "insane", or temporarily incapacitated by drugs or emotion. No, this was a cool, rational belief-based calculation by, most unfortunately, an entirely normal and typical human. He determined that the importance of his message, his goal, was entirely worth the means of sending and communicating it – bombing a building full of innocent people, most all unconnected to what he was aggravated about.

Eric Rudolph planted and exploded bombs at the Atlanta Olympics, at the lesbian nightclub the Otherside Lounge, and at an Atlanta clinic that provided abortion services "because I believe that abortion is murder, I also believe that force is justified ... in an attempt to stop it." An Army explosives expert, his bombs were filled with nails to maximize injuries to people, killing or wounding a total of 120 people at the three locations. The bomb at the abortion clinic was the means of accomplishing his goal - stopping the "holocaust" of abortion - an entirely reasonable and justified response from his perspective. Now Rudolph lacked McVeigh's pristine purity of belief, and in the 11 page justification that he submitted through his attorneys, he claimed that the Olympics bombing "was to confound, anger and embarrass the Washington government in the eyes of the world for its abominable sanctioning of abortion on demand." But since it was indiscriminately located and detonated, most likely people were injured and killed who may have been as fervently anti-abortion as Rudolph, or had never supported or participated in abortion in any way. He later apologized for this, indicating only that he recognized the absurdity of attempting to post facto justify what he had done. Now the bombing of the Otherside Lounge, filled with lesbians, presents a more serious problem. One would guess that it would be a tie between a nightclub full of lesbians and a nunnery full of Carmelite nuns as to who would least be in need of abortion services. Rudolph just refers to their "aberrant sexual behavior" – but since this behavior leads away from abortion, you would think he would send them some kind of reward and not a bomb.

The bottom line is that once you fill yourself with the self-righteous conviction that your end justifies any means, it is easy to get into what the military calls "mission creep" - expanding the scope of what you are doing to cover more and more under your umbrella of righteousness. This enabled Rudolph to pull in the Otherside Lounge because it bothered him – even though it had nothing to do with his cause. The French Revolution is the classic example – what started out as a spontaneous push for liberty and freedom ended in murder by mob rule – using the guillotine for public distraction and entertainment not unlike the way the Roman Emperors used games in the Coliseum.

In 2011 Anders Breivik shot and killed 76 children (and wounded others) whose parents were all members of the ruling party in Norway in order to shock the country into action: "Once you decide to strike, it is better to kill too many than not enough, or you risk reducing the desired ideological impact of the strike.... (my role) is not only a valorous resistance fighter, a one-man army, (but) a one-man marketing agency as well." His goal – to begin a war against all Muslims in Europe. Writing in a 1,500 page document (2083) combining explanation, motivation, and a weapons tutorial, Breivik explained that since in the next decade he expected Muslims to murder 30-40,000 people, and brutalize 3-4,000,000 more, including raping 1,000,000 women, any actions, any means, were acceptable, even causing all the nuclear reactors in Europe to explode, Chernobyl-style. "3.23 Cruel Nature of Our Operations ... Morality has lost its meaning in our struggle... Some innocent (people) will die in our operations... The needs of the many will always surpass the needs of the few.... We should not exceed ... 45,000 dead and 1 million wounded ... multiculturalists in Western Europe." Insane, a few tried to call him; but nothing could be more incorrect. Breivik is the classic belief-driven individual that has not the least reluctance to pursue any means to accomplish his goal, no matter how heinous or barbarous it might seem to an "unbeliever". Dedicated, driven, dangerous and deadly, perfectly capable of putting together and carrying out a flawless plan – sadly society is not always lucky enough to have people like this also visited by insanity.

Belief-driven cognition works because you first establish a belief which is the sieve or strainer or colored glass through which everything else is interpreted. You then add on to this belief a self-consistent set of logical steps that provides a payoff to the individual: "You need to join this Crusade to rescue your soul from eternal damnation," or "Join the crew of this slaving ship and we will be rich after a few trips to Africa," or "These Indians keep stealing our horses and cattle – they all have to go."

"The world has done just fine so far": even if you have some issue with it as a complete generalization, this is the point the skeptics will use to argue that things, taken in totality, are fine. But just over the span of the last 80 years, in the zenith of man's maturity as a civilization-refining sentient being, we have counted up on the order of 100 million civilian deaths due to belief-based thinking, with probably many times that injured and made homeless, and property damage that is inestimable. As the statisticians would point out, it is a bit unfair to query only the survivors if they think things are "fine". Those who were murdered or tortured to death are not getting a chance to vote. But for argument's sake let's assume for the moment that they are correct, that to date man has "overall" been able to manage his way to increasing relative mastery over nature, disease, and famine. But it is the qualifier "so far" that is in fact the critical concept – the key to everything. The unsaid implication is that the next 60,000 years will be, with a major change in technology, just a repeat of the last 60,000. As the clichéd analogy puts it, this is continuing to steer the boat by looking at the wake. Put another way, the author's father was from the mid-West and had many mid-West jokes, like the man who jumped off the ten story building: "How's it going?" they asked him as he passed the third floor. "So far, so good," he replied.

Most unfortunately, the future will not be anything like the past, neither qualitatively nor quantitatively, for a variety of reasons. All of man's 60,000 years of experience and skills will suddenly become not only obsolete but a handicap. Is man up for changing? It is his very nature that must change. If it took 60,000 years to get us here and a significant fraction of that to change again, we will run out of time.

In the last .1% of man's existence as a race, man's sustained success has removed all need for a belief-driven world. There are things not known to man certainly, but man now knows what he does not know. Man has weather models that work well for about five days, and then he has to drop back to macro models that defer to general trends and historical patterns. Forecasters know what makes the weather tick. They just can't tell for sure if all that means it is going to rain on you three weeks from today. Researchers and doctors know just about everything about how people function when they are well and when they are sick, except for syndromes that are rarely seen. They just don't know how to fix everything. They know in general the biomolecular processes that control life; not every single specific process but how general classes of processes work. They just can't control them (without making a bigger mess). Scientists and engineers know about metals, non-metals, materials, machines, electronics, equipment, and buildings, and can just about do whatever someone wants to pay for. A few things still seem "impossible", but most everything else is just an affordability issue. Economics, politics, sociology, even psychiatry are reasonably well-established. Refinements and new learning are added constantly across the board, making things work better and more affordable for more people, but there is no area left where belief is the prime mover, save for religion, but that is tautological.

For 60,000, or 4.5 billion, years, take your pick, the world was such a daunting and dangerous and unscientific place that it could only be successfully-faced when approached with a belief-driven set of perspectives. But now, science and logic and reason can address most every problem. But man is a belief-driven machine, proofed and validated over 60,000 years. You cannot engage in a discussion, or overhear someone over the media, or read a quote, and not on a daily basis come across the phrase "I don't believe in ...", and not in a religious context. But this statement is a self-declaration of obsolescence, of cerebral irrelevance, a confession of incompetence. The world is no longer a belief-based world – it is all facts and science, even if some of the science is very complicated and the data is diffuse. The world is round yet most everyone is huddled fearfully in one place, afraid they may fall off the edge. The pharmacy is full of antibiotics but everyone is still running around looking for a chicken for the blood offering to cure their children. The last ice floe has melted yet we are still optimistically paddling, hopefully searching the horizon for that white dot of ice. Belief is an anachronism; it is so "yesterday", yet belief *is* man. How embarrassing. How ominous.

So we have not a colossal collision, but a massive miss. It's now time for brain surgery and our man drives up in a bulldozer. Our man shows up for full hand-to-hand combat in the octagon and finds a chessboard. It's a Bayesian statistical inference challenge and our man arrives with his big black gun. Almost every problem today is attackable with rational and logical tools, but most problems today are at the same time complex, subtle, and nuanced.

152

But man's belief-based tool kit is not fact-based, or logic-driven, and so this mismatch means today's problems will either be kicked on down the road, or slapped with some belief-consistent, feels-right, politically-correct inappropriate "solution", either further postponing improvement or fostering further degradation.

Afterwords: Belief-Changing

Yes, as many of you are already noting, you can and do change your beliefs. Sometimes it is a gradual, time-based process – some people become more tolerant with age; others less. In other cases it is event-driven, sometimes facilitated by a person who has special credibility in general or in the context of this belief.

The most common way that people change beliefs is when they hold some general, social belief and then some event takes place that affects them personally. What before was an abstract concept is now intensely real, and attitudes can swing 180 degrees. You might be harshly anti-gay until your child announces they are one, or do not believe in mental health as a disease until it affects someone in your family, or do not believe in incarceration until a habitual criminal assaults your spouse, or don't think twice about health insurers until your child gets cancer and your insurance is dropped, or have positive feelings about human nature until a trusted friend disappears with half of your retirement money. All this was discussed in Chapter 8, Cognitive Dissonance.

This chapter is about belief-driven cognition. To first order, if you used to be driven by Belief 1, and suddenly you change and are now driven by Belief 2, you are still belief-driven. Wandering all over the belief landscape, as long as you do not leave, still leaves you belief-driven. Only by escaping into rationality land, populated with facts and logic, do we move away from this aspect of human nature.

Chapter 10
Hard-Wired Capabilities

I/O (Input/Output) Limits

You can go and purchase a vanilla computer nowadays with a quad-core processor – four individual CPU cores on one chip working in parallel, each core able to perform one instruction on 64 bits (8 bytes) of data at a speed of around three gigahertz, or three billion times a second, so your machine can eat data at the rate of just about 100 gigabytes per second.

Pretty damn impressive until you pop the hood and read the fine print that says that the disk buffer to CPU data rate is about 100 megabytes a second, a factor of 1,000 times slower. The transfer rate from memory is a little under two gigabytes per second, still 50 times slower. So you can process the data at light speed – you just can't get the data there in the first place. It's the same predicament that some lucky owners found themselves with when they acquired some of the most exotic muscle cars in the late 1960's – cars like the Shelby Cobra GT500, Chevelle 396, and Plymouth Hemi Barracuda. With 500 foot-pounds of torque but no traction control, touching the gas pedal generally meant the back tires were going to break loose and spin. Like the computer owner, it's an imbalance between the power processor and the input/output device. It's just not nearly as dramatic when the byte wheels spin.

The major reason for vehicle accidents of any type – aircraft, automobile, bus, train - is a distracted driver/pilot. If the driver is simply looking somewhere else, and vision is critical, then that is the whole story. But if the driver is paying "attention", and you begin adding in more and more sensory input, at a point that is very difficult to quantify numerically and may vary from person to person, the person can no longer absorb the information that is coming in, and begins to discard it in unpredictable ways.

You do not really "see" the visual information that enters your eyes – it is way more information than your brain can process. So it has developed all kinds of short-cuts that use the brain to fill-in the information that it cannot process. Like computer software that cannot afford to recreate each scene moment to moment from scratch, your mind decides for you that certain objects are effectively "unchanged" from moment to moment and leaves them as they are in your mind. It decides that other images are extraneous to what you are doing and you do not "see" those objects at all. Scientists have all kinds of fun with this, running experiments where they present subjects with images that stress these brain processes, and getting results that most everyone has seen. People see things that aren't there and cannot see things that are there. The problem is of course that you and your brain may not always be in agreement about what should be ignored and what should be tracked.

Studies of drivers who are texting on cell phones while driving show that they simply do not see certain objects in front of them – pedestrians and other vehicles for example. The brain just gets overloaded and has to be selective about the sensory information that it accepts from the outside world. This explains why distracted driving is the cause of accidents – drivers may be looking but simply do not "see" what is in front of them – the light turning red, a pedestrian, a car pulling out or changing lanes. Every sensory input – conversation with passengers, listening to the radio, talking on the phone, interacting with a video display, reading a map, newspaper, or anything else, or watching non-driving related activities outside the car (accident, fire, emergency vehicles, scenery) – are competition for and displaces what the driver really needs to be paying attention to – other vehicles, pedestrians, signage, and road hazards and conditions.

The Air Force is acutely aware of this. It minimizes and carefully engineers the sensory input that is presented to fighter pilots, because it knows from past experience that pilots would actually turn off critical systems because they could not deal with the information overload that they would face in combat situations. Training for professional pilots includes measuring their ability to maintain situational awareness at all times, meaning during emergencies and similar instances where the cockpit displays are giving constant error messages, the radio demands attention, and they have to fly the plane. Situational awareness is lost if a pilot cannot adequately keep track of everything that is going on and begins to miss critical information that threatens the safety of the flight. Many crashes have been caused by this. Because the ability of people to absorb data is limited, it is fairly easy to pass this limit, and not only are pilots in training rejected, but even pilots who are trained and experienced will lose their way. All it takes is for the pilot to spend too much attention on one system or problem, his input abilities will be saturated, and his awareness of what is going on in total will be impaired, sometimes fatally. This phenomenon is not fundamentally different from that of the driver of a ground vehicle, but it is studied more intensively and has a fancy name.

The average person with reasonable comprehension reads at about 200 words per minute. A few really good readers can do twice that. Through a combination of rigorous training and excellent memory a handful can do better than this, but at some point for everyone there is a rate/comprehension trade-off. Were we the cute little aliens in Close Encounters, we could listen to the eighty or so people playing in an orchestra or the 48 digital tracks within a popular music recording and absorb huge amounts of information aurally, but unfortunately it is not to be. Instead, we find that we have about the same limit for comprehending spoken words as we do for written, about 250 words per minute.

There were a lot of words available two thousand years ago – tens of thousands of works just in the Library of Alexandria, and it was not the only library in the city – and an almost uncountable number today. Yet man's reading speed appears unchanged.

Why? For 60,000 years, man has been designed to do one thing well, and that was not reading or listening. For most people for most of this time he was hunting, or foraging, or planting, or tending, or harvesting, or guarding, or building, or protecting, or carrying, or digging, or cutting, chipping, grinding, fishing, scraping, sewing, or walking. In other words, he was working on something important, trying to feed or clothe or house himself, stay alive, better himself and his family. Man is a problem-solving machine, a learning machine, and above all, a short-cut machine. Once someone found a way to do something, someone else found a way to improve it. Bows and arrows went from fire-hardened wooden points to bone and then to pressure-shaped flint. Native Americans could put an arrow the depth of the feathers into a buffalo; the distance record in the midst of the Renaissance for an arrow was about one mile. They had barely figured out how to work stone 4,500 years ago and then the pyramids at Giza were constructed, an engineering marvel even for today. But man's skills that are the basis of his species superiority are also short cuts – he does not waste time in a lot of analytical study to determine if the bear and her cubs are something that he should eat or vice versa, or if off hunting or fishing he does not agonize over the appropriate time to fire the arrow, throw the spear, or hook the fish. Man is a decision machine – he can size up the situation before it overwhelms him or disadvantages him and take the requisite action.

Language – The Advantage to Die For

What is the key discriminating difference between man and dolphin, or whale, who have similarly-sized brains and make vocalized communications? And why did man wholly displace Neanderthals, with whom he shared the planet for over 100,000 years, as well as Denisovans, probably for just as long, as well as other man-like species that we have not yet identified? And for that matter, why did all these other earlier versions of man completely vanish, with no small cluster or foothold remaining intact anywhere, not a vestige? Argue if you must, and you will, but the unbridgeable advantage man has is the ability to create, think, speak, write, and read complex symbolic languages. Neanderthals, had they just been lacking a little bit of this or that, would still be around today – there are tribes and cultural groups of mankind who fit this description perfectly. But

156

language-less – no human group has so survived intact. Imagine the contact between a language-incapable group and man – trade (barter-based: how many of this for that), planning, hunting together, division of labor, avoiding conflict, conflict resolution – all would be extremely difficult if not impossible. So these non-language groups would be avoided, shunned – benign neglect, nothing vicious or malicious, just not worth the hassle and confusion to deal with. And they would be out-competed, out-hunted, and lack the opportunity for sharing technology advancements (weapons, clothing, hunting techniques). In spite of the communication impasse, a few Neanderthal women would be secured as mates, and vice-versa, for good and for unpleasant reasons, which would account for their five percent presence in our genes today (although it currently seems that only male offspring were fertile). The same thing occurred with the Denisovans in Russia, which have a five percent representation in some Pacific Islander genes. Survival 60,000 years ago was not automatic – saddled with a measurable disadvantage, you would slowly wither and vanish, and the Neanderthal could do no other. Language was an advantage to die for, and they did.

The latest modern spin is that humans violently made war on Neanderthals, Denisovans, and other non-human hominids, and thus erased them from the historical record. But that is not the perspective that you would have if you were trying to survive 60,000 years ago. At that time, there was about one person for every 10,000 square miles of usable land. It took 3,750 years for a family of two, on the average, to increase to the size of four. It was a dangerous, threatening, lonesome, inexplicable, unanswerable time. Bumping into another small group of human-like people, violence would be the last thing you would be thinking – there were already sufficient threats for everyone courtesy of Mother Nature. Imagine arriving at a stream where 1,000 pound Kodiak brown bears are fishing salmon out of the water – will your first instinct be to rush in and try to steal the salmon from the bears? Well, unfortunately, today it might well be (see Chapter 18), but 60,000 years ago, humans would have simply moved to a bear-free stretch of stream. So it would be with human-like contact – if they presented a threat, they would just be avoided. But the much more likely goal of human and hominid contact would be what they could gain from each other. But if one group could speak and the other could not, the relationship would not work well, and the most likely result would be love, not war, with the most eligible women from the Neanderthal and Denisovan groups joining the humans, since the human males would appear to be much better providers and mates. This loss of reproductive capacity may have hastened or even caused the demise of these other groups, since the normal attrition rate was so high in these times.

So Mother Nature provided man with an unassailable advantage, one that all previous versions of himself, lacking, had blossomed, flowered, fruited, but then were left to fall on fallow ground, forming the foundation for the next incremented improvement. But with the gift of language, a tool, a skill of incredible power, Mother Nature slipped in one tiny caveat, one unnoticed and unremarked on by man for all of his 60,000 years. The rate at which words can be moved through man's consciousness was capped at 250 per minute. 60,000 years ago, man signed this contract without a hesitation – he may have thought a 250-word-hour was a busy day – and having the power of the tool of language was the key to kingdom of the Earth.

The Information-Driven/Knowledge-Gated New World

Reading, and having your survival based on reading – this is a phenomenon relatively new (on a 60,000 year scale) – and one impacting a very small percentage of the population. For most everyone, the 250 or so words per minute of everyday speech was sufficient for most purposes. Beginning about 3,500 year ago, only the monks, scribes, writers, and historians ever dealt with words full-time until the printing press got into full-swing about 3,000 years later. People began to read after that to be sure, starting with religious scripture, but they did not read to survive in the sense that the fast readers lived and the slow readers died, or that they earned a living by reading. Eventually books became inexpensive enough that they were used in schools and home libraries. To get to a time where people made their living using information in any significant way, where you could make a case that reading speed is germane to survival in some vague, soft sense, you really have to get to within 50 years of the present. In other words, the speed at which information is gathered has never been one of Mother Nature's priorities for man.

But today, in just a flash of time for Mother Nature, the hard limit on the ability to absorb written information has become a fundamental limitation for man. Not only is there enough existing written material to keep someone reading non-stop for their whole life, there is enough absolutely critical information that they must know to keep them reading for their whole life. And to make it worse, there are enough written and video distractions to keep them distracted their whole life, so they could be engrossed and occupied forever on entertainment and irrelevancies, never learning a thing of constructive value. So where even just a century ago the only issue would be making sure that the citizenry, primarily through schooling and parental coaching and example, read the proper books along with a few improper ones, today the problem is indescribably worse. Technology has made distractions that compete with reading socially and personally helpful and constructive materials so attractive and ubiquitous and easy to find that the distractions appear to be the clear winners.

The world is much more complicated and inter-connected today; the sciences and technologies much broader and deeper. Just to keep up, one would have to learn about more things more intensively than ever before. But with all the distractions, the opposite is occurring. If man's ability to absorb information, his reading speed, were to have expanded over the centuries by a factor of five or ten to compensate, then a balance might be expected, but that is not the case. Man is using the same 3/4" garden hose to fight fires just like his great-grandfather did, but instead of the campfire his great-grandfather had to douse he now faces a forest fire, and on top of that he keeps turning around to see the cool new movie previews and user videos on the massive screen behind him, letting the water spill uselessly on the ground each time he does.

Statistics are just numbers, but they help put some vague perspective on the dimensionality of the challenge. Maybe there were a million different scrolls in all the libraries back 2,000 years ago – we will never know. Most were fiction – you could read the history and science (what counted for science) works fairly readily. Until the printing press made them affordable, books were hand-copied and unavailable until a few hundred years ago, and even then found only in public libraries and the private homes of wealthy individuals. Today there are well over 100 million books. Who cares how good many of them are? Even if only 1% of them are highly valuable you are never going to get to them. Even a list of the most important books of all time to read is much too long to deal with. Then there are journals, one or two for every specialty you can imagine, whether science, economics, political science, or medicine. There are survey articles contained in weekly and monthly magazines that encapsulate for non-specialists the latest state of a particular discipline, like how the immune system works, or how the universe got to where it is today (dark energy et al), or all about epigenetics. There are new books, and articles re-examining people, history, and economic and political theories that are one year old or a thousand years old that are published daily. Then there is the news – newspapers, TV news, cable news, radio, satellite, web-based news and opinion sites, blogs – in 190 or so countries. You have a challenge to keep current on the news in one subject area in one country if you spent all your free time on it.

You used to be able to get a degree say in electrical engineering, and to first order any two electrical engineers were interchangeable. Today, saying someone is an electrical engineer is about as helpful as saying they are human and breathing. They could be analog or digital or RF; control systems or power systems or AI systems. They could be Java-fluent, or HTML-fluent, or fluent in C, or none of the above. How about doctors? Like engineers, most doctors used to be be general practitioners. Then a few obvious specialties began to show up - surgery, neurology, ophthalmology, internal medicine, orthopedics, obstetrics/gynecology, pediatrics, psychiatry. But those have become even more finely divided, and there are now sub-specialties within specialties, like surgeons turning into neurosurgeons, and then into surgical neuro-oncologists. What does this all mean? To cope with the increasing complexity that the modern world presents, man cannot learn faster, so he has to be content with covering a smaller area well. Whether it is medicine, or science, or engineering, or finance, or history, or economics, man has to keep dropping back, reducing the footprint he has to digest, to prevent himself from drowning in details that a wider perspective would require. And all this is driven by his fixed ability to read and learn, a limit installed 60,000 years ago that then was never remotely strained, and now is a constant bottleneck.

Well, not to worry, say the optimists (belief-driven individuals from Chapter 9), what we will do is line up everyone, each with their 3/4" hose, and have them all play it on the same forest fire at the same time – that will solve the problem. In other words, everyone will just learn a little bit about the world (but enough so they personally will be saturated) on some coordinated basis, pre-planned and organized by some unspecified super-wise intelligence in the sky, and through this carefully-orchestrated effort all the bases will be covered. Sort of divide and conquer taken to the extreme. And that is in fact what is done in companies and organizations with a common purpose, tied together with a charter or financial incentives or some combination. Everyone at a law firm or financial institution all gets rich together by agreeing to do things in a certain manner – that does tend to work fine.

But these organizations have a narrow charter and focus. What about everything else? Societies, cities, states, countries, the world? There is no charter that everyone signs up for, or financial incentives for performance. There are just the very-hard-to-read fine-print responsibilities of being a good citizen to your town/borough/county/state/country/continent/world. The benefits even for your country are often intangible and the obligations can be tangibly onerous, unless your country has a very strong social safety net. Are people going to repeat the mistakes of the past, recorded in easy-to-read form if you bother with history, that they have no apparent time or motivation to read? Are people going to take the time to do research on complicated problems when 140 character solutions are so easy to find? All you have to do is look around you for the answer. People are not spending their free time cramming on science and economics. They are much more likely to be using some incredibly important app on their phone like checking in, or checking a price, or texting, or involved in critical correspondence with a social networking site, or watching a video, or playing a video game, or listening to digital music. There are too many distractions, and people feel they are already too busy and tired, to feel responsible to be doing more civic

160

"homework". If they say "clean coal" aren't you most likely just going to buy it since it rolls nicely off the tongue and sounds so heavenly, like "worry-free weight-loss", or "20% annual returns on your investment", or "guaranteed to ...."? What about politics in the U.S. where literally over one billion dollars are spent in a national election, all of it targeted at man's irrational side? You will not find detailed fifty-page position papers produced with this money; instead ads that either judgmentally-tag (Chapter 7) their proponent with positive values or the opponent with negative values. Disinformation, misleading information, deceitful characterizations – these are the meat and potatoes, the sushi and sashimi, the burrito and taco of political campaigns. Yet to make an informed decision, an immense investment is demanded – studying the issues, the positions, and the strength, weaknesses, and capabilities of each candidate. Not only do few have the time to do this, but campaigns do not want this to be done, and take pains to ensure that all campaign and issue ads stay away from facts and heel closely to emotion. And in American politics, electioneering does not just happen near elections; it is a continuous process. Even global issues – trade, currency valuation, tariffs, pollution, piracy (both up-close-and-personal and at-a-distance), trademark infringement, global climate change, water issues, arms reduction, control of nuclear material – are often subject to national politics not to mention the daunting problem of dealing with the complexities of the issue itself.

It is the worst of all possible scenarios. Man's ability to absorb information is a hard-wired limit, bred into him by Mother Nature through 60,000 years of experience. The modern world is not only full of complex problems and innumerable technologies that require proportionately more information to comprehend and master and to remain current on, but it is replete with the most appealing distractions that are instantaneously and ever available, no matter your location. Messages purposefully designed to appeal to man's irrational side and force him to make judgmental and not logical decisions abound, often outnumbering the boring unattractiveness of facts and statistics. To keep up with today's world, man needs the ability to absorb information at a rate that is at least ten times his actual capability, if not a hundred times. But this is not going to happen for – what – another 30,000 years; 60,000 years?

Can the model work where everyone gets their 3/4" garden hose and plays it on the same forest fire at the same time in order to extinguish it? In principle, on singular global or national challenges, sure. But as has been pointed out elsewhere in this book, man has conquered the planet unconditionally, absolutely, but has left it ungoverned, in chaos, with no one in charge, no one steering, no one navigating. There is a United Nations, but to pretend that it is "running the world" has no real traction. Ad hoc international bodies to deal with problems like global climate change and carbon emissions fare poorly, since most countries are taking their 3/4" garden hose and using it for their own internal benefit. Eliminating refrigerants based on CFC technology, which were destroying the world's ozone layer, was the only global victory that can be claimed. Unfortunately, this was probably due to the very few companies involved and relatively minor cost impact (when spread over everyone). If the forest fire gets so large and close to everyone's homes that the wallpaper inside starts peeling off the walls, will that be the catalyst that will get everyone to point their garden hose at the same fire? Maybe, but it might also be too late, and the water pressure might have fallen to too low a value by then (too many problems to solve at the same time).

Chapter 11
Self-First Orientation

The game show <u>Jeopardy</u> has been on network television in the U.S. six days a week for over 40 years. In the final round, contestants can wager all of their earnings during the game on the final question, doubling them with a correct answer, or losing them all (or the amount they elect to wager) if they answer incorrectly. The winner will generally take home between $15,000 and $40,000, so there is a lot riding on the final question and the wagering.

The typical situation, going into the final round, will find that if the person with the second largest total wagers all of his money, and the person with the most money wagers enough to match the person in second place wagering all their money. Assuming they both answer correctly, they will end up tied. In this case, they will both receive, not split, the prize money, say $30,000, and both come back the next day to play again.

But if the person in first place wagers one additional dollar, so if both he and the person in second win, his total will exceed the person in second by that single dollar, so say in this case $30,001 versus $30,000, then the person in second will only take home $2,000, and will not come back to play again. The difference for the second-place person is $28,000 and the opportunity to play again.

With about 250 games per year, how many times would you expect the person with the largest amount of money to allow the person in second place to take home the money that they earned in the game, rather than betting the extra dollar and taking all of it but $2,000 away? 50% of the time, 20%, 10%? No, not even close. Maybe once a year does someone with the most money allow the person in second place to keep what they earned. All the other 249 times the person in second place is screwed out of their money by the person with the highest total winnings going into the final round.

Now what does the person with the most money in the game personally gain in exchange for taking this money away from the person in second place (and the extra $1 that they wager)? If they are consistently taking $30,000 or more money away from them, it must be a powerful tradeoff. Well, what the winner gets is the elimination of the second place person from the next day's contest, and their replacement with someone drawn at random from the pool of future <u>Jeopardy</u> contestants. The person with the most money is guessing that the random contestant that shows up the next day will be a less-competent competitor than the person that they faced in second place that day, a person who was capable enough to be able to tie them in the game's final round.

Now this is no artificial experiment performed in devious fashion by college professors on starving college students with $5 up for grabs. And this is not one of those same experiments where the winner has an opportunity to share some of his winnings with someone else. No, this winner keeps everything. And these are really smart adults, all employed, and huge amounts of money are at stake. And they are all judging that the possibility of a slightly weaker competitor tomorrow is worth depriving their fellow competitor today of tens of thousands of real dollars. Only slightly generalizing, this says that the slightest potential advantage for an individual, even an extremely smart one, is worth depriving his fellow citizens of huge amounts of real money. In other words, man is inherently and essentially self-first oriented. It is his nature to take any advantage for himself, no matter how minimal, even if the cost to his fellow citizens or society at large is massive. Or, put another way, not only do "I" have to win, but everyone else has to lose, or else it is not really a "win". If the winner decides to tie with the second place contestant, he has to tell himself and all his acquaintances that he did not win – he tied. A tie - a murky, vague, on-the-fence, who-knows-what outcome. But if he adds one more dollar to his wager, he earns a clean win – he is the winner – unmistakable, unambiguous, untarnished, unimpeachable. It is man's nature to put himself first, and everyone else second. No cleaner test exists.

If you are interested, you can go and endlessly read about variations of the Jeopardy game in the literature on game theory, a branch of applied math. There are both theoretical treatments as well as experiments, using mostly college students as mentioned earlier. But it is not clear that college students, being very young and playing for small amounts of money in clearly an environment that is artificial, are representative of man in general. So the author is not going to cite these results, which may not appear convincing. For what it is worth, their results also show that man is inherently "selfish."

One special case, often called the "tragedy of the commons", is where a group of people share a limited but common resource. If they individually manage their consumption, the resource will last. If one or more people over-consume or hoard, the resource will be depleted and everyone will suffer, or in the extreme case, expire. The classic extreme examples are people with limited water in a lifeboat at sea, or stranded in a desert environment, or with limited fuel or oxygen and snowed in at high altitudes. But more boring and much more common cases historically are holding back some wheat (or equivalent foodstuff) to plant the next year instead of eating it all now. This may sound simple unless there is a famine and little else to eat. A more current version are water rights – everyone taking as much as they can from the river or groundwater so that the people further downstream or later in time find that they have nothing.

In all of these "commons" cases, the result is just as you would imagine - enough people always maximize their own share so that the common resource vanishes - unless some explicit constraint is placed on the group. That usually takes the form of the group agreeing to put the resource under the controlled issuance of some person or committee where an allocation scheme can be developed and implemented. The only other exception is a group that has agreed to all live under some rigid set of standards that will honor the preservation of a "commons" store of unguarded goods; for example, monks in a monastery. But for everyone else, only through this technique of sequestration and control of the common resource can the common good be preserved. Left to his own nature, man will quickly sack any shared resource save it is limitless. All the computer game theory models show this to be true, all the lab experiments confirm this, and all historical cases support this without exception.

Simplistic moral judgments that some flaw in man may lie behind this should be withheld for the moment. The reasons why this "tragedy" occurs first need to be explored – and a tragedy it may not be. Here is how it would look from the perspective of 60,000 years of experience:

The first reason that one person would take more than their share of the common resource is, as they say in the movies, just business, not personal. If Thog takes as much as he can of a limited resource, he can then trade it to his fellow citizens for other valuable commodities, since its worth will greatly increase as it becomes more scarce. The second reason is a peremptory action – Thog is thinking about taking more than his fair share so he can use it for trading later, which means his neighbor Rog is also thinking about it, which means Thog better act now before Rog gets to it first. The third reason is equity – Thog has 11 people in his family group; Rog has two. Thog either feels the allocation method is "unfair," or is concerned that the method that will be suggested/imposed will be "unfair," since Rog's brother is part of the group making the allocation rules, and so he takes what he feels is the appropriate amount for his group for his needs, which is different from what Rog would think he needs. The fourth reason is also equity, and is the reverse of the third reason. Rog sees that Thog seems to have more of this scarce resource than he should, and realizes that he is probably "cheating" on the allocation rules; so as to not have his own family deprived inequitably, Rog starts taking more of the resource so he feels he is on an equal footing with Thog. Whether he "needs" it or not is irrelevant – research has shown that man judges much more on an relative/equity basis than on an absolute basis.

Now, the four reasons above are all rational. They have nothing to do with being "unethical", or being "bad", or "anti-social". In each case man is making a calculation, and determining what is best for himself and his family. But man is not going to allow himself and his family to come out last, or even taking the risk of last. He is going to make sure that he is worst-case tied with everyone else, and best-case on top. In the forefront of his mind, survival is the issue.

Now let's look at the more normal situation – just a typical day over the past 60,000 years. Every situation had potential risk, whether it was just a short walk to collect water; or a longer one looking for game, fruit, or vegetables; or the birth of a baby; or surviving illness; getting everyone through the winter; judging the intentions of the new group of humans a mile away; everyone sleeping through the night or taking turns with a watch. For most of the past 60,000 years, it was extremely tough going. The population growth was almost unnoticeable. Even if you tried your best to put the welfare of yourself and your family first, you would not always survive. But if you chose not to put yourself first, most likely you never made it. Acting casual, or blasé, or even magnanimous, would have left your genes in the dust. So eventually the only people who were left were those who were most competent at putting themselves and their families first; those who were self-first oriented. Not because they were bad, or evil, or selfish, but because it was a prerequisite for survival. And as was pointed out in Chapter 7, for much of this time each little group of people were in islands of territory 2,000 to 4,000 square miles in extent, so they spent most of their time struggling against nature rather than each other. Plus, almost every prey out there was less dangerous and provided more value than taking on another man, who for most of the time had very little to offer but could put up quite a fight. And as male lions appear to have quickly learned, nothing is more dangerous in a dangerous world than being injured – you cannot hunt food, and you cannot defend yourself. The lion's solution of course is to have the lionesses do all the dangerous hunting work for them, a course of action not plausibly feasible for man. So until man came a soft target – lots of value and not well-armed – which would have been within about 7,000 or so years of today, man would have expended all of his efforts to better himself by pounding against the elements that Mother Nature arrayed against him. The self-first nature that man thence developed was not at the expense of his fellow man, but simply a natural result of making the best of the hand that Mother Nature had dealt him. It has only been recently, recent when using a 60,000-year clock, when man suddenly explosively filled the world with his kind, and his constructions, that man's nature of putting self-first meant that another human, instead of Mother Nature, was most likely to bear the consequence of any action of his. It is not malice, or evil, it's just statistics – there used to be just 70 thousand people, and if you captured all the deer, or dumped your garbage, or ate all the grapes, or set the forest on fire, no one got hurt or even noticed. But today, there are 7,000,000 thousand people, and if you do any of those same things, it's on the news and you're cited, indicted, and possibly spited.

Like the raccoon, coyote, bear, wolf, great white shark, and mountain lion – man means man no harm. Man has just reproduced and built structure upon structure so that he has filled up much of the livable (for man anyway) world with his footprints. Today, if a great white shark, bear, wolf, or man just acts like he has been acting for the past 60,000 years (or 10 million years for some of the others), there is bound to be a conflict, because man has put himself in harm's way. Said another way, it is just a "degree of crowding" problem. Man's societal word now for this behavior in man is "selfish" - but that is only in reference to the other 7,000,000 thousand humans crowding the world of today. 30,000 years ago man was just trying to survive, and this behavior, a self-first orientation against the world surrounding him, was not only appropriate but a necessity for survival.

But today, what was appropriately an asset for the past 60,000 years – man's self-first nature – now abrasively grits, abrades, shackles, encumbers, and aggravates the operation of modern societies, as this trait flourishes as selfishness. Best case it is what game theory terms a zero sum game – what an individual gains from his selfish behavior is equivalent to the collective loss on the part of everyone else. Worst case, through leverage an individual's selfish actions cause societal damage that far outweighs the gains that they obtain. In game theory, that is a negative sum game.

Watching a bird's egg hatch, a miracle of nature unfolds. What was just the raw material for an omelet a few weeks earlier cracks open the shell and emerges as a baby bird; damp, featherless, unable to feed itself, fly, or even walk, it is helpless against any predator. It is capable of only one thing – murder. Centering its back against each remaining unhatched egg in the nest, it slowly pushes the egg up the side of the nest, keeping its back tilted toward the edge of the nest so the egg stays in place. When the egg reaches the top of the nest the chick nudges it over the side where it falls to the ground, ending any chance of life for its sibling. The process is repeated until all the eggs are removed. The bird that does this is the cuckoo – blessed at birth by Mother Nature with the innate desire and drive for fratricide, the most supreme form of self-first behavior in the animal kingdom. If Mother Nature will go this far, it should not be too surprising that less emphatic forms of self-first behavior are built into man as well as other creatures.

Chapter 7 discussed man's compulsion to seek short-cuts, and that the world's oldest profession - crime - was a product of this drive. It is much faster and easier to just take what your fellow man has worked for than to perform the same work yourself. But this tendency toward crime as a short-cut is reinforced and enhanced by man's self-first attitude, which says that he is naturally going to take from his neighbor's store of goods if that will benefit himself and his family. So these two aspects of man's basic nature – seeking short-cuts and a self-first attitude – align and converge and add, making crime the most prominent and consequential example and symptom of man's self-first attitude playing out in a world full of his fellow man. For 60,000 years, man could step out of his lodgings and take anything that he could catch or find for his own betterment, and it was at Mother Nature's expense. Today, for most men, when he leaves his house or apartment he is surrounded by the property of others – it is hard to find anything valuable offered by Mother Nature. Social standards and physical penalties work for many, but where they do not, crime against property and people are the perpetual consequence.

Other examples are more limited in scope but just as devastating for those affected. An individual elects to either not maintain the automobile they commute in; or drive while texting; or reading, or speeding, or under the influence, crash into a big-rig truck, and add one hour to the commute of 50,000 other commuters. A few drivers elect to drive without any liability insurance, or hit-and-run if they get in an accident, and they raise the rates for every other driver in the country. A few physicians practice unprofessionally, and a few attorneys make a living by suing, and everyone's medical costs are raised excessively. A few large financial firms decide that leveraging their investments 20:1 (borrowing $20 for every $1 the firm chips in) is not enough to earn a sufficient number of millions of dollars in pay per partner, so they go to 30:1; and then they realize that they could make a few million dollars more per partner by going to 40:1 in leverage, which they do, and then it all crashes, and everyone in the country loses literally trillions of dollars in value from their investments that they depend on for their retirements, and many lose their jobs, and many local and state governments lose investments of public monies that had been accumulated, causing a reduction in public services for all those affected.

Mortgage brokers receive a commission when the loan papers are signed and the loan goes through, regardless of whether the borrowers can afford the loan or it is a wise investment for the lender. So using so-called Alt-A loans which do not require income verification, some mortgage brokers suggest income levels to their applicant borrowers that will allow them to qualify for the loan, even though they are higher than their actual income, write them on the application, and when the loan is approved, the broker obtains his commission. Banks collect these loans into large pools and sell them to buyers as investments, who have not a clue that they are buying a portfolio laced with vaporware. When the large financial institutions crash, they cause the job and housing markets to stumble, putting all these borrowers in a position where they not only cannot afford their house payments, but their mortgage exceeds their home's market value. This creates a runaway unstable scenario – the recession caused by the financial collapse freezes the housing market, which then has an inventory of houses dumped into it by people who either cannot afford their houses or walk away from a negative equity situation. This excessive inventory causes house prices to drop, which puts more owners in a negative equity situation, which puts more houses on the market. People who have lost their jobs or see others lose their jobs and see house prices falling decide this is a bad time to buy a house, so demand falls. The constant demand that had been coming from speculators who had been buying and selling while the market was rising vanishes abruptly. So all on account of a few selfish brokers, most everyone in the country has lost 25% (some as much as 70%) or so in the value of their home, for most people, their largest single asset.

Most critically, the U.S. Treasury Secretary and his advisers, arguably either possessing or having access to the most insightful and sophisticated financial acumen on the planet, have to assess the relative impact of "saving" Lehman Brothers or letting it fail. Now while Lehman to the average American sounds like just another financial company, for someone in the business Lehman is to the U.S. banking and financial services sector like the cardiovascular system is to you - it is everywhere and does everything - if it shuts down, you die. But these ultra-complex interactions and dependencies, a poster child example of what the modern world is all about, are not part of the decision-making. No, it is the 60,000 year-old man who is doing the considering, deciding that they cannot save "everyone", so they will just let Lehman fail. Every single banker and financial sector worker in the world that night then looks in the mirror and says "If Lehman can fail, my institution can fail," and the next morning they all become ultra-conservative, ceasing to grant credit and loans or only giving them if you do not need them. And so the economy contracts viciously as people can no longer obtain credit for their businesses or personal lives. If you remove the decisions that led to world wars, this was plausibly the single most costly and disastrous decision in the history of the world. And it was made not by amateurs, or imbeciles, or through some accident or mistake, but by the most experienced, knowledgeable, and sophisticated people about modern, ultra-complex economic systems, and they could not get it right.

Every year in the U.S., several thousand people, who were in the wrong place at the wrong time, have a driver under the influence, driving distracted, speeding away from the scene of a crime, or speeding for some other reason plow into their car or their bicycle or themselves, and a family loses a mother or daughter or father or all three. These drivers are intentionally doing what is good for them – acting self-first. Were they the only ones on the planet, there would not be a problem. But with the world full of others, any given individual's rights end where the next individual's rights begin, and this consideration does not match up well in a self-first world.

It is probably a waste of the reader's time to make long list of self-first, or selfish, behavior that is evident in modern society. Each of us is in contact

169

with an aspect of it many times of day, whether some form of road rage, discourteous driving, people cutting in line, people being deceitful to gain advantage, or people selling things that do not work as advertised. The cohesiveness and common backgrounds and cultural norms of a given society can suppress this facet of human nature depending on their relative strengths, but it is "treating the symptom, not the disease." Like all the other fundamental natures of man, the characteristic of self-first has remained unchanged; it is the world itself that has changed – and changed through man's own hand.

Chapter 12
Ease of Adaptability

Background

Recently <u>The Wall Street Journal</u> had an article about red deer in a wildlife preserve that straddles the old Cold War border of Germany and Czechoslovakia, which until 1989 was bisected by an electrified, very serious, steel fence. As you might imagine, deer approaching the fence from either east or west would have to eventually meander back toward their approach direction, since the fence was impassable. Biologists today track the movements of the deer with radio collars, and you might wonder whether the deer have any memory of the fence. Any memory, no; only memory, yes. Only two deer out of hundreds, and out of twenty years, have ever crossed the border. Both deer are probably seeing the deer psychiatrist as this is written. Part of this behavior is attributed to the deer, like other grazing animals, always following in the tracks of their predecessors, wearing a deeper rut in the same trails. The other is just retained memory of where their mothers' took them, incorporated and conserved.

Mother Nature had a decision to make when she invented animals, and she went to one extreme on adaptability – zero, none. Animals are a perfected execution machine – they will perform the required response to each situation precisely as Mother Nature programmed them to. Adaptability would imply some built-in variability, some degree of self-programming competency, but that is absolutely absent. Mother Nature determined, most likely through the inherent elimination feature of evolution, that the most effective expression of her design concept was purity – the optimal animal paradigm was the pure blend of instinct and stimulus/reaction, unchanged and unperturbed by modifications in the world around them. Deep, strong, pure consistency proved superior to a shallower but possibly somewhat more flexible nature. Now the risk is, should the world change dramatically, 90% or more of these species disappear, but while the world is stable, they excel. Mother Nature went with climate-specific optimization.

There may be objections to this by people who say, wait a minute, look at rats and racoons – they are extremely adaptable – they are completely at home in modern urban and suburban environments. While it appears that they have "adapted," they actually have not, if by the word "adapted" you mean that they have made a "change" in their fundamental behavior. While the author detests getting into Clintonesque word-splitting discussions, because the word "adaptable" is being applied to humans, the word has to have its definition re-confirmed here. Adapt means to be able to change or transform to meet a new set of conditions. Used here, it means that after the adaptation, there is a substantive, fundamental difference in the thing that adapted; it is not the same item as the pre-adaptation version.

So for an analogy, let's compare a sheet of plywood, a sheet of ice the same size as the plywood, and a blanket. Say you want to wrap yourself up with something because you are cold. Neither the ice nor plywood are helpful because they are rigid. But the blanket, because it is flexible, can be wrapped and folded to fit any form. But the blanket did not adapt itself to your form, any more than the plywood refused to adapt. It is still a blanket – it is just that by its very nature, made of thin, woven fabric, it could readily conform to any shape. The plywood and ice cannot, due to their nature. But, if you want to melt the ice to turn it into water to drink to stay alive, or into steam to run a turbine to make electricity, you can. You cannot do that with the blanket or plywood. So the ice can adapt to different situations by heating it, or cooling the water and making ice again. It can be transformed into something completely different from what it was before – with no resemblance or memory of its earlier version. So the ice/water/steam are adaptable; the blanket and plywood are not.

There are just not enough words to be able to narrowly restrict their usage to only certain meanings. But for the purposes of this chapter, adaptable is being used to mean a fundamental change in the thing being changed, in this case man. If something retains and conserves what it is, and instead utilizes its inherent nature to cope with and work around the changes in its habitat, then it is not adapting. It is succeeding, but only because the habitat changes are within those that its nature can absorb.

What occurs in the case of animals like the rat is that their fundamental nature is such that they can successfully cope with a variety of habitats. They are nocturnal, omnivorous, have high reproductive rates, and need no special environments for their living quarters. Rats have spent millions of years developing the skills that enable them to avoid foxes, coyotes, wolves, hawks, eagles, snakes, and other predators, all more competent and dangerous than man. They have had to endure climate changes and resulting environmental shifts much more severe than having to live inside a building or sewer.

An analogy might be finding yourself marooned on a desert island and finding one steel tool with you. Would you rather have a knife or a hammer? Most everyone would choose a knife, as it can do many more things than a hammer can do if it is all you have to fall back on. But the knife is not more adaptable than a hammer, since neither one can change its form; it is rather that its basic nature enables it to be put to a wider variety of uses in such a desperate and needy situation. The knife is more useful, on a wider scope of critical tasks; but the knife itself is technically not "adapting" - it remains immutable. In the same sense a rat is like a knife and a mountain gorilla is like a battleship; none change their nature, but a knife and a rat can be used on or are able to use a much greater variety of things or circumstances than a mountain gorilla or battleship, which by their very nature require very restrictive environments and narrow uses.

But if this seems too hair-splitting subtle, it does not really matter. Human adaptability is all psychological, mental, while animal adaptability, even if it were to exist, would have to have been behavioral. Humans do not change their fundamental nature either; their innate skills enable them to cope with an unlimited set of circumstances and challenges.

The Grass is Greener

Ask someone the time period, including today, that they would choose to be alive if they had the choice. A variety of answers will result, but a large number of people will select a historical period - classical Athens, or Rome in the height of the Empire, a Middle Age of knights and castles, pre-revolution France, or early twentieth century. Often the preference is to live as a member of the royalty or nobility. Seldom would someone choose their current situation.

The reason that a previous time is selected is that the person has adapted to their present situation, regardless of how good or bad it really is when compared to the past. Once adapted, today becomes the baseline, the starting point for evaluating any other time. People assume that they can maintain what they like about the present time, and they then look to improve the things that they dislike about today. Hordes of servants, living in castles, luxurious furnishings - whatever sounds attractive about an earlier time sways your opinion.

How about an honest, objective appraisal? In general, earlier times were terrible when compared to today. A few examples:
- the average lifespan was thirty or forty years until the 20th century
- many children died in childhood
- there was no treatment for most diseases until the 20th century
- bacterial diseases/prevention was unknown until the 19th century
- anesthetics were unknown until the 19th century
- crime was often widespread, especially for travelers
- there was no control over contamination or adulteration of food
- travel was expensive and dangerous and took forever
- the gap between rich and poor was much larger than today
- education was very limited aside from the rich
- rights of speech, religion, property, and political representation were non-existent

- wars, famine, and pestilence were the rule

Adapting to one's dominant environment, regardless of its absolute condition, is part of man's fundamental nature. People without money are convinced their problems would be over if they were but rich, yet there are rich people killing themselves, addicted to drugs, committing crimes, and possessing appalling morals in large numbers. People without freedom are willing to die to obtain it, and people with freedom will not even bother to vote or pay much non-cynical attention to their governance. People without education will effectively sell themselves into slavery so their children can get an education, and highly educated people buy their children everything but counsel and love. People that are starving will go through garbage for food, placed there by people who are wealthy enough to order it and leave it uneaten. People are struggling to get into the movie business in Hollywood, while those in the business are struggling to be free of the absence of privacy that it brings. Marie Antoinette's famous suggestion about eating cake was not made out of some vicious callousness, but rather from someone who just could not imagine a life where you could not get anything you asked for.

Maslow wrote about a hierarchy of needs. The idea is that the most basic needs, like food and shelter, come first, and once they are satisfied, others come into prominence, until the last one is reached - self-actualization. The significance of the hierarchy is that each step is the focus of a person's attention, their goal, until it is reached. It then disappears, to be replaced by another that will dominate until it too is attained. This can only occur because of man's adaptability. This allows a goal to be at one moment a dominating force, and the next to be forgotten as if it had never been.

There is an old tale by the brothers Grimm about a fisherman and his wife. The fisherman catches one of those fish who is really an enchanted prince, and seeing that the fish can talk, releases him back into the sea. Upon hearing of this, the fisherman's wife insists that he go back and get the fish to change their little hovel to a cottage. This is done, and two weeks later the wife has noticed that both the cottage and garden are too small, and so the fisherman is sent back to ask for a castle. The next morning, having had only one night in the castle, the wife realizes that the land surrounding them is not theirs, so the fisherman is instructed to return and ask to be king. This also is granted, but no sooner had the fisherman returned home than his wife asks to be made emperor. This continues until the wife asks for power over the movement of the sun and moon; returning home the fisherman finds himself back in his hovel again, and forever there to stay.

That the fairy tale is about greed is pretty obvious. But it is really about adaptability, just as greed is often just about adaptability. With each elevation in comfort, the fisherman's wife immediately adapts to that condition, and longs for one which will address its apparent shortcomings.

"Look here, husband, the cottage is really too confined, and the yard and garden are so small..." the wife observes after two weeks. Since the hovel had neither garden nor furnishings, it could not be too small - it took a cottage and garden to be able to observe that. Never is the situation compared to their starting point - the broken-down hovel. The frame of reference always shifts to the current situation, with all other previous situations forgotten. Of great strength of character is the person who can retain their view of their original circumstance after it significantly changes.

Everything is relative to the vantage point of the observer. There are an abundance of ancient sayings and proverbs about this - the Native American saying about refraining from criticism until you have walked a mile in the other man's moccasins, and "beauty is in the eye of the beholder." Jesus refers to those who are intent on pointing out the mote in their neighbor's eye while overlooking the beam in their own. There is the saying about the self-pity felt by the shoeless person until he met someone who was footless. And there is "a man is as old as he feels," and "every man is a king at home," and "no man is a hero to his valet." The old Finnish proverb says "the satisfied man knows nothing of hunger, and the laughing man nothing of tears." Jesus noted "a prophet is not without honor, save in his own country, and in his own house." Even off in the land of complex physics, Einstein's Special Theory of Relativity is about how the laws of physics and what you observe are only dependent on the relative motion between you and the object you are observing. In other words, there is no "absolute" or "right" or "real", but only relative differences. The simplest example would be that you wake up in space and go whizzing by someone else; neither of you can tell who is stopped and who is moving, or even if both of you are moving.

Man's senses are intensely relative. The day seems extraordinarily bright exiting from a darkened room, yet so does the full moon. The food someone was dying to eat while they were hungry will seem nauseating once they are full. Adults still dislike foods they remember they were allowed to eat without limits, even only once, while they were a child. A house full of cooking smells is unnoticeable to the occupants but overwhelming to a visitor. The same general thing is true when visiting a ranch. Everything tastes sweet after rinsing you mouth with vinegar or lemon juice, and the volume setting on the car radio that seemed fine at freeway speeds will scare you to death when you start the car first thing in the morning.

An Israeli observer has pointed out that, fifty years after its founding, the state of Israel state has surpassed all of the goals that its founders would have had for it. Yet many in Israel are not satisfied, wanting more territory, security, control, and restrictions. They have perfectly adapted to an ever-rising state of affairs, consistently always wanting more, and never being satisfied with what a decade ago would be considered ideal.

"Time heals all wounds" is not about time. It is about adaptability. As time passes, adaptability sets in, and what was unbearable or delightful before is greatly softened with the passage of time.

Many have commented on the different faces of war, depending entirely on the local situation of the observer. Crews on bombers at altitudes of several miles have no contact or feeling with what their bombs are doing on the ground. The horror of war for them comes from casualties on their aircraft from enemy action. Those fighting on the ground in hand-to-hand or house-to-house conditions have a much more terrifying experience, yet it is all the same war. The combatants quickly adapt to the conditions in which they are immersed. The same thing happens in non-combat situations with personal cars. People who would be more than civil and polite in a personal situation become rude and selfish when moved to the relative anonymity of their personal car. Like the bomber crews, drivers become detached and uncaring when they do not have to look into the faces of those they are contesting the roads with. Calling these people bad drivers or jerks or worse is wide of the mark - these people are instead great adapters, rapidly adjusting to the lack of personal contact with the other individual.

Consequences

It is said that in the cooking of lobsters and frogs, if the water starts at room temperature and is then slowly heated, the frog or lobster does not notice that things are turning out unfavorably. It is adaptation, moment to moment, taken to the extreme. Eleanor of Aquitane, one of the most powerful women of all time, sort of a hybrid of Hatshepsut, Cleopatra, and Boudicca, married Henry II both for political as well as emotional reasons, since she had dumped her earlier husband Louis VII of France for being lifeless, and together they created a major pseudo-state (Britain and part of France - these were feudal times) in Western Europe. But it was almost not to be, when Matilda, Henry's mother, trying to take back his kingdom which had been stolen by a usurper, Stephen, on the death of his father while Henry was but a boy, found herself trapped by enemy forces in Oxford at the beginning of December, 1142. Dressed all in white, she was lowered over the city walls, crossed the Thames on foot, and trudging through the snow made her way through the enemy lines all the way to Abington. Wait a minute – crossed the Thames on foot? Yes, it was frozen solid in the first week of December. Turns out this was not only not unusual, this was normal. In fact, the people in London had what they called Frost Fairs on the ice on the Thames River for hundreds of years until it froze no more starting about two hundred years ago.

Mother Nature is slowly cooking man, but since he lives in the moment, relatively speaking, like frogs and lobsters, he seems not to be noticing. He readily adapts to the ever-warming Earth, since for any given human, the rate has been low enough that until recently the changes have not been all that perceptible. Of course, if you live in places like Greenland or Alaska, or near glaciers, or where there used to be glaciers, you are cheating, since you can clearly see the changes.

Several observers in the United States in the early twentieth century discussed the apparent consensus that society was decaying, that on any social measure the quality of life was declining rather than increasing. Their interpretation was that, in fact, society was continuing to improve, and that the feelings of decay were due to ever-increasing expectations of what was socially-acceptable. Historians even give this a name - the theory of rising expectations. This time reflected a unique point in the history of the United States. The exploration/frontier phase of several hundred years had basically ended, and the negative impact of monopolies in rail, oil, and finance had created dramatic and obvious social problems. The muck-racking movement was at full-steam, not only in newspapers and periodicals but in books like The Jungle. Railroads and telegraph communication had suddenly brought a much more universal feel to the U.S. as well as many European countries, as compared to the local village view that had predominated since the beginning of civilization. Technology and knowledge were beginning their explosion that has been accelerating through today. This explosion demonstrated that accepting the world without question was no longer relevant or necessary. Whether in the areas of employment, medicine, food, shelter, transportation, safety, or education, technology could both prevent and solve problems that had always been taken for granted. Whether in building railroads, ocean liners, skyscrapers, hospitals, dams, schools, highways, electric lights, motor cars, automatic looms, typewriters, high-speed printing presses, photography, the telephone, or sanitation and water treatment facilities, there appeared to be no lack of solutions to needs and problems.

With this new attitude about technology, people now looked at the same world and instead of being grateful for what they had, subordinated this to dismay and concern about issues that did not yet benefit from such solutions. In most cases this was first aimed at social issues - working conditions for women and children, food, voting rights, freedoms, food safety, medical treatment, economic fairness - issues that defied easy technological solutions. The combination of a national if not a world view, relatively rapid communication, and no easy solution for these social problems brought about this cynical and negative view of the quality of life, highlighted by the muck-racking movement.

Were things getting worse? They were not, but the rate of social improvement had fallen behind the rate of social expectations, and the juxtaposition created the negative view of the world. Much of this situation has continued to the present day, where society contains a mix of summary opinions that are often a consequence of a particular individual's weighting of problems versus expectations. Some people tend to dwell on what is missing, what is uncorrected, the part of the glass that is half-empty, based on their expectations of what should be. Others look at what has been accomplished, the rate of progress, the part of the glass half-full. Both can see the same world, differing only in their expectations, to have opposing opinions about society's relative progress.

This is all a story of adaptation.

In many areas of the United States, houses are built in areas that are dangerous from a geological or weather perspective. Building in flood-prone areas would be the most obvious example. Other examples would be building on earthquake faults, on hillsides where ocean or rain erosion is natural, near seashores where high tides and storms occur, and downstream from dams or in levee-protected areas. In some cases, people in these areas seem genuinely surprised when their houses have problems. Sometimes you can find an identical problem ten years earlier, sometimes forty years earlier, sometimes 150 years earlier, and sometimes 300 years or more.

Because people adapt so well to what they see everyday, if it is dry today and dry yesterday, they tend to act as if it will be dry forever. Following a major catastrophe, even ten years of non-catastrophic success can sometimes be a sufficiently long a period to enable adaptation to settle in. Written, photographic, and even movie records are available, as are personal recollections, but this is almost uniformly ignored. The geological processes in the world that create problems that affect housing are pretty well-established. Earthquakes and volcanic activity in the Pacific basin, the Ring of Fire, driven by plate subduction processes, are indisputable. Yet there will be surprise and indescribable disaster when the San Andreas fault finally lets go in the Los Angeles area, releasing the stress developing since the Fort Tejon quake in the mid-nineteenth century. Mt. Saint Helens exploded in Washington and killed people who refused to believe that it would, even with the fine example of Crater Lake National Park sitting a little way to the south, where somewhere on the order of 25 cubic miles of the mountain exploded in a similar fashion a few thousand years earlier. People experience drastic flooding on the Mississippi, yet such problems are commonplace on the historical record if you go back 100 years or more. There was drastic flooding in Australia in 2011, but it was much less severe than flooding that had taken place as recently as 1974, and both were like gentle showers compared to the floods of 1893, 1844, and 1841. Problems with a 300 to 500 year cycle, like a major earthquake and tidal wave in the Pacific Northwest on the Cascadia Subduction Zone or earthquake in Missouri, are almost impossible to get anyone to pay attention to. The Japanese keep meticulous records – the Jogan earthquake in 869 AD was of magnitude 8.6 and was estimated to re-occur every 800 - 1100 years. The tidal wave associated with it went 2.5 miles inland. The Sendhai earthquake and tidal wave of 2011 were a repeat of this event, at the high end of the range in both time and magnitude, with of course a much higher population density. Lisbon and the surrounding areas were devastated in 1755 by an earthquake and tidal wave, and smaller quakes have occurred both before and after, but another large quake and wave will most likely re-occur and cause significant damage. People who live there feel that California is earthquake country, since significant quakes occur there in five year or fewer intervals. It seems that if the period of the natural disaster begins to exceed five years, people begin to adjust and adapt as if it had never occurred.

If adaptability in man were just limited to natural disasters, it would be bad but not terrible. But economic systems are prone to speculation-driven frenzies repeatedly, and each time it is as if it were the first time. It could be stock market bubbles, housing bubbles, dot com bubbles, a froth in various commodities, or financial scams of one sort or another promising either outsized returns or guaranteed returns. No matter how many times these kinds of things occur, no matter how many warnings are provided, no matter how much history seems to be repeated, people have completely adapted, adjusted, and assimilated all of the past events and happily leap into the next near-identical situation, somehow assuming that this one case will be uniquely different. Of course, it never is. Or it could be the de-regulation of once-regulated businesses in the U.S. that serve sensitive areas in the public sector – areas such as banking, electrical power and the like. Every time this is done, these businesses, always in oligopolistic positions, start doing things that disadvantage their customers, force their stockholders to unknowingly accept large amounts of risk, and the results are often very bad or disastrous. But people are adaptable, these things are quickly forgotten, and they repeat, without fail. Millions of dollars aren't lost, but billions.

Dealing with the consequences of criminal activity is one of the most obvious displays of human adaptability. Unfortunately, criminals are maybe the subgroup most aware of this. The old adage is "justice delayed is justice denied"; but this is not just descriptive, it is causal. If you were to take any jury, and put them at the scene of a crime, watching it unfold, seeing the pain and suffering and innocence of the victims along with the callousness, purposefulness, and viciousness of the perpetrators, trials would last a few hours. No matter what lawyers would say, you would not be able to distract jurors with doubt, the standard strategy. And in some countries, Saudi Arabia and China for example, crime commission and trial are very tightly coupled in time. But in a country like the U.S., where often years pass between the crime and the trial, and the jurors have no contact with the crime, no matter how severe the crime is, and its impact on society, the adaptation feature in man takes over and pushes almost all of those memories, feelings, and learning to one side. Lawyers can then readily sidetrack the jury with irrelevant red herring comments, so that individuals who kill and chop up their neighbors and bury them somewhere can be found innocent using the excuse of self-defense. Or have diminished capacity because they had a bad childhood, too much TV, were on medication, ate the wrong foods, whatever. Even if they are convicted and are imprisoned, no matter how brutal their crimes, if at a later date they appear to have re-invented themselves, become religious, read books about saints and martyrs, answer letters from widows and orphans, then a subgroup of society will begin to measure these individuals by their current behavior, and not by the actions that put them in prison in the first place. People adapt so well to what they see today that they are simply unable to visualize this same person chopping up children with an axe ten years earlier, even though that is why they are in prison. All this group sees is a nice person in prison – seemingly a miscarriage of justice. Now if you could take all these sympathetic supporters, put them in a time machine, take them back and watch this person commit the crime that put them in prison, they would probably all be clamoring for the right to shoot them on the spot. This adaptation force in man is relentless.

If the the damaging behavior appears not to be illegal, but the societal consequences are sufficiently severe, such as financial scandals, then immediately following the problem develops a push for legislation to prevent a recurrence. But as time goes by, the vested interests who make huge amounts of money without the restrictions that the legislation will impose begin to lobby hard, both with legislators and directly to the public with issue ads. With legislators, campaign contributions are the lobbying tool of choice. As long as a suitable delay has occurred, legislation most often will either be reduced to an ineffective level, or it will be eliminated as a solution altogether. During the time delay, things "seem" OK now, the arguments opposing legislation are the primary ones that people are exposed to, and so adaptation sets in.

There is one more example in the legal arena that is a sophist's dream, an Alice-in-Wonderland example of how you can build a fortress on a cloud using human nature – ease of adaptability - and that wondrous feature of the English common law system – precedent. Precedent means that if you show that vermillion is effectively a red, and faded vermillion is like international orange, and faded international orange looks like coral, and faded coral looks like orange peel, and faded orange peel looks like amber, and faded amber looks like gold, and faded gold looks yellow; that therefore red looks like yellow, and so when the traffic camera photographed my client driving through a red light, it was really the legal equivalent of a yellow light, and therefore no violation of the law took place. Of course, it takes many years and many cases to do this. But precedent enables small, gradual steps to eventually walk you off a logical cliff, since there is no rational or sanity check on where the precedent vector is taking you.

The U.S. Constitution bans the use of "cruel and unusual punishment", and those opposed to capital punishment are utilizing this clause to question the legality of injected drugs for serving capital punishment sentences. If you actually go back into English history and see where this phrase comes from, you will find it was not arbitrary but precisely intentional. Kings were beset with traitors who would have their crowns, kingdoms, and heads. The standard punishment, hanging, was not considered sufficiently severe – both because the king wanted those after his head to suffer as much as much agony as was humanly possible, and because he wanted to frighten off anyone else with a similar idea. So the punishment was modified to being drawn and quartered – first you were just slowly strangled by a rope but not dropped, so you were still alive and conscious. Then your male reproductive organs were cut off. Then they made an incision in your abdomen and slowly pulled out all your intestines. After than, they cut off both arms and legs. Then they chopped off your head, and mounted it on a long iron rod by London Bridge as a warning to all others who would pass into the city. Oh, and in case you forgot, this was before the invention of anesthetics, not that they would have been permitted anyway.

But because man is so adaptable, in the five hundred or so years between drawing and quartering in its prime and today, "cruel and unusual" has been slowly and sleekly morphed from full and complete barbarity to something much more benign than a root canal or a colonoscopy. But it was so gradual, like the frog and lobster in the water, that no one seems to have noticed. Were it not about such a serious subject, it would be intensely humorous.

Political elections, especially in the U.S., represent another great case study of adaptation. Nations have been having elections of varying kinds for 2,500 years, so you would think that people would be getting pretty sophisticated about them. But it is not so. Electors in each election in fact behave as if it were the first in human history. No matter what the track record of each of the candidates has been, no matter what special interests are financially supporting their campaigns, no matter what the pattern has been on other candidates running for office saying one thing during campaigns and then doing something quite different once in office, all that most potential voters appear to do is to pay attention to the campaign materials floated in front of them before the election. Often this comes down to negative campaigning, with the most negative with the most funding winning. This of course has nothing to do with the competency or ability of the elected official to deliver results for the voters, or maybe it does; it is just that there may be an inverse correlation. But no matter how often this is repeated, voters cannot help themselves but to be taken in, fascinated, entranced, almost hypnotized, by the "now" of an election, and not the long, demonstrated, historical record. Certainly, it is not this simple, as other factors are at play – party allegiance, automatic rejection/acceptance of the party in power if things are going badly/well respectively, and the ability of the politician to deliver local jobs and money. But on the average, overall, you have an unpopular candidate tossed out in favor of some newcomer promising miracles, who four or so years later is recognized likewise to be a "disaster" only to be replaced by another miracle worker. The cycle repeats endlessly.

There are so many quotations about being forced to re-experience history from which you have not adequately learned that it has become a cliché. To paraphrase Lord Acton, familiarity breeds contempt, and utter familiarity breeds utter contempt. The reason history is not respected is not that people cannot read, or do not understand it, or even that they do not learn from it; rather, it is that their nature gets in their way. Human nature is not a trifle, it is a force that can, has, and does change the world. If the events are old enough to become history, people adapt to today and the history is ignored. People do learn, they just adapt, and the adaptation swamps what they have learned.

For 60,000 years things were straightforward. You forgot to hunt, or hunted or foraged poorly, and you ceased to exist. Not sufficiently careful with regard to predators, or injuries, and you would drop out of the gene pool. Survival rates were low; only optimal performance tended to be rewarded. Adaptation was a precious skill. Every possible advantage had to be exploited. If things were slightly different, or radically different, or problems arose, the unexpected took place – the people who could adapt and excel survived; those that could not disappeared. Flexibility and creativity, inventiveness – these were all valuable skills related to adapting to the challenges that Mother Nature threw at man.

But today the world is completely different. Man lives in a world that he has made, consisting of complex human social, economic, and political systems. Man is adapting not to something that is effectively rock solid stable, like Mother Nature appeared to be for most of the past 60,000 years, but to a constantly moving target, a dynamic set of systems that he himself is operating and controlling. Sure, Mother Nature changed over the past 60,000 years, but rapid change for Mother Nature, except for some specific cases, would have been on the order of 50 years – two or more generations. Today, rapid change is an hour or less. Plus, for most of the past 60,000 years, Mother Nature was changing on her own, and not due to man. Now man is adapting to systems that are changing due to himself, whether they are economic, or political, or social. So man today needs to learn how his systems work, how to optimize them, how what he does affects Mother Nature. If he adapts so quickly that his learning is suppressed, then he fails to benefit from the learning, endlessly repeating the same mistakes and inefficiencies.

It is like man is always destined to row through life in a boat with six inches of cloudy water at his feet. Every time he learns something, he drops the lesson in the water, and it sinks from view in the murky water of adaptation. He keeps looking down, but if he waits longer than a moment or two after he drops the page with his lesson, it has drifted out of sight, and out of mind, smothered by the waters of adaptation. If historians and philosophers and teachers constantly remind us, we adapt to that, and become bored and then contemptuous of the lesson. Engaging in a clinical review of history provides only two lessons - it absolutely repeats itself, and it is absolutely ignored. And for this we can thank our own nature as humans - our innate adeptness at adaptation.

Chapter 13
Alexander the Greatest
or, The First-est of the Worst-est

First, The Greatest

Around two thousand three hundred and fifty years ago a twenty year old and a group of his friends started out to conquer the world, and they succeeded. From a tiny, relatively impoverished country, their leader was further handicapped by only having a degree in philosophy. Herodotus had only invented history about a hundred years earlier, so none of these people had the benefit of knowing anything about the rest of the world; about the successes and failures of anyone else; the right and wrong ways of doing things; or systematic studies of events and systems and methods and practices. Doing what he did today, Alexander would be the most accomplished human ever. But with the handicaps of 2,350 years ago, Alexander's superiority over any other potential competitor is unquestioned.

It was in Alexander's nature to rise to every challenge, and the more difficult the task, the more he would relish its accomplishment. He would not be denied. Fortress cities that had never been conquered due to their strategic position and high walls were unbearably attractive to Alexander – like a drug addict, he could not pass them by. He never failed, not once, to conquer, take, or reach any goal he set for himself, no matter how demonstrably-impossible it was. There is not the space here to describe each such ridiculous endeavor – but this was Tyre: an island half a mile offshore, protected by 150 foot high walls made with great stones cemented together. Alexander, 2,300 years ago, built a causeway 100 or more feet wide through water up to 18 feet deep over to the island, and then found a weakness in its defenses and took this city of 40,000, killing or crucifying 10,000 of them since they had had the foolish arrogance to slit the throats of some captives earlier on top of their city walls and throw them into the sea, in full view of Alexander, and really pissed him off, a very poor decision. And he would not stop, ever. Maybe he didn't know it, but James Cameron simply ripped off Alexander's bio when he wrote the screenplay for <u>The Terminator</u>, except Alexander had a lot more creativity, determination, perseverance, intelligence, charisma, charm, and leadership skills than the Terminator (paraphrased from the movie): "Alexander is coming, and can be neither bargained nor reasoned with. While he has often pity, and sometimes remorse, he has never fear, and will never, ever stop until you submit or are crushed and lifeless."

Or maybe this other modern characterization better portrays Alexander: "Alexander is the perfect organism - his perfection matched only by his determination – one can only admire his purity of spirit and unique sense of fame and history; yet so often moderated by conscience, remorse, and morality." (paraphrased from Alien, 1979)

In a time where combat wounds would often prove fatal since the concept of infection was unknown, Alexander was wounded, often severely, many times. He had an arrow break a leg bone and another penetrate a lung, resulting in unconsciousness. These wounds occurred far from home, some in India, where cholera, typhoid, tetanus, malaria, and who knows what else would have been rampant, especially for one weakened by a major wound. Yet as Alexander's perfectly healthy friends would suddenly drop dead from some disease, Alexander would rapidly recover from his injuries and appear to be unaffected.

Most people who have struggled to lead would agree that leadership skills are innate, and not acquired. Alexander both by words and by action demonstrated the ability to lead in a manner probably unequaled in the history of the world.

Alexander was gracious, magnanimous, egalitarian, generous, unselfish, unassuming, logical, rational, practical, and reasonable, except in one aspect. And that one thing was his weakness, if you want to call it that, which was his inability to resist conquering whatever was unconquerable, to attack whatever was impregnable, to grab for whatever was completely out of reach. But aside from this, as a twenty year old king, or even as a twenty year old general (if you want to take that perspective), Alexander was all strengths and no weaknesses, like no other king, general, or leader at any other time or place.

A little bit of elaboration is necessary here. Alexander did not set out to build a school for orphans with volunteers; all of this took place in the context of war. Alexander was invading the lands of people that did not invite him to do so – if they resisted, in most cases they suffered dearly. Sometimes there were wholesale slaughters of those who fought, with the rest of the residents sold into slavery. Even if there was no violence the cities had to agree to Alexander's terms – generally pretty undemanding: just don't make war on him – but it was still a restriction of their past freedom. In some cases Alexander's criteria, while logical, appeared simply inhumane: violate any of his terms and everyone died - old, young, male, female, sick, infirm, it didn't matter. Passing moral or ethical judgment on Alexander's actions is not what is intended here.

Here is the picture of Alexander that we get from Arrian, using his words paraphrased (the publisher will not allow the book to be quoted directly), not some modern author's revisionist opinion, so you can make up your own mind. Arrian is writing in about 150 AD, and is using all the historical accounts available, including those who were with Alexander during his campaigns. The following images of Alexander's character are organized not chronologically but by common trait.

This first group of selections shows Alexander's exceptional bravery, courage, and leadership by example both to motivate his men and as a battlefield tactic against his opponents. Not only does Alexander risk serious injury, something often fatal at a time where neither internal bleeding nor infection were understood nor manageable, but somehow repeatedly survives major wounds that should have killed him many times over.

At the battle of Granicus, the Persians had massed their troops in strength along the river bank. Threatening their left flank was Alexander, his magnificent armor making him a most obvious target as he charged across the river. Some of the Persians fell back to meet Alexander, but he blew through them at the head of his troops, right for the point where the Persian commanders were bunched. Breaking his spear in the action, Alexander took another from a comrade and galloped in front of his men to strike Darius' son in law in the face, taking him down. Being now exposed, Rhoesaces rode hard at Alexander and striking with his scimitar, sliced off part of his helmet. Instantly, Alexander thrust his spear into his chest, killing him.[13]

At the battle for Tyre, Alexander was poised with his closest fighters to rush through any breach in the wall. As the battle unfolded, Alexander was in the heat of the battle, not only fighting like the rest but on the alert for any act of bravery on the part of his men that he could later recall to reward and motivate his troops. As one of his men, standing on the breached wall, was killed by a spear, Alexander leaped up to take his place. This caused the Tyrian defenders to retreat, followed hotly and aggressively by Alexander in the lead.[14]

At the battle for Gaza, an iron missile from a catapult penetrated both his shield and light armor, driving into his shoulder. The wound was serious and did not readily respond to treatment.[15] In action near the Don, casualties were high, including Alexander, who was shot by either a arrow or catapult right through his lower leg, breaking the smaller bone, the fibula.[16] At the battle for Cyropolis, Alexander was violently struck by a stone from a catapult that injured both his head and neck.[17]

In the battle with the Mallians, his troops were using ladders to scale the fortress walls, but not quickly enough for Alexander, who impatiently and impulsively grabbed a ladder and raced to the top, standing alone in his

13 The Campaigns of Alexander by Arrian, translated by Aubrey de Selincourt, Barnes and Noble, Inc., 1971, pp. 73-74
14 Ibid., pp. 141-142
15 Ibid., pp. 145-146
16 Ibid., pp. 199-200
17 Ibid., p. 204

dazzling and brilliant armor, an unmistakable and magnetic target for every enemy in the neighboring towers. Realizing instantly that he could die alone on the wall, purposelessly, or heroically fighting, he leaped down alone into the Mallian fortress. Waves of Indians came at him, and he cut them down, fighters and commanders alike, fighting on until an arrow pierced his light armor and his lung, causing him to hemorrhage, choking and gasping for air as he continued to fight. Finally he collapsed over his shield, and was rescued by his men, who were able to pull him from the fighting and back to his camp. With no physician present, one of his men cut the arrow out of Alexander with his sword. His army, thinking Alexander dead, fell into an agony of deep despair.[18]

While Alexander could be a warrior of the most terrible kind, dispensing brutality to meet the appetite of the most savage observer, he could also be seen at the next battle or town acting respectfully and graciously - recognizing brave, honorable, courageous,and loyal behavior on the part of his opponents. At the battle of Miletus, the town quickly fell under Alexander's control. Some men had escaped to a nearby island, and from there they indicated that if necessary, they would fight to the death to defend themselves. Impressed by their bravery and courage, Alexander allowed them their freedom, conditional on their serving under his command at some time in the future should circumstances so dictate.[19]

After the battle of Issus versus Darius, Alexander heard the sounds of women's voices raised in sorrow coming from near his tent, a most unusual occurrence. He was told that these were the family of Darius, captured by the Macedonians, and they were mourning Darius' death. Immediately Alexander sent someone to reassure them that not only was Darius still alive (although it would only be temporary due to Persian treachery), but that they were to keep all of their personal possessions and status. Incredibly for the ancient writers, the wife of Darius, described as the most beautiful woman in all of Asia, was left unbothered by Alexander, where tradition would have been to take her as a wife.[20]

Facing the famous Rock of Chorienes - 12,000 feet high, seven miles in circumference, with a vertical drop on all sides and only a single track of narrow steps for access that was easily defended, and never been conquered - Alexander nonetheless began to construct fortifications out of fallen trees that would eventually allow him to attack this impregnable fortress. The ruler, Chorienes, asked to speak to another ruler (Oxyartes) that Alexander had just defeated, which Alexander allowed. Oxyartes recommended that Chorienes

---

18 Ibid., pp. 313-318
19 Ibid., p. 82
20 Ibid., pp. 122-123, p. 235

surrender, since there was nothing that Alexander could not conquer, and that he could be most fair in victory. Chorienes then did surrender with effectively no penalty other than agreeing not to attack Alexander, and voluntarily agreed to help provision Alexander's troops with food out of the stockpiles he had in his fortress against the siege he had thus avoided.

Porus, a King of India, had impressed Alexander by his courageous and gallant behavior, both as a soldier and a commander during the battle between their forces. Only when he was wounded did Alexander get the upper hand. Alexander rode out to meet him as he came forward to concede. He was physically impressive, somewhere between six and seven feet tall, magnificently built, handsome, and with the manner of an unconquered king and warrior, making a great impression overall on Alexander. Alexander asked him maybe his standard trick question - what treatment did he expect? And the response from Porus was that he simply wanted to be treated in the manner appropriate for a king. When pressed by Alexander, he reiterated that this would suffice. So pleased and delighted was Alexander with this response that he not only allowed Porus to keep his kingdom but gave him additional lands.[21]

Not by any means simply a steroidal and suicidal warrior who would force his troops by way of threats to follow his lead, Alexander excelled as a motivational speaker when addressing his troops, treated them more as equals or family than simply subordinates or soldiers:

Speaking just before the crucial battle of Issus against Darius and the armies of Persia, Alexander called together both the commanders of his infantry and cavalry to speak of the forthcoming battle. The Persians, he told them, have for centuries lived lives of luxury, making men of soft and cowardly nature. Macedonians, bred and trained in the tough ways of hardship and war, have produced men of iron. Macedonians are free, and fight for the glory of Greece; the Persians are slaves, and fight for money - a handful of copper coins. He personally singled out commander after commander, mentioning for each one the specific risks and gallantry that each had demonstrated in past actions, and that Alexander himself had noted. And he went over the accomplishments that they, as an army, had made so far in their campaign. He spoke of their bravery, how proud he would be to lead them into battle yet again, and they crowded around him, thanking him for the opportunity and privilege to fight for him and Greece one more time.[22]

As the two armies closed to within striking distance, Alexander rode rode up and down his ranks of troops, addressing each by name and rank, reminding them and those around them of their previous acts of bravery and

---

21 Ibid., pp. 280-281
22 Ibid., pp. 112-114

courage, pushing his army into a frenzy. Officer and soldier alike were singled out, even the paid mercenaries were not overlooked by Alexander. He then led his troops in orderly fashion against the Persian lines, but as soon as they began to be struck by missiles from the Persian catapults, Alexander dashed into the lead, crossing a stream and into the Persian lines. As he had planned, the left flank of the Persians collapsed as soon as it was hit by the Macedonian charge.[23]

The day after the battle, Alexander visited all of his wounded, even though he had been wounded himself with a sword thrust through his upper leg. Later, the whole army, in full dress, was assembled for a parade and funeral for those who had perished in the battle. As was his style, during the funeral Alexander spoke of the acts of bravery and courage on the part of everyone who had performed heroically during the fighting, and provided them with appropriate rewards.[24]

And at another occasion, speaking to all of his troops after a few of whom had demonstrated disrespect for Alexander's leadership and decision-making, Alexander started by going back to before his father's time (Philip II of Macedon). He told them that their ancestors had been in effect savages, laboring under slavery, whom his father had freed and then civilized. Alexander, upon taking the throne, had inherited but a small amount of money and along with it debts eight times as high; but he had then gone off and borrowed even more so they could set off and conquer the world, since Macedonia was too impoverished to support them in any kind of reasonable fashion. And now, all the riches and wealth they have won has fallen not on Alexander but on his men - Alexander keeping only the title of king as his reward. Alexander eats the same food as his men, sleeps on the same ground, is struck by the same arrows, missiles, stones, and clubs. Alexander dares any of his men to show that they have more sword or arrow wounds than he - that every exposed part of his body is scarred - and his men collapse in embarrassment and agony. They plead forgiveness that they have questioned Alexander, realizing that he has spoken truthfully and forthrightly, and has given far more than they, for their benefit and not for his.[25]

Simplistically, if you are someone who insists on one-dimensional characterizations, you would classify Alexander as just focussed on conquering. But he was also interested, insightful, motivated, and skillful in managing the territories that he had conquered, including the provincial governors that he had set in place

---

23 Ibid., p. 118
24 Ibid., pp. 121-122
25 Ibid., pp. 360-365

He appointed Peucestas, the head of his Personal Guard, as governor of the Persian empire, since he demonstrated an affinity for their customs and traditions. He adopted their way of dress, their language, and lived as they did. This pleased both Alexander and the Persian people, who appreciated that their new governor preferred Persian ways to his own.[26]

But abuse this privilege, and there was hell to pay. Traveling to Susa, Alexander had the governor whom he had installed there, Abulites, arrested and then put to death for abusing his office. Oxathres, the son of Abulites, shared in his father's fate, apparently the fruit falling not far from the tree 2,300 years ago as well. Unfortunately it was more common than rare to find reports of governing officials either using inappropriate violence against citizens, or robbing temples or tombs of objects of value. To send a message, Alexander came down hard in all such cases, generally finding for the complainant regardless, and treating even minor infractions as major, feeling that once an official stepped onto that slippery slope of corruption and abuse, problems would only grow in magnitude and number.[27]

It was pretty much a given in Alexander's day that the spoils of war belonged to the king – he after all had to fund the vast costs of feeding, arming, and transporting the army and support staff of baggage handlers, engineers, armorers, cooks, shepherds, and horse managers. But Alexander demonstrated unselfish and unexcelled generosity with his own soldiers, dispensing the wealth he had accumulated through his conquests to a degree unequalled by another sovereign. When, after piling up riches and treasure, Alexander felt it was high time to distribute it to all of his men, he had a detailed inventory constructed, and asked his administrators to develop a list of debts owed by his men that could be paid off first. Very few names were provided, his men fearful that this may be some trap to see who had been spendthrift in their ways. Alexander, furious, went to his troops and chastised them, saying how could they but question his motives and honesty. He was their king, and would and could never act in any way that would bring his honor into question. So he told his clerks to pay off in full the debt of any IOU presented, and to not even make a note of the name of the soldier presenting the IOU. This was done, and the total paid out was an amount totaling 20,000 talents.[28]

Some writers put the total cost at 10,000 talents. With average daily income for an average family of around 4 drachma, and 6,000 drachma to the talent, even at 10,000 talents this would amount to the average daily pay for 15,000,000 families. To try and get a modern equivalency of the value that this

26 Ibid., p. 347
27 Ibid., pp. 352-353
28 Ibid., pp. 354-355

represented, the median family income in the U.S is about $200 per day, so today this would represent a value of about $3 billion. Such an uncatalyzed act of generosity on the scale of the wealth of some major nations at that time is quite impossible to appreciate today, since the standards of 2,200 years ago were that nothing was given save that something equivalent was expected in return. And on the size of the gift, nothing approaching it would be seen until several thousand years had passed, almost unto the writing of these words.

Some insight into Alexander's complex ego, character, and fundamental nature demonstrates that he is good, bad, and ugly; intelligent and stupid; kind and conceited; thoughtless and terrible; honorable and brutal; sophisticated and barbaric; all wrapped up in one unique package.

Writing to Darius, king of Persia, after he has invaded his country, he admonishes Darius to treat Alexander as if he were the lord over all of Asia - his superior in all ways. All that was once yours is now mine, Alexander tells him, and so if he wants anything from Alexander, he has to grovel appropriately, or not only will Alexander not grant his request, but will treat Darius as a common criminal.[29]

When Alexander reaches Persepolis, the capital of Persia, he burns the palace of the Persian kings. His chief adviser had warned him that this was a foolish move; first, because he was now the owner of a fabulous property that he was now burning, and second, because it would send a message to the people of Persia that he was coming not as another ruler but clearly as a ruthless conqueror. But Alexander was angry, furious that the Persians had burned Athens when they had invaded Greece, and he was only making things even for all the damage that they had done. Arrian pointed out that it was a little disingenuous and counter-productive to hold the people today accountable for what their ancestors had done several hundred years earlier.[30]

While assembled on one bank of the Tanais river, Alexander could clearly hear himself and his troops being dissed by the Scythian enemy formations on the far bank. As was the custom, Alexander had sacrifices made to see if omens were favorable for a battle, but they were against him. So, frustrated, he had the seer do the sacrifice again, with the same unfavorable result. But the insults from the Scythians continued, and it was too much for Alexander to take, and so he declared that he would rather face the worst imaginable peril than sit on the bank and accept abuse from a bunch of loser Scythians. So he charged across the river with his men close behind, chasing the enemy across the countryside on the far bank. But water being scarce, Alexander ended up drinking from a contaminated source, contracting a

---

29 Ibid., pp. 127-128
30 Ibid., pp. 178-179

severe case of dysentery that dropped him from his horse and required him to be carried back to camp, seriously ill.[31]

And then maybe his worst personal sin – the murder of his great friend Cleitus during a night of heavy drinking and arguing. Surrounded, like all celebrities, with sycophants trying to please their master by piling on compliment upon exaggeration, someone mentioned that Alexander's achievements were comparable to some lesser gods, and then to Hercules. His best friend, Cleitus, who for quite some time had felt that Alexander had been going downhill from an ego perspective, listening to this kind of rot, jumped in and began to make light of Alexander's accomplishments. He said that the Macedonians, as a group, should shoulder the credit for their victories, not Alexander, and that in fact Philip, his father, was most likely a much better king. As he shook his hand in front of Alexander, taunting him, saying that it was the one that had saved his life in a particular battle, Alexander, drunk, enraged, out-of-control, grabbed a spear and killed Cleitus.

Alexander then raced to his tent, would not come out, eat or drink for almost a week, cried, moaned, calling himself a murderer. But then he called for a philosopher, a sophist, who laughingly told him a story that Zeus always had Justice sit by his side, to ensure that no matter what extreme action Zeus might take, it was right and proper by definition, blessed automatically by the presence of Justice.[32]

Then, never wanting to be accused of not being open to new ideas, Alexander engages his closest commanders, a group of intellectuals that he respects, and members of the court of the Persian king Darius (whom he has defeated in battle), in a discussion of whether or not anyone who approaches him should grovel on their stomach, which was traditional in Persia, but unheard of in the more egalitarian courts of Macedonia or Greece. Alexander had been moving more and more to adopting Persian customs, including dress, and this was starting to really irritate many of his peers who felt all this conquesting had gone to his head. Arrian feels that Alexander wanted to impose prostration in his presence, and initiated the discussion to see if he could get a majority opinion in his favor. He knew he could always depend on a group of court sycophants who would try to please him no matter what the subject.

Anaxarchus, one of Alexander's best sophists, led off with a pro-prostration speech saying since they would for sure honor Alexander as a god once he was dead, why not honor him as such now, while he was alive, so he could get some enjoyment out of it while he was still around? The court sycophants, who knew this was their cue, fell over themselves to loudly give their assent to this wonderful idea, while the Macedonians were silent. But

31 Ibid., pp. 207-208
32 Ibid., pp. 216-217

one of the Macedonians, Callisthenes, objected strongly to this concept of prostration, and was bold enough to speak up. Men greet each other with handshake or a kiss, but people grovel in front of a god simply because it is forbidden to touch a god, unlike a man. Since even Hercules was not given "god" status while alive, it would be reckless and imprudent to award such honors to Alexander. Plus, people back in Greece would never abide by such an outrageous custom.[33]

Since the Macedonians all agreed with Callisthenes, Alexander most reluctantly and unhappily decided not to impose the Persian tradition of prostration. On the way out of this discussion, the Persian nobility all bowed and groveled to Alexander, which caused one of Alexander's commanders to laugh out loud, making Alexander even more angry.

A little later for this and other insults, Alexander had Callisthenes killed, showing both how angry he was about this and how poorly he was able to bear insults at this stage in his career, as he looked upon himself as emperor of the world (and maybe even a minor god).

And, a little old-fashioned butchery, lest someone forget with whom they are trifling - at a town near the river Choes, they were in a battle where a catapult missile penetrated Alexander's armor and ended up embedded in his shoulder. In revenge for this wound to their king, all prisoners from this battle were summarily executed.[34] In activity subsequent to the fighting at Sangala, Alexander sent word to the next two towns that if they took no defensive action and allowed Alexander to enter their towns as a friend, no harm would come to them. But news of the fall of Sangala had already reached the towns, and everyone had fled in a total panic, leaving behind a total of maybe 500 people who were either too old, sick, or infirm to travel. Alexander ordered all 500 to be butchered, obviously faultless, innocent, and helpless.[35]

At one point when his men were arguing about whether they should turn back and go home or keep on pursuing new places to conquer in India, Alexander told them that if you really think yourself to be a man, as long as you are working toward a goal that is noble in character, work is an end unto itself. Glory can only follow from hardship, risk, and danger, and a life lived courageously produces not only joy in this life but a reputation of legendary proportions that will last down through the ages.[36]

Another writer, Nearchus, noted that Alexander so craved glory that when a battle of any sort was imminent, Alexander rushed in, irresistibly pulled into the fighting like a moth to light, regardless of the risk to himself.

---

33 Ibid., pp. 219-221
34 Ibid., pp. 240-241
35 Ibid., pp. 290-291
36 Ibid., p. 294

Alexander took as much pleasure from a battle as other men did from any other imaginable activity.[37]

Alexander's perpetual conquering finally came to an end when his men refused to do any more fighting and demanded that they be allowed to return home. Not ruling his men through force but by a democratic process, Alexander was obligated to support the group consensus. But his nature was undiminished even in retreat, and he selected the most demanding return route, through the town of Gedrosia. The losses suffered by his troops during this march were more severe than on any other time during his whole campaign. And it was not that this was some kind of surprise - Alexander purposefully selected the route since it had historically demonstrated to be impassable. The combination of a lack of water and high temperatures made the sufferings and deaths terrible.[38]

No accurate estimates are available – but various authors guess that from a quarter to three-quarters of his troops died during this march – the worst casualties his army ever suffered during his whole campaign.

During the "discussion" about whether to return home or not, one of his commanders, Coenus, uselessly reminded Alexander when his troops finally rebelled and refused to go any further east: "Sir, if there is one thing above others a successful man should know, it is *when to stop.*"[39] Coenus, in one brief sentence, perfectly summarizes Alexander's greatest weakness that arises from his greatest strength – he does not know, does not care, does not want, and cannot stop. Most ironically, after having the courage to make the speech that everyone else agreed with but was afraid to voice, several weeks later as the army began its journey back home, Coenus fell ill and died, never seeing the home he so longed for. He was one of Alexander's most loyal commanders.

Arrian's overall appraisal of Alexander describes him as unusually handsome, conscientious in his adherence to his religious responsibilities, bright, inquisitive, and adventurous. Addicted to fame and glory, he would persevere, insatiably, in its attainment, undistracted by wealth, women, drink, or power - things that would be the downfall of other men. What riches he gained, and they were great, he lavished on his men, taking none for himself.

He was logical, rational, and scientific, almost always coming to the correct solution in a situation no matter how complex, confusing, or disordered, especially military strategy and tactics. But when a momentary

---

37 Ibid., p. 319
38 Ibid., pp. 335-336
39 Ibid., p. 297

opportunity arose in battle, to choose whether to plunge forward or not, to send in his reserves or not, Alexander would always make the right call, and never squandered such an opportunity through hesitation or indecision.

The one exception is that Alexander was still hostage to his youth, and would sometimes make hot-blooded, impulsive decisions that were personal in nature - murdering his friend during a bout of drinking and bragging and arguing was such a case. Or when his crowd of courtiers smothered him with compliments, attempting to gain favor, he would sometimes fall under this spell of salivating pandering. But in these cases he was truly remorseful and regretful of his behavior, fully accepting that he had made mistakes, not blaming others or pretending that as a king he by divine right could deflect responsibility.

As an inspirational leader he was unmatched, whether by word or deed. And if his men, for whatever reason, ever did become concerned about the dangers they were facing, he could make them instantly forget through some incredible demonstration of bravery and fearlessness.[40]

Alexander started off to conquer the world when he was not yet twenty-one, and continued without pausing until his death a few months before his thirty-third birthday. Raised to be a future king, and tutored by the best in the world at that time, or maybe any other time – Aristotle - Alexander would certainly have had a more focussed, customized, germane, and sophisticated education regime than anyone else. But the qualities in Alexander that Arrian emphasizes above as the key to his uniqueness and his success are clearly hard to teach – Alexander had to be born with them in order to have them be exhibited at such incredible levels at such an early age.

But it is pretty clear that no one before or since has matched both the achievements and coherent behavior of Alexander. His boldness and excellence in combat leadership, in engineering skills, in bravery, in motivation, in creativity, in adaptation, in generosity, in aggressiveness, in perseverance, in egalitarianism, and in humility and brutality at times are simply unmatched in recorded history. Leading by example, he was the most aggressive, bold, fierce, and fearless warrior in his army, seriously wounded more often than any other of his compatriots. And this front-line presence enabled him to personally recognize and recall for later motivational use acts of bravery and courage on the part of his men. His engineering skills, enabling him to build approaches, siege engines, weaponry, and associated structures of all types were superb and unequaled, most likely acquired from Aristotle, but one has to be an outstanding student to benefit from coaching from an Aristotle – think for a moment how you might do. Did you get an A+ + in all of your courses in school? Because that is probably the minimum prerequisite for Aristotle-level graduate work. Able to accomplish all this with

---

40 Ibid., pp. 395-396

only the knowledge available to him in a tiny country 2,300 years ago at the age of twenty makes this an implausible story even if it were fiction. But even if it were fiction, the hero would have some fatal flaw that would bring him down – but Alexander had no real weaknesses, other than an inability to ever curb or bridle his strengths. Capable of making mistakes he was – killing his best friend following a night of drinking after having his competence called into question. But making a mistake once in a while is not a weakness, it just means he was not really a god after all (he thought he might be).

Other potential competitors of Alexander, whether military, political, or business leaders, have had a combination of major flaws and limited strengths so that they are not even in the same league as Alexander. There is Churchill, with great but not outstanding leadership skills, but also critical weaknesses; there is George Washington - good leadership skills, no ambition and therefore no real weaknesses, but fairly modest accomplishments also (on a world scale). Pericles – he led Athens in its Classical Age, an explosion of architecture, art, and democracy that affected the world down through today, but his efforts were in fact confined to a small city-state in the middle of nowhere. Sulla – never defeated as a general, and willingly resigned from the office of dictator of the Roman Republic, something pretty rarely done, but accomplished many of his "reforms" through murdering those who disagreed with him. Then you have Napoleon – really competent, making over for the better most everything he touched, but with weaknesses as vast as his strengths. There is the huge collection of conquerors/dictators/kings – maybe starting with Khufu, Thutmose III, and Rameses II in ancient Egypt; Qin Shi Huang as the first emperor in China; Hannibal, Julius Caesar, Octavian/Augustus, and maybe a few other Roman emperors; Genghis Khan; Charlemagne; Henry IV of France; Peter the Great; Elizabeth I; Popes Innocent III and Julius II. Then there are the tycoons – J.P. Morgan, Rockefeller, Carnegie, Ford, a Rothschild or two, maybe Onassis. And you might toss in Cardinal Richelieu and Bismarck in if you prefer more subtle candidates. Your list could be different, but it doesn't really matter. No one else comes remotely close to matching up to Alexander. You may not like what he did (especially if you are Persian) but like watching a killer whale, great white shark, or lioness in action, it is pretty difficult not to realize that how it was done was close to perfection. It is pretty surprising to think that over the whole known history of the world, close to 5,000 years of history and maybe 50 to 100 billion humans, that Alexander stands distinctly alone.

And now for a slight change of perspective. Alexander was irresistibly drawn to every impossible, unconquered challenge on the face of the earth. At any cost, at any risk, at any effort, at any diversion. As measured by his results, or his legacy, his goal was to conquer the known world, to have everyone acknowledge that Alexander was their master. He accumulated kingdoms and riches to be sure, shared by his fellow soldiers but not by him, but that was almost an accidental consequence, and not his prime goal. Conquering, winning, mastering, beating, defeating – those were Alexander's goals.

Alexander was not conquering to stave off starvation, or to find more arable land, or more water. He was not trying to find safety from floods or hurricanes or wild animals. He was not trying to prevent bands of marauding bandits from attacking his fellow countrymen. He was not just trying to find a better place for his people to live. No, he was just conquering for the sake of conquering. He was driven – driven to dominate, to be everyone's master, to be Number One, the most admired, the most feared, the most famous, the one who was able to conquer challenges that everyone else had considered impossible. It was a little disappointing that a modern science fiction classic had to reach back 2,300 years to use Alexander the Great, a real human, as the model for the robot for their movie.

Where man for the most part for the previous 58,000 years had been focussing on survival, Mother Nature finally produced close to the most perfect man, and he decided that he wanted no part of that precedent. Striving, driving only to dominate, Alexander became most unfortunately the first truly modern man, the poster child for those who choose to take on their hapless fellow man instead of solving problems, improving irrigation, improving sanitation, or other similarly constructive engagements. While there were warrior kings among the Sumerians, Akkadians, Hyksos, Assyrians, and Chinese for 2,000 years pre-dating Alexander, they were on a local and small regional scale, never with Alexander's talents, scope, standards, or goals. George Mallory's famous response to the mountain climbing question, "Because it is there," was in effect Alexander's motto, if there had been press around to ask. Military necessity, economic or strategic value never entered into consideration for many of the targets of his aggression; they just had the unfortunate luck of being there and being unconquered theretofore.

Now it needs to be pointed out that prior to 5,000 years ago, there were few attractive targets for escapades like Alexander's. Sacking the cave or tent next door for their bowl of berries was a minimal incentive. But once there were cities with royal treasuries filled with gold and jewels strewn across

197

the known world, men like Alexander were awakened. Like the police always say, it takes motive and opportunity.

Alexander was the first of the worst – those who recognized that once the world was at least partially filled with man, a sort of inflection point had been crossed. Instead of expending their energies against Mother Nature, the payoff was far better if they went instead after their fellow man - after civilization itself. Crime, the first professional short-cut, had been long in existence, but this was something altogether different. Alexander conquered more than the known world at that time, making every civilization that he found either subordinate to him or dust, depending on his frame of mind and their response to his demands. Whether it were several of the Roman emperors thereafter, or Charlemagne, or Pope Innocent III, or Genghis Khan, or Napoleon, or Hitler, Hugo Chavez, Bill Gates, or Larry Ellison – they are all following to varying degrees this same path – man/civilization as appetizer, main course, and dessert.

Whether a coincidence or otherwise, this distinction is even delineated in the Bible: "Let us make man in our image, after our likeness: and let them have dominion over the fish of the sea, and over the fowl of the air, and over the cattle, and over all the earth, and over every creeping thing that creepeth upon the earth.... Be fruitful, and multiply, and replenish the earth, and subdue it: and have dominion over ... every living thing that moveth upon the earth." Man is given the authority to subdue and have dominion over every plant and animal on the planet, and the responsibility to replenish whatever he takes (always conveniently ignored), but what is specifically excluded is the authority for dominion over his fellow man - the very thing that Alexander and those who have followed in his footsteps have fastened upon.

Today, as over the intervening 2,300 years, we find Alexander the role model, poster child, and progenitor for the economic war lord/king/company president. Not fighting lions, tigers, or bears but just out after the money possessed by their fellow man. The city-states in Mesopotamia were invented over 5,000 years ago. As recently as 500 years ago they were still contending with each other in Italy and parts of Europe for economic sovereignty. Lacking any international rules or reciprocities, possession was everything, so warfare for territory was pernicious and ubiquitous. But once the rules and reciprocities thing was resolved, you could be a war lord, just like Alexander, from the comfort of your home office. You could use money to buy companies, to influence governments, to influence elections, to buy decisions, to manipulate markets, to buy out your competitors, to create in effect monopolistic scenarios that would allow you to do almost anything you wanted and exact almost any price from those who depended on what you sold to them. With 192 countries to choose from, very few would ever challenge what you did as long as you made sure that those in power politically shared economically in your wealth accumulation. Of course in some cases the political leaders became jealous of this wealth and would go after it themselves, but this was overall rare and was seen as a risk worth taking. In countries where the rule of law dominated, as long as you appeared to follow the law, and gave large amounts of money to the politicians, everything was perfect.

Large global companies with market-driving power are now common, and consolidation increases over time. Only 28 countries out of 192 have GDP higher than Exxon Mobil's revenue of $330 billion. The economic power and influence of these companies tends to be completely unrecognized and unappreciated since they are not perceived to be a priori a "problem". But like the city-state of 5,000 years ago, their job is to get as large and as rich and as powerful as possible, without doing anything to unduly compromise any of those three things. Alexander of course was an extremist – he was willing to risk his life for nothing but the conquering, but he was oh so exquisitely close to perfect. These companies, and those running them, are doing their best to emulate Alexander; just staying away from the risking-their-life and the excessive-risk parts. But the game is the same – not Mother Nature but your fellow man. Alexander set both the never-to-be-attained level of achievement and the paradigm itself – leave your fellow man to try to subdue the world; you just take what you need from your fellow man.

Alexander was both the starting point and one extreme. But the difference between the way say Coca-Cola, Microsoft, Philip Morris, and Diageo look at the world, and the way Cortes looked at the Aztecs, Pizarro at the Incas, Sir Henry Morgan at the Spanish, and Napoleon at everyone, is just a matter of degree; and all are just flimsy copies of Alexander. Cortes and Pizarro were not concerned about killing the goose that laid the golden eggs; while all the others have made the calculation that they are better off with a healthy goose. Cortes, Pizarro, and Morgan decided to give nothing and take everything; Napoleon took much but in exchange created modern France; Coca-Cola, Microsoft, Philip Morris, and Diageo provide something that costs pennies to produce and sell it for dollars. All had 100% exclusive control over their product. All operated within the laws of their time. All are customer-centric; Pizarro, Cortes, and Morgan were the most due to the royal patronage that they had to honor. All were the fiercest of competitors. All were not only able to obtain a sustainable competitive advantage, but were world class in what they did. Each one can make an unmatchable value proposition. But all are following in Alexander's footsteps – taking from those who have been fighting against the elements, instead of fighting the elements directly themselves. But these eight are not being singled out for fame or infamy – they are members of a broad constituency that includes Genghis Khan, J.P. Morgan, Suleiman the Magnificent, John D. Rockefeller, Sir Francis Drake,

Andrew Carnegie, and countless others.

Hopefully, your first reaction to this is shock, horror, and disgust; your favorite company that you buy from, hold stock of in your IRA, or work for has just been compared to the knighted privateer, Sir Henry Morgan. Now if this somehow leads you to conclude that the author must be some anti-capitalist radical wing nut, your reaction is quite normal. Bipolar thinking and judgmental tagging (see Chapter 7) require you to think that capitalism in general is either good or bad (and if you are the average person most likely it is good), and that you will have favorable feelings about it that will cause you to defend it if it is being attacked or besmirched. Cognitive dissonance in Chapter 8 generally requires you to cast aside information that you receive about something that you have positive feelings about – in this case capitalism or business since most likely your standard of living depends on it. Either the information is erroneous or the author is prejudiced or an idiot or all of the above. If you reacted emotionally because you thought capitalism was under attack then you helped validate the points this book is trying to make. The author is not attempting to nor does he even want to make a value judgment about capitalism or business; in the modern world, there is simply not enough room nor does the depth of technology allow for everyone to be a farmer, fisher, rancher, or hunter, so it is inevitable that man ends up using all of his energy and talents on his fellow man, and not on subduing nature. This is a no-fault necessity, but notable nonetheless.

Of course, the author is not trying to directly compare modern companies with Sir Henry Morgan. All the top management of these companies collectively for decades could not begin to match the immense talent of Morgan, whose leadership, creativity, inventiveness, craftiness, fearlessness, and boldness were legend. Instead, the point is simply to say that all of these examples are variations on a theme – man can either spend his efforts and his drive working directly against threats and exploiting the opportunities that the world itself presents, or he can drop back and instead target not the world but his fellow man. For most of the last 60,000 years, there was only the world to deal with – if you bumped into another group of men in addition to your small group they would be just as poor and struggling as yours. But for the last few thousand years, man has grown explosively, and collectively become an "opportunity" for the first time, in the same way that the New World appeared to Europeans. Modern companies are part of this movement, just like Alexander was; it's just that he and Morgan were so much better.

Provide the average head of a large multinational corporation with a sword, light mail armor, and a horse, and you have a reality TV comedy show, not the conquering of the world. But the spirit in the man is the same as that in Alexander. Most everyone out there is working for a living - farming, building, making, helping, selling, mining, serving. The job of all these corporations is to take as much as they can from all these other people, spend as little as they can doing it, try to eliminate their competition, and not get in trouble doing it. Now they may or may not have other subordinate objectives, but if they fail to meet any of the prime objectives, they will get replaced by another, hungrier candidate. The heads of corporations today would have run city-states 500 years ago, or 5,000 years ago. They just would have had to adapt to the technology differences – the principles are unchanged. Others, titularly insignificant, are exerting themselves just as hard to accomplish the same results – on their own, in small companies, or even in large companies. Bankers, lawyers, hedge fund managers, doctors, financial fund managers – they are all cut from the same cloth; pulled from the same mold.

5,500 years ago man (Saqqaq culture) arrived in Greenland. Where from? Not Europe. No, from Siberia. That means these people had to cross the Bering Sea, which was not dry or covered with ice, then all of Northern Canada, and then the North Atlantic, a trip of around 3,500 miles, carrying their collapsible boats with them all the way. Was this hard? This is just about the most unlivable, unsurvivable, intolerant, harsh, food-deprived, warmth-absent, and dangerous territory in the world. Man that conquered the world was tough, durable, inventive, courageous, and a survivor to a degree that is difficult to comprehend today. For 58,000 years this man successfully fought off nature in any form, and then Alexander showed that a different paradigm was not only possible, but could be taken to the ends of the earth. Now the same strength and invincibility and unstoppability that enabled man to dominate nature is being applied to the only "challenge" and "frontier" left – and that is the wealth of their fellow man. Men and women attracted to power and influence and riches and challenge and conquering have chosen not the 58,000 year old well-trodden path but instead Alexander's, fighting (competing) to take money from everyone else, from those who are still struggling against nature as well as all others. So if you see the heads of these companies and wonder what makes them run, why after getting paid $100M they want $200M, or after $1,000M they want $2,000M, just remember Alexander, or his modern shadow, the Terminator, who never stop because they cannot stop; are never satisfied; are eternally driven.

Chapter 14
Challengelessness

In The Territorial Imperative[41] Robert Ardrey proposes that the degree to which a group/nation/civilization gets along with itself, a condition which he abbreviates with the word Amity, is proportional to the sum of two other factors. One he calls Hazard, the totality of natural, supernatural (if appropriate), and environmental challenges and dangers facing the group, nation, or civilization. The other is Enmity, the sum of all dangers presented by other people, groups, and/or nations not affiliated with or part of the nation in question.

Simplistically, if a nation has many challenges outside of itself that threaten its survival or its success, then its members/citizens will band together "shoulder to shoulder" to manage or conquer the threats. They will have neither the time, energy, nor resources to bicker, quarrel, argue, or fight amongst themselves. Whether the citizens build walls to keep out flood waters or human marauders, it has the same internally-cohesive result. Contrarily, without some external threat, people have no common focus, and start nit-picking the behaviors, attitudes, values, ethics, religious views, and other such values of each other.

This is so obvious that it does not need any proof. We all see it happen in teams, groups, companies, organizations, and not just nations. Lacking a clear, common danger to take on, or goal to attain that everyone buys into, a group is going to start having internal disagreements, splinter groups, and miscommunications. The only question is the threshold at which the citizens shift from the "me first" mode into the "common good" mode. Unfortunately for most nations, the threshold is high – it requires a threat that can clearly be seen as imminent and potentially (or demonstrably, in the case of something like flooding) catastrophic.

A critical distinction is that it is only the perception of the threat, and not the scientific evaluation of the threat, that goes into the equation. This is the first thing taught in totalitarian school that all dictators find a way to attend, either by getting tutored or by having a good role model. People that have all their rights taken away, that are half-starving, that have secret police watching them ready to take them away in case they say or do anything that the government dislikes, these people are going to be really unhappy and are not going to be cooperative and easy to manage. So you have to produce something for them to fear, a devil, that will make them forget their troubles

---

41 The Territorial Imperative, Robert Ardrey, Dell Publishing, New York, 1966

and pull together to defeat the devil.

In most cases the devil is another country that the dictator can dress up as the Evil he needs to emphasize. The United States, due to its imposing size and blatant symbolism, is often chosen. But Marx and Lenin chose capitalism while Hitler chose the Treaty of Versailles, so even somewhat abstract concepts can work.

Another factor that dictators have to contend with is the adaptability of man. "Crying wolf" chronically, no matter how long the fangs and how fierce the growl, eventually loses its "dread" content. Part of this is just a variation of "familiarity breeds contempt". New ways have to be found to dress up the perception of the fearfulness of the hazards and the threats. This is where the highly sought-after and rewarded propaganda experts come to the fore, and who all send flowers to Joseph Goebbels on the anniversary his birthday.

But the point that is being made here is a qualitative one, not an attempt to invent a new quantitative scale of Amity equals Hazard plus Enmity.

Over the last 60,000 years, it took no effort to come up with candidates for hazards or threats. If anything, these were in a super-abundance, and for this reason lifespans stagnated around 30 years for most of this time. Whether it was weather, or natural disasters, or disease, or wild beasts, or other nasty humans, there was something to fear and good reason to fear it.

Shift forward to today. The threat from wild animals for most people has disappeared. Food and shelter, while still a problem for some, for many is not a consideration. Crime is an issue for everyone, but for most it does not meet the threshold of a material threat to life on a daily basis. Weather while not controllable is predictable most everywhere. Natural disasters from floods and the like occur, but at a reduced rate due to dams and dikes, and much of the rest is by choice – people who choose to live in areas which they know well have flooded historically due to the preservation of historical records. And while there has probably never been a moment over the last 60,000 years when the world has been free of war of one sort or another, today the percent of the world's population affected at any time is the smallest ever, often less than one tenth of one percent.

So to get the Amity level up through Hazard and Enmity today requires the generation of the perception of threats. This is much harder to do, especially in a free country. It is still done for other reasons, mostly political, for example to solidify a political block in order to win an election by hiding behind the flag and patriotism, or religion, but it is difficult to unite an entire nation this way. A totalitarian dictator can still do this, but today it is difficult to accomplish in other than small, very-underdeveloped countries where the military or equivalent militia allows the dictator to remain in power. North

Korea may be the one remaining clean classic example of this, as of the writing of this book.

The bottom line – today nations are not being brought together by Ardrey's equation. The world is just too damn civilized.

Let's try something else.

Turner – The Frontier Coalesced Disparate Citizenry Together

In 1893 Frederick Turner published Turner's Thesis, or more precisely The Significance of the Frontier in American History, which postulated that the era of the frontier in the United States – the challenge/opportunity of always having a contiguous boundary of unexplored territory available to its citizens – was responsible for the success of the United States. With the disappearance of the frontier, due simply to settling and "civilizing" all the territory available to its citizens, Turner implied that the U.S. might become less successful as a nation. So facing and mastering a challenge may have not only individual implications but national ones. Like any other thesis, it's the "why's" that matter. Here is the first one:

"The wilderness masters the colonist. It finds him a European in dress, industries, tools, modes of travel, and thought. It takes him from the railway car and puts him in the birch canoe. It strips off the garments of civilization and arrays him in the hunting shirt and moccasin. It puts him in the log cabin of the Cherokee and Iroquois and runs an Indian palisade around him. Before long he has gone to planting Indian corn and plowing with a sharp stick.... In short, at the frontier the environment is at first too strong for the man. He must accept the conditions which it furnishes, or perish.... Little by little he transforms the wilderness, but the outcome is not he old Europe.... here is a new product that is American."[42]

The frontier, as an irresistible power, transfigures the colonists that pass through, creating a new individual not seen before, called an American. But this process produced unheralded as well Canadians, Boers, Australians, and many other new hybrid groups. Settlers, always coming from different nations with diverse customs, traditions, and values, were cleansed of their previous identities in this baptism of fire provided by the frontier. So the resultant Americans (or whichever nation in question) now had much in common, all given to them by their shared experience provided by the frontier. It provided a powerful but invisible homogenizing force, like Adam Smith's Invisible Hand.

The degree to which this occurred in the United States is

---

42 The Turner Thesis, George Taylor editor, D.C. Heath and Company, Boston, 1956, p. 2

unappreciated in the present day since people perceive that the country has always been as they currently see it (other than population and technology changes):

"Burke and other writers in the eighteenth century believed that Pennsylvania was 'threatened with the danger of being wholly foreign in language, manners and even inclinations.' The German and Scotch-Irish elements in the frontier of the South were only less great. In the middle of the present century the German element in Wisconsin was already so considerable that leading publicists looked to the creation of a German state out of the commonwealth by concentrating their colonization."[43] Obviously none of this ever came to pass, obliterated by the relentless homogenizing force of the frontier.

Three separate and qualitatively different waves of settlers were able to utilize this frontier mechanism in the U.S.:

"First comes the pioneer, who depends for the subsistence of his family chiefly upon the natural growth of vegetation, called the 'range', and the proceeds of hunting.... He is the occupant for the time being, pays no rent, and feels as independent as the 'lord of the manor'.... The next class of emigrants purchase the lands, add field to field, clear out the roads, throw rough bridges over the streams, put up hewn log houses with glass windows and brick or stone chimneys, occasionally plant orchards, build mills, school-houses, court-houses, etc., and exhibit the picture and forms of plain, frugal, civilized life. Another wave rolls on. The men of capital and enterprise come. The settler is ready to sell out and take advantage of the rise in property ... Thus wave after wave is rolling Westward, the real Eldorado is still further on. A portion of the first two classes remain stationary amidst the general movement, improve their habits and condition, and rise in the scale of society."[44]

Turner feels that the expansion of the frontier into the West in pursuit of in effect free land provided an even more critical benefit:

"It was this nationalizing tendency of the West that transformed the democracy of Jefferson into the national republicanism of Monroe and the democracy of Andrew Jackson.... Mobility of population is death to localism, and the western frontier worked irresistibly in unsettling population. The effect reached back from the frontier and affected profoundly the Atlantic coast and even the Old World. But the most important effect of the frontier has been in the promotion of democracy here and in Europe. As has been indicated, the frontier is productive of individualism.... It produces an antipathy to control, and particularly to any direct control.... The result is that to the frontier the American intellect owes its striking characteristics. That

---

43 Ibid., p. 11
44 Ibid., pp. 9-10

coarseness and strength combined with acuteness and inquisitiveness; that practical, inventive turn of mind, quick to find expedients; that masterful grasp of material things, lacking in the artistic but powerful to effect great ends; that restless, nervous energy; that dominant individualism, working for good and for evil, and withal that buoyancy and exuberance that comes from freedom – these are traits of the frontier."[45]

Some of you may remember from your American History classes that some forty years after Turner first published his thesis, a few academicians began to nit-pick his work, saying he made some technical errors, was too bombastic and one-sided in pushing his point. They brought hordes of tiny academic details in support of their disgruntlement, as academicians are fond of doing. If you are looking for an academic fight, you are reading the wrong book, but Turner's main point is unimpeachable. The frontier made America; it made Americans; it made Australians; it made others; and now it is long gone, and it is not coming back, not ever.

Toynbee – The Criticality of Challenge to a Civilization

The historian Arnold Toynbee, in his A Study of History, proposes that civilizations grow in proportion to the challenges that they must overcome. Unchallenged, or impossibly over-challenged, say by an environment that is excessively hostile, and not much of note is to be expected. But a reasonably-challenged civilization grows and develops through a process that Toynbee calls mimesis. This is where a small minority that has trend-setting powers is in a leadership position, constantly breaking and establishing new ground. The balance of society follows, so in a series of small steps the whole society constantly moves forward and upward. These areas of breakout improvement could be farming, housing, hunting, tools, clothing, shoes, writing, metal-working, ceramics, education, ship-building, navigation, technology, government, laws, administrative – anything germane to the efficiency and prosperity of the civilization. And it does not (and would not) have to be the same group doing the leading for each categorical subset.

At some critical point, this mimesis process gets waylaid, sidetracked, dulled, lost, or otherwise becomes ineffective. The civilization goes through a series of stages that eventually result in its demise. For Toynbee, if the reader is interested, only Western Civilization has not yet seen a corruption of this mimesis process. Only it is as yet not doomed as per his criteria. All other civilizations that he studied, 26 in total, either are already gone or are going.

The attraction about Toynbee's point on challenge being the basis of a successful civilization (he calls the process challenge-response) is that it seems

---

45 Ibid., pp. 14, 17

intuitively obvious. The author grew up in Hawaii, and if you remove the pressure and structure of Western society, the fundamental inherent challenge in Hawaii on a daily basis is whether it's bananas or papaya for breakfast, what kind of fresh fish to have for dinner, and at which beach or sheltered tropical spot you are going to spend the day. The climate is so mild that you don't really need any shelter, even when it rains. Food grows so quickly you have to beat it with a stick so you have room to lie down. It is hot and humid enough that too much exertion never seems appropriate. There are no dangerous wild animals, not even snakes. Hawaii is the poster child for being laid-back, which is why the life expectancy there is so high. A great civilization you are not being challenged to create.

When the author was still young but post-Hawaii his father was a banana farmer with plantations mainly in Honduras. They had a terrible time keeping people on the job for any length of time. Pay was the problem, but not what you would think. After just a few months of working, an individual could readily accumulate enough money to buy a bunch of chickens and a few goats, maybe a cow or two, and retire to a small clearing in the jungle in a compound of thatched huts that you can see scattered everywhere as you fly overhead. He was fixed for the rest of his life – no need for any further work. And should some disaster befall him, a few months of work would set it all right again. Like Hawaii, Honduras was in the challenge-free zone (although today it is different).

But where everything that in Hawaii is easily available becomes instead a fight – food, shelter, wild animals, climate – you are going to end up with a different set of a personalities in the civilization. Anyone laid back is going to starve to death or freeze – the population self-selects so that only those who are aggressive, curious, creative, industrious, hard-working, and often tough will survive. With a sufficiently-large plurality, the population has a chance to develop the small core group that will provide that catalytic mimesis effect critical to the genesis and development of successful civilization.

Does this mean Hawaii or an equivalently accommodating locale can never develop an unmellowed personality? Obviously not, it is just that it will not be able to produce enough of them to establish the catalytic effect for the civilization as a whole to move it forward. It will produce leaders, explorers, inventors, and some other iconoclasts. But it is the center of gravity of the civilization that must move, and not just a few unique individuals at the periphery.

An example of where challenge pushed a civilization forward would be in ancient Egypt. The requirement to control the annual flooding of the Nile river (something that curiously they never understood the cause of) to predictably and reliably manage the production of grain forced the Egyptians to work together to create a complex irrigation system, along with a political, religious, social, and administrative system to manage it all. They even had a goddess, Ma'at, representing the order and stability and regularity that the annual Nile flooding meant to their civilization, and these concepts, tied to the reason for their survival, may explain its longevity, a record as civilizations go.

You can contrast this with the Aztec civilization – maybe 15 million people to feed, a not completely dissimilar climate, free from disruptive outside national threats as were the Egyptians for most of the time (for geographical reasons). But the Aztecs were able to make use of agriculture based on lakes which were always present, and not a river which mysteriously would flood once a year. Granted the Aztecs made masterful work of their lake-based horticulture, but the challenge was not sufficiently substantial to push the civilization along. It is possible that man simply needed more time in the Americas - 9,000 to 12,000 years versus the 30,000 or more years he had in the Fertile Crescent – the experiment was interrupted by Europeans so no one will ever know.

Toynbee's thesis is discussed in more detail in Chapter 20, if you want to jump ahead. The context in the intervening chapters is not needed.

Whether we are talking Toynbee, Turner, or Ardrey, this book is not another academic slog at whether these authors got it perfectly correct or not, or how many warts, barnacles, missing digits, and other imperfections fill their works. For the purposes of what drives society fundamentally to stay or fray, these authors got it much more right than wrong.

For Toynbee, challenge alone is clearly not sufficient to produce a society. North Americans prior to the arrival of Europeans had some challenges, but the population density was extraordinarily low – estimates are on the order of just two or so million individuals across all of North America when Columbus arrived. Compare this to a million and half people in ancient Rome and just under a million in ancient Jerusalem. There were close to two million people in the relatively tiny Old Kingdom of Egypt almost 5,000 years ago. So there had to be a sufficiently-large group of people in a compact area struggling to find enough to eat, and in most cases (Egypt, Sri Lanka, Ur) it appears that irrigation was the solution to their survival challenge, allowing them to produce crops of grain on an organized, structured basis. But the fact that there are other necessary pre-conditions for the success of a civilization in addition to being savagely challenged does not remove or minimize the importance of challenge.

The problem today is that the challenges that faced every prior civilization are anachronisms; history book citations; at the most distant thunder. Lions, tigers, and bears are now found on the endangered species lists and in zoos. People know if they live in flood or earthquake zones. Instead of flooding, in some cases people want dams removed because too little water is flowing downstream. Hurricanes and cyclones which used to come with no warning now come with days if not a week. In some cases even tornadoes and tidal waves have had warnings. Food and shelter for most of the world's population, a number in the many of billions, is taken for granted. Producing food, which used to be everyone's business, is now so rare that most readers will not be able to name a professional farmer that they know. Open and common banditry on the roads and high seas is now a rarity. Wars, commonplace on the world scene as recently as 200 years ago are now scarce, and more appropriately termed limited conflicts. Clean water, sanitation, medical care, electrical power – things that people considered luxuries or fiction 200 years ago are now taken for granted.

There are "challenges" today, but for most of the world they are radically and qualitatively different from those that made civilizations great. If the definition of "challenge" is something like the Nile flooding, where a miss causes a large part of the population to die and possibly puts the viability of the whole civilization at risk, then today we have more appropriately "opportunities" rather than "challenges". For most of the Western democracies, the "challenge", or more appropriately the "struggle", or "opportunity" if you like, is how to appropriately allocate the work-product of every person, organization, and corporation in the country, which when converted to a currency basis becomes the GDP for the country. But since that takes too long to write or read, we will abbreviate it here to "splitting up the spoils". Civilizations are now just economic machines of various sizes and efficiencies. How much money comes out of whose pockets performing which activities, whose pockets does it go into under which pre-conditions, and how many restrictions will be placed on all of these and their supporting activities – this is what modern society is fundamentally about. Or you can use Ambrose Bierce's abbreviated definition: "A plunders from B the goods of C, and for compensation B picks the pocket of D of the money belonging to E." Now, Bierce was a self-described cynic (expansively paraphrasing him, someone who sees things as they really are, not as we dream, hope, wish, believe, desire, want, or need them to be), and so to minimize offending those not already offended, his definition will remain sequestered. And had he the opportunity to see the refined and exquisite professional brigandry of modern corporations, banks, and individuals today, a century and a quarter after his definition, he might well have written differently.

Because these societies are democracies, or democratic republics, this process is generally handled gracefully, bloodlessly, and through the rule of law, although often favoritism is purchased. In most other countries, the form of government shifts to one favoring the rule of men over the rule of law, but it is still a contest of "splitting up the spoils". In these countries, the outcome is much more predictable. The oligarchs and those backed by the army generally always get the largest share, and a lot more blood is let. But we are talking about degree, not kind. Even growing economies, like the so-called BRIC countries (Brazil, China, India, Russia), are making the above determination, albeit rather brutally and crudely in one case. China, by keeping its currency and wages artificially low, has made a determination that it will grow its economy quickly in this manner. India, by contrast, has elected to put bureaucratic red tape, administrative fees, and bribes as a high priority. But these are just choices/elections – the struggle, "splitting up the spoils", remains the same. And what is most critically vital is that the battleground for this is not Mother Nature but man and his systems – economic, social, and political. The spoils are not mined from the ground but from other men; money is not fished from the seas but from the pockets of his fellow man. As Will and Ariel Durant summarized, after spending their whole lives compiling a well-respected history of the world, and providing all kinds of delicious examples: "we conclude that the concentration of wealth is natural and inevitable, and is periodically alleviated by violent or peaceable partial redistribution. In this view all economic history is the slow heartbeat of the social organism, a vast systole and diastole of of concentrating wealth and compulsive recirculation."[46] Mother Nature has been relegated to a role now now more like those of a hulking monster on rare episodic drunken binges – dangerous and destructive to be sure should you find yourself in harm's way, but helplessly taken advantage of the rest of the time, lying motionless in a drunken, passive stupor.

Challengelessness

Toynbee's challenges that drive a successful civilization have vanished. Ardrey's Hazards and Enmity have similarly been erased, which means the factors that drive a nation's Amity (a civilization working selflessly together to achieve common goals) are absent. Turner's frontier, the Invisible Hand that cleanses immigrants of their differences and builds a nation of common values, temperaments, and inclinations, is to be found only in the bookstore and movie section. As new people pile into each nation, their identity can remain more with the culture they left behind than with the culture they just joined. They may seek out others with the same cultural background to live and socialize with. Their language skills may remain with their native tongue; their customs and loyalties may follow. Had some attack of Hazard or Enmity sufficient to pull everyone together taken place, this lack of a frontier might be at least partially compensated for, but this equation is

---

46 The Lessons of History, Will and Ariel Durant, Simon & Schuster, New York, 1968, p. 57

equally powerless. Or if a frontier could have had baptized them in the common uniqueness and brotherhood of their new land, but that is also not to be. So there is no assimilation, no acculturation, no bonding, no common ground, no common values, no common experience. And in each modern society, where the "opportunity" or "struggle" is splitting up the spoils, the contest, maybe well-mannered, of how much each one can get for themselves and their family, contains nothing inherently self-governing to preserve order, save the laws of the land and what is taught at home and in school. Common values forged at the frontier, or bled out side by side in defense of enemy or dire hazard, or from a survival-of-us-all battle for their civilization - none of these can be found. Lacking common experience people lack trust; lacking common goals people lack cooperation; lacking common values people lack appreciation. Lacking the factors that produce Amity a society devolves into grudging tolerance; benign neglect; NIMBY (not in my backyard); an unconcern for the greater good; disrespect for public rules, privileges, and assets; disabuse of the core principles of the country (most often patriotism); an undue self-first emphasis; and a hypocritical unconcern about whether the exercise of your "rights" are trespassing on someone else's.

The degree to which this happens depends on the cohesiveness and depth of the starting cultural values and bonds in a society, the number of newcomers who arrive as a fraction of the existing population, how well the newcomers acculturate, and how orderly the "struggle for the spoils" is carried out. So in a country with a homogenous population (not a hodge-podge of smaller nations stuck together after a war), with a common language, near-uniform religious beliefs, common customs, and a combination of high immigration hurdles and relative unattractiveness to new arrivals (social benefits slow to take effect), the immigrant dilution is so unnoticeable that the nation can retain its original cohesiveness. New arrivals become acclimated and "nationalized".

But a country where the opposites are true, it is easy for a flood of immigrants to co-locate with others of their own culture and language, indefinitely postponing their immersive experience. If social benefits are easy to come by (Great Britain), or jobs abundant at at a certain pay level (U.S.), the flooding pressure is enhanced.

But even in an "ideal" case, without considering immigration, with Ardrey's Amity equation broken (Hazard and Enmity have vanished), the innate cohesive forces keeping society together are missing. People go their own way, focus on their own needs, concern themselves exclusively with their own priorities, and do not relate to, identify with, or feel a need to concede anything for the national good. Rather than overlooking faults in their neighbors, they are more apt to be be annoyed by them. Instead of being sympathetic to the sacrifices made to create and defend their country, they are more likely to be apathetic or even aggravated by the same demands if requested of them. Greedily competing for their share of the spoils, without a willingness to make any of the sacrifices that their ancestors made to create the framework that allowed the spoils to be produced, there are soon few left willing to dedicate their lives in the preservation of that framework. Some historians have claimed that it takes but three generations to forget a wrenching, national lesson – war, depression, revolution. With nothing holding the national consciousness in tune, one can see why these historians may be right.

The malady of most modern societies is challengelessness. Oh there are problems, and troubles, and difficulties, and tragedies, and disasters, as well as opportunities, and choices, and tests, and struggles, but not challenges in the Toynbee or Ardrey or Turner sense of the word. Challengelessness produces wallowing on every national dimension, to the point that one can find subgroups within society becoming frustrated and turning against the very principles, values, and sacrifices that made it great, strong, vibrant, and formidable at its founding and expansion. If the reader is looking for fault there is none. The causes for which challenge originated have vanished evanescently, and are now just dust in the dry brittle pages of unread history.

Some countries in the world remain locked in a perpetual stasis – the people poor and right-less; power and money oligarchically-condensed into a tiny minority often backed by the military. These countries will be excluded from any further discussion – the pre-conditions for progress are absent. For the rest of the world, every nation is in a "coasting" mode – where the focus of the society is "splitting up the spoils" - the economic, social, and political decisions of which groups in society keep which share of the economic output of the country. Nations may not be "coasting" economically. But they are coasting with respect to making progress in the holistic, historic Toynbee context – the mimesis process that enables a small creative minority to lead the rest of society by example to continuous improvements, step by step by step. Surveys in Western European countries show that people are most interested in a shorter work week, more vacation time, and an earlier retirement age. Everything else is already paid for by the government or affordable for most. In France, the top career choice for young people is to be a civil servant; that is, to not produce anything of value but to be part of the social system that allows value to be produced by hopefully someone else. In the 60,000 year context, in the hunting party they all want to count, clean, or carry the spears, but none of them want to have to throw one at their dinner.

In Japan the talents that produced the exalted melded metallurgy of the steel in the katana, or Samurai sword, and the didactic discipline of bushido now produce technology for technology's sake. Electronic devices of any imaginable purpose will sell – they just need to have a model life of a few months since the customer tires and expects newness in that time-frame. Even living creatures have been replaced by electronic technology, including people. Only the worst remnants of the emperor periods remain, with government in a pseudo-parasitic, pseudo-symbiotic death dance with major economic institutions like banks and industry, too encumbered by custom, habit, and tradition to escape. All the while the country remains in a persistent macroeconomic slump, with deflation appearing a significantly-probable scenario, and with governments that have a hard time lasting for more than a year at a time.

Half-way between Japan and Europe we find the United States. 250 years ago its founding citizens were willing to give their lives to settle in a wilderness, throw off the chains of colonialism, and then sacrifice whatever it took to have a compromised union, warts, trade-offs, and all. One hundred years later 2% of the population died just to re-affirm the importance of that union in a Civil War. Today 2% would be six million people, a figure most Americans of today cannot comprehend. Sixty years ago Americans, more than exhausted by the destruction that over a decade of terrible economic depression had taken on livelihoods, homes, farms, hopes, and even lives, for the most part willfully shouldered the responsibility to sail overseas and fight two totalitarian empires, enemies that few had any real tangible knowledge of or direct contact with prior to their departure. Almost half a million Americans died in this war.

Now look at the America of today. If most anyone under any circumstance is asked to contribute something of theirs for the public good, no matter how dire and deep the need, the answer is almost always predictably no. Sacrifice has been redefined to be the investment you make with your time so you become richer. Religion has been redefined, for many, as a place you go to pray for riches from Jesus, the guy who said that you cannot serve God and Mammon; that a rich man getting to Heaven had the same chance as a camel getting through the narrowest gate into Jerusalem (or threading a needle with rope, or an elephant through the eye of a needle, depending on your translation). "He who dies with the most toys wins" used to be a funny bumper sticker; it is now a serious goal for many and a rarity on bumpers. Many public employees technically retire on "disability", although you would never be able to tell. Many retire with pensions, guaranteed annual incomes, much higher than their salary while they worked, by taking advantage of arcane overtime rules. These people, while nominally working as public servants, retire as mini robber barons, caring nought for their financial abuse of their country. By contrast many of these same people are happy to stand idly by and allow volunteers in the military to fight and even die to protect them without enabling them to become citizens, or have all the civil rights that they do, or to keep their families from losing their houses while they serve multiple redeployments without their normal income, or have adequate child care when separated from their young children, or to have adequate medical treatment when they arrive back home damaged physically and/or psychologically, or to obtain sufficient help in finding suitable employment when they are discharged. Especially if providing any of this to these veterans might cost them some of their income (in the form of higher taxes) that they never earned or deserved in the first place.

By highlighting this group of citizens the author is not attempting to portray them as somehow "worse" than others. They just make the cleanest, crispest, best-est example of the contrast between the "I only regret that I have but one life to give for my country" attitude of the citizens who founded the U.S. and the attitude and behavior of many citizens in the U.S. today. One has to search for too long today to find those individuals who are careful to make sure that their behavior does not negatively impact the rights, interests, and opportunities of everyone else, unseen and unrepresented, and cheerfully willing to contribute to the common good. Yet this was the shared set of values that enabled a group of individuals with widely-differing views to construct a foundation for a lasting government for the U.S.

Here is how another author viewed his society as its citizens slowly transitioned from a selfless to a self-centered set of motives, set against the backdrop of a civilization that had risen to the challenges facing it to become the greatest in the world:

"When, however, with the growth of their population, civilization, and territory, it was seen that they had become powerful and prosperous... their wealth aroused envy. Neighboring kings and peoples attacked them .... They girded themselves in haste and with mutual encouragement marched forth to meet their foes, protecting by force of arms their country, liberty, and parents. Then, after bravely warding off the dangers that beset them, they lent aid to their allies and friends, and made new friends by a greater readiness to render services than to accept them from others.... In peace and war, virtue was held in high esteem. The closest unity prevailed, and avarice was a thing almost unknown. Justice and righteousness were upheld not so much by law as by natural instinct.... Between themselves the citizens contended only for honor.... In peace, they governed by conferring benefits on their subjects, not by intimidation; and when wronged would rather pardon than seek vengeance....

When Carthage, Rome's rival in her quest for empire, had been annihilated, every land and sea lay open to her. It was then that fortune turned unkind and confounded all her enterprises.... Growing love of money, and the lust for power which followed it, engendered every kind of evil. Avarice destroyed honor, integrity, and every other virtue, and instead taught men to be proud and cruel, to neglect religion, and to hold nothing too sacred to sell. Ambition tempted many to be false, to have one thought hidden in their hearts, and another ready on their tongues, to become a man's friend or enemy not because they judged him worthy or unworthy but because they thought it would pay them, and to put on a semblance of virtues that they had not.... Avarice ... means setting your heart on money, a thing no wise man ever did.... It knows no bounds and can never be satisfied; he that has not, wants; and he that has, wants more.... As soon as wealth came to be a mark of a distinction and an easy way of renown, ...virtue began to decline. Poverty was now looked on as a disgrace .... Riches made the younger generation a prey to luxury, avarice, and pride.... Mansions and villas reared aloft on such a scale that they looked like so many towns .... I need not remind you of some enterprises that no one but an eyewitness will believe – how private citizens have often levelled mountains and paved seas for their building operations."[47]

What is interesting is not just the observation that Rome transitioned from a civilization based on virtue, selflessness, and citizenship to one of selfishness and greed, but that it did so more than 500 years before the formal date given for its actual demise in 476 AD. Sallust was making these observations around 50 BC, while Rome was still a Republic. Does this parallel transition from selfless to selfish in Roman and U.S. civilizations require the U.S. to end poorly as did the Romans? The Romans fell because they lost their way (sure, it's more complicated), and eventually became insufficiently competent. The question for the U.S. would be, if its citizens also seem to be losing their way, how fast are they losing their competency, and can it be stabilized or reversed? And similarly for England, and Japan, and France, and Italy, and so on.

The vicious irony is that the difficulties and problems of today are much more complex, intractable, and convoluted than those of the past 60,000 years. Unfortunately, they are not the challenges that nations and civilizations need to automatically, à la Adam Smith, pull together all members to accomplish the next great thing. 4,500 years ago, in the infancy of mankind and civilization, man developed the tools to build the Great Pyramids, an astonishing accomplishment which even today cannot be adequately explained. Every so often a problem would arise for which man's tools were incapable of handling, like the Gordian Knot, and then, like Alexander, man would simply use his available tools to deal with the problem in quick, sure, and wholly-inappropriate fashion. Today, every problem is a Gordian Knot. Challenges like the need to tame the Nile River to prevent everyone's family from starving are no more. The Great Pyramid or Nile River irrigation tools cannot solve Gordian Knot problems. This mismatch between man's capabilities and the problems of today is reflected in H.L. Mencken's

47 The Conspiracy of Catiline, Sallust, Translated by S.A. Handford, Penguin Books, London, 1963, pp. 179-183

observation: "There is always an easy solution to every human problem—neat, plausible, and wrong." Man's nature demands fast, effective, straight-forward action to fix problems. Complex, convoluted, interconnected problems that require equivalently-deep solutions just engender either frustration or H.L. Mencken's comment. People just aren't designed for patience when facing problems that need solving – it is not in their genes. Many people can remember the old cartoon of the two vultures on a tree branch - "Patience my ass – I'm gonna kill somebody." It is funny because it rings so true for most people. Laboriously unwinding devilishly-complicated problems that present only muddled and confusing symptoms – for the average person, the modern-day equivalent of swords, guns, and violence appears a more enticing remedy.

So is this the end? Are all societies going to slowly simmer unevenly, become increasingly disparate, dissonant, and dysfunctional? You will need to read on to see where this track seems to lead, but bear in mind that man's nature seems to be solidly immutable, and societies and civilization become only more complex, inter-related, and subtle.

Chapter 15
Adjusting to Change

60,000 Years of Experience

Historically, man has been lucky enough to have been presented clearly and directly with the consequences of his actions. He entered Australia maybe 60,000 years ago, and within 500 to 1,000 years all the large animals capable of providing food were gone. Most likely he prayed to all his gods for the animals to come back but they did not. Oops! I guess we need to change our food-foraging style. And they did, plus their stature went to the small side in a reflection of the lack of large protein sources. The same thing happened in North and South America between maybe 12,000 to 14,000 years ago. The large, easy-to-catch animals all disappeared in around 1,000 years, in spite of whatever prayers were directed at the animal-providing gods; leaving buffalo for those on the North American plains; but - oh crap - acorns, pinion nuts, maize, potatoes, roots, berries, deer, fish, racoons, and a bear of two for most everyone else. In both cases, man instantly knew when the easy game was gone and the rules changed. He surely used his beliefs in his gods which had appeared to work for a thousand or so years, but when it was over, his beliefs notwithstanding, that was it. All those who had been driving the boat by looking at the wake had an unpleasant shock – the world as they knew it had abruptly ended.

The Fertile Crescent was the explosion of civilization in the Western world. But a few thousand years later, the global warming that continued after the end of the Ice Age kept cooking this area until it became a desert, and most everyone left for better climes. The Anasazi went through the same thing around 800 years ago across western North America. Just 80 years ago, drought turned the farming areas in the central part of the U.S. into what ended up being called the Dust Bowl. Hundreds of thousands of people left the area, since it was obvious that the land was unfarmable. In all cases, most likely people turned to their beliefs in an attempt to ward off the climate change, hoping that they were seeing a temporary aberration that would soon reverse itself. But Mother Nature was not to be denied, and many of these areas were abandoned forever. Man's beliefs would have failed him, but he moved on.

The same thing happened in Europe and England with the elimination of old-growth forests for ship-building and for fuel. Only old-growth wood had the strength necessary for large ships, especially warships whose sides would attempt to withstand cannonball volleys, or ships designed for use in the Arctic icepack. The expanding population also needed the wood for heat and housing, and so Europe and England basically ran out of good wood, with the unintended consequence of also running out of the game which lived in the same forests. But when the wood and food ran out, everyone knew it. Wood had to start coming from the colonies, and everyone had to switch to farming in order to survive. It was pretty much an immediate, in-your-face calamity, and had to be dealt with in the span of a generation or two.

Undoubtedly, many people simply reacted to all of the new realities listed above by just changing what they ate, where they lived, or how they lived. This was especially true if you had just chopped down the last old growth tree, or came to the end of the vein of copper or gold you were mining. The end was obviously the end. But drought, or the elimination of all the big game animals, may have been more subtle, erratic, and extended. This may have given rise to a difference of opinion: some would claim the problem was transitory – others that it was permanent. Hardened by debate and desperation, in some people opinion would shade into hope and then to belief. Once established, belief is unshakable, since questioning it directly implies that the belief holder is in error, and cognitive dissonance (see Chapter 8), will not allow this mental conflict to take place. So the small groups of men who believe that things are not changing, that everything will turn out OK in the long term, will ignore all the evidence to the contrary, and those who argue with them, and keep waiting.

Eventually of course Mother Nature takes care of everything. Those who held on to their beliefs that reality had not changed, even though it had, either had to finally concede that they were wrong, or they starved to death or the equivalent and disappeared.

The Newer Reality – A Belief-Gated World

The point of these few examples is that in the collision between Mother Nature and man's belief structure, which in the previous examples were his hopes for food, resources, or climate remaining constant and not changing for the worse, Mother Nature always wins if she "wants to". And man, faced with the obvious, will change, and cope, and adjust, and thrive in the new environment. The memory of large game, or rain where there is now desert, is quickly put aside and forgotten.

But where the situation is different - if man does not directly collide with Mother Nature but simply passes silently by large billboards that she has constructed for man's benefit – all bets are off on changes in man's hopes or beliefs. Like a canine, man's nature is such that he responds quickly and consistently to a folded newspaper whacked across his face; but gracefully unroll it so he only gets to read it (no whacking allowed), and with man you often have about the same success as with a bulldog or a boxer – not interested. Like his best friend, man has to taste it and experience it before he will wholesale buy it; before he will change his belief structure. Information, even if he bothers to read it, seldom changes anything. He has to live it, or feel it, to believe it.

Especially in the extreme case where beliefs are all he has – when the choice is between nothing at all and his beliefs, man chooses his beliefs. If some other emotionally-held belief is involved, for example patriotism or religion, then a subordinate or related belief will be similarly tightly held. In the myriad of cases where something less than survival is at issue, man will often hold on to his beliefs way past the point at which they are obviously wrong, especially if there is some external encouragement to do so. Once the belief is established, by social norms or tradition or culture, or parents, it is difficult to wash away and replace, lacking a collision with a conflicting reality. Just passing Mother Nature's billboards, no matter how informative, or colorful, or clear, or repetitive, is most often insufficient. "That's my story and I'm sticking with it" goes the old phrase. It is sort of Newton's Second Law of Believing – once a belief is established, it can only be changed if a specific force is applied to it, and the size of the force necessary to change it is proportional to how strongly it is held (its inertia). Hearing information does not count as a force, unless it triggers the Cognitive Dissonance force (see Chapter 8).

Patriotic and religious beliefs, and beliefs acquired through personal experience, often have large belief-inertia. Beliefs underlined or accentuated with strong emotions, like those tied to fundamental rights, or like freedom and liberty and privacy and honor, or hate, or fear, or prejudice, hold high inertial values. Beliefs acquired through simply habit and repetition can be difficult to move but have discernibly less inertia.

Without over-dwelling on this and embarrassing some number who may still believe otherwise, it was believed for thousands of years after it had been proved and it was patently obvious otherwise that the world was flat. Whether you were just an average person approaching a mountain from a distance, or watching a masted ship go over the horizon, or you accepted the scientists' calculations, it was pretty obviously round. Plus if you listened to the flat-worlder's explanations for what the world was sitting on, or what happened to oceans and rivers at the edge, it was pretty much a train wreck, but people kept on believing nonetheless. Even after gravity was explained (it won't work flat) people kept believing in flat. Even now, with photographs from zillions of spacecraft circling a round earth, some probably still believe it is flat (the photos are fakes).

Or take the earth-centered view of the solar system, and galaxy, and universe for that matter. This one had the major western Christian church behind it – disagree, and the punishment ranged from social ostracism to eternity in Hell or worse. The church felt that the Bible and its doctrine demanded that the Earth be the center of everything. What did the senior church management believe? Only God knows. So as everyone knows, the mechanical astronomical models necessary to explain the observed movement of the planets across the sky with the Earth as the center of the solar system became much more complicated than anything that Rube Goldberg could imagine, and still they failed to adequately mimic the motion properly. But they had to keep trying - the church beliefs demanded it. The more that observational data and theory came to point to the sun being the center of the solar system, the more the church successfully threatened and pressured. It was not until the middle of the 18th century that books containing the theory of a sun-centered solar system were taken off the banned-book list.

The Greeks believed the purpose of the brain was to be a radiator, and there it stood for centuries in some circles. Peddlers and cheats sold cure-alls and patent-medicines for thousands of years, and people paid money that they had worked dearly for in exchange for these worthless liquids that they often firmly believed or at least desperately hoped would bring miraculous cures. People believed in every kind of fortune-teller, whether reading the stars, or hands, or cards, and would pay for their assistance. Good-luck charms still flourish, as do astrologers, along with all manner of lucky objects, including a bewildering variety of expensive magneto-astro-flow star-channeling energy-enhancing wristbands and bracelets, the sellers of which will solemnly attest provide miraculous powers previously available only to the gods.

A point should be made here on faith and belief. Medical science has verified that belief works in medicine – if you are positive that something is going to help you, then it will, at least better than nothing. If you are told it can ameliorate or eliminate a medical symptom, it often can, whether it actually causally does or not. This is the well-known and established placebo effect. If you take a drug, and it works, some of that may be the drug, but some may be the placebo effect also, and the contribution of each cannot be individually assessed. The placebo process is a monument to the strength of belief – it has the power to eliminate medical symptoms and make people feel better. Used in a contrary manner, by those who believe in voodoo and the equivalent, it can have equally catastrophic negative effects. This is one explanation for Newton's Second Law of Belief – it takes a significant force to change a belief because it possesses such dramatic power. And so the magic polyethylene bracelet with the fairy dust from the planet Omigon that channels angel voices into your life force – hey, it most likely will work if you truly believe in it. So will one made with titanium or iridium dust or even just polyethylene, as long as you believe (putting unusual stuff in it makes it seem more magical). Including these items in the previous discussion was to show that people will continue their beliefs wanting hard evidence to the contrary.

Since in these cases, in the form of the placebo effect, there is evidence to support their beliefs, they may stay around forever, permanently enriching the magic bracelet rip-off entrepreneurial class.

In all the previous examples, there was no hard collision with reality or with Mother Nature to challenge these beliefs, so they stick, and are hard to dislodge. On the other hand, if you eat all the mammoths and believe that more will soon show up, you are going to wait until all the believers starve to death and those who remain change their mind and adjust. So the lesson is that man can readily change his beliefs when smashed by reality, but change is indefinitely postponed when man only gets a view of reality, but does not get to feel it or live it.

Sailing into the Future

After 60,000 years of having had the advantage of the most critical and significant changes in the world being brutally obvious, man has entered a new era where voracious subtlety, audacious complexity, and a vicious absence of collisions with reality dominate. None of these will slap man in the face, knock him senseless to his knees, or leave him parched or starving. Coal is slowly killing miners, trees, lakes; bringing unfixable tropical disease and pests further north each year; making bad summer weather worse and bad winter weather easier, but it happens at such a pace and at such a distance that it can be readily ignored for convenience's sake. Plus it's cheap. Setting the right exchange rate with 150 other countries, and potentially having tariffs on 200 different commodities that you import, and another 200 that you export to each of those 150 countries – who has the time, patience, or interest to deal with that? People say the ocean is running out of fish – but they seem to be there when you go and get some so why should you be bothered? The water table keeps dropping in your area and the winter snowfall is less and less due to warming, but you always hear this kind of hand-wringing so you ignore it. Glaciers and icecaps are melting but they're not near you. The enemy of my enemy is my friend – that seems like a really neat idea. Too bad no one remembers to check back in a decade to see if it still seems just as neat – someone else is responsible a decade later. Someone mentions nuclear power and – forget it, that's all you need to hear – we're not having any of that terrible killer around here. We'll stick with coal – the reliable, steady killer that we can all trust. What to do about the rising costs of medical care, and pension costs for public employees and those on Social Security, and entitlement costs as percent of GDP, and national debt as a percent of GDP – who can even grasp all the issues, aspects, and trade-offs associated with these complex problems? No more vaccines for the kids – I heard on the web that they cause autism, along with fluoridation being a secret conspiracy by aliens from the planet Zombie to turn our minds to mush. Plus your religion is clearly wrong – it thinks it is the only right religion, and should be imposed on secular society, starting with the education of children. I know this for a fact because mine is the only right religion, and mine should be imposed on secular society, clearly starting with your ridiculously wrong religious beliefs. And so it goes.

You might have a different list of issues and problems. The above is not intended to be comprehensive, just representative. Contrasted with the last mammoth or the last old growth tree, which when they were gone were gone, all of these issues do not even appear to be problems or challenges unless someone elects to think about them. There is not even a trigger or a flag from Mother Nature that something is up. After 60,000 years, it's just life as normal, as far as man can tell. The great ship of state, with mankind on board, is sailing smoothly on sunny seas, but whether she has already struck a reef and torn out her bottom and is slowly sinking, or is about to, no one seems to know, and maybe few even care. Mankind is waiting for the storm warning, with high winds and waves coming over the bow, and the ship pitching roughly, and then everyone will pay attention. But that warning will never come.

Chapter 16
The Belie in Belief

Some History ...

    In the years preceding the entry of the United States into World War II, one of the most famous and well-known Americans led the fight to keep the country out of the conflict – Charles Lindbergh. This man was known by almost everyone; loved and respected by many; considered worthy of sympathy by a majority of Americans. Lindbergh spoke out against the U.S. entering the war for years, and his fame meant that his speeches were well-attended and widely covered by the print press and radio. He became a member of America First, an isolationist group that formed in 1940 that had other prominent Americans as members. Due to his pre-existing fame as a pilot, and the notoriety and sympathy from the kidnapping of his son, his efforts were quite effective for years, until he began to lose his audience in late 1941 as his anti-war reasons began to sound just too unpalatable: after Lindbergh four months before Pearl Harbor said in Iowa "the three most important groups which have been pressing this country toward war are the British, the Jewish, and the Roosevelt Administration," Eugene Meyer, owner and publisher of The Washington Post, who had served as both chair of the Federal Reserve System and Reconstruction Finance Committee for President Hoover, at the time observed "Mr. Lindbergh's speech in Iowa show(ed) that he practically adopted the Hitler programme ..."[48]

    It is impossible to sit here more than seventy years after the fact and accurately assign motivations for Lindbergh's behavior. But he was the focus of the world's master propagandist, probably the best there has ever been; the man who everyone since has sought to emulate, copy, and mimic. "You will never find millions of people who will give their lives for a book. You will never find millions of people who will give their lives for an economic program. But millions of people will one day be willing to give their lives for a gospel."[49] That was from a speech by Joseph Goebbels, Hitler's Reichminister of Propaganda. And by "gospel" (German to English translation artifact) Goebbels did not mean it in the narrow religious sense that Americans would take it, but as any kind of emotionally-intoxicating theme, idea, or principle. The shorter, sweeter, and simpler, the better. Knowing well the impact Lindbergh (as well as others, especially in Britain) could have on public opinion, Goebbels would have unleashed the best he had at Lindbergh. Fabricated details on all the good the National Socialist party was doing (he

---

48 Franklin and Winston, Jon Meacham, Random House, New York, 2003, p. 127
49 Goebbels, Ralf Georg Reuth, trans. By Krishna Winston, Harcourt Brace & Company, New York, 1993, p. 82

was not the inventor of mis-information, maybe Sun Tzu et al get that credit, but Goebbels made it an art form), how the negative reports on them were all mis-represented, a million reasons why what happened in Europe had no bearing on the U.S., and then the spell – the gospel – the beautiful imagery of a society, unflawed, perfect, with people of only a single racial background - blond, strong, energetic – the master Aryan race.

One gauge of Goebbels' success was found long after Lindbergh's death. Carefully protected by Lindbergh through meticulous planning, he had been able to create three post-war families in Germany with three German women, two of whom were sisters, producing in all seven adult children. Would Lindbergh have attempted this without Goebbels' coaching? Some may say yes, but it is extremely unlikely that he would go through such elaborate and extreme behavior on his own. This was not exactly common behavior in the 1950's. Without getting into the unprovable debate on whether Lindbergh was sold on the "pure race" message, he was clearly sold on having many German families and children. Lindbergh and his wife were key influence-setters in American society, and were targeted by Goebbels as were others in British society. Lindbergh and his wife spent considerable time with Hermann Goering and other key German members of the government, viewing Goering's vast art collection (stolen of course from Jews sent off to concentration camps), and receiving a medal.

What was the return on Goebbels' investment? Impossible to accurately measure due to the number of other factors at play and the lack of a "control", a way to "run the world over again" without Goebbels in it. But Lindbergh and the others were not anti-war, they were, in their words, America-First. Fortress America, impregnable, so strong militarily that no potential enemy would attempt an attack. That might have had some value, if it were only executed to any degree. But the U.S. was a paper tiger, with weapons both in quantity and quality inferior to both Japan and Germany. There was no preparation, no fortress. When Churchill successfully pleaded with Roosevelt to divert U.S. medium and heavy tanks (Grants and Shermans) and 105mm howitzers to fight Rommel in North Africa, the U.S. Army went apoplectically hysterical, as it was all the armaments they had. Hitler had told his general staff that the time frame for war was 1945, and they were targeting their equipment and munitions build accordingly. Hitler was wrong for the first time when he misjudged the international reaction to his invasion of Poland – had they had six more years, they would have been unstoppable. Hitler's military plan was to first produce quality, then quantity. The U.S. never had a gun to match the German 88, nor Me109 nor Japanese Zero fighters until toward the end of the war. The U.S. never had a tank to match the German Panzer IV, Panther, or Tiger. The Sherman tank was an underpowered, under-armored, under-gunned deathtrap, pushed by generals back home that never had to go out and fight in one. Ronsons, the British called them, after the lighter. Early battles in the Pacific saw basically unarmed and unarmored DE's (destroyer escorts) heroically taking on Japanese cruisers. Every single U.S. attack bomber in the battle of Midway was shot down before it could do any damage until the Japanese commander made a fatal tactical error and put all his planes on the carrier decks at the same time instead of keeping half in the air ready for defense. And prepared? All the ships and planes in Pearl Harbor and every airfield on Oahu were lined up in neat little rows. Even the "great" General MacArthur in the Philippines – 10 hours after Pearl Harbor he still had all his aircraft lined up in perfect order, waiting to be blown into ragged pieces - inexcusable incompetency.

Even if you leave to one side the argument about whether the U.S. should have proactively entered or threatened to enter the war earlier, its lack of preparation for the war, which we can lay directly at the feet of these groups and those in Congress who either supported or who were afraid to oppose them, wasted many, many American lives unnecessarily and prolonged the war by one or more years. Sure, friendly fire, bad tactical and strategic decisions and the like also kill men unnecessarily, but this is hardly a moral or even a logical justification. Under the guise of America First, the end result of this movement, regardless of their original intentions, ending up being as anti-American as you could imagine, just as Goebbels intended.

Not that the individuals were anti-American; far from it – it was just that the cumulative effect of their behaviors ended up to the detriment of American interests and the lives of soldiers. During the war, Lindbergh assisted civilian industry in building improved fighter and bomber aircraft, and even flew as a civilian unofficial and unsanctioned P-38 combat missions in the Pacific toward the end of the war. Other America First members most likely enlisted and died for their country.

Like any such group, the motivations of America-First members would have been varied. Some would have been earnestly for a Fortress America and disappointed that it was not to be. Some would be opposed to participation in any European war that was out of sight, out of mind; for American lives to be lost in any distant conflict. Some were secretly pro-National Socialist politically, or some aspect of its politics – its anti-semitism, its anti-communism, its anti-socialism, its pro-Aryanism. Some were anti-war/pro-peace regardless. So it is not that Goebbels' propaganda affected everyone – far from it. But it brought some to the group that otherwise might have stayed away, and reinforced, substantiated, and validated the beliefs of those who were sympathetic to his messages.

Eventually the war was won with the sheer quantity of U.S. men and materiel. But along with Hitler's megalomaniacal excursion into fantasyland, Werner von Braun was a key factor in winning the war, or at least winning it in 1945, or with the casualties as low as they were. His religious fixation on getting into space drove him to ignite a passion in Hitler for his rocket (V2) as a super-weapon, and as a result it was the top priority for resources in Germany, including superseding the Me262, the world's only usable jet fighter. (Luckily Hitler was a sucker for super-weapons – he had instructed his tank people to work on a 1,000 ton [not a typo] tank.) Had the V2 resources instead gone into the Me262, the Germans would have been able to maintain air superiority, possibly indefinitely. At the time this concept (air superiority) was not well understood, but today we know that it would have been pivotal. von Braun ended up in the U.S. after the war, responsible for the Saturn V that put men on the moon, despised in Britain and Belgium for the WWII deaths his V2 caused, without recognition for the lives he saved by stalling the Me262; albeit it was not done intentionally.

Why is this germane? Without Hitler's blundering into Poland, and then into Russia, resulting from drinking his own Kool-Aid as we would say today, and the V2 diversion, the U.S.'s lack of preparation for the war could have proved pivotal, making the war in the Europe appearing too costly to pursue to victory and resulting in a stand-off with Germany there. The U.S. would have turned 100% toward the war in the Pacific and still won it, but Western Europe would likely still be the Third Reich.

Goebbels' propaganda machine did not just work on Lindbergh – he is singled out here only because he was a singularly important figure in America, and because Goebbels knew this and also focussed in on him. Goebbels' efforts worked effectively on many other individuals, and on whole populations, by using the press in free countries, which would report the misinformation that his group would generate. If a gospel or motivating principle was called for it was utilized, but so were simple ideas that would appeal to the average newspaper reader, like reporting that a country or region had "requested" that the Germans send in troops, to preserve order, defend the safety of resident Germans, or some other reasonable-sounding argument that of course was totally fabricated. They would often falsify official documents to support their position.

Of course, if you were non-belief-driven and well-informed you were not taken in by Goebbels' intellectual fluff. "The Führer sends word that he acted because the Czechs would not demobilize their military forces; because they were continuing to keep their contacts with Russia, and because they mistreated Germans. Such pretexts may be good for Goebbels' propaganda, but they should not use them when talking with us, whose only fault is that we deal too loyally with the Germans."[50] So complained Count Ciano, Mussolini's Foreign Minister, about the line of crapola fed to Mussolini about

---

50 Ciano's Diary, ed. by Malcolm Muggeridge, William Heinemann Ltd, London, 1947, p. 45

the German invasion of Czechoslovakia.

In addition to his external propaganda machine, Goebbels also had to work on the German people, first to get Hitler into power and then to marshal the people behind him. People had used parades and marches before, but Goebbels was the first to make them so large that they produced stirring emotional reactions. He was the first to use sophisticated motion pictures for propaganda, taking advantage of some of the best directors and actors available, resulting in classics like "Triumph of the Will" and "Jud Süss". This is not a book on Goebbels, but he was the master of using simple but emotionally-motivating concepts and ideas to grab and sustain the attention of his audiences.

If this is proving a little too subtle and complex, Goebbels never used the truth when a lie/misstatement/exaggeration would better serve his purpose. And he made sure his lies pulled at the strongest emotions available in his target audience. Patriotism was one of his favorite, along with exercising a prejudice of hate. As fans of totalitarianism fondly know, to keep the evil dictator in power you need to find an even more evil "enemy" to hate and despise, to keep your attention off the bad things the dictator is doing to you. If you prefer, sometimes the poet says it best:

> "Thus men give credit, as of old,
> to fantasies of their desire;
> the things of truth will leave them cold,
> but fiction sets their hearts on fire."[51]

Now for some readers, World War II is going to be "so yesterday". So how about the murder trial of OJ Simpson in the United States in 1995? The evidence clearly showed he had murdered the two individuals as charged. The civil suit later found him guilty, although to a lesser civil standard. Even the jurors after the trial said he probably did it, but the prosecution did not satisfactorily prove the case. The evidence available at the time but for whatever reasons not used in the trial made it a dead certainty that he had committed the murders. So what went wrong? Anyone who paid attention to the trial knows the question had to be posed as: what went right? And the answer was, sadly, likely nothing. But the coup de gras may have been prior to the start of the trial, when the district attorney of Los Angeles made a most interesting decision. The murder occurred in Brentwood, California, an extremely wealthy suburb of Los Angeles in Los Angeles County. Normally murders in Brentwood are tried in Santa Monica, another wealthy area, so a "trial by one's peers" can take place. Racially, Brentwood is 80% white and 1% black. Santa Monica is 78% white and 4% black. But the district attorney decided to hold the trial in downtown Los Angeles, with a jury pool that economically did not represent Mr. Simpson's peers. And the jury did end up

---

51 Mary Jane Burdis, Unpublished material, circa 1965

75% black racially, with two whites and one Hispanic, as the district attorney had no doubt intended.

If there is one belief common among large inner city black Americans, it is that black people do not get a fair shake from the police. This is based on years and countless personal stories passed on through relatives and neighbors – everyone believes it. Mr. Simpson's defense team made sure the jury knew that here was a black man who had been able to rise to success in a white man's world, and here were the L.A. police, possibly engaged in a conspiracy to blame this whole thing on him. Voting to acquit would be either righting a wrong in this case, or for any or all previous cases where blacks had been treated unfairly by the police – take your pick. After a nine month trial, it took the jury only four hours to reach a verdict. Considering the time it took to get organized on their first day of deliberations, select a foreman, and conduct a preliminary vote, there was no time to review anything. The jury did not use the evidence, i.e. facts and logic, to make up their mind. They used a much faster, much more reliable discriminator – belief. There is a more familiar pejorative word for this – prejudice.

Gerry Spence learned from the few civil cases he lost, and then when he switched to defending individuals in criminal cases, he never lost a case (although he also never lost another civil case for about 40 years). There are probably not a whole lot of attorneys who can claim the same track record, but Spence had some real whiz-bang challenges from his clients, showing: that Imelda Marcos was just an average in-the-dark housewife put upon by her dictator husband; that Randy Weaver was innocent of killing a U.S. Marshal, a challenge considering the publicity surrounding the disastrous Ruby Ridge events; that Sheriff Ed Cantrell was excused for shooting his own deputy in front of witnesses; and that Joe Esquibel, a not-very-nice-person who shot his wife in the head in front of eight witnesses including a deputy sheriff was not guilty.

But even Mr. Spence concedes that one thing cannot be overcome:

"Prejudice locks the mind. Nothing can enter. Nothing true can escape.... You can drown the prejudiced person in reason, scream, weep, and beg, but your pleas of fairness and justice will go for naught. You had just as well sing to a bag full of jelly beans.... Prejudices, like phobias, are so deeply set that even if we become aware of them we are usually helpless to do much about them.... People who are prejudiced are not only ignorant of their prejudices, they are usually quite comfortable with them. To them, prejudices are the truth - their truth."[52]

For those offended by both of the previous two examples, here is one offensive in a different way. Toward the end of the 19th century a very

---

52 How to Argue and Win Every Time, Gerry Spence, St. Martin's Press, New York, 1995, pp. 74-77

religious and sincere woman came to believe through her life experiences and her own nature, that disease and medical problems were corruption that could be purged through the appropriate use of Christian prayer. At this time, the practice of medicine was much that, although it was making strong progress. In addition, it has been proven that having a positive attitude helps those who are ill, all other things being equal. Mary Baker Eddy founded the Church of Christ, Scientist, and it is still active today in the United States. No membership figures are available by design, but estimates say that more than 100,000 people practice the tenets of this approach, which declares that Eddy's techniques and modern medicine are mutually exclusive – if you go with Christian Science, you cannot use any part of medicine.

Today, almost 150 years after this belief-based activity first was developed, medicine has solved all the problems that Ms. Eddy was frustrated in finding intractable. But instead of simply declaring that she had won and retiring this religion, or at least the part that bans concurrent medical treatments, like an athlete would retire at the end of his career, this religion doggedly carries forward. It is like people insisting that they go to a farm and bring back milk in pails, refusing to believe that milk comes pasteurized in cartons, or go and get block ice for the icebox because they don't believe in refrigerators. The Amish decline the use of many things, but that is by choice, not belief. The tragedy of course for Christian Scientists – to first degree it does not matter if the adults all decide to kill themselves off – is the penalty exacted on their children, children who never had a choice as to how their strep throat or pneumonia is treated. Retiring an athlete is not a disrespecting or dishonoring of their career; just a commemoration of its passing. But somehow this religion feels that this athletic career can continue even as the football sits motionless next to the urn filled with ashes. It is another testimony as to the power of belief – stronger than reason, logic, common sense, intelligence, and even self-preservation.

Driven by Belief

Being driven by belief is to live in a world where feelings, images, emotions, faith, fear, and hate are the controlling factors. Logic and rationality never play a part. Logical thinking takes time and effort to roll out; there are arguments and counter-arguments. Some aspects are readily scientifically-provable; in others, gray areas cannot be overcome.

But those who choose to lead others by using belief, or creed, or faith, know that they have none of the complexities, difficulties, and details of those who try to communicate in the rational world. They need only toss out the magic word, idea, theme, thought, red meat, red herring; wave the right flag, emblem, uniform, colors, symbol; point at the obvious threat, danger, fear, evil, enemy, conspiracy. They know that those who will respond, who are the finest products of belief-driven cognition will move instantly, unthinkingly, and not with the calm, disinterested, passionless lethargy of an impartial observer, but with the hot-tempered fervor and blood-lust of a true believer, willing to assemble, protest, demonstrate, lobby, and/or whatever it takes to support and defend their belief. The logical guys don't have a chance.

This is not to say that the motives of those who use Belief-Driven Cognition are necessarily all improper. Some are probably morally pure. But there is a built-in problem – since Belief-Driven Cognition is not based on anything logical or rational, there is no cross-check, validation, or verification that can be made to test its veracity. It is so easy for someone employing Belief-Driven Cognition to drift over onto the slippery slope of tossing in a concept, a principle, an idea, something that will capture, grab, and move his/her audience over to where they want them to be, and to hold them there. Or to toss out a phrase that will smear or mislead or mis-characterize someone or something else, someone or something that the phrase-tosser wants to diminish for some personal reason. Regardless of the field of the Belief-Driven Cognition practitioner – be it politics, or religion, or self-help, or psychology/sociology, or entertainment, or some combination of the above – the attraction of the power of this technique when used to mislead, as a short-cut for success, is almost irresistible.

And Belief-Driven Cognition has powers not just to convince, to sway, to move. It has the magical ability to inflame, to alarm, to arouse, to anger; to evince love, respect, admiration, adoration. Unfortunately, that makes it a most welcome tool in the domain of demagogues, religious charlatans, cultists, and others who only thrive by using Belief-Driven Cognition to take advantage of those who respond galvanically to a Belief-Driven Cognition-grounded message. The message can be self-selecting – it only has to attract enough people to form a large enough group sufficient for the purposes of the group's leader. Those not successfully influenced will simply not be part of the group. Maybe they will just be incorporated into a group with the reverse message.

The best place to start is to follow the old adage: "Behind the flag and the cross ofttimes cower the deepest of evils." If someone has both a flag and a religious symbol on their lapel or behind their podium, then they often could be speaking Latin backwards, as long as every few minutes they toss out a phrase that "sets hearts on fire". Most Americans can recall William Jennings Bryan's speech of a little over 100 years ago pleading against the gold standard: "You shall not press down upon the brow of labor this crown of thorns, you shall not crucify mankind upon a cross of gold." He was reported to have had his arms outstretched dramatically as he finished his speech. Now the one thing that 5,000 years of economic history has well-documented is that being on the gold standard works really well for people who have a lot of gold, while everyone else gets cremated at regular intervals. But economics is boring and puts people to sleep as these facts begin to be explored; no one who heard or read Bryan at the time was going to be dozing off. It is pretty hard to do much better than this in one sentence, at least from a belief-based perspective.

As Gerry Spence said, even he could not move people who had their mind made up with prejudice. Goebbels knew he could get people to die for the same basic reason – belief. Today Sunni and Shia Muslims still fail to get along from time to time based on what happened in 632 AD – that is a long, long time to retain a difference, but since it is based on religion, it is only yesterday. Almost 2,000 years have passed since the Sanhedrin, led by Caiaphas, sentenced Jesus to death for blasphemy, although their real motive was the fear that since Jesus was creating notoriety, it would attract the attention of the Romans who would come down hard on Judea. Some Christians still feel Jews today bear responsibility for Jesus' death, although Jesus himself declared his death to be foreordained many times. That would be 2,000 years of religious memory. Nothing else has the staying power of belief. More ominously, sadly, and unfortunately, history is full of wars based on religion – in some cases religions defined by people who were anything but war-like. In almost all cases, it was a belief that the attackers' religion was superior to the attackees' religion. This grand tradition continues unabated through the present day – details are not required. And then you have all of the slightly lesser-scale activities than full-up wars – like the Inquisition, where tens of thousands of people were tortured and over one thousand were burned at the stake or worse because it was determined that their "beliefs" just were not good enough. And this by a faith-based organization whose tenets are (theoretically) love, forgiveness, meekness, and charity. History has demonstrated that being belief-driven can result in behaviors that are the poster-child for hypocrisy.

This book is not about religion. This book is about factors that limit man's ability to deal successfully with his society and his man-made environment. But the story of the oppressive and militaristic side of religion, the most obvious and strongest belief-based phenomenon in man, demonstrates the power of Belief-Driven Cognition, one of the factors limiting man. Citing some feature of man's nature, like some obtuse, abstruse psychology journal, becomes simply conjecture. This book is not about conjecture – it is about unchanged behavior patterns throughout all of man's history. "Behind the flag and the cross ofttimes cower the deepest of evils" does not mean that everyone citing religion and/or patriotism has base motives, it is just that the area is a magnet for those who do, since the "requirement to suspend disbelief", as they say about movies, tends to be applied absolutely when religion and patriotism arise (at least for those who agree to listen).

Advertising agencies know about the power of belief, and it is now incorporated into every advertisement in print, TV, radio, or on the web, and in their slogans. There was not any science behind it when Goebbels first used it; now there are people with PhD's supporting what you see. Simple facts are neither memorable nor motivating; ideas that speak to fundamental beliefs and feelings are. Politicians and attorneys are also masters of Belief-Driven Cognition – possibly because like advertising, there is so much money and power at stake. They know that all they will get on TV and cable news is a 10 second sound bite, and they make sure it conforms to the best Belief-Driven Cognition principles – for a politician, they are always for the good, against the bad; their opponent is always soft on crime, a flip-flopper, weak on national defense, for higher taxes, not supporting the troops, pro-abortion, pro-gun-control, for larger class sizes, a tax-and-spend-liberal, a racist, an extremist. Of course they always stand for the reverse. A defense attorney always has a client whose enemies were out to get him, who is being persecuted; who is being accused of things that are completely inconsistent with the client's values, standards, ethics, blah, blah; who is always innocent of the charges; who has not seen any evidence to support the charges; who finds the charges just incredible, unbelievable, shocking, blah, blah; who is completely surprised, stunned, disappointed, crushed, astonished, shocked, and distraught over the charges.

The use of "labels" to characterize either people's character or their positions, mostly by their opponents in a negative way, is a classic example of belief-driven cognition. The label only takes between one to three words to express, does not need to include or reference facts of any sort, and directly pulls on some fundamental belief at the targeted audience's core – usually patriotism, religion, prejudice, conspiracy theory, or the fear that some cherished right is being threatened in unspecified some way. Often it is that targeted audience's individual religious beliefs, which can show up over abortion issues, public school textbook wording, and public display of religious symbols; anything having to do with firearms, usually any administrative procedures associated with gun purchase and/or possession, which ties back to 2nd Amendment rights, which ties back to strict Constitutionalist values, which generally ties to fear of government and desire to see a small government; and ethnic, racial, xenophobic, and illegal alien "them versus us", "like a disease", and "anarchy/lawlessness" connotations.

There are other psychological factors utilized in addition to Belief-Driven Cognition factors – everything is commingled into one big attractant or repellant depending one's intent. But belief-driven efforts are always the most successful since they speak directly to people's core values, where most of the rest of psychology tends to work on amplification and emphasis.

One of the most impressive parts of the Goebbels propaganda inventiveness, parodied in Orwell's book 1984, is what has been later called "The Big Lie." Small lies can be more easily disproved because, in general, there will be some evidence that will contradict them. But a "Big Lie", a complete and utter fabrication, with absolutely no grounding in fact, will have no evidence to contravene it. (It won't have any evidence to support it either, so you may have to push things around to make it look like you have something if you feel that "evidence" is necessary, but that's no problem if your [lack of] ethics allows for it.) But if you just can't be bothered with fabricating evidence and just want to stick with throwing out the concept you are on solid ground, because you know that you have a core of belief-driven people that will buy in, no matter what.

Want to convince people that aliens from other star systems are walking around secretly among us? Just toss out the idea. No supporting evidence, can't be proved, but, since it falls into the "Big Lie" category, there is no evidence out there at all to possibly disprove it either. Many in the conspiracy, government conspiracy, and of course the plain old flying saucer belief camp will jump right on board.

Want to make war on or invade another country? Just call it "self-defense". It is just a variation on the 1984 word inversion process where "war" becomes "peace", "rationing" becomes "plenty", "torture" becomes "love", and the like. But self-defense has that ring of self-justification, needing no further explanation. How can you be against self-defense? – it is a basic right of everyone – even in the animal kingdom.

Want to make sure as a politician you can have an iron-clad defense against any criticism? First choose a country like the U.S. where the head of state and the elected head of the country are the same person (no prime minister), and then make sure you have a war going on. Hide behind the flag and say "if you criticize me, you are criticizing the flag, our country, the boys in uniform dying for our freedom, and you are giving aid and comfort to our enemies." That will shut up all your critics for good – they will agree to support anything and allow you to bomb orphanages without complaint (bad guys were hiding there). In spite of the most unfortunate long history of patriotism being the first and primary hiding place for scoundrels, this continues to work famously. And why? Because being for your country is such a strongly-felt belief that filtering facts through it is nigh impossible.

Has your client been accused of something bad, whether you are an attorney or a PR person or adviser? Get all the TV cameras out there and you tell them that this is nothing more than a conspiracy, a conspiracy of the left wing, or right wing, or anti-gun forces, or special interests, insurance companies, or whichever boogeyman will work the best in your particular circumstances for the audience you need to convince. Many people will believe that yes, in fact, it sounds entirely plausible that a nasty conspiracy is out to get your client – that would explain why the charges against him sound so bad. There does not have to be a shred of evidence – everyone knows that the nature of conspiracies is that they are secretive and mysterious.

Want to invade Austria and Czechoslovakia? Just say they asked you to invade them to restore order and protect German citizens. Then go ahead and invade them and make up some phony diplomatic telegrams to support it. Many really informed people will suspect that this reason is implausible, but the average person may just buy what seems a perfectly plausible reason.

What are you going to do when your political opponent volunteered and served in combat under extremely dangerous circumstances, while neither you nor your running mate volunteered, had any combat experience, and your running mate was never even in the armed forces, receiving instead deferment after deferment? No problem for the Belief-Driven Cognition guys – just smear your opponent by calling him a liar and a coward anyway. The guys that were never in combat, never volunteered, never risked anything for their country – they were really the patriots. Makes perfect (non)sense. Don't worry, it will stick with enough people to make an impact.

What are you going to do if you mine and sell the dirtiest, most dangerous energy-producing substance in the world? It kills more people (miners) than any other energy source by far during its production (both through mine accidents and through black lung disease); it generates twice the CO_2 per kilowatt hour when it burns than say natural gas. The contaminants that it releases into the air as it burns – primarily sulfur and nitrogen oxides - cause acid rain (not to mention the air pollution) that kills forests and fish downwind of it for many hundreds miles, and the fly ash that accumulates after it is burned results in toxic waste dumps that despoil the surface and can cause flows that destroy homes and property. Answer? Simple, just get a bunch of advertising guys together and give them the challenge. They'll take your money and then you've got it - call it "clean coal". (Getting it down to one alliterative syllable maybe doubled your cost.) Your problem disappears. If coal is clean, all problems vanish. (Except for killing miners – somehow that was overlooked.)

The last example is even more effective especially if, as is the case for coal, no offsetting argument is being presented. The fact the coal is not "clean", would not be cost-competitive with other energy sources if it were somehow made "clean", that the technology to make it "clean" does not even exist, are facts that have nothing to do with making people believe that it is now "clean" through an expensive advertising campaign.

If you have access to the World Wide Web, it is unfortunately too easy to find belief-based positions. You can find sites where almost everything imaginable that is wrong with the world is being caused by a government conspiracy, or a multi-government conspiracy, or a conspiracy by a cabal of people who run the world in spite of the governments, or a conspiracy of the Jews, or some other permutation. These people fervently believe in these conspiracies – evidence is not required. If something is wrong, and a conspiracy is a possible explanation, then the conspiracy is the obvious explanation. Anyone with any experience working inside the government can attempt to explain to these people in a logical fashion that the government is so incompetent that it cannot field a working Information Technology system for a government function no matter how many billions of dollars are spent, and a working, effective conspiracy about anything except incompetency would be impossible, but these people will remain unconvinced by logic. They *know* there is a conspiracy. Logic is not part of their equation.

More damaging, most likely hundreds of thousands of parents stopped vaccinating their children based on the belief that the mercury-containing preservative in the vaccines caused autism. This was based on a fabricated medical research paper by a medical doctor that was later discredited. But regardless of the evidence, for example, the mercury (thimerosal) was removed in 2001 and autism rates have since shot upwards, making if anything a case that mercury prevents autism (not true either!), people with belief-based cognition to this day remain unconvinced, and you can still find multiple web sites warning you about vaccines and autism. You can find earnest, serious people who believe that diet can cause and cure autism. Now autism is most likely caused by mis-wiring of the long neural connections in the brain, wiring that begins to permanently take place around 18 months of age in the white matter of the brain that sits below the outer gray matter, which is why autistics report having their senses overloaded and sounds showing up in the visual field, etc., and why autistic children are pretty normal up to around 18 months of age and then go rapidly backwards as this wiring process goes astray. Autistics and people without autism tend to have the same number of deletions in their genetic code, that is, areas where the code that should be there are missing, but autistics have the deletions in the areas that code for proteins, while in people without autism they are in the non-coding areas that generally provide control over the protein areas. Most of the missing areas in autistics are tied to brain development, like the Ras/GTPase pathway involved with cell-to-cell communications between brain cells, or genes tied to synapses, the connections between nerve cells.

Diet management can significantly help children with autism parents do report, but a cause or cure it is not and can not be. But in spite of the science you will find believers that are unyielding.

How prevalent are belief-based arguments? Most unfortunately, it is hard today to find an exception. Belief-driven phrases are too well-matched to a sound-bite, text-message world view. Fact-based arguments fit poorly into 140 characters or a three-inch screen. Politicians, attorneys, public relations firms, and opportunists find the technology boost that today's media gives to belief-driven comments magical.

But we do not want to give short shrift here to other prejudices – race, color, ethnic background, sexual preference, or political views or social views – and to other emotional values that produce belief-based reactions, concepts like home, family, motherhood, childhood, freedom, and liberty. It is just that religious and patriotic prejudices and beliefs can be laundered to appear politically correct, at least to a sufficiently large part of society to appear acceptable. It is harder to do so for other types of prejudice, so you will note that wherever possible, proponents will make either patriotism or religion the basis for their arguments, and not another type of prejudice that will appear to be meaner and less classy. A good example is gay civil marriage – portraying it as being prejudiced against equal rights for a subset of American citizens, like say denying voting to women (which played well for a long time) looks pretty tacky, but instead declaring it to be against God and the Bible, well, that feels much better. You just can't be against God and the Bible, and no thinking is required or even invited, since you would not want anyone to speculate on what Jesus, that firebrand who confounded the Jewish Sanhedrin by breaking every law, ritual, and taboo they had, and who was accepting of everyone regardless of their sins, would opine in such a situation. It is not that people who hold this strong belief that gay people should not marry do not believe it; it is that by using religion as the rubric all rational discussion and logic are out the window. It is no longer a civil rights issue – it is about people holding on to a religious belief that most likely they will never change, unless their religion tells them they can.

As previously mentioned, the U.S. was one of the last major countries to part ways with slavery. Saudi Arabia uses slavery for lazy convenience. The U.S. used it as the basis for an agrarian economic system that without slavery would have provided a lower middle class living with extensive effort. With slavery, it produced excessive wealth and a leisure class. With these massive and irreplaceable economic and social benefits, the catastrophic consequences of the means required to accomplish them – slavery – were completely overlooked, morally white-washed by otherwise religious and law-abiding people. But believing in their right to their economic system and its benefits concurrently produced belief-driven cognition that dismissed facts to the contrary, along with the belt-and-suspenders assistance of cognitive dissonance, purging any thoughts of human rights consideration for the slaves. And even today its vestigial residue can be seen, driven by pride in what the economic and social system of the South once was, in displays of the

Confederate flag and claims that slavery was not all that bad for the slaves. Human nature mandates that you cannot love what the South was, and at the same time concur that it was entirely based on the most evil of practices.

Consequence

So what is the problem with belief-driven cognition? People all have it hard-wired in, and it takes precedence over logical thought for most people, as long as the belief involved is one that is a "hot button" area for the individual. Some people are immune to each issue, but there are always enough to enable a "quorum" for the intended purpose to be accomplished if the proper belief or combination of beliefs is utilized. While believing in things per se is not a problem, because belief-based cognition works so effortlessly and effectively, it attracts those who want to personally profit in some way, and take advantage of those who would believe. It is too easy – like the Nigerian email scams. It is like a magic sphere in the center of town with a small fence around it and a sign that says "do not touch". Touch the sphere and you siphon $1 out of a thousand random bank accounts into yours. Guess what is going to happen? The town will start wearing a groove into the sphere. But even if the malicious charlatans are removed, you have the unmalicious but dangerously wrong, the unmalicious but financially wrong, and the unmalicious but restrictively wrong, where you give up some of your freedoms in exchange for their flawed beliefs.

The other aspect of this is that once people with some commonality on a particular belief are drawn together, there is a reinforcement process that sets in where the "group-think"/lowest-common-denominator on this belief and then often others sets in. Psychologists love to run experiments on this, where they put a group of test subjects in a room who are supposed to observe something and then evaluate it. Except that only one person in the room is really a test subject - the rest are part of the planned experiment. So regardless of what he/she observes, the group of fake observers claim to see something totally at variance with what happens. The real test subject, faced with being the only one in the group out of step, will almost always ignore what he/she observed and go with what the others tell him; i.e. go with what he/she believes the others saw, and not the reality of what he/she saw. It's the old Groucho Marx thing: "Who are you going to believe – me or your lying eyes?", and "your lying eyes" lose most every time. The pressure from the group is strong enough to offset a direct observation by an individual. If this kind of pressure works on a black and white observation, it works even more effectively on something as soft and intangible as a belief or feeling or principle or value. Whether people are formally bound together in an organization, public or private, or in proximity through physical or geographical restrictions, or informally tied by sharing some common activity, event, or publication, this group-think is always present and always at work, forcing the non-conformities down and the consensus up. People today look back in amusement at witch trials, the belief in a flat earth, the comical cosmic gyrations required to explain planetary motion if the Earth and not the Sun were at the center of the Solar System, the Loch Ness monster, the belief in sea monsters, dragons, giants, Cyclops, Leprechauns, Voodoo, witch doctors - but people at those times believed absolutely in these various concepts and powers. In some cases if you did not believe, *you* became *the* problem, and you may have had to leave the group, leave the town, leave the organization, leave the country, lose your freedom, or lose your life.

30,000 years ago people believed that small figurines helped bring the spring rains, herds of animals that they depended on for food and clothes, and fertility for successful childbirth. That these beliefs were misplaced was of no consequence, that faith in a higher power may have helped these tiny islands of humanity keep going until the ice age receded and man's survival was no longer a question mark. This worship expanded to a panorama of gods and ancestors as the flooding of the Nile, crop yields, herd animal fertility, and protection from marauding humans were added to the list of needs 25,000 years later. And a little later dragons, sea monsters, and the list in the previous paragraph were incorporated into man's belief structure. Some of these myths were added to explain things that could not be explained, some by storytellers to enable them to earn a living, but all had staying power due to the power of belief-based cognition. No facts were ever required – just rumor, speculation, stories, fear, dread, and a vacuum – a lack of any rational explanation for what someone thought had happened. Man cannot stand a vacuum. He has to have an answer, and if belief in some (now seemingly ridiculous) device served the purpose, it stuck.

Now there were more serious misconceptions that turned into beliefs, especially in the "practice of medicine" before around 1800 AD. For several thousand years most doctors believed that bloodletting would help sick patients; had nary a clue about the importance of antiseptics, transmission of disease, causes of disease, importance of vitamins/diet, instead replacing them with beliefs in a lot of other in-effect hocus-pocus treatments. But overall these beliefs collectively, aside from the prosecution of religious intolerance, caused little widespread damage, especially since there was no real alternative at the time.

Today, the head of a country like South Africa can decide to believe that AIDS is not caused by a virus, deny the use of anti-viral medicines to a population of almost 50 million people for nine years, and any of these people can get on a plane and be in another country in an hour, spreading the disease uncontrollably. A country in Eastern Asia can choose to believe that the cases they are seeing are not bird flu, impose no quarantine or other similar measures, and in hours people with a new deadly flu strain are in airplanes and airports over the Pacific and in Hong Kong, Tokyo, Honolulu, and Los Angeles. China with 15% of the energy consumption per person as the United States will build dirty coal-fired power plants at the rate of one a week to fuel an economy that builds exports for the United States, believing that it is only fair that the U.S. reduce its greenhouse gas consumption and hence energy usage first. The U.S. of course believes otherwise since the Chinese coal plants are so polluting and the energy use per GDP dollar in China is roughly equivalent to that of the U.S. Meanwhile both countries contribute to and are impacted by global climate change, helping to shrink the Arctic sea ice down eventually to nothing, permanently and most likely irretrievably changing the albedo (reflectivity) of the Earth. This will warm the Arctic seabed, melting methane ice deposits, and releasing methane into the atmosphere, a greenhouse gas 23 times more effective than carbon dioxide in heating the atmosphere. This heating slowly brings more and more tropical diseases up to the Northern Hemisphere that normally reside in the Tropics – West Nile fever, malaria, dengue fever, schistosomiasis, onchocerciasis, Chagas disease, Leishmaniasis – all on their way as a really nasty surprise that will make everyone forget the mussels and carp. But on top of this many people do not believe in global climate change, or don't believe man needs to do anything about it. Let Mother Nature take care of this as she has done in the past. Of course, Mother Nature's track record is a little unsettling – she has no problem eliminating 90-95% of all species on the planet at one swell foop.

Even a hundred years ago, what happened inside one country tended to say there with some exceptions – a few plagues and pandemics did run world-wide. Today, it is hard to contain a sneeze. With seven billion people, wireless everywhere, relatively cheap air travel (by 1800 AD standards), food and raw materials moving halfway around the world without anyone noticing, the world is hopelessly interconnected. With every passing year the interwoven interdependent sensitivities only increase. A hundred years ago, foolish beliefs often were just that. Today, foolish beliefs can forever damage the lives of many people, and remove the lives of many others. Belief-driven cognition could get a pass a century ago. Today this part of human nature will gore some part of your world and you may not know it until it is too late.

The pollution pouring from the coal-fired power plants in China eventually drops down into California. Water from the Colorado River seldom even makes it into Mexico anymore. A poorly-organized group of drillers, multiple companies with no clear chain of authority and responsibility, furiously rushing to move a leased platform off to the next well, select the least-robust design and execution choices again and again, and using a fail-safe device that will never so perform, create an unmitigated disaster for people in four states and the wildlife in a small sea, including the ever-so endangered bluefin tuna. There are seven billion people that all understandably have a NIMBY attitude on reducing man's contribution to greenhouse gas production. No one wants it to crimp their (country's) economic growth, so they do the cognitive dissonance thing, and simply go the state/planet/universe of denial, saying that this is nothing to be alarmed about; insisting that rapidly increasing CO_2 and CH_4 (methane) levels are perfectly normal since they were higher in the past (several hundred million years ago) without man.

Chapter 17
Maslow Melancholy

Abraham Maslow was a psychologist who produced what he called a pyramid or hierarchy of human needs. The most fundamental needs rested at the bottom – these would be the sole focus of a individual's attention until they were reliably met. Once a person could turn his attention from these, he had the luxury of devoting some time to the next layer of needs, and so on up the pyramid; five levels in total.

To reduce confusion, note that Maslow's needs are not drives, and they are not wants, and they are personal and individual, and not aimed at group or organizational collective needs reflected back into the individual.

At the bottom of the pyramid are elemental, basic necessities – needs that reflect life and death, feed or be fodder, fight or flight – the decisions that determine whether you are present or absent on the morrow. Food; shelter from the elements; clothing; protection from lions, tigers, and bears; and avoiding other humans that might take these other things away from you. Encompassed within these are all activities that support any of these basic needs: making fire; making cloth, clothes, and shoes; making knives, arrows, spears, and axes; making tents, walls, roofs, bricks, cut stone; digging wells and irrigation canals; making plows, harvesting tools, threshing tools, and grinding wheels; and making pottery, baskets, boats, carts, and wagons.

Technically, Maslow, writing at the end instead of the start or the middle of man's 60,000 years of experience wrestling with the world, separated all of the safety and security issues out from the others in his original work. In a modern society, where fundamental safety and security can be taken for granted, this was a rational segregation. But for almost all of man's existence, this was not the case. So for the purposes of this book, basic security (life and death security) is getting smooshed back into the bottom of Maslow's pyramid, where it must lie.

Now while the author does not intend to engage in a critique of Maslow's pyramid (in general it is fine), it is necessary to point out that Maslow did overlook one critical need at the bottom level of his hierarchy. This is most likely because Maslow was writing from a perspective of modern times, and this book is aimed at all of the last 60,000 years. This omission does not change any of the conclusions, but the author feels obligated to include it since this book is describing human nature. The other missing need at this basic level is man's desire to know why things happen. Even small children can drive their parents batty asking "why" forever. The pursuit of why is the basis for religion, philosophy, history, technology, science, and other related fields. This drive may not reside with equal force in every single individual, but the sum total of it across all of man is sufficient.

The fundamental criticality behind the concept of "why" as a need is that it represents two key concepts: the intolerance of the current condition (why do I have to accept things as they are), and the explanation for events that man observes (why do these things happen). Man observes that his feet hurt on rough ground and asks why; he sees that animals have either hooves or thick pads which he lacks, so he fashions hides into booties. When lightning causes fires man notices that the heat provides warmth; he asks why he cannot make fire by himself, and eventually finds a way. He asks why his crop yields vary so much from year to year and eventually devises an astronomical calendar to measure the coming of the spring equinox. He observes that animals pick certain plants to eat when they are sick, and he asks why, and mimics their behavior. Man asks why he cannot have rights, cannot be free, cannot be treated fairly and equitably, cannot escape onerous taxation, cannot have the ability to acquire and own property, cannot have a say over those who rule over him, cannot ask for and receive security for his family, cannot be free to find and hold an occupation of his choice, cannot read and listen to what he wants to, cannot worship as he sees fit. Many scientific and technological discoveries, going all the way back to basic pottery and metal use, came about through failures, mistakes, and accidental occurrences where instead of ignoring what appeared, someone asked "why". No one set out to make glass for the first time, or fused pottery, or tin, or copper, or iron – no one knew they even existed - it was the accidental result of a hot fire and the right combination of raw materials, plus someone curious enough to wonder why and to follow up. There most likely were prior occasions where the same effect was just ignored. But the drive to find a better way, or to explore why it happened in the first place, or to avoid it altogether – this drive needs to be inserted on Maslow's little list.

The second level of Maslow's pyramid then becomes all primarily-comfort-based security issues – car theft, burglary, vandalism, identity theft, fraudulent schemes, car repossession, home foreclosure, and other similar ills prevalent in a civilized society; job security, financial security, retirement security, health insurance security; and other concerns due to local, regional, national, or international policies (e.g. currency devaluations; structural unemployment; racial or other prejudices in hiring, pay, or promotions; non-competitiveness of local industry globally; global embargoes).

The third set of needs are man's needs as a social being – those of belonging to a group and being accepted by that group, by a mate, and by a family. Even introverts seek some external confirmation of their worth – they just prefer that it come by way of an announcement, or posting, or otherwise distanced display of their contribution, and not a packed auditorium with reporters and cameras. All interpersonal relationships that overall provide affirmative positive feedback (although sometimes obviously there are setbacks) are a fulfillment of this need.

The need for being respected, for being seen as having value, for having contributed, for being esteemed, even for being recognized or being famous, all of this is part of the fourth need. This takes the third need, which is simply belonging, acceptance, and relationships, and elevates the nature of that relationship to one that leaves the recipient not just with the feeling of comradeship or intimacy or brotherhood or friendship, but with the knowledge that they possess something of special value. They are a unique person, a recognized specialist, an expert, a virtuoso, one-of-a-kind, a master, a true artist. The critical distinction is moving from being recognized as just one (equal) member of the group to being recognized for your uniqueness by the group.

"Be all that you can be," most surprisingly as it may sound, is the top of the Maslow pyramid of needs. Hopefully the U.S. Army did not pay a bucketful of taxpayer money to the advertising genius that coined that phrase for them. Maslow called it self-actualization, not nearly as descriptive. The fourth rung for Maslow is recognition for your difference; the fifth and top level is being able to take this difference and nurture it, culture it, develop it, feed it, luxuriate in it, revel in it, spoil it, lose yourself in it, even drown yourself in it. The model for this is Nero who certainly luxuriated in his poetic, thespian, and singing skills, making them a central part of his rule, putting on both private and public displays of his talents, which in some cases were pretty fair. Of course, he had to take time to allow his attendants to wash him clean of the blood of his friends and fellow patricians before each performance.

For Maslow, a pre-condition before moving up to the next level of needs on his hierarchy was to have the needs in all the lower levels first fulfilled. The needs were strictly ordered, and each was a necessary and sufficient condition for the next.

A couple of comments on Maslow before moving forward with this.

Some critics take issue with Maslow's categories and methods. He studied a modern Western society. A look at a different society with different cultural norms, say Japan for example – might reflect more emphasis on group or societal needs and less on individual needs. Some people's "selfish" personal focus is ironically directed at the welfare of others – people like Mother Teresa. In fact, in this summary this author has already split Maslow's life and death safety needs away from his other security needs, and put them into two different levels in the hierarchy. While Maslow's work may have issues, they are not germane for the purposes of this, since academic perfectness is not our goal here. Maslow was making the point that man's needs, rather than just being jumbled together homogeneously, can be parsed and ranked and ordered. The most basic, life-and-death needs come first, and the softest, most intangible, furthest-from-survival needs come last. You do not worry about your need to compose your opera if you are competing with the local wildlife for your next meal, trying to keep from freezing at night, trying to survive smallpox or malaria, wondering if it is going to rain so your crop will grow or if you are all going to have to move and try to find something to eat.

For 60,000 years, man collectively has been focussed on the bottom of Maslow's pyramid, on survival. Towns appeared maybe 4,000 years ago, cities a thousand years later. But this was not much more than a veneer – disease, drought, and warfare could and did eliminate towns and cities in a moment. For a family and individual there was no social safety net. If the material you depended on to trade to survive vanished, or your personal skills degraded due to an injury or age or disease, both you and your family most likely just disappeared. To draw a fairly arbitrary line in time, maybe it was 200 years ago that for the first time a significant percentage of mankind could begin to take survival as a given, and address the next level in the period. Of course, even today there are hundreds of millions of people who not only do not take survival for granted, but do not have any idea how they will be able to survive.

Today, with modern medicine, wars limited to local conflicts, food and shelter and a social safety net automatic in Western society, the first three levels of Maslow's hierarchy are satisfied for most people. Give or take a need or two, exactly what needs are in there, who cares. It matters not. If you prefer a different needs mix than Maslow then make your own calculation. What remains are the top two levels, being recognized for the thing or things that make you special, and then being able to exploit that specialness for yourself as far as you want to take it. Why is this important? You can tell if you are starving and you get enough to eat, or if you need shoes and you make or trade for a pair. You don't have it and then you have it – it is black and white. But what about the top of the pyramid? You are not fulfilled as a salesman or a Java programmer or an engineer or a doctor or a manager or an artist or a musician or an actor or a comic or a writer – how do you fill that need? How do you measure if you have accomplished anything? It is all way too subjective and smooshy-wooshy.

But after 60,000 years, this is the stage to which most of humanity has progressed, away from one where they know for sure when they have met their needs to one where they have not much of clue, except that they feel unfulfilled, unhappy, unsettled, drifting. It's the Maslow Melancholy, the bane of modern society, the lifeblood of psychiatrists, psychologists, psychotherapists, and pharmaceutical manufacturers, occupations and businesses that never existed 200 years ago. Man is designed to look at his hungry family, go out and find dinner, bring it home and watch them eat, and know as clearly as he knows anything as he falls asleep that he is a good provider. But how to deal with someone who does not feel fulfilled, who has caught Maslow's Melancholy? He has no way to measure the problem, no way to calculate a solution, no way to gauge if he has even made any progress. It is all so frustrating, and so apparently un-human. It is just one more reason that mankind's nature today is out of synch with his world, and these reasons just keep accumulating.

Chapter 18
Mother Nature's Keeping Track

Epigenetics (or OMG! Stalin was Right)

You of course remember where you were on that critical date in history – June 24, 2000. Like the assassination of President Kennedy or the Challenger and Columbia disasters, people can clearly remember their surroundings on the dates of these unforgettable historic events. Having some trouble with this one? It was the joint announcement by President Clinton and Prime Minister Tony Blair of the successful completion of the full sequencing of the complete human genome, lauded by all those involved as the beginning of a new era in medicine. The genetic basis for disease would result in all kinds of new ways to diagnose, treat, and cure conditions that had sickened and killed man since the beginning of time. This was the great Human Genome Project.

Over a decade later everyone is still trying to deal with the scope of the results. Nothing. Nada. Nichts. Now you might think that this is because it turned out to be harder than everyone thought, or more expensive, or there were side effects, or unexpected consequences. Well, actually, no. The scientists just basically got it all wrong.

Now saying this does not quite manage to convey the impact of the amount of drooling that these scientists had pre-drooled in anticipation of the completion of this genome sequencing. This was going to be the greatest thing ever, and so the scientists had convinced the Federal Government to fund this research. A cynic will comment that this kind of hype is required by scientists to get the Federal Government to support anything, and to cut the scientists some slack, but even if that is the case, the scientists blew it big-time.

Here is the background, simply. Genes are the blueprints contained in every cell in every living thing that do two fundamental things – determine what its physical and chemical structure will be, and determine how it will operate along with every other cell in the animal or plant that it is part of. The genes are strung out on long chains that get bundled into chromosomes, and people have 24 different ones mated into 23 pairs. Humans have between 20,000 and 25,000 genes, and these genes, if their chemical structure were to be completely defined (hence the human genome project), would then tell scientists everything about how the human body is made and how it works.

Humans are the most complex of all beings on the planet by far. So it would seem logical if humans had more genes than any other animal. Well, let's see. Scientists have determined that the foundation of the evolutionary tree of multi-cell animal life is the sponge. Sponges are missing many fundamental building blocks found in most all other animals, like skin, muscle, and nerves, but they are still considered the common ancestor. So, how many genes does this lowly sponge have – 100, 1,000? Well, shockingly, they have between 18,000 and 30,000 genes, the same number as humans. So after 100 zillion years of evolution (actually only about 440 million years, sponge fossils having been found in the Trezona formations in southern Australia, it just feels like 100 zillion), the gene count was completely conserved. So what does this tell us? Some may say nothing, but another interpretation is that the gene count is meaningless.

Well, sadly, this seems to be the conclusion of the great Human Genome Project also. It is not how many genes you have, it is, as the old saying goes, how you use them. And this is the rub. You can put someone's chromosomes into fancy machines that tear them into tiny pieces, duplicate these hundreds of times, and then match all these pieces up against established, known segments so that eventually you can get an almost complete chemical map of someone's genes. Scientists do this all the time. It is "just" chemistry – it is reliable, consistent, predictable. And pretty much useless.

Summary of the Next Three Paragraphs

The next three paragraphs describe in relatively-simple but still technical biological terms how the control of genes works. If you do not want to, have the time for, or otherwise elect not to read through these paragraphs, here is a summary of what is being said. Later on some of these terms will be referenced, especially acetylation or methylation, which are controls that your body uses to enable genes to be used more or less respectively. So if you see them, don't worry about what they mean, just remember that acetylation means gas pedal and methylation means the brake pedal.

Having genes, the blueprints for what you are, is a relatively small part of the whole story. Each of these genes tell the body to produce a specific protein, and these proteins are the building blocks of everything in the body – all the cells that make up a person as well as all the biochemicals that we need to operate – things like hormones, neurotransmitters, and cholesterol. The body can do things to the physical shape of the genes by adding small chemical groups to the genome near them that affect whether or not copies of them are made in the cell, and how many copies are made of them – this determines how many of these proteins are made. This is how, always with the same set of genes, the body builds itself from scratch as a fetus, then never does it again; grows until it is an adult, then never does it again; has brain cells make neurotransmitters and pancreatic cells make insulin, but not the reverse. And this is why some cancers run amok – these controls are all removed so the cancer cell can do anything it wants with the genes. These controls in your genome can and do vary with your life experiences – stress, exercise, eating, and chemical exposure.

There is a lot more complexity than this – even if the cell goes ahead and fabricates the protein that the gene said to make, there are many opportunities for it to be waylaid on its trip to the job site and never accomplish its intended function.

As this study of how genes are controlled expanded, it was found, much to everyone's surprise, that these gene management controls could be inherited, passed on from parent to offspring. This means you could have two identical twins, meaning their genes could be absolutely identical, but they will not be identical at all, because the way in which their genes will be used will be completely different. Using a restaurant analogy, two restaurants with identical ingredients in the kitchen, if they have different chefs and different recipes, will come up with quite different offerings for their customers. For a long time, scientists thought that genes were everything, that if they just knew what raw food was in the kitchen of the restaurant, then you could determine what was going to be served for dinner.

This means that during your lifetime, Mother Nature is marking your genome with changes based on your life experiences. She is not changing the genes that encode the proteins that make you; she is changing the controls that tell your body when to make which proteins where, in what quantity, and how to use those proteins. And some of that can and is being passed on to your children. So Mother Nature is keeping track - of what you are doing, how you are acting, what challenges you are facing, or not, and recording the results in your genome.

Back to the Details Again

But how genes are used in someone's body is incredibly complicated. You are certainly not going to find a complete explanation here – first of all there is as yet nothing close to a complete explanation anywhere. It would take a book that few would want to read to detail the mechanisms already uncovered. But here are some of the factors. First, the activity of genes depends on their topography – the physical shape of the genes, not just their chemistry. When the cell needs to use the genes, they get unwound from a tight, compact structure where they are inaccessible into one that is more loose. But the specific geometry of this openness, a combination of the genes all strung together with proteins called histones, is not predictable. It depends on the specific differences in genes from person to person. It depends on how well proteins called promoters that are necessary to enhance the gene's usability are able to physically attach to the chromosome upstream of the gene that the body wants to use. It is also impacted if the proteins with the opposite function called repressors attach to the gene and shut everything down; and if access to the gene is blocked by being "methylated" - little chemical chains that attach to the outside of the gene. Or, the histones themselves can get methylated, or can have their acetyl groups removed (deacetylation), which mashes them together so tightly that the genes are buried and are not able to be accessed and used at all. This is called being silenced. Stem cells, those miraculous little guys that can almost magically become any specialized cell type in the body, operate with relatively wide-open histones in their chromosomes, so they can get easily accessed all the time. In addition, they have special markers (methyl and acetyl groups) on their genes and histones so the molecules that come in to make copies can readily find their bearings. Contrast that with mature cells whose histones and therefore DNA is more tightly locked up, or others whose DNA is completely silenced. The silencing can be accomplished by one type of a multitude of what are called non-coding RNA's, or ncRNA's, called short interfering RNA's or siRNA's. These stick to genes and make them uncopyable, so their protein and its function are stopped, or silenced.

But even if the poor gene does get used, all that happens is that something called messenger RNA (mRNA) is generated with a copy of the information on the gene. Usually the information tells the cell to go and make a protein. But this messenger RNA is defenseless. Other ncRNA's, tiny little cellular production managers called microRNA's, lie in wait, jumping on board matching sections of the mRNA, making it useless, no matter how hard the gene works to pump out buckets of mRNA. If it is lucky, it can get help from pseudo-genes, genes that make non-functioning copies of mRNA which cannot be used to make proteins, but whose function is to soak up microRNA's so they allow the real mRNA's to do their thing unimpeded. These pseudo-genes, your own pseudo-genes, are in effect using mimicry and trickery on your own genes, a rather interesting concept.

Even if the mRNA gets over in one piece to the ribosomes, the protein factory site in each cell, and its target protein is manufactured, there is still no guarantee that the gene is going to get what it wants. If the gene has even one change (termed an SNP) in one nucleotide in the sequence of four nucleotides, taken three at a time, that are used to code for amino acids, the building blocks for proteins, the protein that gets built may not be quite right. It may not have the optimal physical shape or have its electrical charges in the right place – and it won't do the work that the gene intended it to do. Or, if the gene that made the receptor that the protein is supposed to fit into did not make it correctly, then the protein, even if made perfectly in the ribosomes, will not engage properly (they are supposed to fit like a hand in a glove) and not perform the function that its gene wanted it to. Or if some other sneaky imitation matching protein is first into the receptor slot, blocking all the usable sites but not doing anything useful, then the correct proteins just float around uselessly.

When the chase to establish the identify of all of man's genes was undertaken, scientists found that there were long spaces of apparently unused DNA between genes. The Genome Project did not bother tallying these, since they seemed to be "junk", a pejorative term actually used by many scientists. They were treated like spacers between genes – dead areas, although surprisingly containing lengths with multiple repeats of the same identical sequences of nucleotides. What percentage would you guess of the total number of nucleotides, the total amount of DNA, in the human genome had their identity determined by the Human Genome Project? You would think it must be significant – 70% or 80%? Actually it was only about 2%. Yep. They carefully identified 2% of the DNA in everyone's genes, even though Mother Nature had carefully conserved the other 98% in man as well as all other plant and animal species, and called it a day, a job well done, broke out the champagne and Snapple, called Clinton and Blair.

A passable analogy for all of this is to imagine the greatest restaurant in the world. In the kitchen are staged all the fresh ingredients. In the dining room are served dishes of unimaginable delight. In between is where all the magic happens. All the preparation, the ingredient combination, the herbs, spices, seasonings, fragrances, innumerable sauces and reductions, searing and sauteing, braising and baking, time and temperature combinations, plating timing and artistry – all flawlessly and consistently done so the customers are captivated by their dining experience. Yet you can walk into the kitchen and pick up each ingredient – each raw food that is a part of the final perfect meal, and study it, smell it, taste it, put it down and pick up the next, and no matter how long you spend on this futile exercise, you will never make the slightest inroad into your cluelessness on what it took to make the food you enjoyed taste like it did. Because while you can certainly ruin the meal if the ingredients are not fresh and tasty, it is in the preparation and execution that the meal is made. You can put the identical ingredients into a thousand restaurants, and out of one will come no-longer-hungry Army boot camp recruits, and from another diners who thought their $500 was well-spent. Along with the ingredients you need the recipes, the kitchen equipment, and the skills and techniques that the chefs bring before you have a dish. Presented with just the ingredients, you have nothing.

And so it is with genes. Genes are just the ingredients. If you just make an inventory of them, you are missing the recipes, the chefs, and how everything is cooked and blended together. The genetic difference between a man and a chimpanzee is almost not apparent. There is hardly a difference between man and a mouse or a pig. Only when you get down to say a butterfly do you get to significant differences. It is how the genes are expressed – how and when they are used that matters. And that information is not in the genes proper – it is in the 98% of the genetic information that scientists initially thought was just wasted space between the genes, and in the proteins like histones that help the genes fold up into structurally-compact bundles.

June 24, 2000, Human Genome Breakthrough Day, turned out to be a little like August 10, 1428 in Sweden, which is why you cannot recall it. Nor can the Swedes. On that day they launched the <u>Vasa</u>, the greatest warship of that time. Fitted with 72 24-pound cannons and room for 300 soldiers for boarding, it would be almost 200 years until another ship would be able to deliver as much firepower with one broadside. Crowds of citizens and foreign dignitaries lined the bay as the <u>Vasa</u> set sail for the first time, majestically moving along the shoreline, heeling to port as a gust of wind hit the sails, then filling with water and sinking, leaving just the top of the masts remaining above the water. An unmitigated, total disaster, as no one had calculated the impact of two decks of heavy cannon on the stability of the shallow-draft vessel. The Human Genome Project Breakthrough Day was not a disaster, that would be a little unfair; it only seemed that way in comparison to all the histrionic hype that preceded it. It was akin to the sundry groups who from time to time announce the end of the world, only to be met with yet another sunrise.

Now genes do provide some useful information, just like the raw ingredients in a restaurant do, so to completely diss this Human Genome effort is a mite unfair. You are not going to be able to make a pasta dish without pasta, or guacamole if the avocado is not ripe, or serve sole if you only have bass. Defects and variations in the genes do cause diseases and conditions, or make you more prone to to those diseases, and so some value has come out of this work. Cystic fibrosis is a genetic disease caused by three missing nucleotides on both genes (so the backup gene is also bad) that results in a missing amino acid in position 508 on the protein that the gene is making. The protein, just due to this one missing piece, does not fold up properly so it fails to do its job in the cell, which is to allow molecules to transit back and forth through the cell wall. It also tends to be attacked and degraded by the cell so too few of them are around. So it is like you are going to make bread and the yeast will not grow – what you end up with will not be able to be sent on to the diners. But while there are other conditions that are straightforward like this – one clear-cut gene deletion or change results in a genetic disorder –

there are many others where it is much more gray. Twenty, fifty, or two hundred genes may have elevated activity in individuals with certain diseases or conditions – and if everyone is responsible then no one is responsible. It is estimated that the average person has 300 to 400 genetic differences that result in some loss of functionality and/or some degree of genetic disease. In terms of the total amount of variation, it appears that there are on the order of 100 million SNP's across man, SNP's being the single nucleotide changes in DNA. So when "the human genome" is sequenced, it is just reflecting one possible version out of those 100 million different choices out there. All of this makes using gene identification per se as a tool daunting

Now that we have shoveled sufficient shame on the poor Human Genome Project, let's move to another victim.

A few generations before Darwin, a biologist from France named Lamarck proposed that plants and animals can internalize into their genetic code, and then pass on to their offspring, traits that they acquire through life experience. So if plants are exposed to drought conditions, or people to famine and disease, and they develop capabilities that allow them to better resist or overcome what they have faced, they can pass these advantages on to their children (or plant children). This was accepted at the time.

Then Darwin came along and placed the emphasis on genetic inheritance, so that the role of Lamarckism, while not eliminated, was substantially diminished.

Then in the Soviet Union under Stalin a gentleman named Lysenko refreshed Lamarckism, although this time it came to be called Lysenkoism. For a variety of typical Stalinesque reasons, Stalin wanted the Lysenko approach encouraged. It enabled him to short-circuit scientists who wanted to perform scientific studies which cost money and time, plus they were "elite", while Lysenko could just slap some experience on something and declare it reborn. So the Soviet Union, by fiat, formally adopted Lysenkoism. It is even possible that some aspects of it were valid, but you would never know. Stalin was just too good at misinformation, learning too well from Goebbels, plus his unique method of refreshing the higher ranks of the civil service staff (shoot everyone every four years in case they are thinking of overthrowing you) tended to diminish any effective lessons-learned program.

In Western Europe and the United States, scientists thought that this was the funniest thing they had ever heard. Every respectable scientist knew that life experiences were not inherited – you could not train someone to play the piano and expect that their children would either know how to play the piano or be better at playing the piano. Or grow apples in hot weather and expect that their cuttings will better tolerate heat. The Soviets had lost their mind once again. After Stalin died Lysenkoism faded under Khrushchev and then seemed to disappear.

Now flash forward a bit to the previous discussion about the Human Genome Project fiery train wreck. It's not about the ingredients (the genes); it's about the recipes (the other 98% of the DNA not in genes). Once the scientists were able to scrape the massive amounts of egg off each others' faces, like fiends they began to study what went on in the restaurant kitchens – how genes were turned on and off, used a little or a lot, or never used at all, and by which cells when; and all the factors that likewise affected the production and usage of messenger RNA and the proteins that the genes were supposed to be coded to make in the first place.

As the study of gene expression progressed, it was found that many of the little controls (like methylating or acetylating) that the body puts on chromosomes, messenger RNA, receptors for proteins, and other biological machinery in the body are done during a person's lifetime. Your body inherits mechanisms that it uses to solve problems and control processes, but exactly what it does with those during your lifetime are autonomous and individualized – a function of how you live, the environment you are exposed to, the foods you eat and don't eat, the stress you are under, and so on. In other words, you incorporate your life experiences into your genome, and then can potentially pass these on to your children.

In other words, it looks like during the Cold War Joseph Stalin was right, and all the righteous American scientists who scornfully, pejoratively castigated his Neanderthalish stupidity were just reflecting their own. The Soviets then actually won this part of the Cold War. Now isn't that a bummer?

Of course, it doesn't matter much since the (ex-)Soviets for sure aren't keeping score. Only the scientists that got it so wrong are. But it certainly is ironic. A cynic will point out that Stalin was right for the wrong reason, but the other cynics will point out that it is always, always, much better to be lucky than good.

The science of changes in gene expression that can be inherited was finally given a fancy Greek name - epigenetics.

Now to be fair, but to refrain from sounding like a biotechnology primer, not all of this experiential epigenetic coding gets passed on to offspring. People, like all mammals, (but unlike plants), systematically remove much of the methylation from their DNA and histones during two different phases – in the first three days of growth just after the egg is fertilized, and just after the primordial germ (egg/sperm) cells are formed in the developing fetus. But a portion of the methylation is retained, and the methylation removal process is gradual (the mother's is kept long after the father's is removed, demonstrating again Mother Nature's consistent maternal bias), so exactly how much of this is inherited is not known at the present time. Of course, anything that the mother experiences during the nine months that the baby is developing and is powerful enough to cause epigenetic maternal changes may have those similarly reflected in the baby. But since the degree to which changes in genetic regulation are inherited is generally unknown at this time, and this is not a research paper, we will not dwell on this distinction and just move on. The important concept to remember is that Mother Nature is permanently making changes in how your genes work based on your life experiences. In other words, based on feedback from customers in the restaurant, the chefs are changing the recipes and cooking, although the ingredients remain the same.

As in other fields, scientists look at identical twins to gauge the impact of epigenetics. Take lupus, an autoimmune disease that mostly affects women (90%). If one twin has lupus, chances are between 40% and 75% that the other twin will not. And because the twins are identical, lupus is not caused by the protein-coding genes, but something else, and that "else" is what happens in the kitchen. The twin with lupus has fewer methylation sites on their genes than the healthy twin. Methyl groups added to the genetic DNA serve to shut-down DNA replication, which means that lupus victims have excessively-active genes. Since lupus is an auto-immune disease, it means that immune system genes are too active in lupus victims. When the immune system is too active, it starts attacking things indiscriminately, including a person's own tissues, hence diseases like lupus, diabetes, and arthritis. For some reason, tags that should be put on genes to slow them down either do not get added or are later removed. The result is that, staying with the restaurant analogy, the chef is adding way too much cumin, red pepper flakes, chili powder, garlic, onion, and paprika to the meat loaf, and the diners are complaining.

The genetic methylation patterns on the twin with lupus matches those on others (non-twins) with lupus, which confirms that these epigenetic codes appear to be conserved in this disease. The same pattern has been found in rheumatoid arthritis. Note that this under-methylation involves many hundreds of genes, indicating how challenging a gene-oriented approach to these conditions is.

People do not start off with a clean slate, and then just develop epigenetic markings from birth forward. They certainly do accumulate them due to their life experiences, but they also inherit their parent's experiences, and grandparent's, and so on. In some cases there is what might be called species epigenetic coding, meaning everyone has the same coding, and this is termed imprinting. In many cases only the mother's gene is used, which is called maternal imprinting, and in fewer cases there is paternal imprinting, where just the father's gene is used. Mother Nature has and plays favorites.

While you certainly can find a way to directly damage your genes during your lifetime – the most likely way would be through exposure to nuclear radiation – that kind of direct change in a gene happens to few of us. Instead, everyone accumulates changes in the biochemical machinery that turns their genes on and off, reads them, processes them, produces proteins from them, and then uses the proteins to make the body function properly. 98% of your genetic code, and all of its daily activity, is aimed at doing those things. The 2% of the genes that create "you" just sit there, like a reference library. Some of these changes, like aging, are "normal". Aging involves dropping the repeating nucleotide sequences that sit at the very ends of chromosomes each time the chromosomes are read, until these sequences get too short for reading to occur and the cell can no longer reproduce (you're toast). Some of these changes are accumulated errors that the error-correction machinery built into all these processes fails to catch and rectify. But many changes are induced by how each person lives; what they eat and drink; how they act, behave, and live, how much stress, idleness, and exercise they receive. These markers change in roughly predictable ways as people age, and family members tend to all develop similar age-related changes.

PTSD, post-traumatic stress disorder, is genome-marked, which is why it does not just go away when the person is removed from the stress. It is not clear how to remove the methyl groups in the DNA that cause this reaction to prolonged stress. It is also implicated in Type II diabetes, people with major depression who commit suicide, people with eating disorders, with alcohol dependence, and people who have suffered abuse as children. This knowledge helps explain the difficulty of curing these conditions – the methylation (or acetylation) would have to be removed, and there is no known mechanism to do this at the present time. Methylation is suspected in schizophrenia based on indirect evidence. In some cases environmental triggers may assist in precipitating the epigenetic marking. Cancer is heavily dependent on epigenetics – current thinking is that epigenetic changes prime a cell to go cancerous once a genetic change occurs. Epigenetic changes in the expression of anti-cancer genes like p53, due to the hypermethylation of so-called "CpG islands" in the genome may lead to cancer directly without any genetic abnormality. Most remarkably, Mother Nature even seems to take note of how you were conceived. So far about 70 genes important for growth and metabolism have been found to be methylated in children who were conceived using IVF, or in-vitro fertilization, versus normal conception. The methylation of these genes would lead to slower growth and weight gain, which is what is typically seen in IVF births. Embarrassingly, Mother Nature even knows when you over-visit the refrigerator or the pastry counter. Scientist have found 13 genes that are excessively methylated over an eleven year period in overweight people compared to those of normal weight. So it is not just fat cells that remember your weight and make it hard to lose it; your genes are helping. No wonder weight loss is such a bear for many.

It may take until 2400 AD for scientists to completely figure out what is going on in restaurant kitchen that is the human being. On a relative basis it is "easy" to figure out all the raw ingredients in the kitchen – the genes – they are all the same, more or less, and they just sit there waiting to be counted. But everything else is part of a dynamic, ever-changing set of processes, different in every specialized cell, varying with the cellular environment, which varies with diet, stress, exercise, hormones, and age. It's a ballet of unimaginable complexity that you cannot watch, cannot hear or read the music, do not know all the instruments being used, do not know how many dancers and what movements they utilize, what sets they dance against, and that is constantly being re-set by many unseen directors. You can pull apart someone's cells and eventually create a library of their genes; but the activities in cells are living, dynamic, nano-processes. You cannot fiddle with them to figure them out without interfering and disrupting them.

What is the point of all this? Mother Nature is remembering everything you do. Much of it is folded into your genetic machinery, often by the placement of methyl and acetyl groups on genes and histones. It can be a major determinant of the quality of your life and the quantity of your life.

For 60,000 years Mother Nature remembered a man who was constantly struggling to survive, who often did not have enough to eat, who was challenged just to find food, shelter, protection from the elements and predators - those on two legs, four, and legless. This unbeaten and unbroken survivor is no more. Replaced by a copy, a stand-in, whose only exercise may be pushing buttons, opening doors, and using silverware. A stand-in who takes food and shelter not as a necessity to struggle for but as a luxury to pleasure in. A copy who moves from place to place not as a matter of survival, exhausting himself and risking his life against the threats of wild beasts and marauding humans in the search for food and shelter, but who finds transportation as another luxury to be consumed and prominently displayed. A replacement who used to watch helplessly as his family disappeared though famine and disease, and now expects to live feeling like a teenager forever. A replica who for the most part remains mired in Maslow's Melancholy (see the previous chapter), struggling in the top two levels of his hierarchy, frustrated that even though he has "everything" he needs, he still feels that he is missing something; that he is not complete; that he is not fulfilled. And now, this is what Mother Nature is going to be remembering, incorporating into man's genetic machinery. A different kind of man, a softer, unchallenged, overfed, entitled, self-oriented, over-indulged version. Mother Nature will pour this new man into the genetic structure of billions of people from now on, generation after generation, century after century, until all vestigial memory of that other primal man is erased.

Is it a better man? It's not the same man that got him this far; if things suddenly went very, very wrong, many would not know how to survive. It is a man whose fundamental resourcefulness and depth of experience on basic survival is thin if not absent. It is a man who today classifies as challenges things that for historic man would seem like heaven on earth. Today's man is better at solving the problems of today, unquestionably. But man for man, how would he stack up solving the average problem over the last 60,000 years, using only the technology available at that time? There are only two day jobs that have not changed excessively over the last 1,500 years – that of farm worker and of priest. Everything else is unrecognizable to someone from today, demanding excellence in countless skills and a toughness and durability unfamiliar to most anyone today. In removing just one modern support, modern medicine, most prominently vaccinations and antibiotics, many would succumb instantly to the diseases prevalent a few thousand years ago. The new man may be handy with his thumbs, but hardy he is not. Nonetheless we are at the mercy of epigenetics, relentlessly noting our condition and filing it away in our genetic coding, providing a pre-conditioned platform for the succeeding generation. It is not clear if much can be done to change this, but awareness is supposed to be half or more of the solution to a problem, so maybe modern man at least can settle with a partial credit.

The Gene Cesspool

From time to time most of you can recall seeing live TV coverage of someone who has managed to get themselves into some outrageously dangerous predicament, and then needs to be rescued by the authorities. A few years ago there was an occasion in Australia where a tourist had scaled down a steep cliff over the sea reportedly to get a good view of the sunrise, and had fallen asleep in a precarious position. If they rolled over they would fall into the sea and most likely drown or worse (rocks). Consumption of substances may have been involved. A helicopter was launched and rescue personnel woke him up and winched him up off the cliff face.

Long ago, no one would have noticed, he would have rolled over into the ocean and that would have been the end of it. No one else's life would have been risked, no public money would have been spent, and those valuable resources could have been deployed doing something else.

Most critically, this tourist's genes remained available to be passed on to his children (unless he is successful in killing himself the next time before any children arrive). Long ago, the gene pool had some built-in controls to ensure that there were some barriers to entry; today, everyone gets to fling their genes in.

For years, pirates have been able to operate out of bases in Somalia in general without consequence, holding for ransom any vessel they can board within a couple thousand miles of Somalia in the Indian Ocean. Even sailors possessing only rowboats are aware of this problem. Farmers in Iowa are aware of this problem. Yet every so often, private yachts with unarmed civilians on board have sailed happily into these dangerous seas and – surprise! - have been captured and held for ransom along with these other commercial vessels. Once held, some have issued dramatic video pleas for ransom money to free themselves and avoid some dire consequence. And in some cases ransom money has been raised and paid. You have to ask yourself – what would go through someone's mind, or better yet, not go through someone's mind, to set sail in an unarmed yacht within range of the pirates in Somalia? Were they the parents of the tourist in Australia? And like the tourist case, spending resources and money to rescue these people prevents the resources from being better utilized elsewhere. And once rescued their genes remain in the gene pool (although in some cases these individuals fortunately appear to be past child-bearing age).

In the second <u>Die Hard</u> movie, Bruce Willis' character is instructed to go to Harlem in New York City in his underwear, wearing a sign that made incendiarily-offensive pejorative statements about the residents of that area. Willis was sent there purposefully by the villain who wanted him chopped into fish food, and made him the biggest target he could imagine (consistent with the scope and theme of the movie). Americans know that they can be similar lightning rods for resentment, anger, and even targets of groups and nations because of the U.S.'s unique prominence and history. So, when overseas, Americans realize they need to be alert. Wearing shorts and athletic shoes when everyone else is in black, for example, is equivalent to carrying a large flashing helium balloon. When you travel to potentially hostile countries, even more care is recommended. Yet there have been several cases recently, one on the China/North Korea border, and the other on the Iraq/Iran border, where Americans were blundering along, in one case with video cameras recording information unfavorable both to China and North Korea. Now to say that loose Americans, wandering unprotected, not safe inside M1 Abrams tanks, along their border would be attractive to North Korea and Iran, for both propaganda as well as potential horse-trading value, is the understatement of the millennium. You need to ask yourself how unaware of your surroundings would you have to be to put yourself in the way of this much harm. A direct quote by one of these individuals long afterward summarized the problem exquisitely, blaming Fate instead of themselves: "I think we were extremely unlucky. I guess I never believed there would be so many hundreds of people close to a border." Apparently this person remembered from the maps in grade school that countries were all painted different colors so you could readily tell where the borders were. And somehow missed the U.S.'s two international borders, where there are regularly crowds on the order of a million people per square mile. (This same individual admitted that they never even thought of consulting a map, and that they purposefully left the "safety" of the hundreds of people and walked off on their own until they reached a military checkpoint, along a route where someone had removed all the border colors, and where there was no one except them.) Many years ago, everyone who decided to go play with the cute grizzly bear cubs, or black mambas, or hold the target for the archers, or jump off a cliff to prove they could fly, would just disappear. Eventually, the human race was cleansed of all those individuals who felt the need to do really dumb things. But today, these people are tolerated, even encouraged, helped, saved, welcomed, praised, rewarded, go on morning TV shows, get movie and book deals.

Now available for those who want to mountain climb, or go off into the wilderness, are locator devices based on GPS that will send out an automatic distress signal with your location if you find yourself lost or in need of emergency assistance. If you do not want to purchase them, they can be rented for dollars a day. They are especially valuable on the mountains along the Pacific coast in Oregon and Washington, which are well-known for being hit with dangerous weather during climbing season, storms that bring heavy, wet snow, whiteouts, and avalanches. Both climbing and rescue is impossible until these storms pass. Yet many climbers refuse to take the GPS locators with them, saying that their knowledge that they possessed this safety device would make them take excessive risks.

OK, let's go over this a little more carefully. Storms are likely; every year climbers die. With a locator, a rescue team can find you; without it, it is almost impossible, based on history. Having a safety device for emergency use only, so these climbers say, would encourage them to try harder to get into an emergency situation. This is like saying that you would drive more safely in your car without your seat belt on, because putting it on makes you speed excessively, pass with no visibility, and do text messaging while driving. Or putting life preservers on your family while in your power boat makes you immediately consume a six-pack of beer, since everyone is now excessively safe. Or having someone hold your ladder will make you climb all the way up and stand on the top step. People who think like this are simply self-destructive.

Let's go back to the mountain climbers in the Cascades. When climbers do get lost in snowstorms, a full-scale rescue is deployed. Helicopters, ground climbers, the whole deal, at a great cost in time, money, and resources. Almost always these are unsuccessful, but sometimes someone is rescued. But in either case, society is investing valuable resources in keeping genes in the gene pool that Mother Nature, when she was in charge over the last 60,000 years, allowed to be selected out.

These are just a few examples. People shoot themselves constantly because they did not follow the most basic principles of gun safety and society takes care of them. It does the same for drunk drivers who injure themselves and often injure and kill others. People drive without their seat belts on; drive motorcycles without helmets. Gasoline makes for a great way to clean automobile engine parts, especially inside your garage, and as an ancillary benefit, it will almost always blow up you and your house. Zoo visitors will climb over the first fence, which has a virtual sign on it that says "Do not cross this unless your IQ is under 50," and then the second fence, with its virtual sign that says "Do not cross this unless your IQ is under 20," and then press themselves against the bars of the lion, tiger, or bear cage, which has a third virtual sign that says "Do not stay here unless your IQ is negative," and then will apparently act surprised when their arm or leg is chomped on by the cage occupant. Note that our closest primate relative, the chimpanzee, is way too bright to cross any of these fences. Thieves steal electrical wiring for the value of the copper in it, not apparently bothered by the fact that electricity can be somewhat dangerous, and are electrocuted in the thieving. Visitors to houses whose arrival is unexpected, finding no one there to let them in, determine that the best entry is to be made by way of the chimney, and after making this most original determination are even more incredibly actually able to reach the chimney without falling off the roof, only to be impossibly stuck, sometimes to be rescued and other-times not. People purposefully and willfully inhale polonium-210, the poison that the Soviet and Russian secret police use to kill their enemies, along with other less toxic poisons, and yet society happily takes care of their medical costs (you know these people as cigarette smokers, getting an annual dose of around 14,000 mrem, or 140 milli-sieverts, of radiation just to their lungs, versus about 350 mrem, or 3.5 milli-sieverts, that the average person gets in total from all sources per year. A chest x-ray is 10 mrem.) People go off onto the ocean and into the wilderness without a care for the expected conditions, without any previous experience, without any knowledge of the dangers, and without any humility about the power of Mother Nature.

Mother Nature has a "social" standard that differs from most everyone else's, with maybe only the Lacedaemons (Spartans) coming somewhat close. For Mother Nature, it is survival of the fittest, period. No matter how cute, or how tragic, or how unfortunate, it is survival of the fittest. The weaker disappear, the strongest always remain dominant. Strong and weak are defined by whatever Mother Nature is tossing at the world at that moment – it could be feast; it could be famine; it could be hot; it could be an ice age. And from this simple algorithm, Mother Nature has come up with the killer whale, the great white shark, T Rex, the cockroach, the rat, the HIV virus, and, man. What you do not want to do is to replace Mother Nature's algorithm, refined over maybe three billion years, with something else without carefully testing it to make sure that it is at least as good or, that you can live with the other consequences of the alternatives. Note that it might take a long time to verify this, possibly as long as three billion years.

But man has in fact replaced Mother Nature's plan, tossed it in the wastebasket, and there was never a consideration, a test, an evaluation, an Environmental Impact Statement. Man just eased Mother Nature over out of the driver's seat. But who is driving? And where are we going? The irony is, man just made the most important decision ever made on the face of the planet, aside from his decisions on the ozone layer and global climate change, and he is not even aware a decision was made.

The struggle of man versus Mother Nature was pretty even for a long time. The world population was roughly 200 million in 0 AD, and only doubled to about 400 million a thousand years later (around 1000 AD). Yet 400 years later, due to the Black Death and other problems, the population of the world was still about the same (around 1400 AD). It was not until the explosive growth of oceanic exploration by European countries post-plague and into the Little Ice Age and the concomitant growth in wealth that human population began to show significant increases in the face of Mother Nature. It rose to about one billion by around 1850 AD, the magic date at which bacteria as the cause of infection was first widely recognized. In an almost magical coincidence, at just about the same time, around 1800 AD, what is termed the Industrial Revolution exploded onto the world's scene, led by the steam engine and steel-making. This push in both technological as well as in medical competence finally overwhelmed Mother Nature and allowed the world's population to explode from that point in time forward. It has not stopped since, and only man himself or some global catastrophe will be able to stop it now.

It took about 80 years for the world population to double to two billion (about 1930 AD), and then only about 45 years to double again to four billion (about 1975 AD), with both of these doublings including the catastrophic effects of a world war. Projections say it might take about 60 years to double again to eight billion (since many countries have slowed their population growth) – around 2035 AD, although who knows what may happen if global climate change goes non-linear. So with science, medicine, and technology on his side, man is now in charge of his destiny, not Mother Nature. Mother Nature's rule, survival of the fittest, is out the window, replaced with a social safety net that protects as many people as possible – the poor, the weak, the enfeebled, the blind, the deaf, the crippled, the sick, the mentally troubled, victims of accidents and crimes – few modern (or even ancient) societies allow these people to fall into the cracks and disappear.

Now society has not changed its moral compass, its just that it could not make much headway against Mother Nature's headwind until the middle of the 19th century. So with Mother Nature conquered, and man in charge, almost everyone gets a second, or third, or fourth chance. With Mother

Nature, it is one strike and you are out. People dismissively smile at male lions, lounging in the shade while the females hunt. Well, this is because lions are actually slightly smarter than people, and understand Mother Nature's rules quite well. Hunting is intrinsically dangerous; get injured, and you will surely die from an inability to either hunt and/or to defend yourself. The male lions have logically delegated the task to the females. The male lions not bright enough to comprehend this have all disappeared long ago, their genes now out of the pool.

But humans thoughtless enough to drive while intoxicated are saved by seatbelts, safe cars, and great medicine. Humans who try to walk across freeways at night, or climb electric power poles, or ride motorcycles in traffic without helmets, smoke cigarettes, get lost while hiking, drive without seatbelts or while speeding, or any number of other anti-Mother-Nature behaviors are almost always saved by society.

A moral judgment on man's moral judgments is not the point. It is just that Mother Nature does not make any moral judgments – she just has her simple survival algorithm.

Now it has only been a few hundred years since man changed the rules on Mother Nature. Who know how long it will take for the impact to take hold, and what the effect will be? Will man evolve anyway, or just remain the same, or maybe de-evolve? Most amazingly, we will be running this experiment for the first time in the known universe on ourselves.

Hopefully, there will be someone that we can report the result to.

Those readers who prefer living in the warm glow of denial (from Passive Cognitive Dissonance – see Chapter 8) will tell themselves that this does not matter anyway, that the innate nature and personality of man is not going to be affected by what is in or out of the gene pool.

Only people without children, or parents who have identical personalities, will tend to make these observations. Others will have experienced children who, coming from the same parents and having been raised identically, act as if they were adopted and raised in different countries. To tell these parents that personality is not in the genes activates the other Cognitive Dissonance, ACD, (A for active), because these parents experientially know that you cannot raise out what Mother Nature has put in. But because many parents do have similar natures, and "nature" in an individual is a difficult assessment, scientists do not look at single children in regular families but at identical twins, separated at birth and raised in different environments (usually due to adoption). They find that the twins conserve their personality traits, in other words they still act the same, have the same interests, and end up in the same professions. Beyond this, Mother Nature so loves personalities that she preserves them on a maternal generation-skipping basis, meaning that a daughter can have much of the same personality traits as one of her maternal grandmothers. Unless scientists start working into their 100's, they might not ever find this one. But perceptive mothers and grandmothers know all about it, as long as you have the fundamental personality differences generation to generation that will enable it to rise to visibility.

But this is not limited to just behaviors. Modern medicine attempts to rescue everyone from conditions and disease that for the prior 60,000 years would have meant an early death and no descendants. Every year medicine succeeds in doing better, keeping more people healthy that would have never made it with Mother Nature in charge. Many medical conditions are genetic-based, and many diseases are aided by some propensity in the individual, so these all now remain in the gene pool. Every year the original crystal clarity of the pool is increasingly cessed by these genes that had been banned for 60,000 years by Mother Nature. Slowly the pool will lose its translucency and darken.

There are 34 countries in the OECD, consisting of the most developed, highly-civilized societies on Earth. The average high school drop-out rate for all of these taken in the aggregate is 20%. If this is just restricted to European Countries, it rises slightly to 17%. Looking at the U.S., it is actually worse than the average with a 23% drop-out rate. Spain is in the high 20's, Mexico the high 50's, and Turkey close to 75%. Countries like Italy, Slovenia, and the Czech Republic have lower rates than the U.S. In a desperate attempt to remedy the situation, the U.S. has imposed standardized testing on public education, and in a predictable response, principals whose careers are in jeopardy have modified their curriculum to teach to the test, reducing the time spent actually teaching anything useful. Tennessee and Texas lead about a dozen states in reducing the scores necessary to obtain a passing grade on these tests to significantly below a score that demonstrates basic comprehension. In other words, an acceptable education is not mastery, nor a comprehensive understanding, nor even a basic grasp of a subject, but just some spotty partial muddled half-understanding is good-enough. This is enhanced by grade inflation – where obtaining a 4.0 GPA used to be a rare achievement, it is now looked down upon as embarrassingly plebeianly banal, and today only a 4.4 GPA will suffice. Many parents, suffering from Maslow Melancholy, are not really concerned about whether their children learn anything, but just how "good" they look, how "well" they appear to have performed, since that is a direct reflection on them as "good parents". None of this helps improve the drop-out rate problem, produce citizens better educated, or inhabitants better prepared to take on the complex problems of a non-Mother-Nature-ruled world.

In today's societies, representing human civilization, with technology exploding in most every area, with the amount of knowledge needed to be a competent citizen rising dramatically, these high drop-out rates are an anathema. And somewhat surprising – it was only a few hundred years ago when parents would do most anything to provide their children with the best education possible. The difference – no social safety net back then. If you were not as prepared as you could be, you might starve to death, or live right at that edge. Now there are some exceptions – Germany, Finland, South Korea, and Japan all have relatively low drop-out rates. But overall, things look rocky for gene pool fans.

Back when Mother Nature was in charge, gazelles and wildebeests who did the equivalent of dropping out of high school, say by wandering away from the herd, or dawdling by the river's edge, ended up nourishing hyenas, lions, crocodiles, and cheetahs. For most of man's time on Earth, those who did not pay close attention to their instructors and learn well how to hunt, fish, scavenge, make weapons, make shelter, make fire, treat injuries, stay safe, and other basic lessons also failed the equivalent of the high school GED, and kept the gene pool clarity pristine. Life was very tough and they would not make it.

But today, those who cannot pass even the minimal educational challenge of high school, whether due to willful, environmental, or competency reasons, or some combination, are protected by civilization and society. The safety net may be the family, or unemployment payments, or some form of general assistance benefits. Few, in a modern civilization, are truly left by the side of the road to starve, die, and leave the gene pool.

As has been said to the point of nauseous redundancy, the author is not intending to make a moral judgment. The reason this book is titled The Civilization Trap is that this is a staggeringly difficult problem to cope with. If not, the subtitle would have been A Chalk Circle on the Sidewalk. There is no easy solution, nor hard solution. That is the nature of traps.

If you read the Introduction, it noted that Mother Nature has a track record of replacing her versions of modern man every 200,000 years, and since our version of man has been around for 200,000 years, it is just about time for us to be replaced with a better version. But since man has interrupted the evolutionary process by keeping all his genes in the pool, most likely, nothing better is going to materialize; although something worse might.

For 60,000 years Mother Nature patrolled the gene pool for us, but now the human race is in charge. Actually, no one seems to be in charge. Someone just decided to tear down all the gates and let everyone through. What used to be pristine, clear, translucent pool is now fouled with all matter of genes from people who are hell-bent on self-assassination or just plain defective. For the first time in 4.5 billion years of evolution, man just changed all the rules. And there were no discussions, no hearings, no vote.

This is not a moral argument. This is just a formal announcement of a change in ownership, like those legal announcements that you see and ignore in newspapers and on the front door of restaurant. Old human gene pool owner: Mother Nature. New human gene pool owner: Abandoned.

Mother Nature's Keeping Track

Whether it is through our genes themselves, which determine our many of our direct characteristics (restaurant raw ingredients), or the processes that control gene expression (the chefs and the recipes), Mother Nature is physically changing our DNA and histones to match what we do in our society and civilizations. You may not have noticed that you just took over control of man's gene pool, but Mother Nature knows, and she changed the rules instantly as a result. Compared to the last 60,000 years, we lead relatively unchallenged and dis-hardshipped lives; and societies' norms now keep people contributing to posterity that never made an appearance in the past. No other species over the last say 2.5 billion years of life on this planet has had the opportunity or the power to be able to run such an experiment as this. Man, incredibly, never bothered with the experiment, and simply switched the whole planet over to the new rules in a few generations; an instant from an historical perspective. Based on animal studies, it may take generations before there is a macro population-wide impact. But like D&T (death and taxes), it is safe to say that Mother Nature is not going to be forgetting and there is no going back.

Chapter 19
Dis- Acceptance of Individual Responsibility

Background

Over the last several decades, there has been an acceleration in the move away from acceptance of responsibility for actions taken by the individuals themselves.

In 1912, attitudes reflected the extreme of individual responsibility – no matter what happened to you, you were responsible for the results. The textbook example for this was the sinking of the <u>Titanic</u>. If there was ever something that was not the fault of the passengers and crew, and was the fault of the captain and the ship owners, this was it. Steaming full-speed in the pitch-black darkness in sea ice conditions without the lookouts being given binoculars was never attempted before, and after the <u>Titanic</u> sank in less than two hours, you can see why it was such a terrible idea. Yet no damages were paid to anyone as a result, no refund on the price of their tickets, no offer of another cruise free to make them feel better. In fact, the crew members that lived had their pay stopped the second the ship sank – so as they sailed back to New York on the RMS <u>Carpathia</u> they were in effect already on lay-off status.

Just about exactly one hundred years later, representatives in one U.S. state drafted legislation that would make any injuries suffered by visitors at locations identified in guidebooks about the state the personal financial responsibility of the author(s) of the guidebooks, no matter how much warning and cautionary language they provided in their text. No liability for the state, and none for the tourists themselves. Have yourself ten beers – jump off a cliff with your last two – and the whole thing will be paid for by the author of the guidebook in your backpack. Better yet, get as many guidebooks as you can, in case one of their pockets is a bit too shallow. (Now at the time this book was written, this bill had not yet passed, nor had the state's governor signed it.)

As this book is being written, just about a century later, U.S. society and culture have moved a considerable distance away from the <u>Titanic</u> treatment toward a general abandonment of individual responsibility in many situations where responsibility is most obviously appropriate. Part of this seems to be the escalating use of attorneys to rescue wealthy clientèle, whether in the sports, business, entertainment, or political arenas, from self-created problems and scandal. The explosive growth of wealth in these groups has attracted the subset of the legal profession who is motivated in the same fashion (fame and money), and this partnership has in most cases succeeded, increasing its attraction for more clients and attorneys. A second factor that has helped has been a general thrust by psychiatrists and psychologists both as expert witnesses in trials and in the public press over the last half-century of excusing the behavior of individuals based on their accumulated life experiences, and often their childhood. In contrast to the mindset a century ago, today when something happens to an individual, if an attorney or paid public relations professional is involved, their first action will be to seek out some other person, substance, group, or set of circumstances to blame the illegal or socially-unacceptable behavior on. In the entertainment and to a great extent the political arenas, it has almost become automatic, and hence a cliché, that when something really bad, illegal, or embarrassing happens, the spokesperson, practiced in sincerity, immediately comes out and says that the individual involved "regrets the behavior and is going into rehab." Today, at least in the United States, this seems to suffice for most anything.

One has three choices in a criminal case – aside from the old standards of pounding on the evidence, the law, the witnesses, opposing counsel, and the table – the defendant did not do it, did it but was justified, or did it but can be excused. The movement away from acceptance of individual responsibility often places all the emphasis on the third option. Characteristically the claim will be that the defendant was abused or traumatized as a child or adult in some way, or has some mental condition that results in a diminished capacity (not insane), or was on prescription medicine that had uncontrollable side effects. But, if the attorney is excessively bold and competent, a justification defense can be successful even in cases where the victim was killed and then chopped up in little pieces – all in the name of self-defense. All it takes, after all, is one juror to buy what the defense lawyer is selling, and the jury is hung.

Because of the marriage made in Heaven between lawyers looking for new business areas and this move toward dis-acceptance of personal responsibility, the civil or liability portion of the U.S. legal system has grown exponentially. Most popular with attorneys are class action lawsuits, where individual "damages" for some perceived loss in value may be on the scale of $100, but when aggregated over a class of a million or more defendants their payoff is $30 million while the class of "victims" gets a near-useless coupon. This is not to say that some individuals are not damaged by surgeons who amputate the wrong leg, or by radiation-producing cancer therapy machines that are set-up improperly and over-radiate hundreds of patients who are expecting help instead of terrible damage. But awarding huge sums of money for spilled coffee and the like is logically absurd.

In the regulation of food there is a category called GRAS, which is an abbreviation for Generally Recognized as Safe. Now you can drink enough water and eat enough salt to hurt or kill yourself, but you cannot sue anyone about it – it's your problem. No warnings needed on the salt carton or the bottled water container. There are a large number of other foods and spices "grandfathered" into accepted use in this way. You can stab someone in the eye with a carrot, but you cannot then turn around and sue the carrot farmer. Sorry. If you walk into the average kitchen in the average house, you can damage or fatally wound yourself with just about everything in sight. Knives galore, glassware abounds; fiery death awaits you in the range and oven; the toaster can provide electrocution along with immolation. A few inches of water in the sink and you can readily drown. But if you attempt to go and sue any of the manufacturers of these products, or your builder, or the gas, electric, or water companies for damages, you will be as unsuccessful as your efforts against the carrot farmer.

As you can see, it is not about logic, it is just about what the legal system enables you to get away with. Everyone knows that soup is hot, coffee is hot, and a knife is sharp. But you can sue for coffee, not for a knife, and the author really has not a clue where the silly law is on hot soup, be it thick or thin. But the dis-acceptance of personal responsibility has now established quite a beachhead, and English common law does not work on logic, it works on precedent, so retreating will be nigh impossible.

Consequences

Chapter 1 draws analogies with the concept of this book and the sinking of the <u>Titanic</u> and the accumulation of mistakes made during aircraft landings. Catastrophes and disasters often result from a multiplicity of factors that are always present, some in your favor and some not, but only when these factors all align in an unfavorable way does the result become unrecoverable. The dis-acceptance of personal responsibility is one such ancillary contributing factor. In a perfect world it may just be a pothole, but today's world is not such a place.

60,000 years ago if you tried to pretend that you were not responsible, you just disappeared. Mother Nature was pretty brutal. Maybe it technically was Mother Nature's "fault", but she made her rules abundantly clear, and should you fail to abide by them, it was you who bore the consequence. Mother Nature created everything, and set it all in motion, but it was your responsibility to figure it out and make the best of it. You had the skills and resources to do it (most of the time) – it was your problem. Plus, trying to sue or otherwise get recourse from Mother Nature was tried from time to time, and in general was found to lack traction.

So for most all of man's existence, through the time of the <u>Titanic</u> for sure, he took it for granted that it was his own personal responsibility to deal with whatever was thrown at him, no matter who did the throwing, or why.

Now for straight-forward personal and property crimes, the legal system was invented so that do-it-yourself vigilante justice could be dispensed with, but for everything else, man took responsibility for himself. The key ingredient here is attitude. Man was constantly surveying the landscape for any threat that could negatively affect himself or his family. It might be a something that he would have to deal with, or it might take the combined efforts of all his neighbors. It could be weather, famine, disease, firewood, game, marauding humans, or marauding animals. But man was on guard – always alert. He knew that no one else would be looking out for his welfare or his interests.

But as man built civilizations, he built legal systems, and laws, and rules, and social and behavioral norms. Initially designed to maintain fundamental order and dispense rudimentary justice, over time these systems slowly became more protective and encompassing. Armies and police forces made walking outside one's home safe. Walls, windows, locks, electricity, street lights, smoke detectors, and fire protection made the inside of homes safe. The "Stop/Look/Listen" signs at all railroad crossings had to be replaced with automatic arms not only for cars but for pedestrians. In cities, train tracks had to be lined with fences to keep people from crossing the tracks with their eyes, ears, and mind in another universe. If they smoked, the medical system would take care of them. If they over-ate, and under-exercised, someone else would have a solution for that. If they somehow were sick or injured, the system would take care of them. Before their gene mix or bad habits could hurt them, medicine could intervene and in advance prevent them from getting sick. Fluoride could help prevent their teeth from getting cavities and having to be pulled out, contrary to the fate of their ancestors for the prior 60,000 years, and if cavities or other problems did develop dentists could remedy them. If they lost their job, hopefully the system would take care of them. When they were old enough to retire, hopefully the system would take care of them as well – income, a place to stay, medical coverage. Eventually, well post-Titanic, people began to walk across streets without looking either direction, without even pausing first. People stopped signaling in their vehicles when they made turns, or when they changed lanes. If something went wrong driving, their seat belts and air bags would protect them from trouble. If they want summer fruit in the winter, they can get it. If they want summer weather in the winter, they can get it. If they want their car to act like a living room, or an entertainment center, or a dining room, they can get it.

In today's world, whatever you want, you can get, and you expect to get. You are entitled. You are equally entitled not to get injured or harmed, and on the rare occasion that it should happen, it is not your problem. Your job is to work hard and earn money. The world's job is to provide an endless panorama of choices for you to spend your money on. Your responsibility is to get rich or richer. The world's responsibility is to meet your demands; your needs; your wants.

Is this an overstatement? In some cases, certainly. But what is undeniable is that the center of mass of modern society has qualitatively moved away from personal responsibility for everything to personal responsibility for almost nothing. We can argue endlessly about the content of the "almost nothing", and which sub-groups of society feel more responsible than others – maybe stratified by age, or age and culture, or age and culture and political philosophy. Even the most ardent anti-government advocates expect to have police, fire, and schools to work well, to be able to renew their driver's license smoothly and efficiently, to not have chaos on the roads or in the air, to be able to do their taxes with a minimum amount of effort, to have the military work effectively, and (if they are 65) to have Social Security and Medicare work efficiently. These people are not hypocrites, it is just a reflection of the fact that in today's world you cannot be personally responsible for everything even if you wanted to – the world is just too damn crowded, sophisticated, demanding, and unrelenting.

The Problem

So what's the point? Starting 60,000 years ago, man knew that only he was looking after his own interests. He was constantly on guard, 24/7 as we now would say. Now what was in his best interests were not necessarily in Mother Nature's, in fact they may have often been in opposition, but until the last few thousand years, man's global footprint was rather small and not of great import. But man's footprint today envelops Earth; Mother Nature shudders every time man takes a step, or a drink, or fills his gas tank. Resources, even water and arable land, are limited. Disease and pests can now freely spread globally where before local containment was automatic. Air pollution is no longer local; carbon dioxide levels are building to levels that last produced wondrous varieties of dinosaurs. And coincidentally, man is now no longer on alert. Someone else is supposed to be watching, guarding, providing assistance and care. Someone else is responsible. It's always someone else's problem.

40,000 years ago the small groups of people who were destined for long-term survival would sit around every day and review the relative availability of food, the relative state of the weather, whether wolves or other predators appeared to be more or less a threat, and whether any other groups of humans were more or less a danger. As soon as there were enough people permanently banded together in one place one of the first community structures they would have built would have been one to track the spring and fall equinoxes, keys to farming success and animal births. The technology available to them was extraordinarily limited. When it failed, their fallback was some form of religion. But it was not for a lack of trying, or a lack of listening, if some long-term climate change trend got the best of them.

Now, at the precise, exact time when it is most critical that man pay close attention to Mother Nature's health and welfare, he has turned inward, expecting at most internal accountability. No one is responsible for the world's overall welfare. Sure, a haystack of scientific disciplines have subdivided and compartmentalized the listening to and studying and analyzing of Mother Nature. But no one has the responsibility for listening to all to their findings, and taking collective action. Maybe there will be a resonance on a few issues, if they find proponents that secure some traction with the public, and taking action is not too costly. But these actions will be most often country-specific, and not global. For most people, it is left to these scientists and governments to debate these arcane, complex international and often global issues.

Now would the alertness that man possessed toward Mother Nature for most of the past 60,000 years be the key to solving the problems of today? It's impossible to make a solid argument one way or another – only speculation, which has little tangible value – so the author is not claiming or even hinting that this is a pivotal factor. It is simply one contributor – it is the moonless night or the lack of binoculars for the <u>Titanic</u>. But the change in man's attitude from years past to today is a black-and-white undeniable shift. Taken alone, as one change in an otherwise perfect world, it might not have been all that noticeable. But as background for the wider context, for man's nature working against him, it is prudent to point it out for consideration.

Chapter 20
Other Perspectives on Man's Run

Explanatory Note

    Spengler and Toynbee are two other historians who presented theories about societies rising and then crashing, primarily because history repeats itself. Since they both predict the fall of civilization(s), it seemed only prudent to include a summary of their conclusions and the mechanisms driving the demise. However, the sound and feel and flavor of both of these works are quite different from this book, so there will be a bit of a culture shock moving into this chapter. This book has emphasized the fundamental causes for the mismatch between man's nature and the world he has remade. Both authors, on the contrary, speak more to cyclic patterns and trends across civilizations and societies that bring about their rise and fall. Toynbee does provide a mechanism, but it is not at all clear how the mechanism turns on and off – the examples he provides are conceptual and the events often extremely subtle. Spengler is a poet/philosopher, as you will note ten words into his material, and says some things that will best case appear remarkable.

    If you start into this chapter and feel that the discontinuity is too great, or the material too irrelevant, and cannot be bothered with any of this, then you can skip this chapter.

Spengler

    Surprisingly, maybe(?), there are only two non-religious works that claim civilization cycles through phases in some predictable way. The Decline of the West by Oswald Spengler, first published in 1918, is a dazzling intellectual field trip through the ages, spanning cultures and societies in making a case that Western civilization, like others before it, has moved through phases and is now in a downward arc, approaching this final end state:

    "With the formed state having finished its course, high history also lays itself down weary to sleep. Man becomes a plant again, adhering to the soil, dumb and enduring. The timeless village and the 'eternal' peasant reappear, begetting children and burying seed in Mother Earth – a busy, easily contented swarm, over which the tempest of soldier-emperors passingly blows. In the midst of the land lie the old world-cities, empty receptacles of an extinguished soul, in which a historyless mankind slowly nests itself. Men live from hand to mouth, with petty thrifts and petty fortunes, and endure. Masses are trampled on in the conflicts of the conquerors who contend for the power and the soil of this world, but the survivors fill up the gaps with a primitive fertility and suffer on. And while in high places there is eternal alternance of victory and defeat, those in the depths pray, pray with that mighty piety of the Second Religiousness that has overcome all doubts forever. There, in the souls, world-peace, the peace of God, the bliss of grey-haired monks and hermits, has become actual – and there alone. It has awakened that depth in the endurance of suffering which the historical man in the thousand years of his development has never known. Only with the end of grand History does holy, still Being reappear. It is a drama noble in its aimlessness, noble and aimless as the course of the stars, the rotation of the earth, the alternance of land and sea, of ice and virgin forest upon its face. We may marvel at it or we may lament it – but so it is."[53]

At least with Spengler you are not always confined to the dreary monotony of the historian. And of all the writing in his book, this is without doubt the best, the most inspired, the most poetic. Except that the sentences are way too short, it sounds a little like Faulkner.

Spengler on the surface weaves an abstruse web of connections between modern and ancient times, across science, politics, religion, sociology, and economics, citing innumerable individuals and their contributions to make his case. Sometimes these references are beyond obscure. Spengler's command of his source material is astonishingly impressive. His argument that modern civilization is cycling in a manner similar to that of ancient civilization fills 375 pages densely-packed with people, events, and ideas in support of his thesis.

Here is an example of Spengler's connections, still retaining some of the poetic ring:

"The method common to all the great Cultures – the only way of actualizing itself that the soul knows – is the *symbolizing of extension*, of space or of things; and we find it alike in the conceptions of absolute space that pervade Newtonian physics, Gothic cathedral-interiors and Moorish mosques, and the atmospheric infinity of Rembrandt's paintings and again the dark tone-worlds of Beethoven's quartets; in the regular polyhedrons of Euclid; the Parthenon sculptures and the pyramids of Old Egypt, the Nirvana of Buddha, the aloofness of court-customs under Sesostris, Justinian I and Louis XIV, in the God-idea of an Aeschylus, a Plotinus, a Dante; and in the world-embracing spatial energy of modern technics."[54]

---

53 The Decline of the West, Oswald Spengler, Trans. by Charles Atkinson, Oxford University Press, 1991, p. 381
54 Ibid., p. 60

The extent of Spengler's span is on display in just this one sentence.

The difficulty comes in finding brief quotes that typify Spengler – note that the above is just one, 115 word sentence. But it does portray the reach of his arguments, bridging time, space, cultures, and disciplines effortlessly. Spengler seems to have the ability to weave a flawless fabric with yarns and cord of infinite disparity, so as you read this book and watch in semi-amazement as the names and ideas flow by, you expect to be ring-side to a junk collector and not to an artist.

"When the form-world of the springtime is at its highest, and not before, the ordained relation is that architecture is lord and ornament is vassal. The warrior figures of Diptylon vases are conceived in the spirit of ornament, and so, in a far higher degree still, are the statuary groups of Gothic cathedrals.... Then comes the gleaming autumn of the style. The 'return to Nature' which already thinkers and poets – Rousseau, Gorgias and their 'contemporaries' in the other Cultures - begin to feel and to proclaim, reveals itself in the form-world of the arts as a sensitive longing and *presentiment of the end*.... So it was, too, with the free, sunny and superfine art of Egypt under Sesostris III (c. 1850 B.C.) and the brief moments of satiated happiness that produced the varied splendour of Pericles' Acropolis and the works of Zeuxis and Phidias. A thousand years later again, in the age of the Ommaiyads, we meet it in the glad fairyland of Moorish architecture with its fragile columns and horseshoe-arches that seem to melt into air in an iridescence of arabesques and stalactites. A thousand years more, and we see it in the music of Haydn and Mozart, in Dresden shepherdesses, in the pictures of Watteau and Guardi and the works of the German master-builders at Dresden, Potsdam, Würzburg, and Vienna."[55] This paragraph you will note spans close to 4,000 years and many cultures.

To paraphrase, "I know Gibbon, and Spengler is no Gibbon." It is not the same style by intent, as you can see by the few quotes above. Spengler is more of a political philosopher; sometimes almost a poet; if you get a little dazed, he once in a while seems something of a mystic. Here is a bit where he turns almost Hegelian:

"Modern physics, as a science, is an immense system of indications in the form of names and numbers whereby we are enabled to work with Nature as with a machine.... But as a piece of *history*, all made up of destinies and incidents in the lives of men who have worked on it and in the course of research itself, physics is, in point of object, methods and results, alike an expression and actualization of a Culture, an organic and evolving element in the essence of that culture, and every one of its results is a symbol. Its discoveries, in virtue of their imagined content, (as distinguished from their

---

55 <u>Ibid.</u>, pp. 104-105

printable formulae), have been of a purely mythic nature, even in minds so prudent as J.R. Mayer, Faraday and Hertz... Even if an investigator puts on one side every hypothesis that he knows as such {Note: Spengler is saying for the reader to set aside the 'meaning' of the particular expression distinct from the numbers themselves}, as soon as he sets his *thought* to work on the supposedly clear task, he is not controlling but being controlled by the unconscious form of it, for in living activity he is always a man of his Culture, of his age, of his school and of his tradition. Faith and 'knowledge' are only two species of inner certitude, but of the two faith is the older and it dominates all the conditions of knowing, be they never so exact. And thus it is theories and not pure numbers that are the support of all natural science.... All Laws formulated in words are derived from experiences, typical of the one – and only the one - Culture.... The pure mechanics that the physicist has set before himself as the end-form to which it is his task (and the purpose of all this imagination-machinery) to reduce Nature, presupposes a *dogma* – namely, the religious world-picture of the Gothic centuries.... There is no science that is without unconscious presuppositions of this kind, over which the researcher has no control and which can be traced back to the earliest days of the awakening culture. *There is no Natural science without a precedent Religion.*"[56]

In a few cases Spengler appears both prescient and accurate, although in this case it only took a single generation for the whole world to end up at war:

"With this enters the age of gigantic conflicts, in which we find ourselves today {Note: today for Spengler is 1922}. It is the *transition from Napoleonism to Caesarism*, a general phase of evolution, which occupies at least two centuries and can be shown to exist in all the Cultures. The Chinese call it Shan-Kwo, the 'period of the Contending States'.... The place of the permanent armies as we know them will gradually be taken by professional forces of volunteer war-keen soldiers; and from millions we shall revert to hundreds of thousands.... *These* armies are not substitutes for war - they are *for* war, and they want war. Within two generations, it will be their will that prevails over that of all the comfortables put together. In these wars of theirs for the heritage for the whole world, continents will be staked, India, China, South Africa, Russia, Islam, called out, new technics and tactics played and counterplayed. The great cosmopolitan foci of power will dispose at their pleasure of smaller states – their territory, their economy and their men alike – all that is now merely province, passive object, means to end, and its destinies are without importance to the great march of things."[57]

---

56 Ibid., pp. 188-190
57 Ibid., pp. 375-376

Spengler is also attributing the cause of the conflict to volunteer professional soldiers who needed war to justify their existence, but that of course had nothing to do with the second World War or any subsequent major conflict.

But in other cases, it is not so clear. The preceding quote dogmatically dictating that science must come from religion – it is quite ironic since physicists in particular, whom Spengler most often chooses by way of example, tend to be most un-religious. While cosmology tends to touch on subjects spoken to by religion, almost all scientists in the deep execution of their work think of nothing but their science. Even lunch and dinner are challenging concepts for most – religion is just not in the mix. Anyone who knows a scientist most amusedly understands this – Spengler may not have known any personally. Spengler might argue that his cultural factor of religion is buried so deeply in the psyche of the scientist that he cannot recognize any aspect of it, but that could be said of any argument.

"Every atomic theory, therefore, is a myth and not an experience."[58] Best case, here Spengler is taking the role of a philosopher and is not expected to be taken literally. Worst case, this material needs to be relegated to the entertainment category.

"The application of the word 'time' to the imaginary and measurable time-dimension of physics is a mistake. The only question is whether it is possible or not to avoid this mistake. If one substitutes the word 'Destiny' for 'time' in any physical enunciation, one feels at once that pure Nature does not contain Time."[59] This seems to be a philosophical statement, not a scientific one, and is out of place in this work (assuming the work is about the real world, and not musings about the world).

And here is a summary of the decline within which Western civilization now finds itself: "It remains now to sketch the last stage of Western science. From our standpoint of today, the gently sloping route of decline is clearly visible .... The tyranny of the Reason – of which we are not conscious, for we are ourselves its apex – is in every Culture an epoch between man and old-man, and no more. Its most distinct expression is the cult of exact science, of dialectic, of demonstration, of causality .... Now the question is: What form will the down-curve assume? In this very century, I prophesy ... a change of feeling will overcome the will-to-victory of science .... There is a path to the 'second religiousness' which is the sequel and not the preface of the Culture. Men dispense with proof, desire only to believe and not to dissect."[60] This means that the time he terms the "age of reason", where facts and reason dominate, is coming to an end, to be replaced by a time when belief will dominate, a belief that is independent of

58 Ibid., p. 193
59 Ibid., p. 194
60 Ibid., pp. 220-221

any particular set of facts. This period of faith is Spengler's "second religiousness", serving also as the emotional support for the downtrodden in the final end state of Western civilization (see the first quote in this chapter), as warring nations trash each other fruitlessly and endlessly.

While it is not unusual to find an author with mastery of his particular subject matter – political economics, philosophy, military history – it is rare to find someone who has seemed to have mastered most of the world. The logical ties and analogies across cultures and time periods effortlessly flow from this author like idle water-cooler conversation about sports, celebrities, or reality TV. As readers can assess for themselves from the preceding quotes, one bit of unease for a reader of the English translation is the feeling that either something may be getting lost in translation, or that whatever was "in" from a stylistic perspective in German literature in 1918 just falls slightly off the mark in English a century later. Spengler sounds often like a philosopher-poet, but that is not the difficulty – Nietzsche and even Hegel write in a more straightforward and clear manner than Spengler does. This guy is on a roll, but he is not always rolling toward the reader.

As you get through maybe half of this masterful work, there is another reaction, altogether different, that can arise.

Imagine that you have asked to meet with an expert on a particular country who has agreed to transfer his competence to you, to make you just as much of an authority as he. You just know some key highlights about the country – a few major leaders, historical events, and the like. Proceeding with your personal tour through the country, as you drive along small country roads he points out several older, heavy individuals and comments that the population is aging and of relatively poor health. The dearth of large cities that you see he attributes to a largely agrarian-focused economy. Pointing to several houses with the flag flying, he points out that nationalist feelings currently are running strong in the population, coupled with a moderate xenophobia. As you drive through the capital, he points to several political figures that he says he knows – the head of the loyal opposition, a past president of the country, the vice-chair of the central bank, and a few others. Each one is described in detail – their backgrounds, strengths and weaknesses, and prospects. Exiting the capital, he describes how the constitution has been modified over time in response to various challenges from political groups. As you pass an open-pit coal mine, it becomes an opportunity to talk about the sources of energy generation. And on the way back to the airport, the churches that you see are primarily Catholic, and he confirms that the country is predominantly so, and how it has influenced art, literature, and politics.

On the flight home, as you are consolidating your notes, you start to develop that mildly ominous "Chinese dinner" feeling about your immersion experience. Your guide did seem to know everything about everything. But you did not get the opportunity to challenge anything; to get out and question or interrogate anyone; to see if what you were looking at was indeed representative or not. You were not able to see if anything critically important that might present a contradiction, or simply another concept, activity, group, or portion of the country was missed in its entirety. Most importantly, you could not assess whether your guide's conclusions and judgments about the country were properly drawn, meaning driven by demonstrated cause and effect, or just met the plausibility test based on the portions of the country he selectively chose to show to you.

This same "missing" feeling can also show up while reading Spengler's work. Spengler's declarations are easy to find, but the support, the justification for his claims are not in the book. You basically have to take him at his word – and it is not that he does not sound competent. But conclusivity, believability, credibility, assuredness – to make a sweeping claim that modern civilization has passed its peak and is on a graceful swoon back down to peasants and dictators, requires a suitably strong case. All the rocks have to be stumbled over and at least peeked under. Causality must be demonstrated for the cited evidence, and for the "non-evidence", if it's of consequence, it must also be addressed, to make sure nothing significant has been missed. For events spread over cultures and time, citing coincidence and concurrence does not guarantee causation. So with this missing in Spengler's work, it takes some of the shine off, depending on how important justification is to you as a reader.

Spengler asks you de facto for trust - trust in Spengler that is. Nowhere will you find backing for any of the countless complex connections from one person's or culture's actions to another – just an implication that the author's declaration seems sufficient, based on his encyclopedic grasp of people and events. He may be correct, but you have to believe that he is so.

This does not by any measure make him wrong. As the egocentric (and likely competent) math writers always say "the proof is left to the reader." But this does not compromise the integrity of their postulates; just muddies the validity of the explanation; the justification; the reasoning.

Are Spengler's observations correct? Well for sure we cannot tell based on what is in the book. We can look at a few of his predictions, but need to keep in mind that without the justifications grains of salt may be needed. Of course, he could also be right for the wrong reasons (or without any reasons if that is the case).

Going back to this last stage of Western Civilization that Spengler says we are in, he declares "In this very century, I prophesy ... a change of feeling will overcome the will-to-victory of science .... There is a path to the

278

'second religiousness' which is the sequel and not the preface of the Culture. Men dispense with proof, desire only to believe and not to dissect."

The general consensus is that Western science started with Copernicus in the early 16th century, was accelerated by Descartes, Leibniz, and Newton in the 17th century, began to have wide societal effects with the Industrial Revolution at the end of the 18th century, and reached a furious level with the medical, electronic, and technological innovations in the mid-20th century (which interestingly is after the time of both Spengler and his book). The subsequent phase, where belief supplants the logic of the scientific period, is relatively easy to find – just look for Western societies where the "I believe" phrase tends to preface statements instead of logic or reasons. Religion is an obvious driver, but there can be other mindsets that cause people to simply fall back on belief. In the United States, religious revivals have occurred every few decades, and in the early 21st century, the denominations often classified as evangelical/fundamental were very active. Members of these groups were comfortable taking social and political positions based on belief. While these religious groups represent a relatively small minority of the U.S. population (under 10%), their adamancy and vociferousness enabled their influence to extend to a larger footprint. But is this what Spengler meant, and is this 21st century movement any more significant than similar movements in the 19th and 20th centuries in the U.S.? A number is not to be found in The Decline of the West – being more of a work of philosophy than a scientific work with quantitative statistics – so there is no normative percentage of the population operating in the "belief" mode that Spengler provides as a threshold for reaching his "Second Religiousness" phase. And then there is the issue that the U.S. is only about 20% of the population of the West, as it is most commonly defined, and this religiosity is not a feature in these other countries. Another interesting point is that the U.S. was never really featured in Spengler's book – it was just not significant enough (for him) to be part of the "West" that he was writing about. So maybe the happenings in the U.S. are not even germane in the context of trying to analyze Spengler's predictions.

Let's try another prediction. Here is a sentence from the summary of the end state of Western man: "The timeless village and the 'eternal' peasant reappear, begetting children and burying seed in Mother Earth – a busy, easily contented swarm, over which the tempest of soldier-emperors passingly blows." This is a little more challenging. The last time Western Civilization collectively could be found in such a position was probably at the start of the 16th century, coming out of the depths of the Black Death and before the wealth of the New World had any impact. Viewed from today's perspective, the forces of industrialization, technology, high yield farming techniques, and the growth of the service economy have just about erased all traces of this prior paradigm. Re-establishing it, à la Spengler, would require something close to an apocalyptic event. Possible sure, but more in line with science fiction and Hollywood than the probable outcome of some foreseeable future path that Western Civilization is on.

We have noted before that Spengler, as more of a philosopher-poet than scientist, is not always to be taken literally, so maybe we need to back-off his specific description of the final end-state. Of course, once one moves away from the author's words, then one is on a slippery slope and can end up most anywhere, and unfortunately they may often be places that the author never intended. But let's ignore the "eternal peasant" end-state, and consider just the "tempest of soldier-emperors." From a 1922 perspective, this may have made sense. But a century later, soldier-emperors are no longer to be found. Pirate-dictators do abound, pirating either from their own people or companies residing within reach. Economic piracy is much more profitable than warfare – warfare is very expensive and risky; economic piracy generally costs nothing and pays off richly. Dictators are not often bright, but this lesson was easy to learn. Economic piracy does require someone wealthy to steal from – generally the natural resources of the country – but also a strong anti-democratic tradition, so it is problematic to see it applicable to other than a few Western Civilization countries. Another variation would be a tariff-intensive world where the pirate-dictators keep all the tariff money, leaving the people in the economic equivalent of the "eternal peasant" end-state. But since greed tends to be unbounded, this scenario is probably unstable and so would be a transitory condition. Are either of these the likely destination for Western Civilization? Doesn't seem like a high probability, and again it is not clear if Spengler would accept either scenario anyway. So we are left with no real clarity on Spengler's vision for the future – the most we can say is that Western Civilization may be on the decline to some ignominious future end-state, but like the rest of the book, we have to take Spengler's word for it.

Toynbee

The other forecaster of the future, Arnold Toynbee, is a real historian, and presents his material in a systematic and scientific manner. A Study of History, published in 1946, one additional world war more learned than Spengler's book, reads completely differently, and explores the rise, fall, and disappearance of 26 civilizations over 5,000 years. Toynbee searches for commonalities across these civilizations that resulted in their successful growth, success, stagnation, decline, and then dissolution.

Like Spengler's, Toynbee's work is most difficult to summarize, but for other reasons. It is not poetic but dense; not philosophical but pragmatic; not arcane but deeply specific. Spengler's detail is often distracting – the reader is a little unsure how it contributes to the point being made, or what the point even is. Toynbee by contrast provides if anything too much detail, too many factors. In statistics, which most readers do not want to recall or have explained again, if you can add in a sufficient number of independent variables, you can show (on paper) that all the variation in any particular thing can be completely accounted for by all these factors (variables), and you are edging into this area with Toynbee. The other similarity with Spengler is the lack of rigor on definitions. Terms critical to the book's fundamental case, like "universal state", which a civilization enters into after it has stagnated, is never defined. Toynbee, like Spengler, will also pick out one single event in a civilization's history and identify it as *the* critical, seminal turning point, but without any explanation as to why it and not one of ten other similar events was selected.

Here is a summary by Toynbee on how civilizations successfully develop: "We have now completed our investigation of the process through which civilizations grow and, in the several instances which we have examined, the process seems to be one and the same. Growth is achieved when an individual or a minority or a whole society replies to a challenge by a response which not only answers that challenge but also exposes the respondent to a fresh challenge, which demands a further response on his part. But although the process of growth may be uniform, the experience of the various parties that undergo the challenge is not the same. The variety of experience in confronting a single series of common challenges is manifest when we compare the experiences of the several different communities into which any single society is articulated. Some succumb, while others strike out a successful response through a creative process of Withdrawal-and-Return, while others neither succumb nor succeed nor but manage to survive until the member that which has succeeded shows them the new pathway, along which they follow tamely in the footsteps of the pioneers."[61]

"Challenge and response" is the term used by Toynbee for this. As long as the civilization responds positively, adversity in most any form is a good thing, and up to some point, the more challenging the threat to the civilization the better it responds. This concept takes the Ardrey Amity (Chapter 14) idea one step further – predicting that it creates value and progress and not just bonding. Some groups of people are left behind, as they stay with what they know, which may mean retreating to a holding action in the face of climactic challenges, or coming up with unique but

---

61 A Study of History, Arnold Toynbee, Abridgment by D.C. Somervell, Oxford University Press, New York, 1947, p. 241

encumbering solutions to societal challenges, or giving in to the ways and standards of an armed or cultural invasion from outside. The Aleut society in Alaska is an example of what Toynbee calls an "Arrested Civilization", as was the Spartan civilization in ancient Greece. The almost unimaginable difficulties of trying to just secure food and shelter in Alaska against the climate there was the challenge that the Aleuts could not surmount. The basically inhuman social system that the Spartans set up, one that made communism look mild by comparison, caused its stasis and then demise.

But while most civilizations succeed in response to challenges, they eventually break down and disappear. Of the 26 total that Toynbee starts with, five were termed Arrested and went nowhere, and 11 have already collapsed and disappeared, leaving only ten alive today. Of the ten remaining, Toynbee feels two are on life support, and another seven are on a severe downward path toward dissolution. The one civilization not apparently yet in decline? Remarkably, it is Western Civilization, the civilization that Spengler has in decline on its way to a pathological future.

Civilizations that constructively grow do so by a process that Toynbee calls mimesis, adopting a term that Toynbee uses to indicate that the society as a whole copies the behavior of a small group of cultural leaders: "The essential difference between civilizations and primitive societies *as we know them* (the *caveat* will be found to be important) is the direction taken by mimesis or imitation. Mimesis is a generic feature of all social life. Its operation can be observed both in primitive societies and in civilizations.... It operates, however, in different directions in the two species of society. In primitive societies, as we know them, mimesis is directed toward the older generation and toward dead ancestors who stand, unseen but not unfelt, at the back of the living elders, reinforcing their prestige. In a society where mimesis is thus directed backwards towards the past, custom rules and society remains static. On the other hand, in societies in the process of civilization, mimesis is directed towards creative personalities who command a following because they are pioneers."[62] Toynbee means by this "mimesis" term the adoption of an idea or invention that will move the society constructively forward. It could be a political idea, such as those that resulted in the American and French revolutions, universal suffrage, or the elimination of slavery. Or technological inventions like the steam engine, internal combustion engine, and electrical power; antiseptics, antibiotics, and vaccines; or telegraphy, telephony, TV, and radio. The ideas can of course be smaller. "All acts of social creation are the work either of individual creators or, at most, of creative minorities; and at each successive advance the great majority of the members of the society are left behind.... Our Western

---

62 Ibid., p. 49

scientific knowledge and our technique for turning it to account is perilously esoteric. The great new forces of Democracy and Industrialization have been evoked by a tiny creative minority, and the great mass of humanity still remains substantially on the same intellectual and moral level on which it lay before the titanic new social forces began to emerge."[63]

While Spengler describes the end-state of Western Civilization in poetic terms, Toynbee never does, simply touching on the process and the causes: "One of the most conspicuous marks of disintegration ... is a phenomenon in the last stage but one of the decline and fall, when a disintegrating civilization purchases a reprieve by submitting to forcible political unification in a universal state. For a Western student the classical example is the Roman Empire into which the Hellenic Society was forcibly gathered up in the penultimate chapter of its history.... If we accept this phenomenon of a universal state as a token of decline, we shall conclude that all the six non-Western civilizations alive today had broken down internally before they were broken in upon by the impact of the Western Civilization from outside.... A civilization which has become a victim of a successful intrusion has already in fact broken down internally and is no longer in a state of growth.... Of the living civilizations every one has already broken down and is in process of disintegration except (for Western Civilization). And what of our Western Civilization? It has manifestly not yet reached the stage of a universal state. But we found ... that the universal state is not the first stage in disintegration any more than it is the last. It is followed by what we have called an 'interregnum', and preceded by what we have called a 'time of troubles', which seems usually to occupy several centuries.... We have already defined the nature of these breakdowns of civilizations.... as a loss of creative power in the souls of creative individuals or minorities, a loss which divests them of their magic power to influence the souls of the uncreative masses. Where there is no creation there is no mimesis.... We have seen, in fact, that when, in the history of any society, a creative minority degenerates into a dominant minority which attempts to retain by force a position that it has ceased to merit, this change in the character of the ruling element provokes, on the other side, the secession of a proletariat which no longer admires and imitates its rulers and revolts against its servitude.... The nature of the breakdowns of civilizations can be summed up in three points: a failure of creative power in the minority, an answering withdrawal of mimesis on the part of the majority and a consequent loss of social unity in the society as a whole."[64]

---

63 Ibid., p. 214
64 Ibid., pp. 244-246

While the preceding discussion is more straightforward than Spengler's would be, the specifics of things like the "time of troubles" for each civilization differ widely, and are never precisely defined. One can follow Toynbee's characterizations civilization by civilization – they seem plausible. But the difficulty is going forward - using the examples in the book to pick out Toynbee's key events for the next civilization, which in the current case is Western Civilization. It is not clear how one would do this – staying with this example – what would constitute the "time of troubles" for Western Civilization? Toynbee feels that neither World Wars nor the Great Depression, taken singly or collectively, were sufficient. However, the events in prior civilizations that he counted seemed more benign. One conclusion could be favorable and reassuring – something much worse than two World Wars and an intervening Depression must occur before Western Civilization is threatened. The other conclusion is that maybe Toynbee is just a little too subjective. Western Civ being after all *his* civilization, and he just could not bear, at the end of the Second World War, to come out with his life work announcing that his Civilization had just failed the test and hence was doomed.

To put this in context, contrast Western Civilization with the fall of the Roman Empire, or Hellenic Civilization as Toynbee refers to it, wrapping the Greek and Roman contributions together. Discussing the singular event that was "the beginning of the end" for the Greek/Roman Civilization, Toynbee dismisses out of hand all of Gibbon's Decline and Fall of the Roman Empire, declaring that Gibbon missed the point entirely, which is somewhat difficult to accept if you have read this work. Rather, Toynbee points to the start of the Peloponnesian War in 431 BC as the critical event that brought the downfall of Rome. Now considering Rome was a tiny homogenous republic at this time, and not the sprawling empire it was to later become, Toynbee makes no attempt to prove, and it is difficult to accept, this at best imaginative proposition. But if a war that preceded its Empire configuration by four centuries was sufficient to cause the Roman Empire to collapse, it is hard to see how Western Civ passes unsullied through two World Wars and the Great Depression. Like Spengler, Toynbee is long on declaration but short on justification, so the reader must either accept or reject this, along with the other conjectures.

The most critical transition point in Toynbee's modality is where the mimesis effect in the civilization loses its magic. At this point the large majority of the population ceases to follow the creative minority that is providing the leadership. This begins the downward spiral. But the factors or causes of this transition are not elaborated, yet they are vitally critical to a civilization. With the loss of this mimesis, the civilization is effectively doomed. So knowing exactly how this comes about is terribly important, yet there is no further explanation by Toynbee, leaving the reader with nothing at a point where their suitcase should be full. Another parallel with Spengler - forcing the reader to trust in the author on a key point.

Almost half the book is spent on a discussion of why civilizations break down. At first glance, this sounds encouraging – a substantive evaluation of an important issue. But with the number of reasons that Toynbee gives for the initiation of decay in civilizations, it seems that any number of factors can cause a civilization to start to fall apart. In fact, there are more causes than civilizations. And that leaves us in that undesirable position that if most every factor is a potential cause then they cannot impart much value added. With so many potential factors at play, it is going to be difficult if not impossible to predict the future course of any particular civilization, since it is likely that some or most of these factors will be present.

Here is a sample, a summary from Toynbee of one way that the growth process of mimesis can break down, using examples from past societies, including Western Civilization: "Ideally each new social force released by creative minorities should beget new institutions through which it can work. Actually it works more often than not through old institutions designed for other purposes. But the old institutions often prove unsuitable and intractable.... If it results in a revolution, growth becomes hazardous; if it results in an enormity, breakdown may be diagnosed. Then follow a series of examples of the impact of new forces upon old institutions... :

> the impact of Industrialization on slavery, e.g. In the Southern States of the U.S.A.;
> the impact of Democracy and Industrialization on war, i.e. the intensification of warfare since the French Revolution;
> the impact of Democracy and Industrialization on the parochial state, as shown in the hypertrophy of nationalism and the failure of the free-trade movement;
> the impact of Industrialization on private property, as illustrated by the rise of Capitalism and Communism;
> the impact of Democracy on education, as illustrated by the Yellow Press and of Fascist dictatorships;
> the impact of Italian efficiency on the Transalpine governments, as illustrated (except in England) by the rise of despotic monarchies;
> the impact of the Solonian revolution on the Hellenic city-states, as illustrated by the rise of *tyrannis, stasis,* and *hegemony...*"[65]

---

65 Ibid., p. 580

Another five examples are left out. But this is just one narrow aspect of how civilizations can lose their momentum and fade. Toynbee has another score of factors, with some of these subdivided even further, along with other scenarios that can arise that can temporarily ameliorate or distract from the inevitable deterioration. Elaborating these would be distracting – a summary would take almost as much space as the original work.

But Toynbee is fundamentally simple. As long as a civilization is challenged, it will respond to that challenge. A tiny minority produces original work in social, political, agricultural, medical, scientific, technological, and even artistic fields. The rest of the population mimics this leadership, growing by the adoption of these new ideas. But for any number of reasons, if the challenge vanishes, if the creative minority loses its way, if the "Pied Piper" call of the minority fades, or if internal social problems cause the majority of the population to dysfunctionally abandon the minority's leadership, then the magic of mimesis is broken. It is only a matter of time until there is an everlasting Ozymandias moment.

Keeping score over the last 50 centuries, it is Western Civilization 1, Everything Else 25. Based on the historic record, and the factors arrayed against Toynbee's mimesis process, it is difficult to see how the fate of Western Civ can be anything different from all other civilizations. Toynbee does not claim otherwise; he actually refrains from a forecast. He simply professes that the degradation process did not start on his watch. So while Toynbee may be abstaining on the specific of Western Civ, if there is a takeaway in the book, it is that every civilization is more evanescence than permanence. Whatever man assembles another power will soon diss-assemble. Now this could mean an endless Groundhog Day- deja vu scenario rather than eternal peasants and the tempest of soldier-emperors, but neither gentleman portrays what could be termed a positive and constructive outcome for the future of civilization, and hence Man.

Chapter 21
A Monochrome Tiptoe Through a Polychrome World

After a many-chapter descriptive slog through human nature, a few examples should have much more value in clarifying and cementing these points than a new spew of lecturing words. So let's take a brief walk through some of the major landmarks of modern human society, showing the limitations that man's nature places on his ability to comprehend, assess, and take action on those ideas and institutions with which he engages on a daily basis.

What is Human?

An advanced alien intelligence lands and classifies man. Human? Well, if if it's a name you want, like Rover or Max, then human will do. But if you want something even moderately scientific, then humans are a multi-species platform. Homo sapiens as the primary host with two primary obligate endosymbiotic species – mitochondria, the adapted bacteria in every cell - and about 500 different species of bacteria in the intestines. Without the former, man is lifeless. Without the latter, he is a basket case. Two more parasitic bacteria colonies in the mouth and on the skin complete the species load for the human platform. But since they are parasitic they contribute only health issues and not functionality. Man is a fully-integrated animal/bacteria hybrid organism, an example of how Mother Nature has optimized her use of the biology available to her. Mother Nature considers this biogenetic innovation so important that the adapted cellular bacteria, the mitochondria, are exclusively maternally-conserved. Only the maternal copy is passed on to the children; the paternal version is always suppressed. Scientists use the genes in the mitochondria to trace common ancestry, since it only comes from the mother's side.

If this sounds bizarre and simply implausible to you, you have not heard the half of it. Scientists estimate that the human genome contains about 80,000 genes that have been inserted by retroviruses (germs), which from a percentage perspective amounts to about 8% of the total amount of genetic DNA in the human genome. Since the genes that contain the blueprint information for us as humans only take up 2% of the human genome, that means that the viral content is actually four times larger than the human blueprint portion. That means we are primarily viral, with a minor amount of human content. So the next time you get a cold, or the flu, you are not really getting "sick", it is just a unique way of celebrating a kind of family reunion. Retroviruses insert their RNA into our cells which in turn instructs the cell to make DNA copies with the same viral genetic information. Over the millennia, most of this DNA has been effectively silenced one way or another, so it seems to not be creating a major problem, as far as scientists know. However, if people do get sick, or get cancer, some of this viral DNA does get activated and utilized to our disadvantage. So the moral is – stay young and healthy.

If you were to ask a scientist why we do not classify man, or every other species for that matter, in this fashion (as a composite species), you would have a 90% chance of hysterical laughter as their response. Bipolar thinking in Chapter 7 demands that everything is cleanly one thing or another – man is either homo sapiens or homo bacterians. But he cannot be both at the same time. Yet he is both at the same time – it is just that no one, not even a scientist, can deal with the chaotic cerebral complexity that this kind of classification scheme would bring. So we just drop all the complexity and go with the easiest over-simplification, and call ourselves man. Also at work from Chapter 7 is judgmental tagging. No human wants to be thought of as a hybrid bacterial organism – bacteria are horrible, dirty things that cause disease, are to avoided, eradicated, cleansed, and sterilized. And cognitive dissonance enters in from Chapter 8, complementary to judgmental tagging – if humans are good and bacteria are bad, how can humans be made of bacteria, a bad thing? It would make us bad, and this cannot be, so it cannot be so. As a consequence we end up just plain human, forget all this hybrid nonsense.

So at first contact, right off the starship, the sentient beings from a distant galaxy have their first lesson in what is distinctive about this intelligent race of humans they have stumbled upon.

The lesson is that Mother Nature is a master bio-geneticist/biochemist. Man is not some pristine, clean-slate, stand-alone invention but a hybrid of the same bio-technologies that Mother Nature has expertly wielded and polished throughout the living world for billions of years. Understanding and acknowledging that man is such a product of an accomplished Mother Nature leads one to further explore what she brings to the party. She is wisely parsimonious with what works – the RNA/DNA coding that controls cell fabrication, function, and operation is conserved over all known life. Mother Nature packaged the same partnered co-species bacteria into the mitochondria in each cell of most every species. The control techniques – promoters, repressors, methylation, acetylation, microRNA's, and others – that are used to control gene and protein expression and production are conserved across all living beings. The BOULE gene, which is more than 600 million years old, is utilized in all animal sperm from sea anemones to people. It is the first human gene that has been found conserved in insects and mammals. The genes that are used to make blood vessel walls in people are used to make cell walls in yeast. The genes that are used to produce the template for the nervous system in people are the same ones that mustard plants use to sense gravity and grow straight up. The gene that determines the relative sensitivity of people to pain codes for a calcium channel that serves the exact same function in the fruit fly.

This understanding of Mother Nature, as seen in man's biochemistry, provides a set of "genetic-colored" glasses through which man should view the world should he elect to accept this view. Many people are concerned about anything that is associated with man inserting genes into genomes, feeling that this is artificial and unnatural and risky. But Mother Nature does this about four times a second, 24/7, with of all things humans, arbitrarily combining the genes of genetically unrelated males and females and hoping for the best. And this does not always go well. More than once a second one of those combinations will have gone so wrong the combination will have miscarried, giving Mother Nature a success rate of only 70% or so (of course some failures are due to placental problems). One out of one hundred of those born still have some kind of genetic defect, and about one-third of those result in childhood cancer, cementing Mother Nature's somewhat rocky performance record. We have to get a flu shot containing three different virus strains once a year not because our immunity wears off, but because Mother Nature on purpose created really sloppy RNA replication machinery in the influenza virus so it constantly produces different genes, so our immune system sees a "new" virus each year. This is called antigenic drift. She also invented a process called reassortment, where if two different flu viruses occupy the same cell at the same time, they make a tossed salad out of their RNA. This gives us flu viruses that have pieces of for example avian and swine flu, and different strains of the same flu mixed together, which is called antigenic shift. And this is not just for the flu – around 40 million years ago Mother Nature decided that the bornavirus, a RNA retrovirus (like AIDS) that now only infects cows and sheep), was magic, and incorporated the bornavirus N gene in four separate places into what is now the human genome (only our distant ancestors were present 40 million years ago). Mother Nature embraces genetic modification and genetic tampering.

The polychrome, or the real-world lesson from all this is that taking a position that man should not engage in molecular biology to improve his lot is certainly acceptable, but not because it is unnatural or risky or never been done before. Mother Nature already has a total monopoly on that. In our simplified monochrome world, human nature has trivialized man into often a belief-driven picture of created perfection, or a bipolar whitewash as 100% human, and we then make decisions and judgments based on those simplified views. But by letting our perceptions of ourselves be filtered through our own human nature we in fact fail to comprehend the true nature of what we are as human.

Christianity

The most conserved cultural values and traditions in human society are those associated with religion. Jewish scripture is 2,300 years old; Christian almost 2,000, but we seldom see actual documents that old. But you can still see today tefillin, the small leather boxes with leather straps containing scripture, worn by Jews on their upper arms and heads just as they did 2,300 years ago, as well as the seven-candled menorah, which is at least as old, if not 1,000 years older. On the Christian side, the censer that is used today in Roman Catholic and some other Christian churches to dispense incense was most likely almost identical to the thurible that was used in front of (or by) Augustus Caesar, who was Emperor of Rome (as well as sharing the title of Pontiff) at the time that Jesus, the namesake for the religion, was born. The only other more conserved physical object still in continuous, unchanged use may be chopsticks, a little over 3,000 years old.

Just about everyone in the world is religious in some form or another – the figure is over 95%. The largest subset is Christian, with about 30% of the population of the world and over two billion adherents. There are five different versions of Christianity: the literal words of Jesus recorded in the books of Matthew, Mark, Luke, and John in the New Testament of the Bible; the interpretations of Jesus by his disciples and others, primarily Saul of Tarsus (St. Paul), recorded in Acts of the Apostles and the letters in the New Testament; the written scriptures, doctrine, and beliefs that each organized Christian church uses to define itself; the written material over the last two thousand years by all other Christian writers; and the personal positions of each individual minister and preacher who speaks to his congregation on a weekly or more often basis.

Out of the countless churches and preachers with two billion members, you would expect to find the largest number following the core teachings of Jesus directly. After all, Jesus' name is on the religion, and it would seem almost self-evident that any Christian would have to at least follow what Christ said before moving on to other concepts or ideas. But maybe only nominally shocking, no one is literally a Christian. Most everyone who claims to be a Christian is really a Biblian or Paulian of some form or another, in that they believe in some selected parts of the Bible. The Roman Catholic Church, as seen by someone from another galaxy, would, based on behaviors, seem to be called the Church of Mary. Even the other writers in the New Testament were already re-interpreting Jesus. And why is that? It is because of Chapter 8, Cognitive Dissonance. Here are some of the challenges from Jesus:

> "Blessed are the poor in spirit, those who hunger for righteousness, the merciful, the pure in heart, the peacemakers, those who have been persecuted for righteousness' sake.
> Love your enemies.
> Love one another, as I have loved you.
> Do good to them that hate you.
> Swear not at all, neither by heaven nor by earth.
> Take heed that ye do not your alms before men.
> When thou prayest, enter into thy closet, pray to thy closet which is in secret.
> When ye pray, use not vain repetitions.
> Whatsoever ye would that men should do to you, do you even so to them."

It is pretty hard to find anyone who can consistently meet these requirements. Loving your enemies, doing good to your enemies, and realizing that Jesus is blessing those who are being persecuted for righteousness' sake (sadly a lengthy and notorious list) are the most difficult of these to consistently execute. Often, Christians themselves are helping with the persecution for righteousness' sake, making it more messy. If you say you believe in the teachings of Jesus, and therefore agree to follow them, you are immediately faced with the fact that you cannot comply with these. So you have a built-in conflict, a cognitive dissonance. You think you are a Christian, you want to be a Christian, but you are clearly failing to be one. And so cognitive dissonance says you have to trash one of these ideas, and usually it is the last one that goes out the window. But we will get to that in a moment.

But Jesus is even more demanding:

> "If thy right eye offend thee, pluck it out.
> If thy right hand offend thee, cut if off.
> Whosoever looketh on a woman to lust after her hath committed adultery with her already in his heart.
> Greater love hath no man than this, that a man lay down his life for his friends.
> Whosoever shall put away his wife, saving for the cause of fornication, causeth her to commit adultery, and whosoever shall marry her that is divorced committeth adultery.

But I say unto you, That ye resist not evil
Lay not up for yourselves treasures upon earth.
Ye cannot serve God and Mammon.
Take no thought for your life, what ye shall eat, what ye shall
    put on.
Take therefore no thought for the morrow.
He that loveth mother or father more than me is not worthy of
    me, he that loveth son or daughter more than me is not
    worthy of me.
Be ye therefore perfect."

Now as you can see these are much easier to meet except maybe for the last one.

Actually, everyone is familiar with a small group of people who can meet some of these, especially the ones about not caring about the morrow, their clothes, eating, and their life – we call them crack cocaine or speed addicts or street people. Or just all around insane and we have them committed or halfway-housed or medicated or left on the street to fend for themselves. Not only do we not find any Christians meeting these requirements, we do not even find anyone trying to meet them. They just bail on the whole thing.

This is because the cognitive dissonance mechanism would be incendiarily savaged by this – on the one hand you are claiming to be a Christian; on the other, here are demand upon demand right out of the mouth of Jesus Himself that you cannot meet, nor do you even make an attempt to attain. Human nature says you cannot tell yourself you are a thing, but have a huge pile of evidence in front of you that at the same time that proves that you cannot be that thing.

Psychologists know this, and religious people know this, so here are the solutions available:

The first is ignorance, as in ignoring. While the challenging words of Jesus are clearly printed in every Bible, they are never featured in any sermon, nor are they quoted on the large message boards outside churches designed to draw the interest of potential visitors, nor are they in the foundation of any organized church. These requirements are not even touched upon in the balance of the New Testament by the other disciples of Jesus or by Saul of Tarsus.

The second is reinterpretation. Even though many Christians believe that the Bible is the literal word of God, they are willing to accept that when it comes to Jesus, a lot of windage is acceptable. So "love your enemies" means to be a courteous driver and a good neighbor if possible. The Golden Rule becomes conditional on not conflicting with any of your other prejudices or beliefs. The rest must be typos and translational problems – Western Aramaic colloquialisms misinterpreted.

The third avenue is an alternative approach. Saul of Tarsus and most all modern churches and preachers have taken this avenue - Jesus meant something entirely different from everything that he said during his lifetime. Most all of the requirements listed above by Jesus are measured by actions on the part of an individual, and not by thoughts or feelings or inner activity of some other sort. Jesus mentioned the word "faith" many times, but it was always in two contexts: curing someone of a physical handicap (e.g. blindness), or demanding that his disciples have faith that things would turn out favorably or as Jesus predicted. Jesus never used the word "grace". But starting with others in the New Testament, the meaning of faith was changed and the concept of grace was added to give: "For by grace are ye saved through faith; and that not of yourselves: it is the gift of God." To emphasize the distinction: "And if by grace, then is it no more of works: otherwise grace is no more grace. But if it be of works, then it is no more grace...." Rudely and over-simplistically, if you work your damnedest to follow Jesus' guidelines, or if you make little attempt to follow them, it doesn't matter; only through the grace of God can you be saved and enter Heaven. What you do – works - is only of value if done within the construct of faith and belief. This is peachy, because it means you can skip over all the basically impossible stuff that Jesus demands, and go straight for grace instead. There is only one little wrinkle – generally grace can only be obtained by meeting the requirements of each particular religious institution. But overall, they are always much less demanding than those of Jesus. So all those impossible requirements established by Jesus can be ignored.

The fourth avenue is whatever your minister/preacher tells you will bring you grace, the blessings of God, entry to Heaven, get you saved, relief from your sins, and so on. Many times this preacher is not part of an established religious denomination, but has established his own church/denomination/group. Since there is no limit, restriction, boundary, or control on the messages presented by this group, you can find that each preacher/minister has certain themes that they press, and they quote relevant passages from the Bible in support of these themes. Other portions of the same Bible that are in conflict with their message are simply not discussed, nor are Jesus' requirements mentioned, as most of these people are, using the modern vernacular, CINO's, Christians in Name Only. They are more accurately selective Biblians, generally focussing on messages that emphasize that individuals should always take a positive view and not give up, as God is always helping, facilitating, presenting opportunities, opening doors, and removing obstacles. Often, they hint or even clearly state that receiving and/or praying for material benefits – money, wealth – is perfectly acceptable. It's a good thing that they are not conferring with Jesus – he had some strong beliefs in this area.

The fifth avenue is the extensive literature on Christianity; about 1,800 years worth. You can find almost anything here – academic studies of the whole Bible, background information behind the Bible scriptures, interpretation of everything in the Bible, significance and meaning of everything in and not in the Bible. Some books in the Bible, like the Book of Revelation, are written in such a manner that everything in them is open to interpretation. Most often these writers did not represent a particular denomination or church, so you can read their work without having to look for and subtract out some net bias toward a particular Christian path.

All Christians follow one, or maybe some amalgam, of the above five paths. Human nature, through the specific trait of cognitive dissonance, ensures that literal Christianity, which is following the direct commandments of Christ as recorded and not as re-interpreted, is never practiced or attempted. Over two billion Christians but not a genuine one to be found. Every so often one can see the faded bumper sticker "Jesus is coming and boy is He pissed." The serious question is – will He be? Knowing man's nature, could Jesus truly be surprised that no church is attempting to follow His literal commandments? Probably not. But did He not then expect some at least to try, to utilize rather than discard cognitive dissonance and see how far they could take it? It would be troubling, unsettling, dismaying, frustrating, discouraging, and maybe frightening, but it would be paying homage to Jesus' commandments versus blissfully ignoring them. At some point, we will all see. In the many mansion's of His Father's House, some mansions may be much emptier than others, and some people may feign surprise at the mansion assignment they have so faithfully earned.

In our polar monochrome world, man's nature calls everyone a Christian but no one actually is one. In a world that tolerated or celebrated or at least could see in the polychrome, there would be Christianity A through Christianity Y, Biblian A through Biblian Y; Paulian A through Paulian Y. People would be comfortable with the number of Jesus' or Paul's or the Bible's guidance that they decided to set to one side and not meet, or only partially attain, or re-interpret in a specific way, and these would be explicitly spelled out in the doctrine of each branch. And it's not just Jesus that presents unmeetable requirements – Leviticus 20.9 says you have to kill your children if they curse you, and this will always bring the authorities calling.

The Christian reader who at this point feels his religion or his faith is being attacked and belittled needs to note that this is not the case nor the intent. This is an affirmation of cognitive dissonance, not a condemnation of Christianity. This is about human nature. No other outcome is possible, since human nature is fixed, constant, and unchanging. Getting upset at this is also human.

The significance of all this is that Jesus' words prescribe a certain way of behaving. If followed by two billion people as closely as possible would result in a different world than what we see today, one that certainly would be more humane, caring, and less selfish and violent. Because of the complications that cognitive dissonance brings, all Christian churches have elected to completely dispense with facing up to all of Jesus' requirements on a daily basis. As a consequence, Christian-dominated societies could be looked upon as in effect being less "civilized" than their predecessors. 2,000 years before Jesus the ancient Egyptian civilization was focussed on the afterlife, and in The Book of the Dead were the 42 Negative Confessions, a comprehensive list of actions that an individual had to attest that they had not engaged in to be allowed to move forward to the afterlife. These covered sins that would both damage themselves as well as other citizens. Unlike Jesus' commandments, in principle these are attainable. 1,500 years later the Stoics produced the same kind of philosophy, which is easiest read in Seneca or Marcus Aurelius. Reading either of these authors you basically find Jesus with the impossible bits removed – doing the best you can with what you have. They required you to try as hard as you could and then you were measured and judged. But what none of these philosophies had was an "escape clause", a way to get full-credit without meeting all or even any of the requirements of the philosophy. Only Christianity supplied that – you can mess-up big time and still get a pass from your church. Ironically, displacing both the 42 Negative Confessions and the Stoics with Christianity may have made man in terms of his behaviors less "Christ-like".

Is this the "fault" of Jesus? Hardly - more like in spite of Jesus. This is human nature. Jesus, either due to His extraordinary talents or His non-human capabilities, most certainly knew human nature, knew about cognitive dissonance (for example: "No man can serve two masters: for either he will hate the one, and love the other; or else he will hold to the one, and despise the other"), and most likely believed in the concept that "an unexamined life is not worth living," maybe because of being widely-read and speaking Greek in addition to Western Aramaic, or maybe due to His innate skills. Jesus answered questions and gave guidance most frequently in the form of non straight-forward parables, which forced his listeners to constantly think and question. Many of the commandments and much of the advice of Jesus were either unmeetable or nearly so. Not because Jesus was unrealistic or off-base, but because he appeared to have the intention of creating constant cognitive dissonance in the minds of his followers. He seemed never to want them to rest on the comfort of their beliefs – that they had followed all the applicable rules and procedures and so were "home free". That was the Sadducee and

Pharisee mindset that Jesus was committed to overthrowing and displacing. He appeared to have always wanted to produce a dissonance, a gap between what each follower was and what Jesus expected them to be. They would eternally question what they were doing, how they were acting, and strive to be better. Just look at the last thing Jesus said to his most fiercely-loyal disciple at the Last Supper after he told Jesus he would lay down his life for Him: he would soon deny his relationship with Jesus three times – a vicious cognitive dissonance. It was not Jesus that removed this dissonance, and the resulting self-questioning and self-examination from Christianity. Jesus, based on what He has said, appeared to have wanted and expected and hoped that His followers would forever live in a self-challenging, polychrome world. It was the different branches of organized Christianity that all elected to de-emphasize the teachings of Jesus that would have provoked this perpetual cognitive dissonance. As an alternative they provided their memberships with an easier, attainable set of requirements that would not produce any inherent dissonance. And it was coupled with a "get-out-of-jail-free card" (sin amnesty) in case any dissonance or difficulties arose. So Christians today can awaken every day to an unchallenging, supportive, all-is-forgiven monochromized Christianity.

The single largest denomination within Christianity is the Roman Catholic Church, with about 60% of all Christianity in its ranks. The leaders of this church understand that man is going to view their organization in a bipolar fashion, and obviously want this view to be favorable. Since religion is fundamentally personal; is aimed at your relationship with God, Jesus, and your potential arrival in heaven; is all about doing good and being good; all opinions will be judgmentally tagged, and need to be as positive as possible. Any cognitive dissonance about a church representing Jesus, salvation, God's grace, and Heaven being associated with anything bad, like torture, repression, greed, or gluttony is also to be avoided at all costs. The problem for church leaders is that since feelings and beliefs can be good or bad, if too much bad news is reported or bad behavior is observed, beliefs and feelings can switch over to unfavorable, and that means lower attendance and no donations.

So human nature has made the job of successfully running the Catholic Church as close to impossible as any in the world. The Church amassed uncountable wealth in spite of Jesus' directive that one could not serve both God and Mammon. One only has to stroll through the public areas of the Vatican to observe that. The Church so commercialized collecting money in exchange for the forgiving of sins, by selling indulgences, training its agents on how best to extort the faithful and how much to ask depending on their net worth, that it pushed Martin Luther over the brink. The Church then made war on Protestants for the next 300 years, killing and persecuting hundreds of thousands of them. Then there was the nasty business of the Inquisition, where lots of people were tortured and a few thousand burned at the stake, all for the sake of religion and holiness. And more recently, we have priests using their positions to take advantage of young boys with whose responsibility they were entrusted, rampant global unmitigated sexual abuse.

None of these negatives could be allowed to leak out and perturb either the cognitive dissonance equation or flip the bipolar view of the church from good to bad. Well, for most of the last 1700 years, that was dead on arrival. So anyone who was put off by the behavior of the church was simply threatened, ever so gracefully, with having their soul tossed forever into Hell. And if that was ineffective, there was always the same treatment that the Protestants or the participants in the Inquisition benefitted from. But for the last few hundred years, torture and blatant threats began to have much less of an effective impact and more importantly, began to demonstrate negative backlash ramifications. So what are the church leaders left with? Obfuscation and silence. Hide everything, admit to nothing. Plausible (maybe) deniability. There is no other tool or avenue left to them, other than coming clean, which would be a disaster. Or attempting to mount a defense, which would be just as catastrophic. Hence you find the Catholic Church behaving as it does, entirely in consonance with human nature. Now as the author has said before, this is not a book about making value judgments about the Catholic Church, or any other church, or any other example being utilized. That would be an entirely different book with a goal just about the opposite of that for this book. No endorsement or condemnation of any church's policy or practices is intended. They are simply being displayed to demonstrate that man's nature is so commonly recognized that it is deeply and wholly entrenched in the fabric of even the oldest and most revered of our institutions – religion.

In a polychrome world, the Church would be able to simply put the good on one side, the non-good on the other – two separate, unrelated, uncorrelated lists. Both would be acknowledged, but the one would not detract from the other. In a non-bipolar-thinking, non-judgmental-tagged, non-cognitive-dissonanced world, people would still love, embrace, and attend their church while at the same time acknowledging the countless amount of un-Christian and un-Jesus-like activities it had engaged in throughout its history. But in a monochrome world, it is one or the other. And as a result, problems that should be dealt with are buried by church management who, accurately reading human nature, feels they have no other choice. Damage that should be limited in time and depth is extended, not due to any malicious intent, but by this heavy drop-cloth of silence.

While the Catholic Church was used as an example because of its unique size and longevity, problems like this can be found in many other churches as well, all stemming from the same common cause – man's nature.

"Now I will have to say that, if we don't have the same daddy, we're not brothers and sisters. Anybody here today who has not accepted Jesus Christ as their savior, I'm telling you, you're not my brother and you're not my sister, and I want to be your brother." So stated the governor of a state elected in 2010 (but not a Catholic, making sure it does not look like Catholics are being singled out). Now apparently, this is the same Jesus who, in response to a question of how to obtain eternal life by, of all people, a lawyer, said that you should love your neighbor the same way you love yourself, and when asked the President Clintonesque question of who their neighbor was, Jesus responded with the well-known parable of the good Samaritan. This analogy was chosen, for those who have forgotten, for his Jewish audience for whom the Samaritans were black sheep with whom they were not only not allowed to associate but with whom they were not even allowed to speak. The purpose of the parable was that merciful behavior was what Jesus and God expected and demanded, without any litmus test or preconditions about the individual's credentials for receiving mercy; in fact, even if they were deemed the least worthy of receiving mercy. After some controversy arose following the governor's remarks, not for the reason here but for their apparent exclusion of non-Baptists/non-Christians, the governor said: "I will never deny being a born-again Christian. I do have core beliefs and I will die with those core beliefs," confirming that his views reflected belief-driven cognition framed by the standards of his branch of Protestant Christianity, in this case Baptist. While the governor's position is highlighted since he is a public figure, it is typical of many other Christians, as news coverage surrounding the remarks clearly showed. Now this has nothing to do with a lack of sincerity on the part of the governor – his beliefs are genuine, heartfelt, and aligned with the tenets of his church. The divergence is between the beliefs of the governor's church and the teaching of Jesus – another classic example of how belief-based thinking can overwhelm and displace facts that are in plain view, printed in a book possibly opened and read from daily by every person possessing contrary belief-based views. In the exquisite play of ironies, most certainly the parable of the Good Samaritan is discussed in the governor's church, and others like it, and the message absorbed and taught, but the portion of the parable that applies to the church's own beliefs – that part is just skimmed over, ignored, blissfully passed by as if it were not there. Belief-driven cognition can be surgically compartmentalized, so two incompatible thoughts can pass effortlessly and unentangledly past one another without a hint of distress or displeasure.

The inability to see one's native country in anything but the pure, pristine, brilliant white light of immaculate perfectness was discussed in Chapter 8 on cognitive dissonance. People have their personal identity tied to their image of their country. If the country is flawless then they are proud. If the country has a track record of doing bad things to its citizens and other countries, patriotic people will either feel bad about themselves or will have to stop being patriotic.

Some specific unsavory behaviors on the part of the U.S. are detailed in Chapter 8, but these can be found in any country. The polychrome world is a balance of legal, constructive, positive, uplifting actions on one side of each country's ledger and an unsavory accumulation of polar opposite actions on the other side. Both sides are equally embraced and accepted by the citizenry. The illegal and negative actions take nothing away from the positive side of the balance – they are unrelated.

But in the human nature world, the monochrome world, it is one or the other, you are either for your country or against it – there is no having it both ways. If you are patriotic and someone begins to list actions that your country did that were clearly wrong or illegal, then that person is either clearly wrong or clearly unpatriotic. This dialogue is impossible in a monochromatic world, yet this is reality. This discussion needs to constantly take place. Yet in even the freest country there is no rational freedom of discussion on the report card of the country as a nation. Any such attempt is met by heat, anger, resentment, distaste – only emotion, and not logic. All this is consistent with human nature. Judgmental tagging and bipolar thinking in Chapter 7 back-stop cognitive dissonance to make sure that one's view of their country is only held in emotionally-laden black and white terms. So the opportunities of learning from the mistakes of history are missed. Identifying systemic weaknesses that need correcting are ignored. Preventing the repetition of the previous folly is foregone. Resources, money, time, and lives are invested where a more reasoned, polychrome view would say otherwise.

In the study of totalitarianism that followed World War II, the term "cult of personality" was used to describe how the totalitarian regimes in the USSR presented Stalin to their citizenry, how China presented Mao-Tse-Tung (Mao Zedong), and especially, how Germany presented Hitler. Cult of personality emphasizes to an extreme that the overall welfare of each citizen is tied inextricably to the personal characteristics of the dictator of the country. Without the personal, meticulous, daily intervention of this glorious leader, the nation and its citizens would be lost in the wilderness, defenseless against foes both domestic and foreign, unable to make any progress in any area important to the nation. In turn, the dictator is portrayed as interchangeable with the nation itself, wrapped in the flag and the history of the country, representing every past patriot and patriotism itself. Pictures and murals of the leader are everywhere; every school and a street in every town are named for him. Children are drilled on this concept from their first year of school. Every thing that you want in the country can only be obtained by declaring public gratitude and loyalty to the fearless, all-powerful leader.

While Joseph Goebbels certainly did a masterful job in perfecting the cult of Hitler in Germany, he did not invent this concept. While it is difficult to tell who should get that credit, the Egyptian Dynasties were using this 5,000 years ago. The Pharaoh was the king, but also the state, and also a god. Everything depended on the Pharaoh successfully carrying out his duties, otherwise the Nile might not flood on schedule and many would starve, or foreign invaders might come and turn the meticulously-organized civilization upside-down. The Roman emperors picked this up and ran with it 3,000 years later, fighting for the emperor/state/god title. Like the pharaohs, each emperor would pillage the temples of his predecessor for building materials, have his workmen chisel out the images of his predecessor on walls and statues depending on his ego issues, replacing them with statues and images of himself. That is why for the hundreds of statues of emperors in existence during their reign only a handful exist today. "L'État, c'est moi," apocryphally attributed to Louis XIV, carried on the same idea 1,500 years later – the sovereign is the state.

Why this approach works is because it applies positive, patriotic attitudes toward the state, and services that the state provides (food or other subsidies, government jobs, transfer payments), to the dictator. This utilizes judgmental tagging – since people feel positive about getting things they often desperately need from the government, and about their flag, and country, they assign/transfer these feelings to their leader during the cult of personality process. These positive feelings are then used as a shield by the emperor/dictator against the negative feelings that his policies against his citizens often engender. An example today is North Korea, where the leader of the country uses the cult of personality to insulate himself from a citizenry who in general are miserable from their isolation from the economic benefits of the modern world, lack of any freedom, and starvation.

Modern politicians know all this and utilize the same concepts to various degrees. Some ignore the whole thing and just stay with detailed issues and policy. You will not find these individuals very often in the "news". Others embrace this to an extreme, staying only with strongly-resonant often patriotic concepts intentionally bereft of any detail or specific. An astute observer has termed this class of politicians "celebrities in suits", and in fact some have been actors or famous for some other activity first. It is fairly easy to classify each politician on the "cult of personality" scale – you just need to weigh the amount of supportable, verifiable detail behind each pronouncement versus simplistic, emotional, belief-resonant, slogans. If the politician is just for the motherland/homeland, against enemies of the country, for the flag, for all patriots, for a strong national defense, for freedom, for individual rights, for a rule of law, for small government, for lower taxes, for free enterprise, for the Constitution, for family values, for capitalism, for the American way, for no government interference, then they are wrapping themselves in the flag and the country's founding principles. Everyone is for these basic ideas – they only represent positive concepts. So by just tossing them out and moving on you are appealing to judgmental tagging, hoping your listeners will associate you with those feelings and lock that mental relationship down. Committing to details would most likely create a cognitive dissonance – something in the details would be unattractive – and the voter would change their opinion. So the politician of this persuasion avoids specifics at all costs. Complimentary to this are citizens who engage in Belief-Driven Cognition, who have settled on their particular set of strong political beliefs and now use them as a screen for political candidates as well as ideas. If a candidate speaks of generalized but galvanizing issues that are the basis for a person's belief-driven values, then acceptance and support will automatically occur. It is like the north and south pole of a magnet getting together – no thought or evaluation is required. William Jennings Bryan and Huey Long were adept in this area. And if the politician can successfully cultivate the cult-of-personality-themed positive feelings through belief-driven and judgmentally-tagged associations, they will buy the "teflon-coating" often ascribed to Ronald Reagan as a politician (who ironically only mildly unconsciously utilized this technique), where their weaknesses and problems and errors are overlooked by their supporters, as was the case certainly with Huey Long for example. Politicians who make good use of this technique can be found empirically by the combination of very strong unconditional support by their backers, and relatively high negative views by their opponents, both measured as compared to other politicians.

A cute semantics, 1984-like twist that is often used by politicians who either are or act belief-driven is to claim that they are driven by "principle". No matter what happens in the world around them, they can proudly claim they are consistently and bravely standing on principle. But, of course, the time for standing on principle is when there is no incentive for and no penalty for not. For example, if the power goes out in town, all the police are tied up in a hostage situation, and everyone else is out looting the local stores, and you refrain because, as a matter for principle, it is wrong. Or, if you find yourself in a lifeboat, or in the aftermath of a regional or national disaster, and must decide if you should share equally the limited resources that you find at your feet, or sequester them and let everyone else die of thirst first. And the time not to stand on principle is when you receive actual facts that make you realize that your belief-based position is in error, like believing the Earth is the center of the Solar System but finding out it is not, or learning infections come from germs and not random acts of unkindness by some higher power. So when you hear a politician claiming they are standing on principle, do a quick fact check to see if the politician has calculated that you live in the monochrome world where you will buy "principle" as an explanation for being pig-headedly wrong and fact-deaf.

Politics in the United States is unusual for democratic republics. The head of state/prime minister is elected directly rather than people voting for a party, and the party then choosing their leader, and the amount of unrestricted money spent during elections, much more than that in any other country in the world. In any given election one can find quite a few candidates who take the patriotic/belief-driven/no details approach. Whether they win or not often depends on each local race, the qualities of the opposing candidate, how much money was in the race, and the amount of negative advertising. But if the candidate is weak in other areas, it can be an effective strategy.

Were we in a polychrome world of details and facts, relatively little money would be attracted into politics. You can only show the average voter your positions on the issues by mail, on the web, and over the media so many times in so many colors before he loses interest. But in a human nature world, where everything is belief-driven or judgmentally-driven, it is an entirely different story. You cannot incite people with position papers. But you can with emotionally-tuned arguments that resonate with those key belief or judgmental values. If you can create a cognitive dissonance using these emotional arguments, you can change attitudes on your opponent from favorable to negative. And by filling the air-waves with sound-bites about freedom and taxes and less of this and more of that, concepts that you know the electorate will galvanically respond to, you can reinforce the wonderful appropriateness of your candidacy. Now this you can throw money at, since you can roll out one issue after another, in both positive and negative terms, going after different sub-groups of voters that make up the constituencies whose votes you need. Unlike long lists of details, short flashy emotional highlights can be repeatedly reinforced, pulling at the judgmental tagging and belief-driven aspects of human nature, and actually changing voters' attitudes, beliefs, and how they vote (and/or if they show up to vote). Because this has been demonstrated to work so well, it is a magnet for money. But as any U.S. citizen can attest, it is very hard to discern a tangible, detailed position out of the barrage of emotional appeals in election messages.

Having put such an investment into candidates in U.S. elections, these backers insist on a return on their investment. After all, the only reason they had money in the first place to invest was because they were successful in their line of business. They know precisely what ROI (return on investment) means. It makes a good marriage, since the candidate that ran on appeals to emotion and not reason is pre-committed to few details, and can move their positions around to accommodate what their backers need. Of course, in most cases it is pretty simple. Those with lots of money want to keep as much of it as possible and want to make sure no one interferes with their ability to make a lot more. This probably has nothing to do with the messages that allowed the candidate to get elected, or for that matter, what is best for the electorate overall. But since it is not inconsistent either hopefully no one will notice. But this aspect of human nature makes for a particularly unrepresentative electoral system, probably not what most voters intend, expect, nor desire.

In a polychrome world, judgmental tagging and belief-driven cognition would not be enabled. No matter how much a politician would prattle on about motherhood and apple pie, the citizens would still want to hear about the politician's detailed positions on each program that they were interested in. No matter how many flags the politician would wave it would not have anything to do with policy specifics. In a monochrome world, just the mention of freedom and lower taxes and the politician is the voter's new best friend. Of course what happens is that the politician may in fact do nothing specific about those ideas, or take freedom and taxes away from that citizen and give them to another one more "deserving". But neither judgmental tagging nor belief-driven cognition demand that specific to be further elucidated.

What is lost in the monochrome world is that by appealing to style over substance, countries like the U.S. end up with politicians whose success depends on the continual feeding of this judgmental tagging process. No specifics, no concrete actions, no detailed positions, just the continual re-hashing of the same sloganeering that will reinforce the belief-driven or judgmentally-tagged views in the citizenry. Like the old metaphor of riding the tiger, once aboard, dismounting is fatal. This is especially true if you have made the tiger more and more hungry by goading it and racing it around. So issues that need national attention, that affect not only the lives of each citizen but now the rest of the world, since the economic, environmental, and health interconnectedness of the world is today so great, are unaddressed and languish, twisting slowly in the winds of monochromaticity. A few hundred years ago when everyone was a farmer or a journeyman making shoes or candles, to first order it did not matter much if the king and his cabinet wasted time diddling and fiddling. The mass of the country would move along regardless. But today this is not the case. Economic policies and international actions can have drastic and decade-long impacts on almost every country in the world. So politicians committed only to image and style add no value where value is needed, and the world is the worse for it.

To reinforce the point made in the Preface, this is not to infer that all politicians behave in this manner, nor that all supporters of politicians do so for these reasons. Using an old naval analogy, if the flagship of the opposing (for example incumbent) politician is under attack, and the only one within range is a single person in a rowboat with a shotgun, firing blast after blast that harmlessly slam against the thick oak planking on the flagship, this person may receive a singular amount of support and popularity. He has no crew or team, no plan (other than to set fire to and sink the other guy's ship), no resources, is completely vulnerable to a counter-attack or even a wave or storm, is not doing any real damage but only making a loud display of aggressive behavior, but since the warships of every other competing politician are either out of range or their salvos seem to be missing their target, this lone individual will get all the attention and support. The rowboat guy may have even taken off all his clothes, covered himself with green Jello, and claim that he is a reincarnation of Genghis Khan – no matter – he is taking on the other guy. So it can be with politicians – one who is the loudest and most aggressive can get all the attention, because it is a "feel-good/making-a-statement" experience for a frustrated voter. They believe in supporting this politician he will make the largest splash/impact – the largest bull in the china shop. Selecting china is not the voters' objective. Or people will just vote for the anti-incumbent, an expression of their frustration with the status quo or to "send a message". And sometimes these factors align – a politician utilizing purely emotional factors will also appear the noisiest and most message-iest, and so attract voters from many camps.

One thing that politicians have figured out is that man engages the world through belief-driven cognition, and not with rational thought. Unique insight they may not have, but in the Darwinian struggle for political success it is soon clear which approaches are successful and which crash and burn. Facts fail, but fiction is dazzlingly and alluringly a winning strategy.

As of the writing of this book (2011), the U.S., like most Western European countries, has the problem of a high and increasing national debt, resulting in interest payments taking a significant portion of the annual budget. In the U.S., in the national discourse of how to deal with this issue, often you hear the cute sound-bite phrase "We don't have a revenue problem; we have a spending problem," since in the middle of a recession, with home values depressed and people concerned about their jobs and finances, no one emotionally wants to face the prospect of higher taxes. You might have vague uneasiness about this statement, since the U.S. was still suffering from the effects of recession second only to the Great Depression in duration. But

Senators and Representatives who have leadership positions in the House and Senate made this statement, and you figure there is no way they are going to come out and just boldly lie to the American people. These people aren't commentators but representatives of the people. So what do the actual numbers show? Well, there was a census in 2000, and if you divide the total U.S. government revenues in that year by the population you get a figure of $7,196 per person. Ten years later, in 2010, there was another census, and if you do the same thing, but first adjust for inflation, meaning you divide the 2010 government revenues by the change in the Consumer Price Index over that ten year period (through June, 2010, the mid-point of 2010), then the government revenues in 2010 in year 2000 dollars were $5,627, a 21.8% decrease from 2000. So, in fact, what we have because of the recession (and the Bush tax cuts), just as common sense would tell you, is a giant revenue short-fall, a major revenue problem. This drop in revenue, if you turn it into dollars, is roughly $450 billion per year, or $4.5 trillion over ten years. Now spending is up also, since the initial invasion and then retreat from Afghanistan, the occupation of Iraq, the re-invasion of Afghanistan, the prescription drug program for seniors, and Homeland Security were all unfunded programs passed by Congress. But it turns out that in our monochrome world, our Congresspeople in fact have also come to the same conclusion as the author. The average person is so unable to understand or comprehend the complexity of modern society that you can simply say that black is white. A 21.8% reduction in revenue, $450 billion per year, is "not a revenue problem" - and expect that no one will notice or complain that you have boldly lied. People want to *believe* that there is no revenue problem, that there is only a spending problem, and so politicians tell people what they want to believe. And they get away with it, even though it has nothing to do with the facts; reality; the truth.

Politics on a national party scale is the distillation of these individual positions of politicians and political commentators, issue experts, and political entertainers on a nationally-recognizable basis into one or more consensus positions that appointed or self-appointed group leaders then use to represent those of the group. In a polychrome world, these positions would be logic- and fact-based. But in a monochrome world, human nature is ofttimes forcing a Darwinian competition between whoever has the most pure, polarizing positions that will best incite bipolar judgments and belief-driven thinking. So sometimes ideas that are nowhere near the center of gravity of all collective positions and appear less practical and specific become adopted as major platform planks by large political groups. In other words, in a monochrome world, logic and facts wash harmlessly and ineffectually over a human nature driven by emotion and feelings. So if you find yourself in a very tiny minority, wondering why politics is all ten second fiery sound-bites of blood-in-the-water rhetoric rather than pages of position papers with numbers and alternate scenarios, blame both human nature and Mother Nature.

Public Safety Institutions

Several years ago, in a large West-Coast city, occurred one of the robberies that you might expect to find on one of the TV shows about the world's stupidest criminals. Three gentleman, having partaken of significant quantities of beverages sold only to those over 21, decided that it would be a most outstanding idea to attack two other gentlemen coming out of a bar in order to obtain, without their permission, their bag of food, in this case fajitas. After severely injuring one victim the other called 9-1-1. Once the police arrived, they all observed the three attackers brazenly driving by in a white truck, and so they were detained by the police.

It all would have quietly ended there had not one of the attackers been the son of the assistant police chief of the city, and all three were off-duty policemen. Omertà, the Sicilian code of silence, never met a more friendly environment than inside a big city police department. A black hole, the condensed gravity well from which even light cannot escape, is more airy than the police department under threat of embarrassment, and was this ever such a case. Not a word about this case was heard from the police department for years – it was continuously under investigation. You would have thought five foreign heads-of-state had been assassinated by five different terrorist groups simultaneously in the city. Eventually both the police chief and assistant police chief lost their jobs. One of the policemen in the incident self-destructed and lost his job. The victims won civil damages, but obstruction of justice and conspiracy charges against the police, although obvious, were unwinnable, since the omertà is understood and unwritten.

While initially they may not seem logical bunk-mates, for ease of discussion this section on Public Safety Institutions includes all the armed forces of the country; the police forces, both state and local; the fire protection services; all doctors and dentists, and the Federal Aviation Administration (which manages the Air Traffic Controllers). All these people are officially owned, backed, chartered, and/or licensed by the local, state, and/or Federal governments, and the common theme that ties them together is they all are supposed to do nothing but good.

The people that run all these organizations, and those who are politically responsible for them, know only too well all about cognitive dissonance, bipolar thinking, and judgmental tagging. They know that their ability to have a steady stream of funding and to operate with a minimal amount of regulation and oversight depends on how well they are able to keep the average citizen in one side of the bipolar mode. They need to stay on the side that says this organization is great and wonderful and just does good things all the time and therefore should never be questioned, even if you might have a question based on something clearly questionable that has occurred. So everything that is written or said is always carefully manicured to present the same uniform message. This organization is dedicated to serving the welfare of the citizens of the country and always puts their interests first, no matter what you might hear to the contrary.

To preserve this, all of these groups ensure that any "problems" that arise with members of the group are always handled within the group itself, and never by outsiders. This keeps all the "dirty laundry" inside the groups so the public never sees these negatives, which would immediately create cognitive dissonance and possibly damage the reputation of the groups. The one exception to this are Police Citizen Review Boards/Committees, but these are generally defeated by the unwritten agreement among police that they do not disclose problems amongst themselves to outsiders. Commonly, problems that arise are presented to outsiders as some variation of: "While undertaking their sworn duties of guarding the hen-house, Officers John Fox and Joe Fox were suddenly ambushed by a renegade band of chickens. In the ensuing struggle, a chicken jumped into the mouth and down the throat of each officer. Both are expected to make a full recovery."

As most people realize, members of these organizations are no better or worse than society at large, and being human make just as many errors, omissions, sloppy work, poor judgments, hasty decisions, are tempted and fall into corrupt and illegal practices, skirt the law, take the law into their own hands, and oppress and hurt those who are defenseless and whom they are sworn and dedicated to protect. But to hear it from these organizations, these things just never happen. No matter how much evidence piles up, no one in these organizations is able to see it. This position is caricatured in movies from Robocop through Repo Men, where theoretically reputable do-good organizations leave legions of bodies and blood splattered all over town, but no one notices, complains, or objects. All of these organizations are trapped in the same position as that described earlier for the Catholic Church. Any admission of negative behavior would create a cognitive dissonance conflict in the mind of each citizen, and these organizations would potentially lose their positive image. This being intolerable, their only course is hide, deny, cover-up. Yes, in a polychrome world, or in a more ethical world, these organizations would let their problems be visible and handled by an external organization, just like everyone else. And these problems would not detract from the positive side of the ledger, because in a non-cognitive-dissonance world the negative side does not talk to or take from the positive side – they stand independently. But in a monochrome world, it is all denial.

Several year ago the author and his wife were in a 757 on a major carrier getting ready to take off. The author was looking out a starboard window, just forward of the wing, listening to the cockpit/air traffic controller conversation. Just as the controller told us to "Cross (runway) 19L and hold short on (runway) 19R" you could see a plane coming in over the water about to land on 19L, maybe six seconds away. If the pilots follow directions, we are all famous. Instead after a long pause, the pilot says "Confirm hold short 19L," which the controller confirms back. The author called the FAA hot line to report this, and was told "Don't worry about this for another moment. Controllers constantly give pilots the wrong information and they just ignore it." In 1981 President Reagan fired all the air traffic controllers because they were illegally striking. Regardless of how you may feel about this, the consequences were a permanent degradation in air safety in the U.S. that has never been rectified. But, no matter how close together two planes come in the air, or run into each other, or run into mountains, or controllers fall asleep on the job, you will only hear one four-word response from the FAA - "safety was never compromised." In other words, "black is always white," "sand is good to eat," or whatever other garbage you would like to substitute in place of this FAA response. Why? Because as a public service agency – they "cannot" take any other position. It would be political suicide. If you saw the movie Airplane, you may remember the scene where a flight attendant is reassuring the passengers, some of whom have been rendered unconscious by food poisoning, that everything is just fine, while at the same time the rest of the attendants are carrying all of the pilots, who are all unconscious, down the main aisle through the cabin to the back of the plane, and, of course, since it is a comedy, the passengers all happily accept the announcement. This scene is the basis for the FAA constantly reassuring the flying public that "safety was never compromised". They figure that if the Airplane passengers bought it, maybe the American flying public will also, and most seem to.

The cost of this is substantial. Systemic problems in these organizations, whether from incompetence, protracted abuse, corruption, or illegal behavior, or financial abuse, or criminal behavior, can continue unabated, resulting in damage both to the societies they serve and protect and the trust that individuals have in these groups. Members of these organizations, seeing that problems or illegal behaviors are tolerated and accepted, turn from idealism to cynicism, poisoning their attitudes and then their behaviors, creating a self-perpetuating sub-standard situation. Everyone has seen examples of this - in the military, the police department, doctors, dentists, and firemen. They are reflected in issues as "small" as racial, ethnic, sexual, and religious discrimination all the way through extortion, drug running, murder, and mass killing of civilians. Every so often a bad apple is disciplined, but this is atypical and masks the untouched problems that are unrevealed and under-consequenced.

It is not a public-safety institution, but the parallel is too amusingly ironic to ignore. Say you were to sign a contract with a state-licensed professional, like an engineer, or engage in an implicit one by going to a doctor. In other words you needed a task or job done that the state said could only be performed by these certain state-registered and certified individuals. And they were to completely botch what they agreed to do – either not do it at all, or do it so terribly badly that it had to be redone by someone else. Yet they still charged you their full fee, or maybe twice their fee, and sued you if you refused to pay it. Of course, you would retain a lawyer, any number of whom would be drooling at the opportunity, and obtain not only recovery of your costs but compensatory damages for whatever the mistakes and non-timely performance cost you. In fact, lawyers are so unreluctant to sue that many feel this in itself is a major social problem in the U.S.

But there is one striking, remarkable exception, and that is if it is a lawyer who is the licensed professional failing to perform the work stipulated in his contract, incompetently executing his tasks so you end up in jail or asset-less, and over-charging you anyway. What would normally be called fraud or breach of contract in the real world, in lawyer-land is called a "fee dispute". Most often it is ignored by the one and only authority sanctioned to deal with the non-performance of or misbehavior by lawyers – your state Bar – consisting solely of other lawyers. Have you ever heard of anyone getting one lawyer to sue another lawyer for taking all their money and doing nothing, or making a giant mess? Like winning the lottery – you know it must happen, but you hardly ever see it. A lawyer will fight too hard, making it too expensive and time-consuming to pursue, but most importantly, it violates omertà; honor-among-thieves. It would part that dark curtain that must never reveal the incompetence, sloppiness, selfishness, abuse, and sometimes criminality that is just as prevalent among lawyers as in society at large. The legal profession must appear virginally-pristine. Nothing would trash that faster than 10,000 lawyers regularly suing each other, even though the potential payoff could be delightfully munificent.

Capitalism

Yelling out "Fire!" in a crowded public building is used as the touchstone for irresponsible and dangerous anti-social behavior. Donning your Ku Klux Klan costume and walking through some inner city neighborhoods yelling out the "n" word on Saturday night can also bring a substantial risk of personal jeopardy. But going to a U.S. Chamber of

Commerce meeting and attempting to enumerate the problems with capitalism might finish in a dead heat with the first two. Nothing more brightly illuminates human nature than taking a shot or two at capitalism in front of steroidal capitalists.

In brief, America was made by capitalism, so it has the emotional tagging of patriotism. It has the emotional tagging of self-interest, of survival, of security, of success, of fame, of self-esteem, of self-actualization. People who accumulate wealth from being successful in capitalism almost always concurrently accumulate power, and power is a tremendous motivator. It has everything you learned in school about it being the best economic system ever devised, and containing none of the disastrous weaknesses that central planning systems like the USSR had. It is held in bipolar terms – you are either for it or against it, and supporters and most participants are for it. It is ripe for cognitive dissonance. Knock capitalism and you are taking a shot at all the positive feelings and beliefs just listed, so any criticism has to be dismissed. Normally critics of capitalism are classified as either socialists, communists, academic idiots, anti-American, or some combination of these labels. Since the criticism cannot be correct, you have to shoot the messenger, attack the witness' credibility, or whatever other analogy works best.

Of course, this is the monochrome view of capitalism. Sure, it is the best economic system, even without splitting hairs over the definition of "best". It is the most effective and efficient economic system, both on a micro and macro basis. A great part of this is due to its self-incentivization. Those who can best operate within the system become wealthy, and everyone wants more wealth and what it can bring. Capitalism as a system clearly works extremely well. You can find countless examples in country after country, century upon century. It is probably the best man-made system of any kind ever devised, second only to Mother Nature. With almost unlimited wealth, fame, and power as the reward, capitalism incentivizes man to find the most creative and original ways to create, design, manufacture, package, price, distribute, support, and market products and services. It drives him to unimprovable levels of excellence and attainment. If it is not impossible, capitalism will probably profitably produce it (and hopefully legally).

But in the real world, in a polychrome world, it is perfectly acceptable to consider improvements, enhancements, adjustments, problems, side-effects, and negatives along with positives when viewing capitalism. DDT was both an effective and efficient pesticide, but it was doing too much collateral damage to be tolerated. The old air conditioning refrigerants R12 and R22 were near perfect. The only problem was they photo-disintegrated up high in the atmosphere and destroyed the ozone layer, which was going to give the world eye damage and skin cancer. So they had to be replaced with something not nearly as effective. PCB's and carbon tetrachloride also performed their jobs flawlessly, but turned out to be too dangerous and had to be replaced. So just being effective and efficient are not sufficient.

X-rays are a great medical tool, used not only for simple pictures for physicians and dentists but also for virtual colonoscopies, CT scans, and fluoroscopy. Today they can be three-dimensional and digital. But x-rays are ionizing radiation, and will cause cancer, based on the accumulated exposure and the area exposed, and so exposures have to be carefully controlled. This danger can be harnessed and used to kill cancer, by selectively treating the tumors to massive doses from specialized equipment. You can receive also x-ray exposure naturally though the environment and by flying, and occupationally, and it all counts. So any intentional x-ray exposure has to be carefully managed, so that its value is not compromised by its inherent risks. No one questions the value of x-rays, nor their risk; they are accepted together.

Why is this? Because there is no particular emotional tagging of x-rays one way or another. They are just a tool like a hammer or a saw. Cognitive dissonance, belief-driven cognition, and bipolar thinking – these facets of human nature do not apply to x-rays.

There are many, many things in the same category as x-rays. Automobiles and airplanes are wonderful modern tools, but misused or poorly maintained they can and do kill people. But their dangers are accepted because of their social benefit. Anesthetics are fundamentally just deadly neurotoxins, and they are carefully applied just short of killing the patient, a most careful ballet between life and death. But they are welcomed because the alternative is so much worse, and their downside risk is tolerated. Just about every tool and aid, mechanical, electrical, and chemical, falls into this category. So do systems, like the legal system in most countries. They do accomplish their objectives but not without creating problems and failing to administer fair justice in many cases.

Man's monochrome nature compels him to condense and commingle the effectiveness and efficiency of capitalism, which are beyond dispute, with the consequences of capitalism, which can range from quite positive to disastrous, depending. But the requirement to mentally categorize capitalism into two distinct buckets – one for its *workings*, and one for its *results*, is too much to ask for man. It has to be all one color, one valuation, one moral finding; right or wrong, good or bad. The complexity of part "good"/ part "bad" - this is territory reserved for philosophers and sophists, academics and those unable to hold a real job.

The best analogy for capitalism is the automobile transportation system in an advanced country like the United States. Capitalism works most efficiently and effectively in an entirely autonomous fashion as does the traffic system; all drivers recognize that adding a human (a policeman directing traffic) makes for a catastrophe. Like Adam Smith's Invisible Hand, drivers constantly make optimization decisions about what route to take, what lane to drive in, when to pass, how fast to drive, without any assistance from a central authority. Like capitalism, drivers have strong built-in incentives – fancy cars and horsepower and speed. Like capitalism, there are many choices available to drivers to reach their objectives – whether to choose a civically-responsible or gas-guzzling vehicle, like a career choice that is socially-minded or self-serving. He can drive in a manner that does not endanger his fellow citizens or drive with abandon, like making ethical business choices versus running Ponzi schemes or the equivalent. He can choose to drive impaired or distracted or not, and decide to take unfair advantage of his fellow workers, clients, and competitors or not.

While some commentators have said that Americans "love" their cars, some of that is driven by the necessity of having no viable alternative. But the automobile traffic system is regarded with reasonable objectivity, hence this comparison. No one would dispute that regulation is required to meet socially-desirable objectives and to prevent unnecessary damage and injury. Drivers are licensed and insured. Vehicles have to meet certain minimum safety and environmental performance requirements. If a truck, maximum weight limits prevent damage to roadways. Traffic rules are plentiful, and speed limits are substantially below the capability of modern vehicles. Provisions are made so pedestrians can safely cross streets, even though the result is substantial traffic inefficiencies. Traffic lights and stop signs allow intersecting traffic to pass accident and disorder-free through common points without any human intervention. Traffic rule commonality enables a driver from one location to safely drive 3,000 miles away without any familiarization. More efficient alternatives are available at higher cost should a driver so desire – toll roads and bridges. Changes, additions, and improvements can be made to the existing system without disruption.

But if one proposes to apply the same regulation philosophy to enhance the operation of or curb the same dangers and excesses in the capitalism system as in the automobile traffic system, instead of simply rolling out the regulations, or maybe some discussion first, the proposer is pejoratively labelled anti-business, anti-jobs, anti-free-enterprise, anti-growth, anti-free market, a socialist, anti-American. This difference is not due to any real difference, or any logical difference; it is all due to human nature. Because any such regulations are perceived to be an attack on the emotionally-held beliefs about capitalism outlined in the second paragraph under this topic of Capitalism, people perceive that their belief structure, their values, and their livelihood are under attack. And people react not rationally but emotionally, unlike the traffic counter-example. So problems and/or circumstances that if they were on the traffic side would be instantly corrected are allowed to continue doing damage or not providing benefits.

Unfortunately but not surprisingly, proponents of capitalism, like politicians, know full-well that people do respond in this way, and so they always color their arguments with phrases that will garner the most fervent reaction from those who are listening. In a sound bite world, they know that calling a proposed regulation or rule change a "job-killer" will get infinite more media play than some dreary technical economic argument, plus it will do a much better job raising blood pressure in their target audience.

A classic example that perfectly illustrates how this works comes from the automobile analogy side, conveniently with business overtones. In the late 1960's, at the peak of the "muscle car" era in the U.S., you could purchase several unmodified (from the factory) cars with 400 to 450 cubic inch V8 engines and around 350 horsepower that delivered about 10 miles per gallon. (Now drivers only really use torque – the only drivers who use horsepower are those either in prison or deceased. But since no one understands torque we will stay with horsepower.) Then came concerns about oil shortages, so regulations with mileage standards were imposed, followed by clean air regulations. Every automobile manufacturer threatened and predicted for years the end of the automobile as we knew it. The car of the future was going to be powered by something between a lawn mower engine and a sewing machine engine, would get about two miles per gallon, and people would have to get out and walk up hills. A little over forty years later – where are we? Well, let's see, you can get a Mercedes AMD CL65 with 620 horsepower or a BMW M5 with 560 horsepower, both with 11 mpg city and 17 mpg highway. A 500 horsepower Corvette gives you 15 mpg city and 24 mpg highway. There are other cars to choose from in this horsepower range, and a zillion at 300 horsepower and up. A 330 horsepower Infiniti G37 gets 19 mpg city and 27 mpg highway, and this is from a tiny 226 cubic inch V6 engine.

So what went so terribly astray? How did this catastrophe come about? How could every competent automobile manufacturer be so woefully, dreadfully, completely, invertedly wrong? What went wrong is that what you heard was not a real forecast, just whining by companies who were trying to get out of any responsibility to do anything, which is their right. Denied that, what happened was the system worked as advertised. The free enterprise system rewards people who make things that meet the rules, no matter what the rules are. And the system works so well, is so powerful, is so not-to-be-denied, that these engine technologies and their performance appeared like magic. But it only seems like magic unless you understand what is behind it – a system that always succeeds, that cannot be stopped. Oh, you can, and should, redirect it, control it, monitor it, restrict it, and punish parts of it when they do bad, but the system will always explosively flourish.

Now let's turn back to capitalism. Unlike the automobile traffic system, where most (but not all) issues are dealt with rationally and quickly, problems and needs in heavily capitalistic societies like the U.S. remain chronically under-addressed. An example might be the ability of company management and sometimes owners to purposefully defraud their stockholders, customers, bondholders, and employees without penalty. (Note this is the layman's definition of fraud – you were told you had something of value, and it turned out to be worthless.) Of course, their defense is always that their *intent* was only to engage in behavior that eventually led to the fraud, and not the fraud itself. This is like a driver saying that his *intent* was only to drive fast, and not to kill anyone while doing it. On the traffic side, this is no defense, but on the business side, it always succeeds. Efforts to remedy this always fail, no matter how many hundreds of billions of dollars are lost by people who could not afford the loss. The number of business people punished in any significant way for this kind of behavior is approaching the number of people reporting whale bites. The impact on society is that with not only the absence of any negative sanction for their behavior but often great rewards (money), people keep acting in this way and society has to amortize off this large cost on an ongoing basis.

But even in the cases where blatant fraud is afoot – say where Enron traders were using their techniques that they called Death Star, Fat Boy, and Ricochet to game the California utility market to enable them to artificially collect higher than allowed fees, or where mortgage brokers intentionally encouraged Alt-A mortgage applicants to "exaggerate" their stated income to qualify for mortgages that the brokers knew they would never be able to afford, the number of individuals that received anything more serious than home confinement for a few months you could count on the fingers of one hand. The contrast between "crimes" in capitalism and any other situation is stark. If someone steals your car or all your jewelry or all your cash they go to jail. But if they steal all the money out of your house value or IRA nothing happens.

Another outstanding example of traits like belief-driven cognition so extreme that it is humorous is the furor on personal tax rates. The argument is put forward, although it is heard primarily in the U.S. and not other industrialized countries, that any tax rate higher than zero for high income earners will discourage them with the result that they will: stop working; stop hiring other workers; stop spending money that helps the economy grow; some or all of the above. In the traffic analogy, this argument is the same as saying that anyone that owns a car that costs more than $70K or has more than 300 horsepower should have a separate speed limit of 80 mph or they will become discouraged and will not buy such cars. Of course, everyone knows that is nonsense. Everyone has the same speed limit and people buy the cars they want regardless. People in business will go after money because they are driven. They do not give a ding-dong about the tax rate, other than they try their damnedest to minimize their taxes.

The maximum personal tax rate as of this writing in the U.S. is 35%. The only time it was lower was during the Great Depression. Most of the time it was between 70% and 90%, and the U.S. did quite well, growing to be the most powerful country in the world. The maximum tax dropped to 50% in 1982 and continued to decline thereafter. U.S. real median household income, meaning adjusted for purchasing power, was about $45,000 in 1978 and was just under $50,000 in 2009, a growth rate of under half a percent a year. So this drop in maximum tax rates actually did nothing for the average American. But it did help make a lot of individuals really really rich.

To understand how someone wealthy responds to the marginal personal tax rate, one has to put themselves in that person's shoes for a day. Say your income is about a million dollars a year, which is roughly $20,000 a week before taxes, and if your state's tax rate is 10% and you have reasonable deductions, would be take home pay of about $13,000 a week. You bought your main house and other two houses with stock options so you only have say $2 million in mortgages that you keep for their tax deduction. You have roughly $5,000 of your first weekly check left after paying off the mortgages. You put on your hand-made bespoke suit, $5,500, made in Italy so no Americans were helped. You get in your chauffeured limo for the ride to work. It was made in Europe. Mid-morning your spouse calls. She is shopping with a designer for two rooms – the bill is $78,000 so far. This is just an exercise in money changing hands buying exotic objects d'art – no jobs are created. You meet her for lunch and then drop by an art gallery to choose a painting for one room - $75,000. Number of jobs created: none. That's $150,000 for the rooms but since the most you have ever been able to spend is a third of your take-home pay in a year, you have $3 million in cash in a brokerage account and can just move some of that over. Later that afternoon your broker calls – he was able to get you in on that IPO you wanted – 2,500 shares at $40 a share. Bragging rights – the money is pocket change. And no new jobs. That night you go out to dinner, and it's the chef's tasting menu – 6 courses, $225 per person. Of course, you brought your own nice wine from your own wine cellar, happily paying the $45 corkage fee. It's a 2000 Haut Brion; you paid $2,300 for it but it is worth way more than that now. But so as not to upset the waiter, you did order two glasses of 2001 Chateau d'Yquem after dinner at $300 each. Jobs provided: none. While you were working, there were crews of people manicuring the yard and cleaning every inch inside the house. Much of the money they made went back to their relatives in El Salvador, Nicaragua, and Mexico. When you get home that night, you leave a voice mail for your agent to ready the villa in Saint-Tropez for a visit in a week, plus travel on a private jet. Jobs created: none.

Now suddenly, the tax rates change and this person's after tax income drops from $13,000 to $11,000 a week. You can ask yourself – what in the above scenario will change? Well, absolutely nothing. At $11,000 per week, you can't spend it fast enough. Even $2,300 for a bottle of wine is about one day's pay. All this talk about tax rates being a catastrophe for the economy is just people trying, understandably, to maximize their greed. It, after all, is their nature.

People that are really rich conceptually spend money just like middle-class people do. It's just that they spend it on things that cost 100 times as much because not only is the cost unimportant, it often says a lot about who they are. LVMH only exists for people like this. You might buy two watches for $79 or $99 – they will also buy two, but one maybe at $12,000 and the other $24,000. You have two cars, $22,000 and $27,000. They have two cars also, $125,000 and $350,000. You bought your wife a nice necklace for $350. He buys his wife a nice one also for $275,000. Your wife buys her outfits on sale – an item for $59 here, $79 there. His wife does the same thing - $750 here, $4,500 there. Your wife has several pairs of shoes, some at $69 and some at $89. His wife has several also, but they are mostly Louboutins at $700 a pair. So the impact is that the quantity of items purchased by the wealthy is often not much greater than that accumulated by the average person. It is just that they buy really expensive things that have exorbitantly-high mark-ups and therefore prices.

As a result of this, the wealthy do not spend much of their income on what would be called consumable goods. They are almost always either investing – stocks, bonds, apartment buildings, land, houses – or buying really expensive car collections, horses, jewelry, yachts, wines, antiques, and/or paintings from other collectors or dealers with lots of money themselves. They have put two billion dollars into hedge funds – available only to the wealthy - designed to employ the best financial minds available to take great risks and make the rich dramatically richer. Vast quantities of money changes hands for these items, and in and out of these funds, but almost no jobs are created. And the money does not go into the economy in any noticeable way – it just washes through the bank accounts of one rich dude or dudess to the next.

Now there are wealthy people who are so careful with their money that they do not spend much more on food, cars, clothes, and jewelry than the average upper-middle class citizen. But the argument still applies – change the tax rates on them and absolutely nothing happens.

If you want specific examples of these kinds of people, you actually know many of them already – you just don't realize it. The average professional baseball, basketball, football, hockey, and top tennis player and golfer in the U.S. all make one million dollars per year or more. So do the average movie actor and pop singer if you recognize their face and/or music, along with many hit TV show actors. About one-fourth of all lawyers in large law firms are partners, and their average pay is just under a million dollars a year. The average U.S. Senator, 100 of them, all earn somewhere close to a million a year if you toss in their spouse's income and their assets in blind trusts. Many specialty doctors, like orthopedic surgeons, along with some dentists earn close to one million dollars a year (often by receiving kickbacks from medical companies for the products they install during surgery). Many well-known national commentators like Sarah Palin, Glenn Beck, and Rush Limbaugh earn several million dollars per year. The presidents, CEO's, Chairmen, and officers of every Fortune 1000 company, if you add in stock options, over time make on the order of one million dollars a year or more. Every investment banker on Wall Street, at places like Goldman Sachs, Morgan Stanley, and JP Morgan, earns close to one million dollars a year. Then there are the 1,500 people with incomes of a million dollars or more who through creative tax planning paid no income taxes at all – for sure they will not be changing their habits if the tax rates change. And we can't forget the managers of hedge funds who earn from maybe $40 million to $2 billion per year – their tax rate, due to a technicality in the tax code, is fixed at 15% no matter what – lower than nurses, school teachers, bus drivers, and many servers. They are also immune from any changes in tax rates.

All of the above people, a few thousand whom you know to one degree or another, would not hire anyone if the tax rate changed. Many probably do not even know how much money they make. They have advisers or accountants who handle that kind of thing for them.

If you don't care for a model or examples focussed on individual behaviors, then you can approach this using macro-economic data. In 2011 The Wall Street Journal reported on this. At the moderately wealthy level ($200,000 per year salary), Russia and then Japan have the lowest effective overall tax rate, including income and social security taxes. Germany has just about the highest, with the U.S. slightly higher than Japan but much lower than Germany.

But the economies of Russian and Japan, the countries with the lowest tax rates, are and have been disasters of the first order. Were it not for Russia's vast natural sources of oil, gas, and diamonds, the country would probably have collapsed and disappeared. Japan has been in a no-growth stagnation for decades. Germany, saddled with integrating East Germany, an economy not much improved over the level of 1946, is an economic miracle. And Haiti, while not in the data, has zero taxes, and has a non-existent economy (although the rich do quite well). On the surface, it seems the inverse is true – the higher the tax rates, the better performing the economy.

Or just use a more recent U.S.-only example. In the eight and one-half years immediately preceding the Bush tax cuts that were passed in mid-2001, the inflation-adjusted compound *quarterly* growth rate in the U.S. GDP was 0.85%. After this large across-the-board tax reduction, favoring the highest earning taxpayers, over the next seven and one-quarter years (until Quarter 3 of 2008) the GDP compound quarterly growth rate was 0.56%. (After this period the U.S. fell into a recession due to the house price bubble and bankruptcies of Lehman and other institutions, so we'll exclude that from the data.) So lowering taxes reduced GDP, the macro measure of the total economic output of the country. You might say, well, GDP may not mirror employment, so what happened there? Over the first eight and one-half year period above, non-farm employment grew by 20.6%. During the Bush tax cut period ending in June of 2008, non-farm employment grew by 3.2%. If you pick the peak employment in this whole Bush period it showed a total growth of just 4.5%, less than one-fourth the growth of the prior period. So no matter where you look, the higher the tax rates, the better off we are economically. Unless, of course, you ask those who are wealthy and are being taxed. They don't like it and so they create imaginary arguments that they spin through the media justifying the need for lower taxes. But they stay away from the real data – it just does not go their way.

Now notice, in case you are reading at the same time as you are tweeting, twittering, and tittering, that the author is not saying or hinting that more taxes across the board are good for the economy, GNP, or jobs. Obviously, and simplistically, if the government takes everyone's money away, the economy is going to do fairly poorly, other than the money that the government sends back again. The countries referenced above that have higher average tax rates and better economies tend to do so by having more progressive tax rates, meaning the people with lower incomes pay a much lower tax rate than really wealthy people do. But without diving into the economic cesspool, if the government of Haiti begins to tax the rich and uses the proceeds to build infrastructure that provides businesses an efficient, viable, profitable, predictable, and safe environment in which to operate, the economy would grow. If, on the other hand, it uses its revenue to build a large military, and confiscates all food production to feed the army and control the population, it simply becomes a North Korea, and people begin to starve to death. What the government does with tax revenues, what its fiscal and monetary policies are, what its inflation levels are, how it sets its currency in relation to other benchmark international currencies, whether it has abundant natural resources for profitable export, whether it has a relatively free economy or one encumbered with limitations and regulations, what its practices are with respect to import and export tariffs, whether it has a sustainable cost advantage in certain businesses or not, whether it suffered from any systemic real estate asset bubbles/implosions during the period in question, what the growth, education level, and relative age of its population are – all these factors go into determining whether a specific country has full employment and solid GNP growth or not, in addition to its tax policy.

You may have noticed that you do not find the presidents of any companies coming out and saying that they are not hiring or expanding due to tax rates, whether personal or corporate for that matter. Wonder why? Well, that's because if they did, there would immediately be an emergency phone call meeting by the board of directors that would go something like "Well, we have a potential disaster. Our president has come out publicly and said he is going to hire based on tax rates. We are either facing an ischemic stroke or major substance abuse problem, and need to a replace him immediately...." Knowing this, no president would ever be so stupid as to say such a ridiculous thing.

A little bit on tax rates and business decisions. Most financial professionals measure companies using a yardstick called EBITDA, which you have probably seen. It is earnings (E) or profit before (B) subtracting out a list of other items, one of which is taxes (T). In other words, No One Even Cares about taxes. Second, people that calculate taxes have thousands of pages of IRS rules and regulations and tax court opinions and cases and are often lawyers and accountants. All they do all day is worry about rules and regulations and laws and restrictions. Company presidents do not want that attitude anywhere near the creative people that make their company successful, so generally they put them in a separate office or building as far away as possible from everyone else. If there ever were colonies on the Moon or Mars, the tax people would be the first ones sent there. Third, there are four reasons why in a business you decide to pay more money to people to do more work. The first is rule or regulation, meaning you have to do it. You have to document your personal protective equipment and forklift procedures for your safety program and hire a contractor to write it up for you. The second is risk-reduction, especially low probability/high consequence events. You find to your extreme embarrassment that your company still has on-line access to its cash in its bank account through a PC that is also used for other on-line activities, meaning it is only a matter of time until it is cyber-hacked and all your money is sent by a guy in Russia or Latvia to his bank in Cyprus. So you hire a contractor who provides you with the unhackable solution – a dedicated, off-line except when used, banking-only, preferably Linux machine. The third reason is cost reduction. The painter, or the furnace operator, or whoever, says that the yield is much poorer than normal when using paint X or glaze Y, and if you can authorize him overtime he thinks he can figure out the problem. The fourth reason is a development in the marketplace you serve

- either an opportunity or a competitive threat. You are starting to see people walk out of the store because of the length of the checkout line, or your video game or photo editing software is aging and is need of an update, or your customer will order 1,000 tops if you can make them in a week, and you either need to work the present staff on overtime, hire temporary staffing, hire a contractor, hire someone part-time, or hire someone full-time. But if you need to buy $15,000 of material to cinch a $100,000 order, and your receivables are already factored, and your payables are so far beyond 60 days that you are on C.O.D. with everyone, and your credit cards are all maxed out, and no one at a bank or CIT or the SBA will give you any help, then you are completely out of options anyway, and you cannot take on any new business because you do not have the working capital, otherwise known as cash. Tax rate – you have got to be joking.

Let's say for the sake of argument you simply eliminated all taxes, and let the economy run for a moment before it fell apart à la Germany after WWI. Would anyone get hired? People in lower and middle class income levels, based on past track records, would pay off credit-card debt and save. People who were extremely wealthy, in the example above, would not notice. But, people in the just-barely-rich category – there might be a few hires here. Some people with just one nanny, or just one housekeeper, might now feel they could afford a second one. They might go see their dermatologist or plastic surgeon or dentist for a procedure that they had previously felt was just not justifiable, and these physicians might have to hire a nurse or receptionist or two. And everyone who could afford it would donate money to the politicians who were promising to keep taxes at the zero levels, so the politicians would have to hire a few accountants to keep track of their largesse. But the national impact would be unnoticeable – maybe in the few thousands.

Or try this perspective – the total assets of the top 2,000 companies in the world are about $120 trillion, and about 7% of these assets are held in cash, which is about $8.5 trillion. If these companies needed to hire someone, and assuming the productivity of the new hire is zero for their first full year after hire, and assuming their total cost of salary and benefits is $80,000 per year, these companies combined could instantly hire 25 million people and only use one-quarter of their cash on hand. Non-financial companies in the U.S. have around $2 trillion in cash. If they used half of it they could hire 12.5 million people, instantly putting the U.S. unemployment rate at zero. So why don't they hire anyone? - because they don't have any work that they can profitably afford to hire someone to do. Tax rates are a complete and utter non-issue.

In no case are tax rates a consideration when making a hiring decision. Only pundits and people in the political entertainment business engage in that kind of wordplay. The stark Emperor's-New-Clothes contrast between the polychrome world disconnect between tax rates and jobs, and what is said in the monochrome world of human nature, is one of the brightest and clearest examples of how effectively these traits of human nature work, and how those who recognize this utilize it to their advantage. It is sort of a variation on "imitation is the sincerest form of flattery" - pushing and presenting ideas in a way that will maximize the response from man's non-rational side.

Politicians push the tax rates/job linkage because it is wealthy corporations and individuals that provide them with campaign funds so they can get in office and remain in office. It is in the individual interests of these people and groups to have their taxes as low as possible (taken collectively; some individuals do not agree). So this linkage (taxes and jobs) is advertised not because it is accurate or true, but simply because it maximizes the amount of money received by both the politicians and the wealthy. But because capitalism, free enterprise, the American way, and all it represents are held in such favorable emotional terms by Americans, and in some other Western countries, the emotion sticks tightly, the facts just slide off the slick slimy surface, and this shotgun marriage concept of tax rates and jobs and the economy appears to have a reasonable foothold, at least if you measure it by taking an attitude survey.

You may wonder why people make such a to-do about lowering taxes on the wealthy if it doesn't help add jobs; that since there is so much talk about this there must be something to it. The owner of a business that manufactures and embroiders clothes in Tampa, Florida was quoted[66] in The Wall Street Journal in 2011 to the effect that lowering taxes would help his 19-person business grow: "We spend more on taxes and insurance than even on payroll." Payroll taxes, workers' comp, and unemployment insurance maybe run to just under 10% of payroll worst-case. If by "insurance" this gentleman means health insurance, and it costs say 15% of payroll, and he pays 80%, that is another 12%, so we are up to 22%. To add another 80% in taxes, income taxes, to get his total taxes and insurance over his payroll costs, and assuming for the sake of simple arithmetic that this gentleman's composite Federal and Florida corporate tax rate is 33%, requires him to have his net profit after all his expenses equal to 2.4 times the amount he pays everyone, including himself, in wages and salaries. In other words, he is making so much money he is soon going to have to start his own bank. But he wants more. Only the cocaine guys from down south can compete with these kind of profits. So is what he is saying technically true? Absolutely. But is it germane? No. It's like Katy Perry or Lady Gaga declaring that a lower tax rate would enable them to put out more songs. Yah, well, OK, whatever.

Here is a concrete example. Say you are claiming that you need a reduction in the tax rate before you can afford to hire another employee, and assume that you will be hiring on the cheap - $30,000 in annual wages plus

---

66 "Private Ideas on How to Create Jobs", The Wall Street Journal, September 7, 2011

another $10,000 (33%) in fringes and benefits like vacation, sick leave, payroll taxes, and insurance for this employee. Let's say that a 5% cut in the tax rate is proposed. For a 5% cut in the tax rate to leave you with an extra $40,000 requires your pre-tax income, that is, profit after all of your expenses including your salary are deducted, to be $800,000. But wait – if your profit is already $800,000, you could instantly hire this $40,000 employee – you don't need to wait for the tax rate to change. So this tax argument is just a red herring, an irrelevant distraction.

Many years ago there was a Dilbert cartoon by Scott Adams that went something like this: "Engineer: What does the customer want? Marketeer: The customer wants all of the latest technology. The customer wants all imaginable functionality built-in. The customer wants the device to be so intuitive and easy to use that no manual or instructions are needed. The customer wants the interface to be so attractive and sexy and addictive that they cannot put the device down. And the customer wants all of this for free." Translated to capitalism – people that are rich want to be richer; they want no rules; no restrictions; no regulations; no impediments; no oversight. They are stuck at the top of Maslow's hierarchy – self-actualization. They are trying to prove to themselves and to the world that they have unique value and merit because of their wealth. Does Oracle's Larry Ellison have a 450 foot, $200 million yacht the Rising Sun to house his software development staff? Does Microsoft's Paul Allen's $200 million yacht Octopus help him hire fishermen? Or was Steven Spielberg's $200 million yacht Seven Seas thrown together to help him house promising screenwriters? Larry Ellison spent another $200 million or so on the BOR 90 so he could have bragging rights on the world by winning the America's Cup. And they may still be working on the ultra-sleek, ultra-cool, ultra-personal-touched yacht of Steve Jobs, years in the building. Most all these and countless others regard taxes, like mortality, as just one more aggravation to work around on their way to smashing Maslow, constructing some flawless, stunning, unmatchable physical manifestation that unmistakably demonstrates their personal universal uniqueness and importance both to themselves and to the world. Maybe Leona Helmsley, a multi-billionaire, summed it up as well as anyone to her housekeeper: "Housekeeper: You must pay a lot of taxes. Leona: We don't pay taxes. Only the little people pay taxes."

Do you think Oprah and Madonna each have six houses because of the enormous size of their families (one and five respectively)? Or how about John McCain with eight houses (two people)? Ellison buys houses in groups - three or more at a time, at $20 million or more apiece - assembling and then reconstructing countless collections of massive estates that he may never visit. Steve Jobs spent years and tens of millions of dollars on an ultra-exclusive New York apartment that he sold before he ever set foot in. And how about the Siegels in Orlando - asked why he built the largest private house in the United States - 90,000 square feet, well over *two acres* of house, about the size of two American football fields without the end-zones: "because I can ... I couldn't spend all the money I was making."[67] These people and most others are competing with each other for relative coolness and richness, whether through yachts, cars, houses, clothes, race horses, wine collections, art collections, airplanes, NFL football teams, NBA basketball teams, Major League baseball teams, and/or Premier League soccer teams. So they (not necessarily these named individuals above) complain about everything that gets in the way, because it is their nature to do so (just like the scorpion in the modern scorpion and frog fable). They are driven, sometimes it seems uncontrollably – like modern-mini versions of Alexander the Great. Urging and silent pleading from a fundamental self-first orientation, Chapter 11, provides additional momentum. They are a testament to the power of human nature described here. Drowning in money they can never spend, they ever want more, accumulating the world's most exquisite material goods in their private race to the grave. In a free country, they are maximizing their use of freedom of speech to maximize their share of income and wealth, fame and uniqueness. They have enormous amounts of money to invest in "encouraging" others to support their positions. The U.S. Chamber of Commerce spends on the order of $75 million in an election year - and you can see the results on a daily basis. And you can be certain that no one will be spending any money advertising the contrary position.

Unfortunately, there are real ramifications to this beyond simply proving that human nature works as advertised. The consequences to the social and economic system are that valuable programs which could be funded from higher marginal tax rates on those with high incomes are permanently delayed, and/or deficits that could be reduced or eliminated through higher taxes remain or become larger. The author is not recommending one or the other – that is a decision made by each individual country. The author is not necessarily recommending any particular tax rate for anyone, as this is not an economics or political science book. It is just that if the reason giving for not raising taxes on the wealthy is that it affects jobs and hiring, that reason is vacuous. It is based on the monochrome view of the world as perceived by human nature.

Abortion – For and Against

On few issues can you find both sides perfectly matched, mirror-images of each other from a human nature perspective. Abortion is one such rare topic - both positions on abortion in the U.S., for and against, are classic

---

67 "The Wild Ride of the 1%", The Wall Street Journal, October 22, 2011

examples of cognitive dissonance, judgmental tagging, and belief-driven cognition.

Both groups, for and against, have their basic principles and core values framed through belief-driven cognition. The reasons are not just because being belief-driven is fundamental to human nature, but are quite pragmatic. Belief-based frameworks for groups like this allow the groups to remain fully in control of their own tenets, agenda, logic, reasoning, explanations, and justifications, regardless of anything that may happen externally to the group. Scientific discoveries, legal opinions, or statements by religious institutions can be ignored if so desired. Just imagine if it were not so. Some fact is discovered, or a legal case is decided, and the group has to revise all of its positions, literature, and web material, and then tell all of its supporters that one of the positions that they firmly believed in yesterday has just been changed. After a couple of these exercises the supporters will start to have major problems – having to first support something and then reverse their support of it. This will make the supporters question whether there is any part of their position that is inviolate and immutable, or whether over time all their beliefs on this subject may be open to collapse or modification. To preclude taking on any of this risk, both the for and against abortion groups assume exclusively belief-based philosophies. The pro-abortion groups generally use the concepts of "the woman's right to choose" or "woman's rights over her own body/own reproductive system." The anti-abortion groups generally utilize some variation on "sanctity of human life" or "human life begins at conception." All these positions are based on philosophical ideas, concepts, beliefs, and not on some set of established facts or science.

Both groups are fully-sensitive to cognitive-dissonance, and so present positions that are free of any implicit conflict, nuance, compromise, or gray areas that might bring on such dissonance. This requires two things – a purity of position, and no compromise or allowance for an exception, no matter now reasonable the exception may be, and no matter how irrational the resistance to granting the exception may appear. Granting any concession presents to the groups' supporters the mental quagmire that they desperately need to avoid. The group is absolutely for something except in this one case it is not for it, or it is absolutely morally wrong to do this except in these two cases and then it is fine. This puts the supporters sliding on the famous slippery slope. If some things are allowed or not allowed, why not more? Where do we stop? So the answer is pristine purity – all yes, or all no; no exceptions, no dissonance. If you have a question, you already know the answer. The pro-abortion groups refuse to admit any circumstance under which an abortion should be restricted; likewise the anti-abortion groups refuse to accept that there is any situation that would allow for an abortion. The positions of both groups work the best at each pregnancy extreme, where the opposing group's argument is the least plausible. They both then get increasingly strained as the pregnancy approaches the other limit – birth in the case of the pro-abortion people; conception in the case of the anti-abortion people. If a woman just after giving birth decides she does not want the baby, and demands an abortion, that is clearly infanticide or homicide. If a woman in the delivery room after a full term pregnancy suddenly decides she wants an abortion, is that OK? At that point you clearly have a baby. As the lawyers say (the author hates quoting lawyers), this is a distinction without much of a difference. It is not that much different from someone a few weeks short of full term, or even a month short of full-term deciding.

Conversely, is the loss of a fertilized egg really an abortion? If the egg does not stick to the wall of the uterus, which is fairly common, it just dissipates. Mother Nature does it all the time. It is quite a stretch to claim that for a few hours it was a "human" who then vanished. Similarly, if the egg does attach, and then the placental attachment becomes corrupted and there is a spontaneous abortion/miscarriage, also common, is that a human? Mother Nature does this regularly also. Then there are ectopic pregnancies, happening about once for every 100 pregnancies, where the egg attaches to the fallopian tube and either aborts at a few months or has to be medically removed (or in pre-modern times the mother died). If your objection to abortion is religious, you would have to take the position that God, in maybe 25% or so of the fertilization cases, is creating "humans" for a transitory period anywhere from hours to months and then destroying them. In the attempt to bolster the sacredness of all human life, and prevent any discussion of abortion, some religious groups will claim that the individual soul or spirit for each person becomes part of them as soon as the egg is fertilized. But in the case of identical twins or triplets, the developing egg (the blastocyst) splits into two or three parts sometime in the first two weeks after fertilization, making problematic the source of the soul or spirit for the second and third twin.

We have no statistics on how high the percentage of spontaneous aborted/lost/miscarried fetuses was if looked at over the past 60,000 years, but considering the stress, diet, and disease problems during this interval most likely it was substantially higher than today.

And while fetuses before around four weeks of full-term look just like a complete baby, many are missing one critical thing – a surfactant in their lungs that keeps the small air-spaces from collapsing. Its absence drops their oxygen levels and increases their carbon dioxide levels until the baby can no longer survive. And Mother Nature is not just spontaneously aborting defective fetuses – much of the time it is placental problems – the fetus is fine. So in spite of what they look like, whenever a mother goes into labor around a month or more before full-term, Mother Nature is allowing babies to come forth who are designed to die. And in the anti-abortion groups, to keep the

325

dissonance at bay, they must also disavow the use of abortion in the cases of rape or incest, which are of course both legal as well as moral and religious crimes of violence, often on women who are unable to defend themselves or who were dependent on those who violated their rights. So adherence to cognitive dissonance forces both groups have to defend their positions at the two extremes of pregnancy. They must defend situations that make their protestations look untenable, counter-intuitive, and illogical to someone who has not already "chosen sides" for belief-based or ideological reasons.

Both groups use judgmental tagging on their positions. Pro-abortion groups base their views on the sanctity of a woman's fundamental personal individual rights, something that everyone can agree need to be sacrosanct and carefully protected. Who wants the government legislating what a person can do with their own self? Anti-abortion groups base their position on the sanctity of human life – that abortion is murder. Who can disagree that cute little baby humans should not be murdered? Both positions ignite emotional responses in supporters, and others for that matter, rather than a feeling-neutral reaction that fact-based positions would engender.

In our monochrome world, on the abortion issue, the confirmation of all this is summed up in the old lawyer aphorism: "If the law is on your side, pound the law; if the facts are on your side, pound the facts; if neither, then pound the witnesses and the table." Since both for and against have belief-driven positions based on philosophical concepts, and they need to maintain the respective intellectual purity of these positions to prevent any cognitive dissonance, and their positions are both backed by emotional content, there is almost exclusively pounding of the table. This drives a more and more forceful reiteration of the righteousness of their positions, and an often savage characterization of the relative unrighteousness of the opposing position. In modern lingo - all heat, no light. But there should not be any surprise, dismay, or distress. This is just human nature at work. Nothing malicious, nor "evil", nor bad. No conspiracy to do terrible things. But few appear to comprehend this, and many act as if either they or the opposing position are engaged in a holy war.

In a polychrome world, these three human nature attributes would not need to be rigidly conserved. Anti-abortion groups would be able to accept abortions where appropriateness (like rape and incest) dominated, or where it was clearly so early in the pregnancy that no "human" was at stake. Pro-abortion groups would be able to concede that the criteria for abortion should escalate in proportion to the term of the pregnancy, with later term abortions requiring all matter of alternatives considered first. Instead of dissipating their energies combating one another, perhaps both groups would work cooperatively in the cases where the fervently pro-life groups would agree to adopt the children produced by those who might otherwise seek an abortion as a solution but would be willing to carry the baby to full-term in exchange for some consideration.

SMACT (Sugar, Marijuana, Alcohol, Caffeine, and Tobacco)

This is an absolutely exquisitely perfect example of man's irrational, monochrome nature, as long as you live in a country like the U.S. where marijuana is still illegal. If this does not for you convincingly demonstrate what man is, then you are in that select group that truly represents man at his most fundamental level.

There are only four major substances that an individual can legally acquire (although there are age and some sales restrictions on tobacco and alcohol) and use that have mind-altering effects – sugar, caffeine, alcohol, and tobacco (without the fat, caffeine, and sugar, chocolate is not quite sufficiently major). Everything else requires a prescription from a physician. Marijuana, while Federally illegal, is in widespread use in some areas and by some subsets of the U.S. population, utilized for both its mild mind-altering properties and for its uniquely-effective anti-nausea benefits for people on chemotherapy and for some other conditions.

For this case, we will start with a polychrome analysis of these five items. Sugar here will for simplicity be restricted to refined sugar or high-fructose corn syrup, although the comments would certainly apply to many other forms.

Only two, tobacco and marijuana, are natural, in that you can use them as grown. The other three must be obtained by processing plants to various degrees. Of all five, alcohol is the oldest - the Egyptians made beer and vintage wine around 5,000 years ago, while coffee is the most recent, maybe only 1,000 years old or so.

Tobacco is by far the most dangerous – it can be addicting with as little as a single exposure, and nicotine addiction is more difficult to escape from than heroin, accounting for why smokers have such a terrible time trying to quit. The health consequences of tobacco are now well-established – cancers in areas in contact with smoke or tobacco are the biggest problem. The nicotine in tobacco makes people feel less tense and suppresses appetite, so many women use it to keep their weight down.

Alcohol is responsible for maybe a third of all automobile accident deaths per year and a similar proportion of injuries. It causes a waste of public resources policing areas, businesses, and people who abuse alcohol, jailing and imprisoning those who violate laws. Families are disrupted and destroyed through the behavioral problems and income devastation brought about by alcohol abuse. Sexual attacks and violence are often attributed to alcohol in excess. Depending on one's genetics, alcohol can be addicting, and can cause medical problems that result in severe disability or death, creating high medical costs. Alcohol makes some people act more relaxed, some people act less inhibited, some act more arrogantly and belligerently, some more violently and viciously, and some to temporarily leave reality.

Sugar has no nutritional value, and its consumption results in a myriad of medical problems – tooth decay, diabetes, excess weight gain in the form of fat that results in high blood pressure, high triglycerides and cholesterol, and the consequent risk of coronary artery disease and stroke. Sugar is unfortunately most often incorporated into foods that also have almost no nutritional value, and derive most all of their calories from some combination of fat, sugar, and some other carbohydrate, foods like desserts, pastries, candy, and beverages. These foods would not even exist without sugar. For maybe the last 100 years, aside from the Great Depression, famine has made but a scant appearance in the U.S., leaving man no time to escape the genetic imprinting of the previous 60,000 (or 60 million) years, placing a premium on the consumption of fats or foods (like sugars) that could be readily converted and stored as fat, imprinting that you can see in meat-eating animals who eat only the fatty portions of their prey and leave the protein-rich but lean meat to scavengers. While technically not addicting, since they do not reset the neurotransmitter levels in the brain's craving circuitry, consuming these sweet, rich foods and beverages provides people with so much imprinted pleasure that many become psychologically dependent and the rest just desirous, sufficient to support a $100 billion market in useless calories and excess weight.

Caffeine appears the least harmful medically, used as a stimulant with the transient effects of a diuretic, and vasoconstrictor. It can enhance problems in people with high blood pressure and atrial fibrillation. While caffeine is not addicting, people can develop a dependence on it so that they will develop severe headaches if they attempt to stop using it. Excessive caffeine can produce serious systemic effects.

Marijuana acts as a strong anti-emetic, glaucoma treatment, appetite accelerator (helpful in cancer), and analgesic. It is a mild hallucinogen, interrupts short-term memory during use, and sustained long-term use may include hormone disruption and some cancer enhancement. When smoked it releases combustion byproducts to the lungs with unknown long-term effects, but probably negative if the marijuana is adulterated.

But neither caffeine nor marijuana bring any of the drastic health consequences of the other three - addiction, poisoning, irreversible organ damage, disease, and even death. And compared to the most commonly used medicines - aspirin and acetaminophen - which can bring stomach bleeding, liver damage, and death in children, all at the recommended doses - caffeine and marijuana are relatively much safer.

There is some anecdotal evidence that some of these substances are used together – tobacco and alcohol or tobacco and food are often co-consumed. Some choose to consume caffeine with alcohol because it enables them to drink more, but that is a choice. Some people feel marijuana or alcohol consumption leads to other drugs, but this appears not to be the case. People who want to use substances to escape reality first try alcohol and marijuana, but should they prove inadequate, turn to ecstasy, methamphetamine, cocaine, heroin, or other designer drugs. But these entail much higher legal, medical, and physical risk, social unacceptability, much higher cost, and the risk of hard addiction.

But marijuana is basically illegal, while the other four, all of which (except caffeine) are either addicting, unhealthy, dangerous, offer no nutritional value, have no health benefits with exception of very limited alcohol consumption, or all of the above, are either available without restriction or entirely legal. Contrasting marijuana, which may have never caused a death or serious injury, to the approximately one million annual deaths from alcohol, tobacco, and sugar, in a polychrome world you would have to admit – this makes no sense at all. But in a monochrome world, it makes perfect sense. There is one key difference between marijuana and the other four items – a difference that explains everything. And what is that? You can grow one marijuana plant at home and cover all of your needs – but you cannot do that with the other four substances. You can make them at home, sure, but they all require a large amount of work, and in some cases high cost. The final result will be a poor imitation of what you can readily purchase at relatively low cost, high quality, and infinite variety. So sugar, tobacco, alcohol, and caffeine all have multi-billion dollar corporations behind them, making huge amounts of profit providing products that people are willing to purchase instead of trying to make themselves. But they cannot make money selling marijuana – people will turn them down and grow it themselves. Without these large corporations and their political donations defending the use of marijuana, when it came time to write restrictive legislation on what would be legal and what not, it was swept up with cocaine and opium and corralled into illegality. But had marijuana been something that only with some special processing large corporations could have put in a bottle with a variety of flavors and strengths, it would have been a completely different story.

So, in a monochrome world, almost by default, lacking a wealthy sponsor, marijuana dies a death by a thousand cuts, tarnished, slammed, cursed, and despoiled by every moralizing crusader out to find a convenient villain for his particular version of why evil befalls society. Fatally judgmentally tagged, marijuana ranks alongside a radiation leak or flesh-eating bacteria for many people. But in a polychrome world, marijuana and caffeine would be OK (except for the standard driving and machinery restrictions on marijuana), sugar rationed and restricted, tobacco banned, and alcohol either banned outright or available only with heavy rationing, restrictions, limitations, and sharp penalties for abuse (loss of privileges).

And Now a Word From the Flat-Worlders

In mid-2011 the Congressional authorization for the total amount of debt that the U.S. could have outstanding needed to be increased beyond the statutory limit of $14.3 billion. In a Reuters poll taken a few months prior to this date, 71% of American said that they did not want the limit to be increased. Many politicians, "listening" to their constituents, came out publicly and voiced their full support and commitment to vote against the debt limit extension.

The theme of this book is that man's skills, developed to handle the world that Mother Nature threw at man for the past 60,000 years, are obsolete and a hindrance in today's world, one of man-made systems and environments. The debt limit for the U.S. is an ideal example – a macro-economic monetary consequence of the nation's cumulative fiscal policies. Economic systems are man-made, not Mother-Nature made. The average citizen, struggling to understand the concept, appears to interpret the debt limit like a weight limit for a person on a diet. Once you reach the limit, for example 200 pounds, you are not allowed to exceed it, so you have to cut back what you eat until you stay below it. It's really simple – you just mandate the limit and then live inside it.

But of course the analogy of the weight limit for a dieter is not applicable, reflecting a complete misunderstanding of basic economics, which man has no fundamental skills in, training for by Mother Nature, aptitude for, interest in, or time for. A dieter, even if they eat nothing, can provide their basic caloric needs of ten calories per pound per day from their fat storage. A germane analogy instead would be you in a huge caged area with a large number of lions. Every day a bin opens and you receive a pile of meat that you toss out to the lions, who ravenously consume it and then fall asleep in the sun. Every so often, they let another lion into the area, and so they have to add a proportionately-larger amount of meat to your daily allowance. Now freezing the debt limit is akin to freezing the meat allowance. The next time a lion comes in, there is only one way there will be enough meat for all the lions, and that is if you personally are included in the lions' meal plan.

If you freeze the debt limit, the first extra lion comes in the next day, since the U.S. is currently operating in a deficit, and so both new debt needs to be sold and old debt needs to be retired and re-issued. If someone comes in to obtain their money from their Treasury note or bill or bond, or an interest payment needs to be made, and the Government cannot pay them, then the Government has defaulted. Ignoring all the verbal anguish that would pour forth, the tangible result of this is that what is called a risk premium would be added to the interest rate of all interest-bearing securities issued by the U.S. Government, to compensate owners for the now-demonstrated risk that they may not be able to get their principal back. Say this risk premium is 2% (it might be more) - this means a bond that is now 3.5% would go to 5.5%, 4.5% would go 6.5%, and so on. The way this happens in bonds is that a bond worth $1,000 drops in value to around $700. So if your IRA is 40% in stocks and 60% in bonds, and half the bonds are U.S. government (the others say are corporate), then 30% of your IRA is going to drop by 30%, or an overall 9% drop in value. If you are all in bonds, it would be proportionately worse. Professionals holding stocks, calculating that the cost of money had now increased (higher interest rates) for the average company, and that equities (stocks) now look relatively less attractive compared to bonds since the interest rate on bonds is much higher, will sell stocks and buy bonds, dropping stocks by 10% to 15%, so your IRA will drop another 4% to 6% in value.

But it gets worse. With $14 trillion of outstanding debt all at another 2% higher rate of interest, the amount of interest that the Government has to pay annually will double, from $200 billion to $400 billion. Now this will not happen in one year, since the due date for much of this debt is spread out over many years, but every year it will creep up, and with no benefit or value gained, just higher cost.

Now hearing about the default implications, the flat worlders will respond with their elegant, 60,000-year-old solution: "No problem – we will just pay off all the debt principal and interest first, and so there will not be a default, and everyone will be happy." Your grandparents may remember this as a variation on an old Depression radio comedy skit – a company announces that to save jobs, everyone's salary is being cut by a third, and when the concerned creditors call the worker, he tells them not to worry. He promises to pay all his creditors first, and stiff everyone else, so this should not affect his credit at all. They thank him for his thoughtful solution and hang up. Then his bookie calls about his money and gets the same story, followed by his brother-in-law about his loan, and finally by Jimmy-Two-Toes, all of whom are delighted to hear that they will be taken care of first. Now flash forward 80 years, to a world of ultra-sophisticated sovereign and hedge funds managing trillions of dollars of U.S. Treasury debt, and ask yourself if the same comedic assurance will suffice. "Sure, we are short of money, but we will make every effort to pay you first. Don't give a moment's thought to the screaming people who are getting shafted." As the rating services like Moody's and S&P have already declared, if the U.S. runs short of money, regardless of whom they promise to pay when, the credit rating will be slammed, and interest costs will jump.

Going back to the lion analogy, the proposal would be – feed the young, strong, active lions first (the Treasury bill/bond owners), and hold off on feeding the older, slower lions (others that the government has promised to pay but now cannot). So you do that, and it works fine for the first day, and second day, and third day, so you feel, holy moly, these people may well be right. You can pick and choose who to pay, and no one is the worse for it. But on the fourth day, fifty of the old, slower lions, who now realize what is going on, desperately rush you as a group as you are trying to feed the younger lions. Feeling they have nothing to lose, they get much of the meat and, of course, you as a special treat. In the financial world, this would be equivalent to getting a court order to block the dispersal of funds to the Treasury owners first instead of a pro-rata distribution to all. Or a distribution based on the date the obligation to pay was established, or to hold up all payment until due process was completed through the courts. These are the kinds of things that you would expect in any kind of bankruptcy action. The party in bankruptcy never gets to determine on their own who they get to exclusively pay and not pay. Or, since the money is not coming out of the Government, some people, being not overly stupid, feel that they are in no mood to keep sending money to the government. So they lower or eliminate their Federal withholding and estimated tax payments, unexpectedly dropping the revenue stream that the Government was anticipating to have to pay its Treasury obligations. And so it defaults anyway.

In this interim period until someone goes to court or tax receipts drop and you go into a hard default (the Treasury bill/bond owners do not get fully paid), the risk premium added to interest rates will most likely be less than the 2% mentioned earlier – probably less than 1%. But no one really knows, the operative rule in the market being "the market can remain irrational longer than you can remain solvent."

For a few of the 71% opposed to raising the debt limit, when hearing these dire consequences, their solution, confirming man's inability to grapple with the challenges of his modern world, is to reduce government spending so that spending matches revenues, ensuring that the debt limit is not broached.

The U.S. budget deficit, at the time the debt limit needed to be raised, was around $125 billion per month. Assuming that 95% of that is eventually spent in the U.S., and 50% of it as wages and salaries, and that the average labor rate is $5,500 per month, eliminating the deficit would result in the loss of jobs for 12.6 million people. Considering that unemployment at that time was "only" 13.9 million people, this elimination of the deficit would increase the U.S. unemployment rate instantly from 9.1% to 17.3%, placing the U.S. effectively into a depression.

But it gets much worse. The other 50% of this spending goes to things like mortgages, rents, medical payments and insurance, credit card balances, and auto loans. If for every six dollars of this activity there is one dollar of support labor servicing this activity, that is another 1.2% increase in unemployment, on top of the personal calamity of all these people not able to pay their rent, mortgages, buy critically-needed medicine and health care, and pay bills. If this condition would last for more than a week or so, people would begin to be thrown out of their apartments, banks would start foreclosure paperwork on mortgages, children in colleges and private schools might have to leave, and the credit ratings of all those affected would be decimated. People most dependent on government money without any personal wealth – those living month to month on social security and those in nursing homes and long-term care facilities – could be placed in life-threatening conditions. And the general rule of thumb is that two indirect jobs are lost for every direct job lost. These would be people who make things or perform services that the person who lost their job and income can no longer afford to buy. This overall impact could push the U.S. unemployment rate up over 30%, resulting in something much worse than the Great Depression. Collective social disruption, shock, frustration, and anger – conditions that a politically-stalemated democratic republic is poorly designed to address. Instead, the executive branch (President) would request/demand sweeping emergency executive powers to deal with the crisis. Unfortunately, in the interest of efficiency and speed, these powers would have to "temporarily" suspend many of the rights citizens have and remove many of the constraints that the Constitution impresses on the government. This is the way all dictatorships start, and the circumstances would be not too unlike the economic catastrophe that brought Hitler to power in Germany.

Man's nature in his monochrome world drives him emotionally, not rationally, Mother Nature's blessing that enabled him to so skillfully survive the last 60,000 years. And so his emotional reaction to complex national economic problems is predictable – just stop it, kill it, end it – no complexity, no nuances, no detailed analyses. Leaving the debt limit in place is just one more example of man's fascination and addiction to short cuts - simple solutions that are easy to grasp by man's 60,000-year-old-nature that not only do not work but bring with them catastrophic collateral consequences. This is not a "failure", or a "breakdown", this is simply man acting as Mother Nature intended him to.

So in a polychrome world, where man was designed to cope with complex economic problems, he would be able to see from miles and years away that even talk of not raising the debt ceiling, of putting the Government into the potentiality of default, was paramount to economic suicide. But in his monochrome world, he is blissfully happy that he can solve many of his problems by this one simple action.

Three additional exquisite examples, while we are on the subject of the debt ceiling (and economics). One member of Congress, also a declared candidate for President as a Republican, made a prime feature of their campaign that they could always be found to be "standing on principle", even where unpopular, and one of these was the critical importance of not raising the debt limit, and themselves voting "no" when it was finally lifted. When a major rating agency, Standard & Poor's, subsequently lowered the debt rating of the U.S. one notch, from AAA to AA+, based on Congress acting like the South Korean legislature without the furniture-tossing, this candidate immediately declared that were they President, they would recall Congress (who were in recess) and mount a massive campaign to regain the AAA rating. Not a campaign to get more jobs, or lower the deficit, or debt, or help with home foreclosures, or something else that Americans at the time felt was really important, but the S&P debt rating.

Now aside from the gallows humor of recalling the same Congress who were already responsible for the lowered rating and expecting them to do anything except make it even lower, the point here is that this candidate had based their campaign on not raising the debt ceiling. If successful, and it had stayed in place, it would have lowered the U.S. debt rating instead of just one notch to AA+, probably six or seven notches to A- or BBB+. But now, this candidate was saying that just a one notch reduction was a national calamity, where just a few days earlier they were fervently promoting a six or seven notch reduction.

Now in a polychrome world, the supporters of this candidate would look at this complete reversal of a fundamental, key position, being against what you were for a few days earlier, and say "Geez, my candidate claimed to be standing on principle, but can't be for two diametrically oppositional principles at the same time. So 'standing on principle' is just another political sound-bite; my candidate is no more than another prevaricating politician." But in the monochrome world of human nature, seemingly not one supporter was bothered. Why? Because their support is based on belief, and its offshoot the "cult of personality" belief/trust in the individual personality. They believe in their candidate, and the "rightness" of what they are saying – and the logic, or rather the illogic, of specifics is never questioned or investigated. Plus, the simple economics linkage between the debt limit position of this candidate and the impact on the debt rating of the U.S. may be too complex a problem for the candidate's supporters. Another confirmation that man's skills are mismatched for even the fairly simple problems of today's world. Thus the evidence that man is belief-driven, and not logic or rational-driven, surrounds us everyday, overloading us in simply unrecognized everyday examples.

Another Republican Presidential candidate, at around the same time, said that any further easing of the U.S. money supply by the Federal Reserve would be treasonous. Now by way of background, in order to keep interest rates low to help get the U.S. out of the recession, the Fed had already executed two programs of so called quantitative easing, QE1 and QE2. These had primarily pro-business impacts, resulting in the doubling of the S&P 500 from the Haines' Bottom of 666 (the Beelzebub Bottom was too hard to pronounce) to over 1350 in July of 2011. Aside from the apparent incongruity of a Republican candidate slamming a pro-business action by the Fed, the "treasonous" appellation was intentionally designed to be as pejorative, judgmental, incendiary, and therefore newsworthy as possible, ensuring sound-bite coverage all over the media. But what was notable was the response by the candidate's spokesman, who, given the benefit of time, can always restate a hasty, ill-tempered, off-base response into something more substantive and statesman-like. But instead, the spokesman said: "The governor was expressing his frustration with the current economic situation and the out-of-control spending that persists in Washington." What this means is that the campaign has calculated that those Republicans who will be making primary voting decisions either cannot tell, or do not care, about the difference between fiscal and monetary economic policy. Spending, which is what the spokesman referred to, applies to fiscal policy. How you manage the amount of money in circulation, and the interest rates on holding that money, is monetary policy. The Fed does the latter; Congress does the former. So even political campaigns know that voters either lack even a basic grasp of fundamental economics, or that they will be making belief-driven and not fact-driven decisions; in other words, they fully ascribe to the premise of this book.

A third candidate in the Republican primary race for President at one point was the first choice of approximately one-third of all Republican voters, based on the fact that he was a successful businessman and not a politician; he was an excellent public speaker; he is a working Baptist preacher; he had a positive, upbeat outlook; he was personable, affable, and likable; he often sang a hymn a cappella at the end of meetings with voters; he seemed like "a good old country boy", meaning he was not a traditional shiny, slimy career Washington insider; he tossed out bold, aggressive, original, simple, down-to-earth solutions to many chronic national problems, including a major revision of the national tax system.

At the same time, he readily admitted he would figure out foreign policy once he was elected; did not know what a neoconservative was (thereby missing the last two decades of contentious U.S. foreign policy, including four foreign interventions - Kuwait/Iraq, Afghanistan #1, Iraq, Afghanistan #2);

would not provide any substantive detail about his proposals; would provide clear, extended statements defending both sides of a particular contentious issue, and then explain that he had simply "misspoken"; and would sometimes declare that a previous position was simply "a joke", as if he were still just a pundit. But none of these factors had any effect on the views of his supporters.

His tax plan, termed 9-9-9, is the one tangible proposal by the candidate with both some detail. It most astutely draws on man's Pied Piper obsession with short-cuts - taken literally as proposed, it represents the most simple, sweeping, condensed, elegant solution to all Federal tax and fiscal policy in just three single digits. It is even faster, simpler, and more sweeping than "location, location, location" in real estate. The details on his website change every few days, making an analysis challenging, but for the purposes here all that matters is to match up the detail offered at one moment with the voter's view of the candidate at that same moment. This plan produced strong positive resonance with his supporters, either because it was a great idea, or because it was a great start that would lead to a much-needed simplification of the federal tax system. At the risk of losing the reader in dreary economics, let's briefly look at 9-9-9 viewed just a couple of weeks after it was proposed.

The candidate's web site says the plan will be revenue-neutral, meaning total tax revenues will be the same with his plan as under the current system. Corporate taxes of 9% will be applied to gross income (sales less the cost of making the products sold), less purchases, investments, and exports. But the cost of making things (COGS in business-speak) already contains purchases and investments, so complex new tax code will have to be written to handle the potential double-counting here. In addition, depending on what they do, the financial structure of companies differs widely, so a one-size-fits-all solution produces illogical and indefensible results. Ignoring the purchase/investment issue, the author went to the most recent 10-K's of four major companies to demonstrate this problem. Caterpillar, a well-performing classic manufacturing company, will have taxes 20% higher under this plan; Apple, a high profit, non-traditional manufacturing company (most all its products are made by Hon Hai in China) would have its taxes cut in half. Safeway, a distributor-type company that just buys finished goods and resells them, would have their taxes more than tripled under this 9-9-9 plan. And JP Morgan, an example of a financial services company that does not buy or sell any products, but just performs services, makes a lot of money and already pays a lot of taxes, would see their tax bill rise by 23%. So these arbitrary imbalances will have to be fixed by writing a bunch of new IRS rules - you can absolutely count on this based on the lobbyists that these companies and their peers will retain to influence those who oversee tax legislation in Congress.

Secondly, gross income is offset by purchases and investments. So say you are a big company and your gross income is one billion dollars. Well, if you got through at least the sixth grade, you purchase/invest a billion dollars, borrowed if need be, in something - anything. You can buy some raw material/parts that you use, or gold, or copper, or palladium, or your own stock, or someone else's stock - whatever the new IRS rules will allow - and presto! - you will not have to pay any taxes. So that will require another new volume of IRS rules, or no company will ever pay taxes.

Looking at the personal tax side, the millionaire used as an example a few pages back, with an income of exactly one million dollars, would have a total Federal tax bill of between 24% and 26% of their gross income, depending on their deductions (assumes a married couple). With the new 9% plan, and ignoring charitable contributions to keep the math simple, 9% results in a $90,000 tax bill, a savings of $150,000 to $170,000 over their current taxes. If they spend say $150,000 of their income buying things that the nominal 9% national sales tax would hit (art, third houses, jewelry, yachts, classic cars - all being used aren't taxed) that is another $14,000, so their net savings are $135,000 to $155,000. At $500,000 of income, these savings would drop to $50,000; at $200,000, it approaches a wash. But since the plan overall is revenue-neutral, if your family income is much under $200,000 the 9-9-9 plan will have to cost you more in taxes. If you do not itemize but instead take the standard deduction, and say you are a family of four with both parents working, then the cross-over point for the 9-9-9 plan is at $100,000 of income - below that, you will pay more; above it, you will come out better.

Looking at the 9% national sales tax, here is an example of where the subtlety comes in. Say a U.S. farmer decides to go with cotton, prices being much higher than normal recently. Buying seed, fertilizer, pesticides, equipment for his tractor, renting a Deere 7760 to harvest it - he has to pay the 9% tax on all these. A U.S. mill buys the raw cotton, paying the 9%, and makes fabric, which a wholesaler buys, paying 9% again. A small manufacturer of women's tops buys from this wholesaler, paying 9% again, silk-screens designs and adds sequins that have the 9% tax, and sells the top to a consumer, who again pays the 9% tax. So you see why in Europe they call this type of tax a VAT, or value-added tax, since it is tacked-on at every step. You do not pay this tax just once, you may pay it five times or more - you just do not see all the earlier payments that were added in to the final cost of what you are buying. So the 9% tax will most likely turn out to be somewhere between 15% and 18%, moving the income cross-over point for who is better off to between $170,000 and $250,000.

Used goods are exempt from the 9% tax, so that will result in a volume and a half of new IRS regulations - 10,000 experienced, competent, well-paid tax attorneys will ensure that takes place, parsing the word "used" with combs so fine that Bill Clinton would beam with pride. Who has to possess the item, under what conditions, with what if any evidence of "use", for how long, with what if any title change, to be deemed "used"? If a company "runs" a laptop, TV, car, etc. to make sure it works, or stone-washes jeans, is it used? What if they transfer it to a contractor who does it? And also transfer title, or even "sells it", for the test duration, and then "buys" it back? Is an unused ticket for an event that is re-sold "used", or new twice? With 9%, or 15%, or 18% of $6 trillion of consumption up for grabs ($540 billion to $1 trillion), you can bet this will be beaten beyond death.

With over $2 trillion in cash on hand, U.S. corporations are not hiring solely because consumers do not appear to be planning to buy more goods tomorrow than they are buying today. Companies have no reason to ramp up production. People look at falling or low home prices, about one-fourth of them with their mortgage under water, and if they do try to buy or sell a house maybe the appraiser comes in from out of town and the house will not appraise for the sale price so it falls through. They see their spouse or themselves or their neighbor or friend having lost their job, or having to take a lower-paying job; having one or more of their kids still at home because they cannot find a job; seeing their retirement savings getting trashed, grow a little, get retrashed again, so that neither home prices nor the stock market seem a dependable way to plan for the future - and people think - I am not spending more money buying things unless I absolutely, desperately have no choice in the matter. Unless of course you are really wealthy.

So what is a tax on consumption going to do - a tax that will make everything not just 9% more expensive but some factor times 9% depending on how many steps it requires to make it? The average person, already reluctant to buy, is going to the store, see all prices much much higher, and say to themselves: "Well, we're not getting that today." And so the economy will slow even more, layoffs will naturally follow, tax revenues will fall, the deficit will increase, everyone will feel more pessimistic, and so on.

If you look back two pages, none of the above discussion entered into the thinking of the supporters of this candidate. And what is the message here? The supporters are behind this candidate for the identical reasons that - 50,000 years ago - they would have chosen him to be the leader of their 30 person group, or the one to lead them on their hunt. But all the issues that modern society brings - complex national and international economic, political, and social problems - none of these are engaged with the slightest degree of depth or analysis. This candidate and his team know that one-third of Republicans, and assuming a similar candidate could be found on the Democratic side, maybe one-third of Americans, are still dealing with the credentials for the person in charge of the most powerful country in the world, with some of the most complex modern problems imaginable, in the exact same way they made choices and decisions 50,000 years ago. While today's world would be unrecognizable to someone from that time, today's version of man is thinking, and deciding, in an manner identical to his ancient ancestors. The parallel is unmistakably brazen.

There have been many crashes on the Airbus series of commercial planes due to problems with the interface between the pilots and the automated computer software flying the plane. Initially, most pilots were unaware that the computer, and not they, were actually making the key flying decisions. If the pilot tried to interfere, or did not pay rapt attention to what the computer had decided to do, the plane would crash. In case you think this was due to probably poor pilots, some of the crashes were by Airbus' own test pilots. Just like your computer at home, things work just fine on the Airbus aircraft until something goes really badly wrong, like the Air France A330 Flight 447 that crashed over the Atlantic in June of 2009, and then, as they say, everyone is toast. Those pilots had to transition from pilots (or, unfortunately, maybe just airplane operators) to computer engineers while in an aerodynamic stall in the center of a thunderstorm in the middle of the night, and ran out of time.

The first documented act of cyber warfare took place in January of 2010, when a huge (half a megabyte) piece of malware (computer virus) dubbed Stuxnet, allegedly written by U.S. and Israeli experts, was inserted into portable USB memory drives which were then allowed to let drift into Iran. Designed to gain unauthorized computer access through the use of four at-that-time-unknown (so-called zero-day) software vulnerabilities, self-limiting its spread to no more than three computers per USB device to reduce the chance for detection, it targeted the control and communication language used by industrial equipment known as SCADA. It was specifically aimed at that used by Siemens for the control of centrifuges separating U-235 (fissionable) from U-238 (kinetic weapons). Once in place, the malware would cycle the frequency of the centrifuges up and down so fast that they would self-destruct, then reset the frequency to a nominal speed so it would appear that nothing was wrong. Iran admitted that over 30,000 computers in the country were hit by this virus, the most sophisticated piece of malware ever written, but claims there was no impact to the centrifuges at the Bushehr nuclear facility, the real target. Other data on the number of operating centrifuges at the facility, however, did show a significant number off-line after the attack.

Jonathan's First Law of Technology says that "Technology use should be restricted to those who fully understand it." That means a lot more than you may realize at first glance. It is not talking about how you download apps and purchase music on-line. It is about every possible thing that can go wrong, whether you can even tell if it is going wrong or not, how it might affect you and your device, how and how rapidly you can recover, and how you can protect yourself in advance. Less sophisticated versions (and improved versions) of the Stuxnet virus float around the Web on a daily basis. People using smartphones have not a clue whether or not their passwords, bank account, social security number, and other information are always held in unencrypted form or not in every application and Wi-Fi transaction they use. People depending on a certain kind of hyper-encrypted digital device appear hysterically surprised and agonized when the system collapses when a piece of hardware and then its backup fails. Cancer therapy and x-ray machines, if they are not set up properly because the man-machine interface is slightly confusing or the doctor did not check everything well enough, can near-fatally over-expose patients to radiation just like they were standing next to the Chernobyl reactor when it blew up.

Whether the technology is electrical, or electronic, or mechanical, or chemical, or biological, or fiscal, or monetary, or taxation, or constitutional, or legal, or geo-climatic, or some other aspect of economic, political, or sociological behavior, the First Law of Technology still applies (i.e. soft technology is included). But man does not apply it, is not concerned about applying it, and so bears fully the consequential problems, repeatedly, unlearnedly.

Roughly speaking, it took Mother Nature about 80 million years to grow all the fossil fuel we have, most of it from fern and tree forests, moss, algae, and bacteria several hundred million years ago. These were then slowly-cooked underground into oil, coal, and natural gas. We have been using these fuels for roughly 200 years now, and let's say that they will last another 200 years at the current rates of consumption. (What will probably happen is that they will last longer, but at a higher price and lower consumption, but that does not matter for this exercise.) If man consumes in 400 years what Mother Nature grew in 80 million years, that is a ratio of 200,000 to one. That means every year we are burning, or putting into the air, the same amount of carbon (in the form of carbon dioxide) that it took Mother Nature 200,000 years to pull out of the air (in the form of carbon dioxide) and sequester into plant material. So you have to ask yourself – whoever thought that this 200,000 to one ratio was a good idea? Didn't anyone think that Mother Nature might react somewhat violently to this imbalance? As has been pointed out before, one of the problems is, no one is in charge of the planet. Man took over, filled all the seats, someone has pressed the accelerator to the floor, but a map, compass, steering wheel, brake, or even window seem not in evidence. We're just rocketing along to wherever we get to. And we will get there quickly.

In a polychrome world, perhaps a more daunting, mentally-challenging issue than global climate change is not to be found. The most fundamental need is to reduce the complexity in a meaningful way so that the average non-scientist citizen can learn, analyze, evaluate, and question the facts, assumptions, weaknesses, and climate model results to whatever depth they are comfortable in exploring.

So questions might be asked about the current projected range of dates for the elimination of the polar ice cap in summer, what that might do from a climate perspective, and whether any cost-effective alternatives to slow the process down need to be considered. Or about the range of estimates on how much methane hydrate (methane ice) might be released as the Arctic warms up, and where it might go (ocean versus atmosphere), and the impact. Someone might want to know the chance and the possible early signs of the Maunder Minimum re-occurring. Others might be interested on the range in estimated values for the acidity (pH) change of the ocean with time as it absorbs carbon dioxide, and the range of impacts on coral reefs and sea life in general. Questions about the weather extremes that different areas of the world could reasonably expect to have to prepare for might be asked, depending on whether it was a El Niño or La Niña year. Some might want to know the local/regional weather consequences of the global climate models for all areas of the world, since in many cases they may run in counter directions to the global trend in terms of temperature and rainfall at different times of the year. Others might be interested in how the relative impact of other regular climate cycles like the El Niño/La Niña/Southern Oscillation, which can last seven years or more; the North Atlantic Oscillation, that can vary on the scale of decades; the Arctic Oscillation, whose cycles can last from a few months to around three years; the sunspot cycle, which affects the heat output of the sun, a roughly 11 year cycle overlay both the "normal" regional patterns and any global trend. The planning for animal and human disease migration due to climate change could be made clear and explicit, as could the preparation for pests that infect farmed and non-farmed plants and trees. The long-term impact on water and water-rights could be of great interest to the impacted areas. Similar to the planning in flood and earthquake-prone areas, long-range planning in coastal regions that could be subjected to flooding and erosion (up to 80 feet a year for permafrosted Alaskan coast) by rising ocean levels might be of interest to residential and commercial property owners and state and local governments. Agricultural planning that might involve genetic modification of crops to make them more optimally-fit for the climate shifts might be undertaken.

But in the monochrome world of human nature as we know it, as Mother Nature has so carefully designed and developed us, from so many people we hear instead just the one response: "I just don't believe in global climate change."

If your favorite example of human nature has been overlooked, the author hereby apologizes, but there is space for only so much. And to rehash an earlier point, the issues that were covered here were not singled out for infamy, nor condemnation, nor special merit, but just for the clarity that they bring to real-world examples of the nature of man's thinking. This is not about making judgments or assigning blame or fault. Man does not need to justify what he is and how he behaves any more than the crocodile or great white shark. Granted, the antelope and sea lion feel greatly put upon, but the great white is just reflecting 15 or so million years of polished existence as an unchanged species, while the crocodile can claim the same constancy for over ten times as long a period, one of Mother Nature's proudest displays of perfection on the planet. Man may not be perfect in Mother Nature's eyes, but he is just doing his human nature thing.

After 55,000 years of successfully battling Mother Nature, without benefit of metal tools, equipment, machines, engineering knowledge, heavy construction or fabrication techniques, or any previous relevant experience, man built the Great Pyramid of Khufu. Made of several million perfectly-shaped limestone blocks weighing several tons each, with some internal granite blocks weighing as much as 80 tons, the entire outer surface was covered with polished white limestone facing stones with a near-mirror finish. Had astronauts or visiting aliens been orbiting Earth back then, the reflection of the sun off this pyramid would have been the only man-made object ever seen by the unaided eye from space. Yet 4,500 years later those same skills that enabled man to conquer Mother Nature so perfectly, and to build this pyramid so dramatically, are an utter mismatch for the problems and challenges of the social, political, and economic systems that man has created for himself in his replacement environment for the world he was designed for – Mother Nature's world. The examples in this chapter are just the most dramatic. The reader can certainly recall his own list from his experiences. As his civilization grew explosively and replaced that of Mother Nature, his skills and nature remained unchanged. And so man went from dominant to dumbfounded; competent to clueless; omnipotent to out-of-it. Boldly, proudly, confidently, even arrogantly at times, man strides through his polychromatic world, happily seeing only the simplistic monochromatic panorama that his nature provides him.

Chapter 22
The Cosmic Catch-22

Inspiration

Is there anybody out there ... Can anybody hear me? ...

If there is one thing that two radically-different groups are confident of, it is that the answer is a resounding yes. One group is the UFO aficionados, for whom there is nothing U about the FO's. These people are positive that advanced intelligent aliens from other star systems – for the most part smooth, slight, skinny, and pale – have visited Earth frequently. Always acting like unsupervised, intoxicated joy-riding teenagers, zipping around houses, towns, airliners, sometimes landing and kidnapping humans for confusing capture-and-release experiments. Physical evidence confirms their presence, to hear these people talk – Area 51 in Nevada for example. And governments have conspired to hide indirect evidence such as radar and visual sightings.

The second group are sophisticated astrophysicists, astro-biologists, and engineers, who calculate that the odds of other intelligent beings in the universe, and in our galaxy, are high, and we should be listening for signs of their presence. They have produced calculations on the probabilities of the existence of these aliens. This math says the probabilities are pretty high, and so there have been and are several programs to listen for radio signals from these civilizations, using single antennas and arrays of large radio telescopes.

Plus, man simply would like to know if he is alone, as the poetry alludes. The universe is oh so very big and we are not ever going to physically get anywhere. If Earth is a small pea, then the sun is a basketball a 100 feet away. The nearest star is still 5,000 miles away. The center of our galaxy is over 30 million miles away. The nearest big galaxy, Andromeda, is about halfway between Uranus and Neptune, about 2.4 billion miles away. That means as a super-being you could move (walk) the 100 feet from the sun (basketball) to the Earth (pea) in twenty seconds, which is 25 times the speed of light (25 times faster than it really takes light to make the actual trip). But look how long you have to walk to get to the nearest star – it's 5,000 miles away, even for you as a super-being moving at walking speed (the equivalent of 25 times the speed of light). A more typical star would be 100 times further away - a half a million mile walk. This is why we aren't really seeing any joy-riding aliens flying all the way here and back from their home star just for kicks. In other words, even if we shrink things down to miniature size, the distances are still unfathomable and unmanageable.

This is the Catch-22 à la Joseph Heller, from one of the best novels of the twentieth century. (Dalton Trumbo wrote a more searing anti-war work, but it is no fun to read.) The cosmic portion comes from a combination with the modified Drake Equation, which predicts the odds of finding intelligent life in the universe.

Since Catch-22 was intended as a logical absurdity, we will loosely translate it here for those who missed out on the book. If you possess some key capabilities that enable you to obtain some very special thing, as soon as you claim it those same capabilities either destroy you, make you impotent, trap you in some way, or otherwise deny you what you thought you had garnered. You can get it, but the getting will instantly make you powerless. In Heller's case, being declared insane by others would get you out of the war, but if you yourself, terrified by the horrors of combat, feel yourself going crazy and ask to be relieved on that basis, you will be judged sane since you recognized the insanity of war, and your request will be denied.

A Non-Technical Option

The following discussion uses something called the Drake Equation as the basis to calculate the odds of finding intelligent life somewhere else in the universe that might be broadcasting a radio/TV or equivalent signal that we might be able to hear (electronically). Due to the nature of the subject, this calculation requires numbers and math, and other similarly bad concepts if you are not a fan of this kind of thing. If for you this is an utter and total turn-off, and you are not going to read it if numbers and math are involved, then this section will summarize it with the math excluded. If you want to try the math version, which is not all that bad, just stop reading here and skip ahead to the section titled "The Theoretical Basis for Intelligent Life Elsewhere."

Frank Drake was an astronomer who first put this equation together that identifies all the assumptions that you have to make about such things as how many stars have a planet that will be in the "sweet spot" like Earth that will allow water to remain liquid on the surface, how many will keep it stably there for say at least two billion years, how many of those will develop any life, how many of those will develop intelligent life, and so on.

There were some problems with the original equation, and some factors were left out, so this all is adjusted in the more technical discussion that you are skipping if you are reading this. For example, intelligent civilizations will probably only broadcast high power radio/TV signals into space for a brief time. Then they will convert to a combination of fiber and low power local RF distribution, like we are doing on Earth. So even if they are there you will only have a small time window to observe (hear) from them. Plus, the power of the radio or TV signal falls dramatically with distance, so even if signals are being radiated we will not be able to hear them.

If you use reasonable assumptions for the modified Drake Equation, then you arrive at one intelligent civilization for every 20 million galaxies. If you then push the assumptions to be as optimistic as possible, you get to one for every 800 galaxies.

The problem is, since light takes millions of years to travel the vast distances between even the closest galaxies, even if intelligent civilizations last one million years, they will be gone before their signals reach the next civilization and have a chance to be heard. So this means that, sorry, we are alone.

So to increase the odds, what we have to do is drop the requirement that the civilization still be around, and simply require that we can hear it, even if it is gone. If we do that, staying with the optimistic assumptions, and target all the stars in our own galaxy that orbit inside our star, which is a sphere about 60,000 light years in diameter, then we have a chance of hearing from as many as 74 civilizations, although all may be extinct by now.

The only remaining problem is that when you calculate the broadcast power that our other civilizations have to be using for us to hear them, it is way more than we would ever be using or ever have used. This means that either they would have to be doing something that we would never think of, or they would be broadcasting an intentional beacon signal to let everyone know that they were there. So the whole thing is still problematic.

But let's say you are still confident that, calculations and estimates aside, intelligent civilizations are out there and we should be hearing from them by now. All this Drake Equation stuff is just wild guesses anyway. Then you can turn forward five pages to the section titled "Cosmic Catch-22," skipping the technical stuff which is next, to continue this discussion.

The Theoretical Basis for Intelligent Life Elsewhere

In the search for intelligent life on other planets, there are physical searches for planets that are Earth-like, which are interesting but will never find any sign of life. The most useful approach is actually theoretical – a calculation called the Drake Equation named for the astronomer who first put the relevant variables in one place. The initial run at the Drake Equation gave a value of ten sets of detectable intelligent civilizations in our galaxy at any time, which we are defining as an advanced developed civilization, one that must have the ability to broadcast high power RF signals that we could receive. Since there are about 100 billion candidate stars in our galaxy, that is one intelligent civilization for every ten billion stars. The only wrinkle is that we have not heard a single squeak from any of these other nine civilizations, either meaning that they are populated with paranoids like some of us who say that broadcasting our existence is the equivalent of blood-in-the-water – it is just going to attract someone bigger who wants to feed on you - or, the equation assumptions are wrong. Unfortunately, if you look at the original Drake assumptions, they were made by people who really wanted to find intelligent life, and so are biased way too optimistically (e.g. they assume an average of two planets with life per star). And they were done in the early 1960's when high power broadcasting was the only way to communicate over distances.

Let's redo the Drake Equation over again targeted at intelligent life in the universe (Drake was just looking at our galaxy). To make it easy to remember, there are about 100 billion stars in an average galaxy (big ones have a trillion), and there are about 100 billion galaxies. (There are actually about four times as many stars in galaxies, but about 75% of these are dwarf stars that cannot possibly have planets with life. So we will just keep the 25% that are reasonable candidates, since that makes for the nice round number of 100 billion).

First we need the chance a star has planets – this is very high – let's say 80%.

Then we need the chance that the planet is in the right temperature range for liquid water to remain on the surface for a long time – say two billion years. Here is where it gets messy. The Earth should be frozen solid except for the fact that it is full of radioactive elements coming from nearby supernovae. These have kept it unnaturally hot for 4.5 billion years. The window in space and time for a planet to not be too cold or too hot, and to remain that way for at least two billion years, is vanishingly narrow. Many stars are double-star systems, and these are too disruptive for stable planets. Crowded star systems, such as globular clusters, may have too much inter-stellar gravitational interference for planet stability, causing perturbed Oort Clouds and Kuiper Belts to constantly bombard planet surfaces with comets, ruining their chances for the development of sophisticated life. Even with orbit stability, if the planet is not in exactly the right location water will either boil off or remain frozen and life won't start, or if it starts, it will stay in the bacterial phase. And if the star is unstable, by being much hotter than the sun (most are), then that thermal variability over time will ruin life's chances. If the planet is too heavy or the atmosphere has the wrong mix of gases, the atmosphere will create a runaway greenhouse gas situation, resulting in an intolerably high surface temperature. Venus, about the same size as Earth, has the equivalent of just about a mile deep of ocean all evaporated and turned into a cloudy atmosphere so that the surface has probably never seen the sun. Yet its surface temperature is higher than the highest temperature on Mercury, which is over twice as close to the Sun and has no atmosphere, too hot for life. Mars has lost so much of its original atmosphere that it is the equivalent to being at an altitude of 56,000 feet on Earth, with maybe 100 feet or less of water locked away as ice on its cold, dry wind-swept surface, probably warm and wet for too short a time for life to have ever developed.

So let's say the odds of a planet being in this narrow temperature range is one out of 1,000. The chance of it remaining stably there for two billion years continuously is one in 100. (Note that some people feel that instead of two billion years, you have to use the time that Earth has been life-tolerant – about 3.8 billion years. Others feel that the conditions on Earth have to be duplicated precisely. That would include periodic mass extinctions of life, the frequency, magnitude, and timing of which are for certain unique to Earth's history. If you want to buy into either of these assumptions, you would have to adjust the above odds to much lower numbers; in the latter case, to just about zero.)

The chance of life on such a planet let's assume is high - one out of ten. Water would have to accumulate and stay, but water seems ubiquitous.

Then we need the chance of sophisticated life – not mats of bacteria and algae, but say mammals. Let's put that at one in a thousand.

Then we need intelligent life. Not dolphins, or Neanderthals, but creatures at least as smart as us. That would be another one out of a thousand.

Then we need probably the most iffy number, the time a civilization stays "intelligent". The original Drake number was 10,000 years, so for the time being we will use that.

Lastly, we need the time, as a percent of the civilization's lifetime, that it will broadcast high power electromagnetic radiation off into space. At some point civilizations will move to either all light transmission (fiber), or local low power RF transmissions. Little will be radiated into space unless the civilization elects to broadcast a beacon signal to let others know of their existence. As an initial value, we will use 2%, which would be 200 years out of a 10,000 year civilization.

Since we have been listening for about 40 years, we need to give credit for that, and multiply everything by 40.

If we use all the above values, we get one planet with detectable intelligent life for every 20 million galaxies. In other words, it's just us for all intents and purposes. And that is why we have not heard from anyone else.

Let's say civilizations last ten times, or 100 times as long. We are still all alone.

The only way to make a dent is to assume that civilizations last 100,000 years. We need to increase the chance of a planet in the habitable zone to one in 100, and to remain there for two billion years to one in ten. Once life arises, we need to push up to a one out of 100 chance both for sophisticated life and intelligent life. And we will push the broadcast percentage up to 500 years, or .5%. The chances of intelligent life near us then go up to one detectable civilization for every 800 galaxies.

Well, as they say in some circles, we are still screwed. Even if a civilization lasts one million years, the average galaxy is over one million light years away, which means by the time we hear from anyone, they are already for sure dead and gone. Plus, another galaxy is so far away that the chance of picking up a signal from a civilization is zero unless they purposely produce an ultra-sophisticated high-power beacon aimed right at us. Big-time bummer. But maybe this explains why we have not heard from anyone.

But if we drop our requirement that the civilization still be alive, or listening, and just demand that we hear something, then all we need is that somewhere in our galaxy some civilization launched a signal and at some later time we picked it up.

Our solar system resides about 27,000 light years from the center of our galaxy, a distance that encompasses most all the stars in the galaxy, even though the spiral arms reach much further out. So if we assume that we can hear anything within the rough diameter that we are in, say 60,000 light years, then anyone that broadcasts anything in the last 60,000 years we might be able to hear. Now obviously the math is much more complex – if a planet 10,000 light years away sent a signal out 50,000 years ago we would have missed it. But let's use the simplistic assumption and give ourselves credit for the full 60,000 years. Since the Drake Equation is full of assumptions anyway, being off a factor of ten or 100 does not matter too much.

If we do this, sticking with the optimistic assumptions, it says that there are 74 intelligent civilizations in our galaxy that we might have heard from by now. Now contact, even if such civilizations exist, is not guaranteed, since the degradation in the signal level travelling a distance of many light years is simply horrendous. A broadcast originating 5,000 light years away will have the power level of the signal degraded by about 400 dB. That figure is used so as not to sound too daunting, since no one thinks in dB's. But it means that if we listen with a giant 70 meter antenna on Earth, and the other guys broadcast with a large (20 meter) parabolic antenna that sweeps right across Earth as their planet rotates, they have to be putting a signal of about 200 megawatts into their antenna. This is way more than we would ever put into one of ours unless we were intentionally producing a beacon signal. Also note that we never broadcast radio or TV programming with parabolic antennae – parabolas are only used for line-of-sight to another antenna on the ground or to a satellite. If the civilization is ten times closer, 500 light years, then the required power into the antenna drops to two megawatts, now only outrageous instead of unimaginable. To bring the broadcast signals down to a reasonable level, say 200 kilowatts, the source would have to be even closer, say within about 150 light years of Earth. But if the antenna is smaller than 20 meters, or not parabolic, both of which would be typical, then the signal level would still be unobservably low. And, this still assumes that the other guys are broadcasting this signal from *above* their atmosphere, since atmospheric losses can be enormous and there is no way to guess what they might be. (All these numbers are based on X-Band signals, which for us represent government radar or communication frequencies – those most likely to be at unusually high powers.)

What this means for those that are not into dB's or megawatts, in other words normal people, is that it is possible that the reason we have not heard from anyone is because the power of their broadcasted signals are so low by the time they get to us that they cannot be detected. It's like shining a flashlight at another star or the Andromeda Galaxy – your photons will get there, no problem. But they will be lost in the bright glare of our Sun as seen from their vantage point, so the relatively dim light of your flashlight cannot be observed separate from our Sun. The signals from these 74 civilizations could be reaching Earth, but they cannot be distinguished from general background cosmic and thermal noise in the universe. Of course, it is also possible that the optimistic assumptions are improper, and the only intelligent life in this galaxy is us.

Now some will say that since the Drake Equation is all assumptions, the results are meaningless. Logically, however, this is a non sequitur. Saying that errors will always add up the wrong way is like saying you will always get heads when you flip a coin. You can make estimates about all kinds of things, and as long as the errors in the estimates are not systematically correlated, the errors often offset each other and the result can be useful, especially to an order or two of magnitude (within a factor of 10 or 100). The results of this estimate are so far away from a useful number that errors are not going to save it.

Cosmic Catch-22

But many people want to believe that there is intelligent life all over the place. And man is a belief machine after all. So let's toss the math out the window and assume that this is true, and we are then left to account for the absence of any signals from all these advanced civilizations. Excluding the paranoia explanation, is there another? The answer may be the cosmic Catch-22, the conundrum now faced by man that may be common to all intelligent civilizations.

Any intelligent species has to subdue all the threats presented by their planet in order to take itself from a few scattered settlements to a heavily-populated world, full of sophisticated technologies. This species must have certain traits and skills to successfully take on the risks and challenges presented by their raw, untamed world. They must be able to size up a situation quickly and act decisively, to out-muscle, out-think, out-last, and out-invent their way out of every possible difficulty they find themselves in. Dealing with nuance, subtlety, complexity, problems with sophisticated global inter-relationships, issues with latencies on the scale of one hundred years or more – anyone with these skills would have been eaten by the first wild animal or swept away by the first flood during the long struggle up the road to civilization. It was Alexander the Great/Genghis Khan temperaments that would conquer their world, not a continent full of Plato's. Yet once civilization was created and spread planet-wide, these nuanced, complexity-oriented skills are the only ones that are useful, and all the talents that were so valuable on the way up become not just valueless but a handicap. It is a little like the movies about the last cowboy, lost in modern society, his skills and values obsolete, useless, and unappreciated.

The Cosmic Catch-22 is that the skills that enable an intelligent race to reach an advanced civilized state then become a self-generated trap, unusable in the context of such a changed world. In other words, since the species itself does not change while it transforms the world in which it lives, it creates a mismatch, it becomes the wrong tool for a different job. It is designed obsolescence, Mother-Nature-style. Even if there are many intelligent civilizations out there, as soon as they reach that stage, they all find that the talents that allowed them to progress to that stage fail them, and they are "suddenly" beset by problems too complex and too subtle to unravel and solve. So instead of dominating their world they find the reverse; progress becomes more ragged and choppy; unchallenged global setbacks take place; a frustrated citizenry discourages international cooperation and even consistent national focus. Rather than one million years or even 10,000 years duration for a civilization, the average lifetime becomes cosmically brief. And so, the universe is silent, a confirmation that this cosmic trap, this universal Catch-22, has befallen everyone.

Of course, it may not have to be so, if the civilizations on the planet could use their intellect to suppress their collective nature, and act appropriately for the new world they have made. Suppressing belief-based cognition, judgmental tagging, and bipolar thinking, gritting one's teeth during cognitive dissonant episodes – if this were conceptually doable for enough people that the world could move forward and not simply dissipatively exhaust its frustrations at the complexities of a world dominated by man and his environments. Unfortunately, this is only an "if".

Otherwise, man will find that civilization, while slick and sleek, is no more than a trap, the Civilization Trap, capturing and constraining man so that instead of an intellectual explosion in this pinnacle of domination of his world, he finds himself trundling down the muddled, monochrome path of sentient senescence.

Chapter 23
A SNAFU-Endemic World

In college, when writing papers for certain courses, the author, like other students, was privileged enough to have access to the historical papers of individuals who had willed them to the library. Selecting Irving Fisher, an economist, and writing about the U.S. recession of 1937, it was dismaying to say the least to read the writings and letters of Fisher, including some to FDR. Fisher declared that the problem was the velocity of money, which had dropped to an extremely-low value compared to pre-Depression values. No one listened, no one did anything except make the problem worse, and so the recession of 1937 put the U.S. back basically to where it was in 1934, rescued only by the spending explosion for World War II.

In the 1930's, even the most advanced nations barely understood the fiscal aspects of economics. About the monetary concepts – the quantity and velocity of various components of the money supply - they had not an inkling. Yet literally billions of people's lives were drastically affected and in many cases ruined by this complete lack of understanding, including the author's grandmother, who carefully packed her three boys and all the clothes they were wearing in a car and drove from a small farming town in Indiana to an unfamiliar California.

And what did Churchill call the Second World War that pulled the U.S. out of the Depression, although at a terrible price? "The Unnecessary War" - catalyzed exclusively by the Treaty of Versailles, whose draconian economic clauses, designed to punish Germany financially so viciously that she would never forget, did in fact do that better than the treaty's framers could have ever imagined. Hitler's popularity strongly depended on the anger, frustration, hurt pride, and economic disaster caused by Versailles. Churchill specifically notes that neither the politicians, nor the people of Britain and France, had a clue about how the economic provisions of the Treaty would work, or not work[68] – in other words, a world war was caused by man misunderstanding how economic systems operate – something his nature provides him no relevant skills with which to address.

Welcome to civilization, crafted by man, crammed full of systems that most all citizens and many leaders do not understand and/or misuse. The consequence is a SNAFU-endemic civilization; the acronym standing for situation normal all fouled up, although when frustrated people often make more colorful word substitutions.

Are you often frustrated by things that do not work like they should? Government doesn't seem to do its job efficiently or effectively; large

---

68 Memoirs of the Second World War, Winston S. Churchill, Houghton Mifflin Company, Boston, 1987, pp. 5-6

corporations seem constantly to be ripping people off; there is an abnormal fascination with self-destructive celebrities; politicians appear to be completely unprincipled and only opinion-poll and moneyed-special-interests-driven; the national infrastructure is wearing out and no one has the courage to step up to the problem; major national problems are deferred in preference to attractive irrelevant emotional nuisance issues; the news profession is now the entertainment business; people appear to be self-absorbed, self-oriented, self-interested, and entertainment-driven; education receives less funding, scores decline, student performance fades. Fortunately, there is a simple solution for all of this – no need for a psychiatrist, SSRI's (think Prozac), frustration, excessive alcohol consumption, or escaping reality into video game playing. Alfred E. Neuman and his 19th century predecessors had the answer "What? Me Worry?"

The Old Testament of the Bible, especially in books like Lamentations, Job, and Psalms, had the Sadducean perspective that all bad things that happen to man (the Jewish nation in this case) came from a less-than-adequate conformance to God's many specific rules, which resulted in God rewarding man with punishments accordingly. No greater authority than Jesus, in one of the most intriguing scenes in the Bible, quotes the classic Psalm 22 lamentation while on the cross. Exactly what you had to do to avoid punishment as a nation, or exactly what the punishment was for, or what the punishment was supposed to accomplish – these were details left as an exercise for the reader.

At this point, it sounds like the human race, due to the mismatch between man's nature and the world he has so radically remade, is in a pickle, and a good lamentation may be in order. But lamenting will not change a thing, since this Civilization Trap is relentlessly deep, and of fierce construction, and the wailing will not help man lift himself an inch from his abyss, nor cause the Trap to be unsprung.

These problems and difficulties are designed into man. They are not some weird, unusual, bad-luck mistakes that just happen to land at your doorstep or in your country or county or local school. Man was constructed and optimized to take-on and defeat Mother Nature, and that he did, without question an unmitigated success; but dealing with the systems that modern society presents – forget-about-it. Man's talents and nature are as home here as a dolphin in the desert or an elephant up a tree. One response by society may have been pin-pointed in a rephrasing of the subtitle of the 1964 movie Dr. Strangelove - "How I Learned to Stop Worrying and Love the Trap". Or, if you prefer something a little more recent, and with a slightly different flavor, say from Star Trek, First Contact: "We are (modern society)... surrender ... Resistance is futile."

The Civilization Trap is a construct of this mismatch between man's inherent nature and modern society – man is the elephant up a tree – the tree he himself has grown and nurtured and manicured. Because it is a trap, railing against it, bewailing man's condition, hardly serves a purpose. Escaping requires a change in man's fundamental nature – and this will not be happening. Making the best of it, implementing coping mechanisms, working hard to understand, to comprehend, taking remedial and corrective action, reacting compassionately and selflessly - entirely appropriate, constructive, useful, and value-added. And since giving up has a draconianly-obvious consequence, it is probably the poorest selection to make. The standard plot line in modern world-wide catastrophe movies is "Don't tell the citizenry until the very last moment - they will run amok like steroidal drunken bull elephants, destroying everything." Yet 30,000 years ago, faced daily with equivalent challenges, the response of our ancestors was "Have no concern - we are all well. Who can know what the morrow will bring. Our fathers and theirs faced and conquered worse, and so shall we. Risk and danger will always be present, but opportunities and gain are there for us to find and take - it is up to us."

While his nature may be immutable, man has a choice about how he behaves. Acknowledging his situation and predicament, implementing as many work-arounds as possible, treating his fellow humans not as Alexander instructed, acting ethically, Golden-Rule-ly, humanely, farsightedly, as rationally as possible - the man of 30,000 years ago would certainly have selected this course of action without delay or debate. It is the man of today, whose attitudes and behaviors, made rusted and dusty from generations of disuse, then placed in cold storage by the distractions of modern society, who is struggling, so far unsuccessfully, to face his situation. But the man of 30,000 years past is there - we just need to reach in and act.

But protestation and lamentation aside, no matter how distracting and exhilarating the monochromatic journey, nor the degree of compassion, caring, grace, selflessness, and rationality that is brought to bear, the name on the destination appears unchangeable – Sentient Senescence.

Sources

The following sources were used directly or indirectly:

Abuse of Privilege, Vertner Vergon, Exeter Publishing Company, Los Angeles, 1986

Against All Enemies, Richard A. Clarke, Free Press, New York, 2004

The Annals of Imperial Rome, Tacitus, Michael Grant, Trans., Barnes and Noble Books, Copyright 1956, 1959, 1971 by Michael Grant Publications Ltd, New York, 1993

The Best and the Brightest, David Halberstam, Ballantine Books, New York, 1969

Born on a Blue Day, Daniel Tammet, Free Press, New York, 2006

Bush at War, Bob Woodward, Simon and Schuster, New York, 2002

The Campaigns of Alexander by Arrian, translated by Aubrey de Selincourt, Barnes and Noble, Inc., New York, 1971

Ciano's Diary, ed. by Malcolm Muggeridge, William Heinemann Ltd, London, 1947

Citizen Soldiers, Stephen Ambrose, Simon & Schuster, New York, 1997

The Complete Guide to Asperger's Syndrome, Tony Attwood, Jessica Kingsley Publishers, London, 2007

The Jugurthine War/The Conspiracy of Catiline, Sallust, Translated by S.A. Handford, Penguin Books, Copyright S.A. Handford 1963, London, 1963

D-Day, Stephen Ambrose, Touchstone Books, New York, 1994

Days of Fire, Samuel Katz, Doubleday & Company, Garden City, 1968

The Decline of the West, Oswald Spengler, Translated by Charles Atkinson, Oxford University Press, 1991

Descartes' Error, Antonio Damasio, Avon Books, New York, 1994

The Devil's Dictionary, Ambrose Bierce, Dover Publications, Inc., New York, 1993

The Emotional Brain, Joseph LeDoux, Simon & Schuster Paperbacks, New York, 1996

"William Faulkner - Banquet Speech". Nobelprize.org. 17 Mar 2011 http://nobelprize.org/nobel_prizes/literature/laureates/1949/faulkner-speech.html

Fiasco, Thomas Ricks, Penguin Books, New York, 2006

Franklin and Winston, Jon Meacham, Random House, New York, 2003

Goebbels, Ralf Georg Reuth, trans. By Krishna Winston, Harcourt Brace & Company, New York, 1993

The Great Documents of Western Civilization, Milton Viorst, Barnes & Noble Books, New York, 1965

Hatchepsut, Joyce Tyldesley, Viking, London, 1996

Henry Plantagenet, Richard Barber, Barnes and Noble Books, New York, 1993

The Penguin Book of Historic Speeches, ed. By Brian MacArthur, Penguin Books, London, 1995

The Histories, Tacitus, Kenneth Wellesley, Trans., Penguin Books, Copyright Kenneth Wellesley 1964, 1972, 1975, 1986, 1990, 1991, 1992, 1993, London, 1993

The History, Herodotus, trans. by David Grene, The University of Chicago Press, Chicago, 1987

The History of Alexander, Quintus Curtius Rufus, Penguin Books, New York, 1984

How to Argue and Win Every Time, Gerry Spence, St. Martin's Press, New York, 1995

"India Graduates Millions, But Too Few Are Fit to Hire", The Wall Street Journal, April 5, 2011

The New Complete Works of Josephus, Trans. by William Whiston, Kregel Publications, Grand Rapids, 1999

The Lessons of History, Will and Ariel Durant, Simon & Schuster, New York, 1968

Letters from a Stoic, Seneca, Robin Campbell, Trans., Penguin Books, Copyright Robin A. Campbell 1969, London, 1969

The Mask of Sanity, Hervey Cleckley, Emily Cleckley, Augusta, 1988

Memoirs of the Second World War, Winston S. Churchill, Houghton Mifflin Company, Boston, 1987

The Nazi Seizure of Power, William Allen, Quadrangle Books, Chicago, 1965

The New Complete Works of Josephus, Trans. By William Whiston, Kregel Publications, Grand Rapids, 1999

Napoleon Bonaparte, J.M. Thompson, Sutton Publishing, Phoenix Mill, 1988

Nature's Mind, Michael Gazzaniga, Basic Books, New York, 1992

The Origins of Totalitarianism, Hannah Arendt, Harcourt, Inc., New York, 1968

Panzer Leader, Heinz Guderian, Da Capo Press, Cambridge, 1992

The Pentagon Papers, as published by The New York Times, Bantam Books, Toronto, 1971

Plan of Attack, Bob Woodward, Simon & Schuster Paperbacks, New York, 2004

The Portable Dorothy Parker, Dorothy Parker, ed. by Brendan Gill, Penguin Books, New York, 1976

The Rape of Nanking, Iris Chang, Penguin Books, New York, 1997

Rommel as Military Commander, Ronald Lewin, Barnes & Noble Books, New York, 1968

Secrets, Daniel Ellsberg, Viking, New York, 2002

State of Denial, Bob Woodward, Simon and Schuster Paperbacks, New York, 2006

A Study of History, Arnold Toynbee, Abridgment by D.C. Somervell, Oxford University Press, New York, 1947

The Territorial Imperative, Robert Ardrey, Dell Publishing, New York, 1966

Terror Out of Zion, J. Bowyer Bell, St. Martin's Press, New York, 1977

The Turner Thesis, George Taylor editor, D.C. Heath and Company, Boston, 1956

The Twelve Caesars, Suetonius, Robert Graves, Trans., Penguin Books, London, 2003

Voices of Power, ed. by Henry Bienen, The Echo Press, Hopewell, 1995

Von Braun, Michael Neufeld, Vintage Books, New York, 2007

We The People, Jerome Agel, Barnes & Noble Books, New York, 1997

What Happened, Scott McClellan, Public Affairs, New York, 2008

Without Conscience, Robert Hare, The Guilford Press, New York, 1993

Witness to America, ed. by Henry Commager and Allan Nevins, Barnes & Noble Books, New York, 1996

Alphabetical Index

About the Author

After receiving a B.A. in physics from Yale University, the author went on to obtain a master's degree in business from Carnegie-Mellon University, at that time a professional hot-bed for research on how people make decisions, solve problems, and form and change attitudes and beliefs, enabling the author the privilege of bickering with professors like Herbert Simon, later to win a Nobel Prize for his work.

A career in the management of high technology operations and projects spanning industry, government, research, and academia, along with the normal social contacts one develops as a parent, neighbor, and volunteer, provided the author with the most fertile of exposures to the myriad of personality types and behaviors that account for the human condition. Sociopaths, serial abusers, people entirely driven by belief, even a sociopathic-like (formally undiagnosed) murderer were known from first-hand experience, along with all manner of "normality". For forty years the author has kept mental notes and categorizations as to what he has observed and why he observes it; for the past decade he put these down in writing, intending simply to document in the most simple and distilled terms what makes man think as he does. But having defined man, and why he was made that way, the premise of this book – the mismatch, the trap – would have been intellectually dishonest to avoid disclosing.

13618266R00220

Made in the USA
Lexington, KY
10 February 2012